Contents

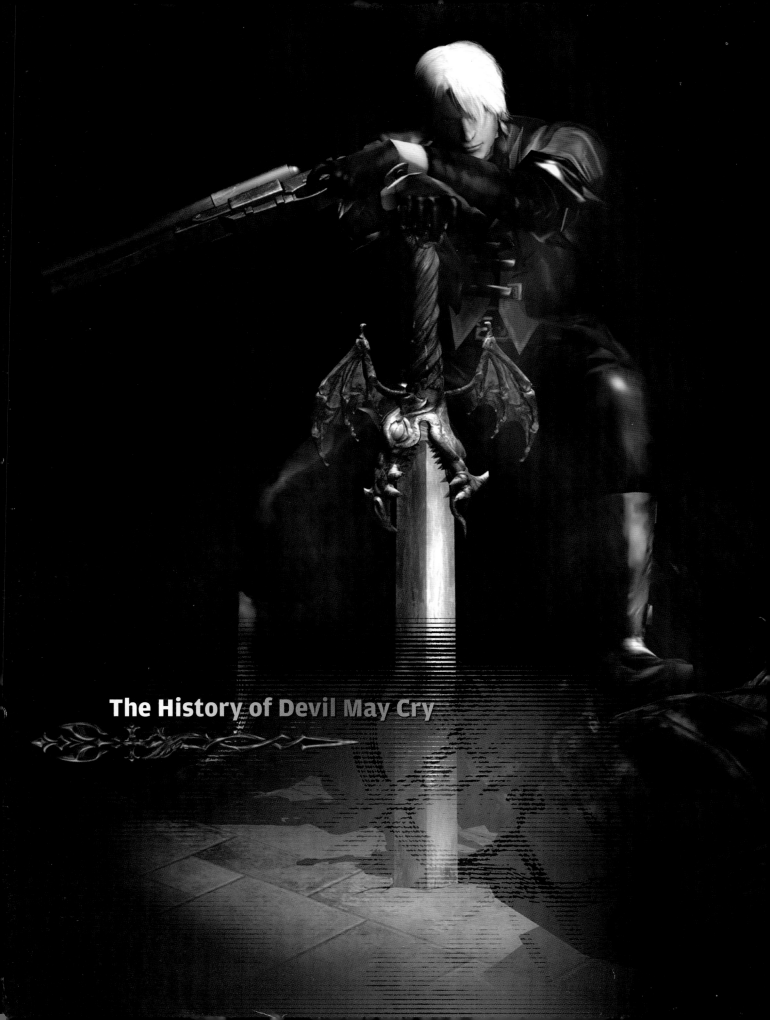

The History of Devil May Cry

Devil May Cry

The Story

The day Dante, the proprietor of Devil May Cry, received a request from the beautiful Trish was truly a red letter day. For it was the day that he was asked to travel to Mallet Island and combat the Demon Emperor Mundus. Just as his father, the Legendary Dark Knight Sparda, did ages before, Dante was tasked with sealing away Mundus. Mundus responded to this challenge like any evil puppet master; he sent his subordinates to exterminate Dante's family. Empowered with demonic abilities thanks to the blood of Sparda coursing through his veins, Dante set off to perform the emperor's last rites. After eliminating the demons sent to end his existence, Dante's journey took him to the immense castle said to hold the slumbering Mundus. It was there that he met a demon named Nelo Angelo, the transformed soul of his departed brother Vergil. His brother's plight filled Dante's soul with remorse and infusing with the power of a true Son of Sparda, his blazing will drove him towards the battle to end all battles - a showdown versus Mundus!

The Cast

Dante

A renowned Devil Hunter born to a human mother and the Legendary Dark Knight Sparda. Dante is the proprietor of Devil May Cry, a shop specializing in the elimination of demon-kind. Two pistols in hand and a sword slung across his back, there are some who say he has even surpassed his father in power.

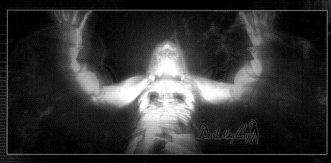

Nelo Angelo

A demonic knight who battled Dante on three occasions. Surprisingly he avoided the dirty tricks and improvised methods for which denizens of the underworld are so often known for. At the root of Nelo Angelo's chivalry lies his origins; for within the demon's body rests the soul of Vergil, Dante's vanquished brother, now a pawn subject to Mundus's machinations.

Trish

The mysterious beauty Trish was responsible for requesting Dante seal away the Demon Emperor Mundus. Closely resembling Dante's departed mother, Trish is actually a demon crafted in that form by Mundus himself. However, in the face of Dante's love, her human heart awoke, and now she works alongside the Devil Hunter as his partner.

Devil May Cry 2

The Story

The beautiful Lucia's sudden appearance signaled the beginning of Dante's involvement with the clan charged with protecting Vie de Marli. It was on Dumary Island that Dante met Lucia's mother, Matier, a woman who once fought alongside Dante's father, Sparda, in the defense of Vie de Marli. Matier hoped that Dante would fill a similar role, and help her defend the island against an encroaching evil by discovering the location of an ancient treasure known as Arcana. However, Lucia found Dante's involvement unwelcome, and sought out Arcana alone. The Uroboros Corporation, which controlled Vie de Marli, and its CEO Arius, were also after the treasured artifact, although for more nefarious ends. Arius hoped to use Arcana to raise the vile demon Argosax, and by doing so achieve absolute and supreme power. Dante recognized the evil in Arius and fought to put an end to his ambitions. Lucia suffered at the hands of her cruel fate... It is within these complicated destinies that the evil known as Argosax was brought back into existence!

The Cast

Dante

With age, Dante has become more fearless than ever, and has embraced the legacy of his father, Sparda, with the hope of one day living up to the Dark Knight's legend. The prospect of the resurrection of Argosax, launched Dante into the underworld to seal the demon away again, just as his father did before him.

Lucia

Lucia is a member of the clan that has for ages been charged with defending the faithful of Vie de Marli from all incarnations of evil. However, she is in fact an artificially created demon, crafted by Arius's own hand. The truth of her origin weighed heavily upon her, until Dante's words reinvigorated her spirit. She now patiently awaits his return from the underworld.

Arius

Using his leadership role of the corporate conglomerate Uroboros as a front, Arius focuses his efforts on research into the black arts, making him a modern day sorcerer. He seeks nothing less than the power of Argosax, a vile demon sealed away on Vie de Marli. Arius came close to achieving his goal; however, the intervention of Dante stopped his dastardly scheme and turned him into the most unsightly of demons.

Devil May Cry 3

The Story

A youthful Dante, still unknown to the larger world, saw his life take a fateful turn upon the appearance of the mysterious Arkham. Arkham was merely a messenger at the time, carrying an invitation from Vergil, Dante's brother. The messenger's disappearance coincided with the appearance of a massive tower inside the city. This tower was known as Temen-ni-gru, a portal to the demon world, long ago sealed by the Legendary Dark Knight Sparda. The man responsible for the resurrection of Temen-ni-gru was Dante's twin brother, Vergil. Raised separately from Vergil, Dante began his ascent up Temen-ni-gru to stop his brother's path towards evil. Dante's path up Temen-ni-gru was littered with the remains of demons, until he met a fellow devil hunter, Lady, inside the halls of the tower. Her mother slain by her father Arkham, Lady climbs Temen-ni-gru to seek revenge for her death. Dante and Vergil. Lady and Arkham. Two families intertwined by fate, and all on a path to the underworld in Temen-ni-gru!

The Cast

Dante

Before he was the proprietor of Devil May Cry, Dante was a brash and arrogant young man, who would fight at a moment's notice and became irritated even quicker.

Vergil

Vergil, Dante's twin brother, forsook the legacy of their father Sparda and proceeded down the path of the underworld. With his katana, Yamato, in hand, only his twin brother stands as any sort of rival to Vergil's power. After their battle, he was left to reside in the underworld, eventually falling under the sway of the Demon Emperor Mundus.

Lady

A human devil hunter who encounters Dante in Temen-ni-gru. Initially suspecting Dante as a demon, she tried to kill him as she would any other demon, stopping only when she realized the sense of justice he held within his soul. For this reason, she entrusted Dante with her beloved weapon, the Kalina Ann. After parting ways with Dante, Lady successfully enacted revenge against her father Arkham, then reunited with her fellow devil hunter after his defeat of Vergil.

Devil May Cry 4

On the coast of a distant land lies the castle town of Fortuna. It is here that the group known as the Order of the Sword practices a religion so mysterious, no outsider knows what happens behind closed doors. In times past, the Order of the Sword fought to protect mankind. They revere the demon warrior Sparda as their god, and their hatred of all other demons runs deep. Their sole purpose is the extermination of these demons. On the day of the annual Festival of the Sword, a powerful man appeared seemingly from nowhere. Before anyone could act, this man assassinated the head of the Order! A young knight of the Order, whose only purpose previously was the extermination of all demons, was immediately ordered to pursue the mysterious assassin...

Nero

Young and fiery, Nero is a member of the Holy Knights, a group charged by the Order with the task of eliminating demon-kind. Always ready for a fight, Nero eschews the other members of his group to carry out his work alone. However, his innate powers have earned him the respect of everyone.

Dante

Legendary Devil Hunter who sealed away the Demon Emperor Mundus. Son of Sparda, the demon revered by the Order of the Sword, Dante stands alone between demons and humanity. His mastery of close-quarter and ranged combat has led some to believe he has surpassed his father.

Credo

Credo is the Supreme General of the Holy Knights, and earned his title due to his ability with a blade. His austere demeanor and ability to lead his forces have made him a beloved leader and comrade. As Kyrie's brother, he too has accepted Nero into his family, despite the youth's insubordination.

Kyrie

Kind and loyal, Kyrie is trusted by everyone. She is renowned for her musical ability, which has earned her the coveted role of songstress for the Festival of the Blade. Having accepted Nero into her family, their relationship can resemble that of brother, friend and lover all in one.

Sanctus

Sanctus is the infallible ruler of the Order of the Sword, and the Vicar of Sparda. Having gained absolute trust from his flock, he has earned a reputation as one of the greatest leaders in the history of the Order. He once served as Supreme General of the Holy Knights, and is known to endlessly crave knowledge.

Agnus

Agnus serves as the Chief Alchemist for the Order. In charge of development of anti-demonic technologies and arms, he is responsible for the iconic sword used by the Holy Knights. Often a lab shut-in and prone to stuttering, he is so rarely seen that his very existence is unknown to some members of the Order.

Gloria

Meteorically rising to a leadership position in the Order shortly after joining the faith, Gloria's exotic appearance and voluptuous assets set her apart from the rest. However, her rise to the top, coupled with her looks and ability have attracted the attention of many detractors.

Trish

A demon with a striking resemblance to Dante's mother. Once a conspirator against Dante on the behalf of Mundus, Dante's decision to save Trish sparked her conversion to his cause, and now they work together.

Lady

Making her living as a Devil Hunter, her previous encounters with Dante are long and twisted; however, the two have arrived upon a mutual friendship. Known to force her dirty work upon her "friend", then demand vast sums of compensation in return.

Chapter 01

Game System

Careful preparation is the key to emerging victorious from Fortuna's perilous, demon-infested regions. This chapter aims to familiarise you with the fundamental workings of the game, providing detailed information whenever possible.

It's divided roughly into three areas of interest: the game interface, basic Player Character controls and the various aspects of the in-game environment. Be sure to read the "Basic Controls" and "Environment" sections, as later chapters build on the information they contain. Once you've gained more hands-on experience and have new questions concerning the above areas of interest, return here for answers.

Getting Started

This section deals with everything you need to get set up properly and start a game. Please note that settings which do not influence the actual game play (such as Sound, Brightness, etc.) and external settings implemented via the PlayStation® 3 XrossMediaBar™ or the Xbox 360™ Dashboard, are left to your own discretion.

Controls: Xbox 360™ | PlayStation® 3

From this point forwards, Xbox 360™ and PlayStation® 3 controls will be shown simultaneously and written as - for example - **Ⓨ** | **△**. The button, or button combination to the left of the "|" separator, applies to the Xbox 360™ version, the one on the right to the PlayStation® 3 version. That way, you can immediately see which input you need for a particular action, regardless of the platform you're using to play the game.

Also, skills and techniques are described using the Default Control setup - if you bind the controls to different buttons (see the Control section on how to do this), you'll have to convert the input mentioned here to one corresponding to your custom setup.

Press START at the Title Screen (some of the introductory scenes can be skipped with **Ⓐ** | **Ⓧ** or START) to start a new game, load a saved game, or fiddle with various options. In order to navigate through this and later menus, use the Left Stick or the Directional Pad to select an option and press **Ⓐ** | **Ⓧ** to confirm your choice. Afterwards, **Ⓑ** | **◯** allows you to cancel the action and return to the previous step. Should other buttons be available in a certain menu, the game will mention them - and their use - on-screen.

The adventure begins.

New Game

Choose "New Game" to start Devil May Cry™ 4 completely from scratch. Before you dive into the action, the game will ask you to make three choices.

Tutorial

Turn this on to receive additional help during the game. Whenever you happen upon a new, significant feature, the game will pause and a Help Screen will appear with relevant information about it. The first few times you play the game, we strongly recommend that you activate the Tutorial, as it provides immediate, in-game help. On the other hand, it also breaks up the pace of the game, so turn it off once you're familiar with its contents. Please note that some Help Screens - most notably those pertaining to usable objects - are not part of the Tutorial and will be shown regardless of your choice.

In-game help is much appreciated while you're getting to grips with the game.

Difficulty Level

Choose the difficulty setting on which you wish to begin the game: Human or Devil Hunter. The former is ideal if you're new to the series - it's the easiest setting for training your skills, gathering resources and beating the final Mission. The latter is more difficult and challenging, because you do less damage to enemies while they're more aggressive and have stronger attacks. Choose Devil Hunter if you've already won Human or are a Devil May Cry™ veteran.

Experienced players should be able to make Devil Hunter their first choice.

These are not the only difficulty levels available. As your skill and mastery of the game's twenty challenging Missions improves, you'll be able to unlock two additional settings - which can't be selected when starting a New Game - called Son of Sparda and the absolutely diabolical Dante Must Die! The main differences between all four difficulty levels lie in the amount of damage you can deal using the Player Character (Nero or Dante), the attack power of the enemies and their aggression. These will discussed later on.

Automatic

Automatic charging and powerful combos with just one press of the button - it's almost cheating.

This setting allows you to enable Automatic Mode, in which the game partially controls the actions of your Player Character. Automatic Mode automatically selects the most appropriate attack or combo as soon as you press an attack button. It can also, without you having to lift a finger, charge weapons and transform the Player Character into its demon form when running low on health. Only the skills that have been unlocked in the game so far can be used.

Automatic Mode is well suited to players who want to use advanced techniques, without having to worry about entering the right button combination at the right time, and to still have the option of entering a combo manually, if needed. However, since your moves are intertwined with those chosen by the computer, your personal playing style will not be able to manifest itself fully during the on-screen proceedings. Also, the time spent watching the computer performing skills automatically could have been better used practising them. So players who want to be in full control of the Player Character's actions should turn this off.

Load Game

Load Game allows you to enter the HDD Access Screen and select an earlier saved game from one of sixteen available slots. As you flip through them,

In Devil May Cry™ 4, you can do a lot with 16 game slots.

the current Mission, difficulty level and total playing time will be displayed and updated to help you find the right game. Once you've picked one out, you'll enter its Mission Menu.

Here is where you customise the game to suit your personal needs. The most important sections are Game Options, where you can change various relevant game features and also Control, which allows you to configure the controller bindings. Options can also be accessed during the game via the Pause Menu.

Optimise the settings for your ultimate game experience.

Game Options

Lock-On Display

When this setting is active, a blue (Nero) or orange (Dante) circular cursor will appear around the point the Player Character is currently locked on to. More about Lock-On can be found in the Basic Controls section.

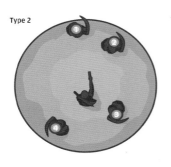

Locked on target.

Lock-On Type

This alters the Lock-On priority, i.e. the sequence telling the Player Character which target to lock on first, which comes next, and so on.

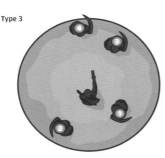

Type 2   Type 3

Three Lock-On types are available. Type 3 is quite straightforward - the first target is the one closest to the Player Character, then the one after that, until the farthest target is reached. Type 2 is also straightforward, as it gives priority to targets directly in front of the Player Character, then targets those that are more to the left and right, eventually reaching those behind the Character's back.

Type 1 is a hybrid of Type 2 and Type 3. By default, it behaves exactly like Type 3. However, if you press the Left Stick in a certain direction,

Lock-On priority will be forced to act like Type 2, with the direction you choose becoming the Player Character's front area.

From the above, it follows that Type 1 is the most versatile Lock-On Type, but at the cost of needing manual input, while Type 2 and Type 3 are fully automated. Experiment a little with each Lock-On Type to find the one best suited to your personal style and needs.

Mini-Map

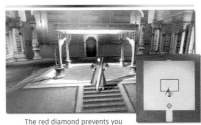

The red diamond prevents you accidentally going back to the previous Area.

The Mini-Map is a small, semi-transparent map of the current Area, displayed in the lower right corner of the screen when this is turned on. The Area may be so large that only a portion of it - the bit containing the Player Character - is displayed. Doors are coloured red, while a small, red diamond marks your point of entry. The starting point and orientation of the red arrow show the Player Character's position and the direction it's facing, respectively. Enemies are not displayed.

Camera

You can choose to invert the camera controls (press left and the camera rotates to the right, press down and the camera rotates upwards, and so on). More on the Camera can be found in the Basic Controls section.

Tutorial

If you want to change the Tutorial setting after starting a New Game, this is where it can be done.

Control

Unhappy with the default control bindings? Change them here.

Here, you can bind the Player Character's basic controls to any of the controller buttons. First, select the Player Character of your choice (if available), then a controller button. Flip through the various basic controls until you find the function you need and confirm. The game will accept your choice, unless one of the basic controls disappears because of it - if you, for example, change "Jump" to "Gun Attack" and there is no other controller button bound to "Jump", the game will reject your input. Select "Default" to restore the default controls if things get messed up.

Mission Screen

The Mission Screen appears just before the start of a Mission. The image you see after initiating a New Game and watching the opening movie, for example, is a Mission Screen. It contains the following data and options:

1 Mission Number
Shows the number of the current Mission, ranging from 01 to 20.

2 Title
The title of the Mission.

3 Objective
A short, sometimes cryptic text, filling you in on what's about to happen.

4 Record Scores
Shows the largest amount of Red Orbs you've collected in this Mission so far, plus your record score and rank. More information about these statistics later on.

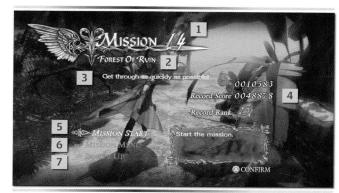

5 Mission Start
Select this option to start the Mission.

6 Mission Menu
The option that takes you to the Mission Menu (see next section).

7 Power Up
Choose this option to buy Items and improve the Player Character's abilities (consult the main Divinity Statue section for more information).

Mission Menu

The Mission Menu is the central hub of your current game. From there, you can select Missions, watch cut scenes, review your performance or consult additional background information, and so on. All of the Mission Menu's content has to be discovered or unlocked to become available, so expect to see more and more features as you proceed through the game.

Mission Select

To play a Mission available in the Mission Menu, select a difficulty level, the Mission you want to play and the Player Character (using Easy Automatic Mode or not). The currently shown Missions are the last ones you completed earlier. Confirm your choices to proceed to the Mission Screen.

You can only access the Missions you've just reached or have completed already, but you can play them as many times as you want. This has several advantages. If you find, for example, that you're getting clobbered in a difficult Mission, you have the freedom to replay earlier Missions - in a different difficulty mode altogether - and gather resources (Items, skills, etc) which may allow you eventually to get through the problem situation. Replaying Missions also allows you to face optional challenges you might have shied away from initially, or find secrets you may have missed the first time round.

Story Theatre

The Story Theatre allows you to view every pre-rendered cut scene you've unlocked so far, without having to replay the Mission they belong to. Apart from a few exceptions, finishing a Mission unlocks all the movies it contains. You can select cut scenes by Mission or flip through them one by one. Finally, with "Play All", every unlocked cut scene is played in sequence.

Watch your favourite movies here.

Lights! Camera! Action!

It's possible to manipulate the camera while watching cut scenes. Press RT | R2 to zoom in on a detail of interest. The harder you press the trigger, the larger the magnification. Reduce trigger pressure to zoom out again. You can also move the Right Stick to pan the camera in the direction of your choice – although the panning range is limited.

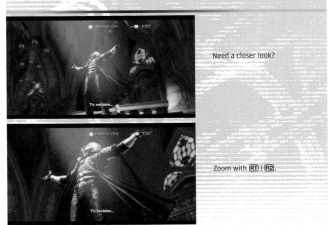

Need a closer look?

Zoom with RT | R2.

Total Ranking

The Total Ranking Screen displays – for each unlocked difficulty mode – the best rank achieved for all the Missions you've completed so far. Select one of them, using the "fiery circle" cursor, to review the Mission Clear Screen of the best performance that led to your achieved rank. Note that the cursor is blue when a Nero Mission is selected, red if a Dante Mission is chosen.

Your finest hour on a single screen.

The numbers on the right are those of the Secret Missions you've found. Whenever you clear one of them, a purple cross will be visible next to the corresponding number. More about Secret Missions and the Mission Clear Screen later on.

Library

This is your one-stop Devil May Cry™ 4 source of in-game information. Every element of the game you've discovered so far is described at length here, complete with interesting background information, illustrations and – when appropriate – movies or rotating 3D models. Be sure to consult it regularly. Knowledge is power, after all.

As if the info wasn't useful enough, small movies demonstrate each skill.

View your enemies from all angles without getting hurt.

Library Updates

As a general rule, the Library is updated with a new topic as soon as you've completed the Mission in which you come across it for the first time, unless you acquire it through a Divinity Statue, causing it to appear instantly. Whenever something new becomes available, various "New" tags will lead you all the way to the topic in question.

Looks like there's a lot of new stuff to go through.

Save / Load

Select this option to save the game in its current state, or to load another saved game. After making your choice, you can perform the desired action from the corresponding HDD Access Screen.

Basic Controls

Basic Controls covers only the most basic movement, attack and environment control skills. These are absolutely fundamental, so memorise them well in order to be able to alternate between skills without a hitch. Once through this section, you should be able to explore most of the environment, have a pretty clear idea about the Player Character's potential and make good use of the Camera and Pause Menu. For an in-depth overview and combat analysis of all other, advanced skills, consult the Combat System from page 90.

01

Xbox 360 Controls

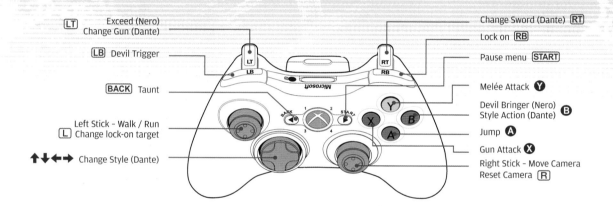

LT — Exceed (Nero) / Change Gun (Dante)

LB — Devil Trigger

BACK — Taunt

Left Stick – Walk / Run — L Change lock-on target

↑↓←→ — Change Style (Dante)

Change Sword (Dante) RT

Lock on RB

Pause menu START

Melée Attack Y

Devil Bringer (Nero) / Style Action (Dante) B

Jump A

Gun Attack X

Right Stick – Move Camera / Reset Camera R

PlayStation 3 Controls

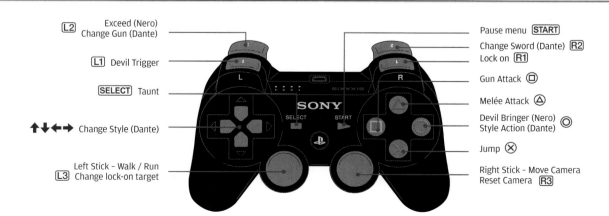

L2 — Exceed (Nero) / Change Gun (Dante)

L1 — Devil Trigger

SELECT — Taunt

↑↓←→ — Change Style (Dante)

Left Stick – Walk / Run — L3 Change lock-on target

Pause menu START

Change Sword (Dante) R2

Lock on R1

Gun Attack □

Melée Attack △

Devil Bringer (Nero) / Style Action (Dante) ○

Jump ✕

Right Stick – Move Camera / Reset Camera R3

The following controls are shared by both Nero and Dante and serve the same purpose. Their physical abilities are executed in an identical fashion – Nero jumps as high as Dante, runs equally fast, and so on. However, since both demon hunters have unique weapons and personalities, their Taunts and Attacks are different.

Walk / Run   Left Stick

Unless the Player Character is airborne, the action always takes place on planar surfaces viewed from a certain camera angle. Push the Left Stick slightly in a given direction and the Player Character will turn to face that direction and Walk towards it, along the planar surface it is standing on and relative to the current camera angle. Push it all the way to get the Player Character to Run.

Hot: Running

Not: Walking

For as long as the Left Stick is held in the direction of your choice, the Player Character will keep Walking or Running forwards, even if a sudden camera change alters the original meaning of the direction you're holding. When the camera changes continually, the Player Character will Run round in wide circles. However, the moment you let go, you'll have to adjust your input to match the new perspective. What was once "left" in the original camera angle may now, for example, be "up". This could be somewhat confusing and cause "movement malfunctions" during camera switches early on- especially for novice players. However, once you've had a little practice and become familiar with the various camera angles in the game, the issue will recur increasingly less often and – hopefully – disappear.

Although Walking is badass to do when you're surrounded by multiple enemies on the verge of an attack, or quite simply when you're relaxing during a stroll through Fortuna's gorgeous locales, it has no significant role in the game. Furthermore, strict time limits need to be respected if you wish to maximise your score, so you're strongly advised to Run whenever possible.

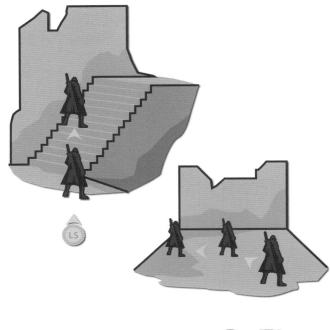

Jump   Ⓐ | ⊗

Here, the Player Character reaches the maximum Jump height.

While the Player Character is standing, tap Ⓐ | ⊗ slightly to execute a Jump with minimal height. To achieve a higher Jump, keep pressing the button for an increasingly longer time – which can be done until the maximum Jump height (more than double the Player Character's height) is reached. In addition to being useful for reaching higher ground, Jump is also good for evading ground-based attacks.

01

Somersault Left Stick + Ⓐ | Left Stick + ⊗

Lean the Left Stick in a certain direction and tap Ⓐ | ⊗ slightly to perform a Somersault. This way, you'll always get one when pressing the Jump button while Walking or Running. Functionally, a Somersault is like a Jump, except that the Player Character also moves over a certain distance along the chosen direction. Pressing the Jump button for a longer period of time increases the Somersault's height (its maximum height is the same as a Jump's) and the distance it moves.

Generally speaking, you'll Somersault far more often than you'll Jump.

Kick Jump

If you execute a Jump or Somersault and, at some point, find yourself directly next to a wall, you'll have an opportunity to use this wall to perform a second Jump or Somersault in a valid direction. The entire manoeuvre, called a Kick Jump, is extremely useful for reaching high places, obtaining a tactical advantage over enemies or creating time-saving shortcuts.

Reach greater heights thanks to the wall.

Instead of Running up the staircase...

... save time and use a Kick Jump.

Side Roll RB + sideways on Left Stick + Ⓐ | R1 + sideways on Left Stick + ⊗

Tap or hold RB | R1, move the Left Stick sideways relative to the Player Character's orientation – not the current camera angle – and tap the Jump button to perform a Side Roll. It's mainly an evasive manoeuvre, as the roll is quick and reduces the Player Character's hit area. Use it to escape from fast attacks when Running left or right doesn't cut it.

This oft-forgotten move is useful against very fast attacks.

Melée Attack Ⓨ | △

Press Ⓨ | △ to attack with the currently equipped melée weapon. A single attack won't do you much good – the real strength of a melée weapon lies in its innate attack combos, as described in the Combat System. Nero carries only one melée weapon, his trusty Red Queen battle sword, whereas Dante eventually has access to the Rebellion sword, the Gilgamesh knuckle-dusters and the Lucifer projectile launcher. Both of them also get to use Yamato - a katana with tremendous powers - later in the game.

Melée Attacks are quite effective against most enemies.

Gun Attack ⊗ | □

To fire the Player Character's currently equipped gun, press ⊗ | □. Although weak compared to melée weapons, guns are ideal for damaging enemies from a distance or even disrupting their attacks with raw firepower. As with melée weapons, Nero has only one gun, the stylish Blue Rose, whereas Dante eventually carries Ebony & Ivory, his handguns, the shotgun Coyote-A and the wonderfully metamorphosing Pandora.

Some foes need to be softened up with Gun Attacks first.

Float like a butterfly, sting like a bee

If you use a Gun Attack during a Jump or Somersault, the Player Character will remain suspended in mid-air for the duration of the shot. Shoot continuously, and it's possible to keep the demon hunter floating for

If things get too hot on the ground, take the fight into the air.

an extended period of time. Handy against ground-based enemies, or when trying to score multiple hits against flyers or targets in a higher position. The effect also occurs with most of the Melée Attacks.

Taunt   [BACK] | [SELECT]

Want to show off your élite skills, humiliate the underachieving opposition and gain subtle, but beneficial effects? Then press [BACK] | [SELECT] to entertain the enemy with a provocative Taunt. Taunts are Player Character animations aimed at enraging the enemy

Thank you! You've been a great audience!

and gaining a little something while at it. They must be executed reasonably close to the enemy. You can cancel a Taunt at any moment by moving or attacking, but you won't receive a bonus unless the animation has finished or run for a set amount of time. The more time a Taunt needs, the more difficult it will be to finish the animation before the enemy attacks, but also the more powerful the bonus will be.

Devil Trigger   [LB] | [L1]

At some point in the game, the Player Character will have the ability to change into a devil by pressing [LB] | [L1].

All of the Player Character's attacks are enhanced in DT mode.

In this Devil Trigger (DT) state, Nero and Dante automatically regenerate health and become more powerful, each in their own, unique way as shown by the tables (you'll learn more about their contents as you read on). The only downside to all this is that the DT form is temporary and should be conserved for emergencies and tough encounters.

Use the DT's regenerative powers to recover health in a pinch.

Nero's DT Powers

Power	Details
Melée Attack	During DT mode, Nero attacks with the Yamato blade rather than the Red Queen
	(the Red Queen sword's Attack Power does not change)
Gun Attack	Demon uses long range attack after Nero's long range attack
	(Nero's attack power with "Blue Rose" does not change)
DT Exclusive Skills	Some skills can only be used during DT:
	1. Maximum Bet: Nero's strongest ranged attack
	2. Showdown: The strongest multiple hit attack (needs time to launch)
Devil Bringer	Devil Bringer (Buster) is much stronger
Snatch	Changes to Devil Snatch, which can pull in multiple enemies simultaneously
Regenerate Hit points	Health Gauge increases by 99 Hit Points per second*
Action Change	The Speed technique activates more quickly
DT Gauge Depletion	Loses 1500 Magic Points during the first 3 seconds, then 330 Magic Points per second*
	The latter is reduced to 255 magic points per second using the Trigger Heart technique

* valid under an average screen refresh rate of 30 frames per second.

01

Dante's DT Powers

Power	Details
Attack Bonus	Melée Attack Power x 1,5
	Enemies are disrupted twice as fast
	Release Power x 1,2 (Royal Guard Style)
Defence Bonus	Enemy Damage is halved
	Dante is hardly disrupted by enemy attacks, even the most powerful ones
Regenerate Hit Points	Health Gauge increases by 90 Hit Points per second*
Speed Up	Dante's speed increases by 10% (x 1.1) except the Dance Macabre finish, which works at normal speed
Action Change	Stinger, Kick 13 and Pin-up skills change to DT only technique
	All techniques of Ebony & Ivory and Coyote-A are stronger
	Pandora PF262: Jealousy is getting stronger
	Easy transform command for Pandora PF124: Hatred, PD398: Revenge
	Series of TrickSter dashes are possible
	Dante can block every technique using the Royal Guard Style (no deflection)
	The Speed technique activates more quickly
DT Gauge Depletion	Loses 1500 Magic Points during the first 3 seconds, then 300 Magic Points per second*
	The latter is reduced to 225 Magic Points per second using the Trigger Heart technique

* valid under an average screen refresh rate of 30 frames per second.

You can stop Devil Trigger at any time by pressing [LB] | [L1] a second time. By the way, in Dante Must Die! mode, enemies also have the ability to enter Devil Trigger. Beware.

Lock-On [RB] | [R1] and [L] | [L3]

Press and hold [RB] | [R1] to lock on to an opponent with the Lock-On priority, determined, as described earlier, by the Lock-On Type. Press [L] | [L3] to scroll through all the enemies. This allows you to select a specific target and put it at the receiving end of all your attacks.

Lock-On: making fighting fast foes easy.

Furthermore, it allows you to keep track of fast-moving targets. Provided you're locked on, the Player Character will point its ranged weapon continuously at the target's latest position.

It isn't possible to Run while the Lock-On button is held, only Walk, Jump, Somersault backwards and forwards and Side Roll to the left or right. Keep this in mind while evading attacks. Also, holding the Lock-On button makes it impossible to Walk or Side Roll off any ledge or elevated location. You can still Somersault off them, though. Finally, please note that it's also possible to lock on to

Lock-On Walking looks badass and keeps you safe from falling.

some background elements, such as Sealing Mechanisms and Battle Statues (more info about them later on).

Camera Right Stick and [R] | [R3]

In most cases, the perspective used to display the game is fixed, only changing when moving from one predetermined location to another. Sometimes, however – most notably during combat – it's possible to change the camera angle manually. Push the Right Stick in a certain direction to rotate the camera that way. Tap [R] | [R3], and the game will try to position the camera directly behind the Player Character. Should your camera work result in some objects blocking the Player Character, the

When an object is about to block the view...

... it turns semi-transparent.

game will render these objects semi-transparent so that you can still see the action.

Whenever you enter a new Area, push the Camera button a few times to see if you can manipulate the perspective. Although this has limitations – rotation is difficult when the Player Character is next to a wall – you should definitely learn to use this feature, since it can be used to your advantage during combat by keeping your targets on screen at all times. Furthermore, looking at the same location from different angles may reveal hidden locations or breakable objects.

Pause Menu [START]

The Pause Menu is important, if only because it allows you to use Items at any point in the game, or to restart a Mission if things go awry. This menu is quite extensive, so there is more information about it later on in the Pause Menu section.

The abilities in this section can only be performed by Nero. Whilst lacking in the arms department when compared to Dante, the young hero more than makes up for it with his powerful Devil Bringer.

Exceed LT | L2

Press and release LT | L2 in a steady, controlled rhythm - pretty much in the same way as you would rev a motorcycle engine - to fill the Exceed Gauge quickly. This becomes visible in the upper left corner of the screen, along with other statistics. It soon runs empty, so don't wait too long after releasing the Exceed button. Once it's full, the Red Queen's first power level will light up, the sword will take on a red glow and the Exceed Gauge will return to zero. You can then refill the gauge a second and third time to activate their corresponding power levels.

Here, the Exceed Gauge is fully charged - the Red Queen is all set to go.

These power levels stay on the Red Queen until you decide to use the weapon for an attack or skill - a single Melée Attack uses one power level, for example. Exceed-enhanced Attacks are much more powerful and destructive than regular Attacks. It's always advisable to get all three Exceed power levels on the sword before and after a fight, since the charges in your Exceed Gauge will remain charged until you expend them by using Red Queen for an attack. Nero can only Walk while charging the Exceed Gauge.

Exceed-enhanced attacks are quite explosive.

Devil Bringer B | ◎

This is Nero's trump card. Stand close to an enemy, then press B | ◎ and watch as a giant, demon hand mimics Nero's motions, picks up the demon and slams it down with tremendous force. The Devil Bringer, in conjunction with other skills, allows Nero to fly large distances, or grab and toss around enemies as if they were fluffy toys. Whilst not so effective initially against bosses or strong, or very large, enemies, these can be weakened in such a way that a single Devil Bringer can initiate a spectacular attack and deal phenomenal damage.

Nero's demonic power is extremely useful. If all else fails, use the Devil Bringer.

That's going to hurt.

01

Dante Exclusive

Dante is all about weapons and skills. With a whole raft of moves available across various Styles, no two fights will ever look the same.

Change Style Directional Pad

It's possible to change Dante's current combat Style on the fly. Simply press your controller's Directional Pad in one of its main directions, and Dante will take on the Style of your choice. The icon that appears in the upper left corner of the screen (along with other statistics) and the pose Dante strikes ensure that you can pick the Style you need without much hassle.

Choosing a combat Style means that Dante will have special attacks available and generally be stronger in aspects of combat affected by that Style. Other aspects weaken or disappear, although basic controls will always be available.

In later difficulties, Changing Styles becomes a must.

TrickSter
Directional Pad ⬆
Activating TrickSter turns Dante into an acrobat. He will be much more mobile, able to perform fast aerial and ground manoeuvres at the cost of a limited offensive repertoire.

This move is only possible as a TrickSter.

Sword Master
Directional Pad →

Sword Master gives Dante full access to all his sword and other melée weapon combos. If you like to deal massive combo damage to nearby opponents, this is your Style.

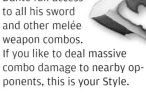

Use Sword Master to perform aerial Melée Attacks.

Royal Guard
Directional Pad ↓

Royal Guards should press Down on the Directional Pad to activate the Style. It allows you to block attacks and fill up the Royal Gauge with Angry Energy, which can be used to strike back at your enemies with tremendous power. Requires practice, but the pay-off is worth it.

Royal Guard: often neglected by beginners, but loved by experts.

GunSlinger
Directional Pad ←

The GunSlinger Style puts Dante's ranged weapons in the spotlight, with exclusive, powerful ranged weapon attacks at your fingertips. Give it a shot.

GunSlingers have very interesting moves at their disposal.

Dark Slayer
Directional Pad

Available late in the game. Press the button of the currently selected Style again to access the Dark Slayer Style. This allows you to attack with the powerful Yamato blade, special techniques included. The Style is pretty much like Sword Master, except that you are bound to Yamato when it comes to special attacks.

Yamato might not have a lot of reach, but it makes up for it by packing a lot of punch.

Style Action   Ⓑ | ◎

The Style Action button is the enabler for all the current Style's special attacks. Pressed on its own, it already yields one special attack, but that only scratches the surface of its possibilities. Consult the Combat System on page 114 to unleash Dante's true potential.

Dante's finest attacks are initiated with the Style Action button.

Change Gun   ⎣LT⎦ | ⎣L2⎦

Press ⎣LT⎦ | ⎣L2⎦ to scroll through all available ranged weapons - your current selection will be briefly displayed in the lower left corner of the screen. You can't move back and forth but, since there are only three ranged weapons available, there's little need to.

It might be a good idea to switch to the Coyote-A against these enemies.

Change Sword   ⎣RT⎦ | ⎣R2⎦

Press ⎣RT⎦ | ⎣R2⎦ to go through all available melée weapons - your current selection will be displayed briefly in the lower right corner of the screen. As with Change Gun, moving back and forth through the list is impossible. Yamato cannot be selected this way.

Heads up - the Gilgamesh weapon icon looks a lot like Lucifer's.

Environment

Now that you know how to start a Mission and are familiar with the basic controls of the Player Characters, it's time to start dissecting the game itself. In this long section, you'll discover everything there is to know about the various elements you come across as the story unfolds. Opponents (Lesser Demons and Bosses) will not be treated in-depth here however, as they have their own chapter starting from page 46.

Exploration

Fortuna's beautiful, lush environments simply beg to be explored, if only to find – and retrieve – all hidden Items and discover its darkest secrets. To that end, it's important to know how the environment is structured and how to navigate successfully through it.

Areas

An Area is a 3D background loaded into memory, complete with object data. Your actions will take place over a large number of Areas, which are grouped into several regions - a castle or a forest, for example. Each Mission begins in a certain Area -clear the Mission Objectives and then proceed to the final Area (which may be the same as the starting Area) to complete the mission. Whenever you enter an Area, its name will be displayed briefly in the lower left corner of the screen.

In theory, it's possible to backtrack to every Area discovered earlier in the game but, in practice, this won't be necessary. Furthermore, previous Areas may be (temporarily) unavailable due to important story events. Areas may be logically connected with each

This is an Area in the forest region.

other in several ways, with doors and passages being the most common ones. Whenever you come across an unblocked door, hallway or something similar, check it out to see whether or not it leads to a new Area. The Mini-Map is invaluable as a reference tool while you're doing this.

Boundaries

While exploring Areas, you'll often be drawn to an interesting location (an inviting ledge, the roof of an intriguing structure, etc), only to be greeted by an invisible wall placed slightly in front of it. Congratulations, you've just found an Area Boundary the developers have put up to make this clear statement: "turn back, it is meaningless to venture here". Occasionally, also, Boundaries may be introduced to prevent easy shortcuts within the Area.

It's very tempting to take an easy shortcut by jumping over this staircase ...

... except that you can't - there's a Boundary blocking your way.

Boundaries clearly show that there is no way into a location - it's as if the place is surrounded by a slippery "bubble" the Player Character is unable get a grip on. Try not to confuse Boundaries with places that are simply hard to reach, or you may miss out on secret Items. Don't let these spoilsports ruin your natural curiosity.

Try to jump on that fountain to experience the Boundary "bubble" surrounding it.

Investigate   Ⓐ or Ⓑ | ⊗ or Ⓞ

Stand directly in front of an object you're interested in and press Ⓐ or Ⓑ | ⊗ or Ⓞ to Investigate it. If you see a Jump or special attack being performed, the object is irrelevant (or you need to adjust the Player Character's position). In all other cases, the

Hmm, what's this?

Player Character will either provide a comment, manipulate the object, pick it up, or do a combination of the above. For example, Investigating a door connected to a different Area will lead you to that Area. Whenever you enter a new Area, take your time to Investigate everything suspicious – you never know what you're going to find.

Cut scenes

During the Mission, various pre-rendered cut scenes may be shown to advance the plot. As with the Story Theater cut scenes, you can press RT | R2 to zoom and, to pan the camera, move the Right Stick. Camera controls are not possible for cut scenes that are rendered using

To skip or not to skip this cut scene, that is the question.

the game engine. If you've already seen a particular cut scene and are in a hurry, press Ⓐ | ⊗ or START to skip it entirely.

Hazards

Whilst falling from great heights doesn't bother the Player Characters in the slightest, every now and then they will encounter a physical threat that may hurt them badly or kill them if they don't escape in time. Watch out in particular for spikes, poison gas, self-destruct sequences and other assorted environmental hazards.

Pointy.

Self-destruct-ish.

Health Meter

The Health Meter displays the amount of health the Player Character has left. It's subdivided into several hit point (HP) levels – each level representing 1000 HP. Initially, the gauge has six HP levels, or 6000 HP

Here, the Health Meter is almost at maximum.

but, by acquiring certain Items, it can be extended to a maximum of twenty levels. Obviously, the longer it gets, the better your chances of survival. Every Mission begins with a full Health Meter.

DT Gauge

This shows the amount of magic the Player Character has left. Like the Health Meter, the DT (Devil Trigger) Gauge is subdivided into power levels, each containing 1000 magic points (MP). At least three levels of power need to be filled completely with magic in order to enter the DT state. When Devil Trigger is active, the DT Gauge will steadily deplete and can only be refilled by using Devil Stars or White Orbs (see later). Once the DT Gauge is empty, the Player Character becomes human again.

The DT Gauge starts out relatively small, with three levels of power, or 3000 MP (just enough to Devil Trigger), but if you acquire certain Items and skills, it can be extended to a maximum of ten levels of power and be made to become depleted less rapidly, greatly improving the time Devil Trigger

Most of the time, you'll refill the DT Gauge by fighting enemies.

can be maintained. Only three levels of power are filled at the beginning of a Mission, even if more levels are available. To fill the DT Gauge during the game, you need to hit or get hit by enemies, Taunt enemies, acquire certain Orbs (more about those later on) or combine any of the above.

Jump Pad

At some point in the game, the Player Character will be able to use Jump Pads. These circular, magical objects have the ability to propel their users to great heights at breakneck speed. Whenever you come across them, don't forget that they are essential for completing the current Mission.

At the apex the Player Character will Somersault. Use this to change direction.

Chrono Slicer

When you've found a certain unique, magical item, you'll be able to activate Chrono Slicers. These strange machines allow you to slow the passage of time, which makes it easier to get past Areas with extremely fast-moving obstacles.

Nice Chrono Slicer side effect: enemies will move in slow motion, but you won't.

Sealing Mechanism

A Sealing Mechanism consists of several blue, glowing stones, arranged in a circular fashion on an ornate stone slab. To unlock whatever it is protecting, the Player Character must attack it without pausing, using a melée weapon. Once it has been dealt enough damage, the mechanism will reveal its secret.

This is a Sealing Mechanism.

At this point, it's almost activated.

Area Warp

Area Warps occur when the act of leaving an Area transports the Player Character to an Area different from the logically-connected one. They often occur in Fortuna's forest region – Dante, in particular, has to face a convoluted Area Warp maze in one of his Missions. In some cases, the Player Character has to step on a special Warp Pad to initiate an Area Warp. Last but not least, there are also enemies with the ability to warp the Player Character to a different Area.

The purple clouds will warp Dante to distant Areas if he steps into them.

A typical Warp Pad.

This creature is about to warp Dante to an underground cavern.

Nero Exclusive

The following abilities and environmental features are available to Nero only.

Auto Search

After a unique, magical item has been acquired, Nero will be able to detect secrets, typically large hidden Orb caches or Secret Missions (more about these later on). Whenever he's in the vicinity of a secret, his demon hand will start to glow and emit a sound. The closer he gets, the brighter the glow. As soon as it reaches its maximum (when a large, glowing, blue orb surrounds Nero's hand), it's only a matter of time until you find the secret.

With Auto Search available, you have the option of entering the Mission Menu and scouring the earlier Missions to make sure you didn't miss anything. Since the location of secrets in an Area never changes, you can use the knowledge you have gathered later on when, as Nero, you visit these Areas with Dante, who lacks Nero's useful ability. Auto Search doesn't work during combat.

The Auto Search reacts. Let the treasure hunt commence.

This is the maximum glow – the secret is really close now.

Grim Grip

Grim Grips are magical background elements which allow their users to move long distances in a flash. Possession of a unique magical Item is required. Usually invisible to the naked eye, Grim Grips manifest themselves when the user stands on an activated Continuum Pad. Only those linked to the pad will appear.

A deactivated Continuum Pad.

An activated Continuum Pad.

This is an actual Grim Grip.

Grim Grip travel is quite exhilarating.

To use the element, lock on to it with the Lock-On button, then press the Devil Bringer button. The Devil Bringer will quickly pull Nero towards the Grim Grip, then release him - at which point Nero will continue his forward flight a little further while slowing down, and then fall. Depending on the situation, you may need to quickly re-orient yourself and lock on to another Grim Grip in order to cover large distances.

Gyro Blades

At first sight, Gyro Blades look like oversized, metal urns. It's not until a unique magical Item has been collected that you're able to discover their true form. Press the Devil Bringer button near a Gyro Blade, and it will transform itself into a floating blade construct with a blue flame on top. It remains active until you leave the Area or transform another Gyro Blade. You can only transform them one at a time.

Press the Devil Bringer button a second time and you'll be able to move the Gyro Blade over a small distance along a straight line, bouncing off walls if it runs into them. To give it a little more steam, hit it with Nero's sword - its blades will spin and, using the Devil Bringer, then propel it over a greater distance. Hit it twice and the blades will spin even faster and will move even farther when striking it with Devil Bringer. Gyro Blades are extremely destructive and can be used to obliterate enemies and certain, magically sealed obstacles - provided that you hit them.

Use the Devil Bringer to activate the Gyro Blade.

This one's ready to go.

Fast blade spin. The Gyro Blade will move a long distance.

Fastest blade spin. The Gyro Blade will move a very long distance.

This magically sealed object will shortly be destroyed by a Gyro Blade.

Orbs

Orbs are crystallised objects of a demonic nature which look like screaming, human faces. They come in several sizes and types, which can be recognised by their colour. When you get sufficiently close to them, the Orbs will automatically merge with the Player Character, who can then use their magical properties to restore power, become stronger or obtain other Items. Below is a list of all Orb types you might encounter "in the wild" while proceeding through an Area. Other Orb types, which must be obtained in different ways, will be discussed later.

Defeating enemies is one way of gaining Orbs.

Red Orb

Size comparison: this is a Red Orb S.

This is a Red Orb XXL.

Red Orb Sizes

Size	Number of Units
S	1
M	5
L	20
XL	100
XXL	1000

Red Orbs are the most common Orb type. Whenever the Player Character absorbs one, the total number of Red Orb units currently available is briefly displayed and updated in the upper right corner of the screen. Collecting them allows you to buy Items at Divinity Statues (more later on) or the Power Up menu. As shown in the table, they come in five sizes, the bigger ones equivalent to a large quantity of the smallest Red Orb – this counts as one unit. The bigger the Red Orb, the rarer it is.

Green Orb

Pick up Green Orbs to instantly refill the Health Meter and heal the Player Character. They come in three different sizes (see table). The bigger Green Orbs heal more HP, but appear less frequently. Picking up any Green Orb with a full Health Meter adds 10 Red Orbs to the Red Orb counter, which is bit of a waste, especially if it's a hidden medium or large Green Orb, which can be collected at any time. Try to save these until you get hurt and really need them.

This Green Orb L will really hit the spot.

Green Orb Sizes

Size	Hit points healed
S	1000
M	5000
L	10000

White Orb

White Orbs refill the DT Gauge and are quite rare, regardless of their size. Like Green Orbs, they come in three sizes (see table). The bigger ones appear less often, but can restore a larger number of MP. Also, picking them up with a full DT Gauge adds 10 Red Orbs to the Red Orb counter, but this again is a waste. If possible, save White Orbs until they can be used to stock the DT Gauge.

White Orbs are not as essential to life as Green Orbs, but useful nonetheless.

White Orb Sizes

Size	Magic points restored
S	720
M	1800
L	3600

Blue Orb Fragment

There are only 32 Blue Orb Fragments to be found in all of Fortuna, and with good reason: if you manage to collect four of them, they will merge into a Blue Orb which will extends the Health Meter - a very powerful and beneficial effect. The table shows how the Blue Orb Fragments are distributed throughout the game. If some terms are unclear at this point, don't worry - they'll be explained later on.

Some Blue Orb Fragments are easy to get, others require serious skills.

Blue Orb Fragment Distribution

Obtainable Where	Amount
Set Orb	12
Battle Statue	8
Secret Mission	12

Gold Orb

Gold Orbs are very rare in the wild.

Even rarer than Blue Orb Fragments, Gold Orbs have the ability to bring the Player Character back from the dead. Unlike other Orbs which are immediately used when obtained, you can collect and store a maximum of three Gold Orbs. If you have a Gold Orb and the Player Character dies, you may opt to use it. This action revives the Player Character at the fatal spot with a full Health Meter, ready to continue the fight as if nothing had happened.

Gold Orbs come in one size only and are quite convenient to use if the Boss you're fighting, for example, has only a little amount of health left and you really want to finish him off. However, a Gold Orb is a penalty item and using one will have a noticeable impact on your final score.

No! And so close to success!

Gold Orb to the rescue!

Hah! Who's laughing now, chump?

This Set Orb wants to tell you something.

Set Orbs

Set Orbs are Orbs that have been placed in an Area. The exact number is always the same for each Area and location where they are to be found. Visible Set Orbs can't disappear. Some Set Orbs - often small, Red Orbs - are placed in obvious locations, usually done to give you a hint about where to go next or to lead you to a secret. Other Set Orbs - mostly larger Red Orbs or rarer Orb types - require a little camera work to find, or are hidden inside Breakables (more later on) or have been dropped in hard-to-reach places. Finally, the largest caches of Set Orbs require the Player Character to stand on a particular spot inside the

Gold Orbs are very rare in the wild.

Area. Finding some of these locations is almost blindingly obvious, while seeking others require a clever combination of skills. Please note that, apart from Blue Orb Fragments, they always fully regenerate themselves at the start a new Mission.

Reaching caches of Set Orbs can be tricky sometimes.

All Set Orb locations can be found on the maps in the Walkthrough chapter, starting at page 142. Whilst you can consult them at your own leisure, you're advised to use them only as a last resort. Obtaining the Set Orbs in every Area is an interesting challenge which you should try to take up yourself initially.

Battle Statue

Need to hone your fighting skills without the risk of getting hurt? Then a Battle Statue, which depicts a snake-like creature holding a glowing shield, is just the ticket. Whenever you find one of these giant, training dummies and can use it, position the Player Character in front of it,

Only Dante may attack Battle Statues with red shields.

show it your best game - all your attacks will work on them - and check the evolution of the Stylish Rank Gauge (more about that later) to see whether or not your handiwork fills it up. If the gauge decreases, it's a clear sign that you need to add more variation to your strategy and mix in a new technique or two.

Raise the Stylish Rank Gauge...

... and reap the rewards!

But that's not all. Depending on the Battle Statue in question, if you manage to attain a certain Stylish Rank, the statue will break and release large numbers of Red Orbs. Regardless of difficulty level, you'll even get an extremely useful Blue Orb Fragment, when you break the statue for the first time. But it will never break if you don't reach the required Stylish Rank. The further you are in the game, the higher this rank will be.

Number Of Torches

Torches	Required Rank
2	B
3	A
4	S
5	SS
6	SSS

You can easily discern what Stylish Rank is required by observing the front of the Battle Statue. On each side of the Statue you will notice small torches. There are 3 on the right and 3 on the left. Each torch corresponds to a Style Rank. The more torches that are lit up, the higher the required rank.

Please note that Nero can only use Battle Statues that have a glowing blue shield. Other statues with glowing red shields are earmarked for Dante. All in all, there are eight Battle Statues scattered around Fortuna - four for each Player Character.

The only way to break this Battle Statue is by reaching Smokin' Sick Style!

Breaking Battle Statues

The code word is "variation". In order to destroy a Battle Statue, you must vary your attacks. As long as the game doesn't believe that you're repeating the same move over and over again, you'll be fine. In practice, try to execute at least three different attack sequences before returning to the original one. An easy strategy, which breaks every statue for both Nero and Dante, is to start with a simple ground-based combo, then propel the statue into the air to perform an equivalent aerial combo. As the statue touches the ground again, finish the cycle with a different ground-based attack. Repeat. The use of melée weapons is recommended.

Basic Battle Statue Breaking Strategy: ground combo one...

... aerial lift and mid-air combo...

... ground combo two. Lather, rinse, etc.

Orb Stone

Whenever you come across a very large, floating red crystal with screaming faces all over it, you've found an Orb Stone. It has the potential to give you a very large volume of Red Orbs if you do things right.

Something must have really scared the poor souls inside that crystal.

Orb Stones work as follows: as soon as you hit one with a melée attack – note that ranged weapons won't dent it – a few orbs come out and you have ten seconds to hit it as many times as possible. Orb Stones don't care about attack power, only the number of hits, and each hit generates Red Orbs. The more hits you can land over a short period of time, the bigger the released Red Orbs become, and the better the pay-off. When the time's up, the statue will self-destruct. In order to maximise the pay-off, study the Player Character's available skills well, pick out your fastest attacks and unleash them on the Orb Stone. As Dante, try milking one with the Prop / Shredder combo (see Combat System) to get a taste of what's possible.

Prop / Shredder for the win.

Breakables

Most areas contain Breakables, i.e. objects that can be destroyed by being attacked with a melée or ranged weapon. Whenever you see an object which looks breakable (a bench, a container, a freakishly large cocoon, etc), have a swing at it and see what happens. With a bit of luck, the object will break and you'll receive its contents - a bunch of Orbs, which might be Set Orbs - for your trouble. If not, then the object is probably empty, or won't break at all. Sometimes, Breakables can prevent you from continuing a Mission by blocking the path to the next Area. You need to get rid of them to get on with the show.

This Breakable contains lots of goodies.

To destroy large amounts of Breakables efficiently, it's best to use a sword and stick to the first few attacks of the Player character's default melée Attack combo. Swing at a Breakable with the first move, get the next one with the second move, and then abort the combo and repeat. With good aim, Nero has the ability to clean them up much more quickly with a Gyro Blade (when available). Breakables can't be targeted.

The large windows are Breakables. Obliterate one to reach the Battle Statue.

Hostiles

The journey isn't just about exploring Areas, finding secrets and gathering Orbs. Right from the start, Nero and Dante have to fight to survive. This section takes a brief look at the Hostiles they meet along the way. For

In this game, if it moves, it wants you dead.

an in-depth analysis of each enemy, together with working combat strategies, consult the Opponents chapter on page 46.

Roaming Demons

Roaming Demons are Lesser Demons (i.e. non-Boss enemies) which appear in an Area - alone or in a group - for no other purpose than to trade punches. Accept the invitation and either defeat them to earn some Orbs, or ignore the lot to save time.

Fight or skip these Roaming Demons? Your call.

Which Roaming Demons you meet during a Mission depend on the Mission itself, the Area and the difficulty level. For example, where you once fought a group of easy Lesser Demons in Devil Hunter mode, you might suddenly encounter several tough Lesser Demons in Son of Sparda mode.

Sealed Doors

During a Mission, it's possible that you'll find the Area, or a location inside it, sealed. When that happens, the Player Character is trapped until a certain condition has been met. This condition depends on the colour of the Seal.

You may have to defeat more Hostiles than those initially present in order to break the Red Seal.

Red Seal

The Red Seal signals that you need to defeat a number of enemies within the sealed Area or location before it can disappear.

Blue Seal

The Blue Seal indicates

Start looking for a puzzle or Sealing Mechanism to escape the trap.

that you need to solve a puzzle before it fades. The nature of the puzzle depends on the location. Consult the Walkthrough, beginning on page 142, to find working solutions for each Blue Seal location.

Bosses

Bosses are extremely powerful demons and are often huge. They have many, very powerful attacks, which they aren't afraid to use. Some of them become even more dangerous when low on HP, so keep your eyes peeled. Most of the time, they'll appear at the end of a Mission in a Red Seal Area. Get your best game out and show these challenging opponents who the boss really is!

They're big, they're bad. With the right strategy, they're also toast.

The new colour is a clear warning: get ready for the 'no holds barred' end-game.

Damage

During combat you'll try to hit the enemy while the enemy tries to hit the Player Character. Your attacks, and theirs, do a certain base amount of damage (expressed in HP), multiplied by a Correction Factor, which depends on the current difficulty level shown in the following table.

Difficulty Level Correction Factors

Difficulty Level	Player Char. Attack Power	Enemy Attack Power
Human	x 1.5	x 0.5
Devil Hunter	x 1.0	x 1.0
Son of Sparda	x 0.85	x 1.75
Dante Must Die!	x 0.7	x 3.0

* When enemies attack other enemies, the Attack Power Correction Factor is 0.1.

The Correction Factors tell you by how much the Player Character and Enemy Attack Power is reduced or increased in a certain difficulty level. As the difficulty level increases, the Player Character's attack power decreases, whereas the enemies become stronger. For example, enemies do only half the damage in Human, but their Attack Power triples in Dante Must Die! Mode, while the Player Character can only deal 70% of the base damage.

Aggression

Enemies become increasingly aggressive as difficulty levels go up. This shows itself in several ways - enemies may have new attacks, move faster, attack more frequently, use more advanced A.I., and so on. The Enemy Aggression table shows you how eager the enemies are to eradicate the Player Character in each difficulty level on a per Mission basis.

Enemy Aggression

Mission	Difficulty Level			
	Human	Devil Hunter	Son of Sparda	Dante Must Die!
1	100	100	300	800
2	115	125	350	800
3	130	150	450	850
4	150	200	500	900
5	160	220	515	930
6	170	240	530	960
7	190	280	550	1000
8	200	300	565	1000
9	220	350	600	1000
10	230	365	615	1000
11	250	400	650	1000
12	200	350	550	800
13	210	370	605	900
14	220	390	635	1000
15	240	430	700	1000
16	250	435	715	1000
17	270	450	750	1000
18	280	465	760	1000
19	290	480	780	1000
20	300	500	800	1000

The numbers shown in the table are only there to give you an idea of the enemies' aggression levels: the higher the numbers in the table (which ranges from 100 to 1000), the harder the fights will be. It's interesting to note, for example, that enemies in Son of Sparda mode start out just as aggressive as the enemies in Human mode's final Mission. Dante Must Die! mode is just insane. The aggression level drops if you die repeatedly and use Continues, but this has its price, as you will see later on.

Stylish Rank

If you fight Hostiles or beat up Battle Statues in a cool way - i.e. by varying different techniques and avoiding getting hit - the so-called Stylish Rank Gauge, displayed on the upper right side of the screen during attacks, fills up. Leave the fight, and it will immediately drop back to zero. Cycles of at least three techniques are sufficient to increase the Stylish Rank Gauge steadily. It's subdivided into six levels, as shown in the table below (S, SS and SSS are considered to be one level).

Nero is positively Atomic!

Default Taunts. Short and unspectacular.

Brutal - Atomic Taunts. Looking good there.

Smokin' Taunts. The crowd goes crazy!

Stylish Rank Overview

Level	Stylish Rank	Name	Stylish Red Orb Multiplier
6	E (lowest)	(not shown)	x 1
5	D	Deadly!	x 2
4	C	Carnage!	x 3
3	B	Brutal!	x 4
2	A	Atomic!	x 5
1	S	Smokin'!	x 7
	SS	Smokin' Style!!	x 7.4
	SSS (highest)	Smokin' Sick Style!!!	x 7.7

The higher the level, the harder it gets to reach the next one, but the pay-off is worth it: you'll receive a higher amount of Stylish Points - in other words, your score, which is displayed beneath the

Stylish Rank Gauge - and a greatly increased number of Red Orbs (multipliers are displayed in the table). Rule of thumb: change techniques frequently and be a general badass to maximise your rewards!

Stylish Rank and Taunts

The Stylish Rank has an important connection with Taunts. Each Player Character has three sets of Taunts and will choose a Taunt at random from a particular set, as determined by the current Stylish Rank. The first set of brief Taunts is available by default, the second will be accessed when the Stylish Rank is Brutal or Atomic. The third, coolest, but riskiest, set will be used when things are Smokin' or better.

Body and Soul Food

Defeating Hostiles usually yields a certain number of Red Orbs. There is, however, also a chance you'll receive some Green Orbs from them, and White Orbs as well. The probability of getting Green or White Orbs is calculated by taking the Player Character's current amount of HP and Stylish Rank, then looking at the Green or White Orb Drop % table

Looks like you got some Green Orbs for your troubles.

(whichever is applicable) to find the probability that corresponds with these values. Generally speaking, the lower the Player Character's health and the higher the Stylish Rank, the better the odds of getting Green or White Orbs.

Green Orb Drop %

Health Meter	Stylish Rank					
	SSS	SS or S	A	B	C	D or less
100%	0%	0%	0%	0%	0%	0%
75% and more	15%	10%	10%	5%	5%	0%
50% and more	20%	15%	15%	10%	10%	5%
25% and more	25%	20%	20%	15%	15%	10%
0% and more	50%	40%	30%	20%	20%	15%

White Orb Drop %

Health Meter	Stylish rank					
	SSS	SS or S	A	B	C	D or less
100%	0%	0%	0%	0%	0%	0%
75% and more	10%	5%	5%	0%	0%	0%
50% and more	10%	10%	5%	5%	5%	0%
25% and more	20%	15%	10%	10%	10%	5%
0% and more	30%	25%	20%	15%	10%	10%

Special Bonus

Performing a special action with the Player Character may result in a Special Bonus for the DT Gauge, Stylish Rank Gauge, Stylish Points, or a combination of these three. Consult further chapters to find out what these special actions are, as well as the Special Bonus involved.

Destroy the healing ice surrounding the Frost to boost the DT and Stylish Rank Gauge.

Proud Soul

Proud Souls are the currency used to buy or sell skills and abilities. As such, they are very important to the Player Characters' development. The only way to obtain them is by fighting Hostiles or completing a Mission - the formula used to calculate the exact amount of Proud Souls will be divulged at the end of this chapter.

Use Proud Souls to turn the Player Character into the ultimate demon hunter.

Continue

If the Player Character is unfortunate enough to be defeated without a Gold Orb being used, the game will end. It will then add the number of Proud Souls accumulated during the Mission and display the Continue Screen. There, you can choose to Continue the game from the nearest, predeter-

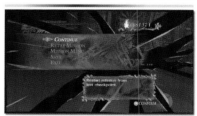

The Continue Screen, aka the Devil May Cry™ 4 Screen of Shame.

mined Continue Point. The options are: Continue with a full Health Meter and a DT Gauge with three power levels filled; Save the current game; Retry the Mission from the start; return to the Mission Menu; or Exit to the Title Screen.

Items are objects which can be picked up and - unlike Orbs - stored for later use. Note that, using this definition, a Gold Orb behaves just like an Item and, indeed, is counted as one by the game. Items can be found in the game and be picked up once per difficulty level. They can also be acquired through Divinity Statues, as described later on.

Vital Star

Vital Stars, when used, replenish Health. They come in three sizes - the bigger they are, the greater the healing power. The Player Character can carry large amounts of them, as indicated by the table.

A free Vital Star S.

Vital Star

Size	Heals (HP)	Max Amount
S	3000 HP	30
M	10000 HP	30
L	Entire Health Meter	30

Devil Star

Devil Stars, when used, replenish the DT Gauge. They come in two sizes only - the larger model can restore more MP. The Player Character is able to carry only small amounts of them, as indicated by the table. Devil Stars become available after Mission 06 has been cleared.

This Devil Star S is semi-hidden.

Devil Star

Size	Restores (MP)	Max Amount
S	5000 MP	10
L	Entire DT Gauge	10

Holy Water

Use a bottle of Holy Water to severely damage a group of enemies within a 100 metre radius (relative to the game). Its Attack Power decreases as the difficulty mode increases, as shown in the table. Unfortunately, all Hostiles - especially Bosses - have a resistance to it. For the best effect, use this rare Item on large groups of low-level Lesser Demons. The Player Character can hold up to 30 Holy Waters.

It's cleansing time.

Holy Water Attack Power

Difficulty Level	Attack Power (HP)
Human	20000
Devil Hunter	10000
Son of Sparda	5000
Dante Must Die!	2000

Key Items

Key Items are a special Item class. They are always found in the same locations and you can't avoid picking them up if you wish to complete the Mission and, ultimately, the game. Some Key Items allow you to overcome powerful, magical barriers, others allow you to use new means of transport, and others still have interesting support functions. Unlike with standard Items, you don't need to enter the Pause Menu to use Key Items. Their purpose will become clear to you in the Walkthrough chapter starting on page 142.

These are the Key Items collected by Nero so far.

01

Divinity Statue

Throughout the game – often near Bosses – you will find statues of a woman with a lion's head holding a huge hourglass. These are Divinity Statues. Investigate them to enter the Power Up menu, where you can use Red Orbs and Proud Souls to acquire new Items and skills. Divinity Statues are marked on maps by a yellow triangle.

She might be Tefnut, Egyptian goddess, mother of the sky and Earth.

Secret Mission

Every now and then, if you search the environment thoroughly, you'll come across a piece of paper with strange markings on it. Investigate it to start one of twelve Secret Missions, mini-quests which require you to take up a specific challenge, sometimes within a strict time limit. Once the challenge has been met, you'll be able to obtain a Blue Orb Fragment. Pick it up to clear the Secret Mission and return to the main quest. After clearing a Secret Mission (regardless of the current difficulty level), you can try to finish it again, but then the Blue Orb Fragment will be replaced by a Red Orb XL.

Whenever you see these markings, Investigate them to start a Secret Mission.

The objective of a Secret Mission can be quite strange.

Success! Hand over that Blue Orb Fragment!

Achievements

As you play the game, you'll unlock a number of Achievements whenever certain conditions have been met. These are shown in the table - coloured entries are already listed in the game. Most of them require you to complete everything in every difficulty level, or to collect as many resources as possible. As such, they are an incentive to playing the game often and intensely, and mastering every challenge there is. In the PlayStation 3 version you do this just for kicks, but in the Xbox 360 version, up to 1000 Achievement Points (distributed as shown in the table) can be earned.

Achievement Table

No.	Achievement	Objective	Points*
01	A Comfortable Pace	Clear Mission 11 in Human mode.	10
02	Easy Does It	Clear all Missions in Human mode.	10
03	Half Way There	Clear Mission 11 in Devil Hunter mode.	10
04	Done and Done	Clear all Missions in Devil Hunter mode.	20
05	Rock and a Hard Place	Clear Mission 11 in Son of Sparda mode.	10
06	Hardly A Simple Task	Clear all Missions in Son of Sparda mode.	30
07	Easier Said Than Done	Clear Mission 11 in Dante Must Die! mode.	10
08	All Bow Before You	Clear all Missions in Dante Must Die! mode.	40
09	Step into the Light	Clear all Missions in Heaven or Hell mode.	10
10	Tonight, We Dine in Hell	Clear all Missions in Hell and Hell mode.	10
11	The Best of the Rest	Clear all Missions in Human mode with an S ranking.	20
12	A Cut Above	Clear all Missions in Devil Hunter mode with an S ranking.	30
13	A Stunning Feat	Clear all Missions in Son of Sparda mode with an S ranking.	40
14	Never Say Die	Clear all Missions in Dante Must Die! mode with an S ranking.	50
15	A Throne of Glory	Clear all game modes.	50
16	Nothing Left Unsaid	Clear all Secret Missions.	10
17	The First Circle	Clear stage 10 of Bloody Palace mode.	10
18	The Second Circle	Clear stage 20 of Bloody Palace mode.	10
19	The Third Circle	Clear stage 30 of Bloody Palace mode.	10
20	The Fourth Circle	Clear stage 40 of Bloody Palace mode.	10
21	The Fifth Circle	Clear stage 50 of Bloody Palace mode.	10
22	The Sixth Circle	Clear stage 60 of Bloody Palace mode.	10
23	The Seventh Circle	Clear stage 70 of Bloody Palace mode.	10
24	The Eighth Circle	Clear stage 80 of Bloody Palace mode.	10
25	The Ninth Circle	Clear stage 90 of Bloody Palace mode.	10
26	Covered in Blood	Clear all Bloody Palace mode stages.	40
27	King of the Palace	Clear all Bloody Palace mode stages with an S ranking.	50
28	Speak of the Devil	Clear the game with Super Nero (Dante).	20
29	Smokin'!	Complete a Stylish Rank S (Smokin'!) combo.	10
30	Smokin' Style!!	Complete a Stylish Rank SS (Smokin' Style!!) combo.	10
31	Smokin' Sick Style!!!	Complete a Stylish Rank SSS (Smokin' Sick Style!!!) combo.	10
32	Simply Spectacular	Complete a Mission with an S ranking.	10
33	Modus Vivendi	Extend the Vitality Gauge to maximum capacity.	10
34	Bat Out of Hell	Extend the DT Gauge to maximum capacity.	10
35	River of Red	Acquire 10000 Red Orbs.	10
36	Your Cup Runeth Over	Acquire 100000 Red Orbs.	20
37	Red Orb Millionaire	Acquire 1000000 Red Orbs.	40
38	Filled with Pride	Acquire 10000 Proud Souls.	10
39	Brimming with Pride	Acquire 100000 Proud Souls.	20
40	Proud Millionaire	Acquire 1000000 Proud Souls.	40
41	Rookie Devil Hunter	Defeat a total of 100 enemies.	10
42	Skilled Devil Hunter	Defeat a total of 1000 enemies.	30
43	Legendary Devil Hunter	Defeat a total of 10000 enemies.	50
44	Item Collector	Acquire the maximum number of all Items.	50
45	Skill Collector - Nero	Acquire all of Nero's skills.	50
46	Skill Collector - Dante	Acquire all of Dante's skills.	50

* Achievement Points applicable to Xbox 360™ version only.

Pause Menu

Access the Pause Menu to use Items, restart the Mission or, read the Map, and much more besides. Regardless of the sub-menu you're browsing, you can always leave and return to the game with a single press of the Pause Menu button.

The Pause Menu in all its glory.

Item

Enter the Item Menu, where you can select and use any combination of Vital Stars, Devil Stars and Holy Waters in your possession. It's also possible to view the currently owned Key Items, Gold Orbs and Blue Orb Fragments.

It might be a good idea to use a Vital Star M at this point.

Skill List

This provides a complete overview of all the Player Character skills unlocked so far, sorted by weapons and abilities. Unsure how a certain combo works again? During the Mission, this is the place to be. Note that the Skill List shows all skills and abilities currently usable by Easy Automatic Mode.

Hmm, how did that Table Hopper work again?

Map

Review all Areas discovered in the current Mission so far in full detail here. Use the Directional Pad to switch from Area to Area. All other controls are shown on-screen.

Check the Map to look for locations you haven't examined yet.

Systems

Here, you can retry the Mission from the start, or quit it altogether and return to the Mission Menu. In both cases, if you earned any Proud Souls, they will be added to your current total before the selected action takes place. You can also save the current game or access Options, which leads to the identical menu to that of the Title Screen.

Not happy with the way the Mission is going? Consider retrying it here.

Divinity Statue

This section takes an in-depth look at the Divinity Statue, which is basically the game's "shop", where Proud Souls and Red Orbs can be exchanged to gain skills and Items (or Orbs), respectively.

The Divinity Statue's menu, equivalent to the Power Up Screen.

Skill Up

Nero's Skills

Arms / Abilities	Skill name	Price*	Available When
Red Queen	Red Queen Combo B	150	Mission 01 Cleared
	Red Queen Combo C	300	Mission 01 Cleared
	Roulette Spin	500	Mission 01 Cleared
	Exceed 2	500	Mission 01 Cleared
	Exceed 3	1000	Mission 01 Cleared
	Streak	50	Mission 01 Cleared
	Streak 2	500	Mission 01 Cleared
	Split	50	Mission 01 Cleared
	Calibur	500	Mission 01 Cleared
	Shuffle	300	Mission 01 Cleared
Blue Rose	Charge Shot	50	Mission 01 Cleared
	Charge Shot 2	300	Mission 01 Cleared
	Charge Shot 3	1000	Mission 01 Cleared
Devil Bringer	Snatch 2	300	Mission 02 Cleared
	Snatch 3	1000	Mission 02 Cleared
Yamato	Trigger Heart	2000	Mission 06 Cleared
	Maximum Bet	5000	Mission 06 Cleared
	Showdown	5000	Mission 06 Cleared
Abilities	Table Hopper	150	Mission 01 Cleared
	Table Hopper 2	500	Mission 01 Cleared
	Table Hopper 3	1000	Mission 01 Cleared
	Speed	300	Mission 01 Cleared
	MAX-Act	5000	Mission 01 Cleared
	Get More Orbs	2000	Mission 01 Cleared
	Enemy Step	5000	Mission 01 Cleared
	Air Hike	2000	Mission 01 Cleared

* Excluding additional skill costs.

Is Calibur not working out for you? Return it and get your Proud Souls back.

Inside the Skill Up Menu, you can buy skills for the Player Character using the Proud Souls earned so far and review the current skill set in the Skill List if needed. It's always possible to undo a skill without losing anything - the game will refund you all the Proud Souls you bought the skill with, including additional skill costs (more about that soon). This allows you to buy a few skills and replace them later on with other skills - better suited to the new situation - without needing to gain a lot of additional Proud Souls. The tables show which goodies are available for Nero and Dante, their prices - excluding additional costs - and when they become available.

Dante's Skills

Arms / Abilities	Skill name	Cost	Available When
Rebellion	Stinger	150	Mission 11 Cleared
	Stinger 2	700	Mission 11 Cleared
	Round Trip	1000	Mission 11 Cleared
Gilgamesh	Kick 13	500	Mission 13 Cleared
	Flush	1000	Mission 13 Cleared
Lucifer	Pinup	500	Mission 16 Cleared
Ebony & Ivory	Charge Shot	150	Mission 11 Cleared
	Charge Shot 2	500	Mission 11 Cleared
	Charge Shot 3	1000	Mission 11 Cleared
Coyote-A	Charge Shot	150	Mission 11 Cleared
	Charge Shot2	500	Mission 11 Cleared
	Charge Shot3	1000	Mission 11 Cleared
Pandora	PF124: Hatred	500	Mission 15 Cleared
	PF398: Revenge	1000	Mission 15 Cleared
Trickster	Style Level Up 2	300	Mission 11 Cleared
	Style Level Up 3	700	Mission 11 Cleared
	Style Level Up 4	5000	Mission 11 Cleared
Sword Master	Style Level Up 2	300	Mission 11 Cleared
	Style Level Up 3	700	Mission 11 Cleared
	Style Level Up 4	5000	Mission 11 Cleared
GunSlinger	Style Level Up 2	300	Mission 11 Cleared
	Style Level Up 3	700	Mission 11 Cleared
	Style Level Up 4	5000	Mission 11 Cleared
Royal Guard	Style Level Up 2	300	Mission 11 Cleared
	Style Level Up 3	700	Mission 11 Cleared
	Style Level Up 4	5000	Mission 11 Cleared
Devil Trigger	Trigger Heart	2000	Mission 11 Cleared
Abilities	Speed	300	Unlocked from the Start
	Get More Orbs	2000	Unlocked from the Start
	Enemy Step	5000	Unlocked from the Start
	Air Hike	2000	Unlocked from the Start

* Excluding additional skill costs.

Auto Skill Up

If you don't want to spend a lot of time powering up the Player Character, you have the option of letting the game do it for you. Select one of three playing styles and Auto Skill Up will power up skills according to the Player Character's table. First, it checks whether or not the highest skill has been bought and, if not, will purchase it. Then it does the same for the skill beneath it and so on, until there are no more Proud Souls to sell.

Auto Skill Up Priorities (Nero)

Orthodox	Variety	Novice
Streak	Streak	Streak
Split	Split	Streak 2
Charge Shot	Red Queen Combo C	Air Hike
Red Queen Combo B	Roulette Spin	Red Queen Combo C
Table Hopper	Charge Shot	Split
Red Queen Combo C	Shuffle	Get More Orbs
Shuffle	Calibur	Trigger Heart
Charge Shot 2	Red Queen Combo B	Charge Shot
Snatch 2	Streak 2	Snatch 2
Speed	Air Hike	Snatch 3
Streak 2	Speed	Speed
Roulette Spin	Table Hopper	Red Queen Combo B
Calibur	Maximum Bet	Maximum Bet
Table Hopper 2	Showdown	Exceed 2
Exceed 2	Enemy Step	Charge Shot 2
Air Hike	MAX-Act	Exceed 3
Charge Shot 3	Exceed 2	Charge Shot 3
Snatch 3	Charge Shot 2	Roulette Spin
Trigger Heart	Snatch 2	Shuffle
Table Hopper 3	Table Hopper 2	Calibur
Get More Orbs	Get More Orbs	Showdown
Exceed 3	Exceed 3	Enemy Step
Maximum Bet	Charge Shot 3	Table Hopper
Showdown	Snatch 3	Table Hopper 2
MAX-Act	Table Hopper 3	Table Hopper 3
Enemy Step	Trigger Heart	MAX-Act

Each playing style has been carefully composed so as to generate a Player Character that is balanced throughout the game. The Novice playing style focuses on mobility first, while gradually introducing attack skills. Orthodox takes the opposite approach, whereas Variety is a mixture of the two.
Spend a few moments figuring out which approach suits you best, then give Auto Skill Up a try.

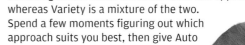

Auto Skill Up Priorities (Dante)

Orthodox	Variety	Novice
Stinger	Stinger	Stinger
Charge Shot (E&I)	Style Level Up 2 (SM)	Style Level Up 2 (TS)
Kick 13	Kick 13	Style Level Up 3 (TS)
C-A Charge Shot	Style Level Up 2 (GS)	Get More Orbs
Pinup	Pinup	Air Hike
Style Level Up 2 (TS)	PF124: Hatred	Trigger Heart
Style Level Up 2 (SM)	Style Level Up 2 (TS)	Charge Shot (E&I)
Style Level Up 2 (GS)	Charge Shot (E&I)	C-A Charge Shot
Style Level Up 2 (RG)	C-A Charge Shot	Stinger 2
PF124: Hatred	Style Level Up 2 (RG)	PF124: Hatred
Round trip	Air Hike	Kick 13
Charge Shot 2 (E&I)	Round trip	PF398: Revenge
Charge Shot 2 (C-A)	Style Level Up 3 (SM)	Style Level Up 2 (SM)
Style Level Up 3 (TS)	Flush	Style Level Up 3 (SM)
Style Level Up 3 (SM)	Style Level Up 3 (GS)	Charge Shot 2 (E&I)
Trigger Heart	PF398: Revenge	Charge Shot 2 (C-A)
Style Level Up 3 (GS)	Style Level Up 3 (TS)	Style Level Up 2 (GS)
Style Level Up 3 (RG)	Speed	Style Level Up 3 (GS)
Flush	Style Level Up 3 (RG)	Style Level Up 2 (RG)
Speed	Charge Shot 2 (E&I)	Style Level Up 4 (TS)
Air Hike	Style Level Up 4 (SM)	Style Level Up 4 (SM)
Stinger 2	Charge Shot 2 (C-A)	Speed
Charge Shot 3 (E&I)	Style Level Up 4 (GS)	Flush
Charge Shot 3 (C-A)	Enemy Step	Enemy Step
PF398: Revenge	Stinger 2	Style Level Up 4 (GS)
Enemy Step	Style Level Up 4 (TS)	Charge Shot 3 (E&I)
Style Level Up 4 (TS)	Style Level Up 4 (RG)	Charge Shot 3 (C-A)
Style Level Up 4 (SM)	Get More Orbs	Pinup
Style Level Up 4 (GS)	Charge Shot 3 (E&I)	Round trip
Style Level Up 4 (RG)	Charge Shot 3 (C-A)	Style Level Up 3 (RG)
Get More Orbs	Trigger Heart	Style Level Up 4 (RG)

Additional Skill Costs

As the number of purchased skills increases, additional Proud Souls need to be sacrificed to reduce the mental strain put on Nero or Dante. The table shows the additional skill costs that have to be paid when a certain number of skills have been bought for the Player Character.

Additional Skill Costs

Number of Equipped Skills	Additional Costs for the Next Skill	
	Nero	Dante
0	0	0
1	100	100
2	150	150
3	200	200
4	250	250
5	300	300
6	400	350
7	500	400
8	600	450
9	700	500
10	800	600
11	1000	700
12	1250	800
13	1500	900
14	1750	1000
15	2000	1100
16	3000	1200
17	4000	1300
18	5000	1400
19	7500	1500
20	10000	1750
21	15000	2000
22	20000	3000
23	30000	4000
24	50000	5000
25	100000	7500
26	-	10000
27	-	20000
28	-	30000
29	-	50000
30	-	100000

Items

In addition to skills, you're able to buy Items with the Red Orbs you've obtained so far. No refunds this time, though. Holy Water, Vital Stars and Devil Stars are all available. The Divinity Statue also has a few exclusive Orbs for sale which can't be found anywhere else.

Blue Orb

A Blue Orb extends the Health Meter by 1000 HP and completely refills it. Fantastic – you can buy entire Blue Orbs without needing to worry about collecting Blue Orb Fragments! Up to six Blue Orbs are available for purchase. Because of the free Health Meter refill, it's advisable to hold off buying them until you reach a difficult Area or a Boss with a heavily damaged Player Character. If you're not into such tactics, just buy them straight away – they're more than worth it.

Blue Orbs – the best thing Red Orbs can buy, unless you're doing a low Health Meter run.

Purple Orb

The Purple Orb is similar to the Blue Orb, except that it adds another level of power to the DT Gauge rather than the Health Meter, and then refills it. You can buy up to seven Purple Orbs. Since Devil Trigger can be a decisive factor against Bosses, only buy them prior to a dangerous Boss fight to ensure a longer, full DT Gauge. Buying them as soon as you can is not recommended since you don't really need the extra level(s) of power in the early parts of the game. Purple Orbs become available after you've cleared Mission 06.

Unleash the demon for a longer period of time with Purple Orbs.

Price List

For game-balancing purposes, the first Items and Orbs you buy are relatively cheap (you shouldn't have a lot of Red Orbs at this point), but the more you buy, the more expensive they become (this prevents you from buying Vital Stars in bulk straight away and waltzing through the game). At some point, the price will peak and will no longer increase. The table shows how much you have to pay the first time you buy an Orb or Item, how much the second time, and so on.

At 3000 Red Orbs, that first Blue Orb is an absolute steal...

... but buying the sixth one will probably take a while.

Item / Orb Price List

Item /Orb	Price						
	1st	2nd	3rd	4th	5th	6th	Beyond 6th
Vital Star S	1000	1500	2000	2500	3000	4000	5000
Vital Star M	2000	3000	4000	5000	6000	8000	10000
Vital Star L	3500	5000	7500	13500	20000	20000	20000
Devil Star S	2000	2800	4300	7800	15000	15000	15000
Devil Star L	3500	5000	7500	13500	20000	20000	20000
Holy Water	10000	15000	20000	20000	20000	20000	20000
Blue Orb	3000	5000	10000	15000	30000	50000	-
Purple Orb	2500	4500	8000	13000	20000	30000	50000
Gold Orb	10000	15000	20000	20000	20000	20000	20000

Mission Clear

So, now you know what the game is all about, one final question remains: how does your performance measure up? After you've successfully cleared a Mission, you will be led to the Mission Clear Screen. Most of your results will be ranked, S being the highest, followed by A, B, C and finally D. When you've finished reviewing them – which is explained in detail below – you'll have the option of Saving the current game, entering the Mission Menu or going to the next Mission Screen. There are lots of formulas in this section, so brace yourself.

Clear Time

This is the amount of time you needed to complete the Mission. The faster you were, the higher the rank. Note that the clock stops whenever the game is interrupted (by cut scenes, entering the Pause Menu, Help Screens, etc), which means you can take a break from the action, whenever you want, without fear of losing time.

Stylish pts.

Stylish pts. (SP) are a measure of how well you've battled Hostiles. Each time you hit an opponent and deal a certain amount of damage, the game calculates your score as follows:

$$SP = A \times B \times C \times D \times 0.1$$

A is the amount of damage dealt to the Hostile in the attack. "B" is a multiplier, which depends on the enemy and ranges from 1.0 to 2.0. Weak Lesser Demons and Bosses have a value of 1.0 or close to it, tough Lesser Demons a value closer to 2.0 or equal to it. "C" depends on the current Stylish Rank, as shown in the Stylish Rank Multiplier table – the higher the rank, the better the multiplier.

Stylish Rank Multiplier

Rank	Stylish Rank Multiplier (C)
E	x 1,0
D	x 1,5
C	x 2,0
B	x 2,5
A	x 3,0
S	x 4,0
SS	x 4,5
SSS	x 5,0

Finally, "D" is called the Enemy Re-spawn Multiplier. It's a value which rapidly decreases to zero in order to motivate you to seek out new Areas and Hostiles. If

Enemy Re-spawn Multiplier

Re-spawn #	Enemy Re-spawn Factor (D)
1	x 1.0
2 to 3	1 / (Re-spawn # x 2)
4 to 6	1 / (Re-spawn # x 3)
7 to 10	1 / (Re-spawn # x 5)
11 to 100	1 / (Re-spawn # x 10)
Over 100	x 0

it didn't exist, it would be very easy to get the Stylish pts. total as high as you wanted, simply by staying in one Area with re-spawning Hostiles and defeating them ad nauseam. The Enemy Re-spawn Multiplier table shows how "D" decreases as the number of enemy re-spawns (Re-spawn #) increases.

The resulting SP value is added to the Stylish pts. score which, at the start of each Mission, is zero. The more Hostiles you battle, the higher the score. The Stylish pts. total you managed to rack up at the end of the Mission is ranked according to Mission and difficulty level. In order to get the total as high as possible, use attacks that do a lot of damage, fight tough opponents, get the Stylish Rank Gauge up and refrain from repeating battles against the same opponents.

Orbs Found

This shows the total number of Red Orbs you've collected over the course of the Mission, as well as the Red Orb Collect Percentage (or Orb %). The higher the Orb %, the better the rank, as shown in the table.

Orbs Found Rank

Orb %	Rank
Over 95%	S
75% – 94%	A
60% – 74%	B
45% – 59%	C
44% or less	D

The Orb % is calculated as follows:

$$Orb \% = Orbs\ Found / (U + V)$$

In this formula, "U" is the sum of all the Red Orbs belonging to the Set Orbs in all the Areas you've visited during the Mission. "V" is the sum of all the Red Orbs which have spawned from other sources, such as defeated Hostiles, destroyed Battle Statues, etc. The Red Orbs you get from Orb Stones aren't counted.

For example, if you collected 5400 Red Orbs in a Mission where there were 5000 Set Orbs in all the Areas you visited and 1800 Red Orbs spawned from other sources, then

$$Orb \% = 5400 / (5000 + 1800) = 0.79 = 79\%$$

The Set Orbs term U is very important here. It's possible get the highest Orbs Found Rank without collecting Set Orbs, but then you'll need a truly gargantuan number of spawned Red Orbs. So, as a rule of thumb, collect as many Set Orbs as possible in every Area you enter and try to pick up all the Red Orbs generated by other sources.

Bonus & Penalty

If you were able to beat the Mission while meeting certain special conditions, these will be mentioned here. Two of these can be considered a Bonus, whereas three are a Penalty. As you'll see, each of them will affect the Devil Hunter Rank. The list of Bonuses and Penalties and a short description can be found in the table.

Bonuses & Penalties

Type	Name	Description
Bonus	No Damage	Finished the Mission without taking damage. Bravo!
	No Item	Didn't use an Item. Not so difficult to achieve.
Penalty	Gold Orb Used	Used a Gold Orb. Do this with moderation.
	Continue Used	Used a Continue.
	Enemy Level Down	Used several Continues in a row, making enemies less aggressive. Consider trying this Mission again.

Devil Hunter Rank

The Devil Hunter Rank is both your total score for the entire Mission and the most important statistic, as it "measures" your overall performance. It's calculated as follows:

> **Devil Hunter Rank =**
> **(Stylish pts. + Mission Clear pts.)**
> **x W x X x Y x Z**

The "Mission Clear pts." value is a constant, depending only on the Mission. "W", "X", "Y" and "Z" are multipliers. The first three depend on the difficulty level, Clear Time Rank and Orbs Found Rank respectively, while "Z" is determined by the Bonuses and Penalties you have achieved. For each Bonus or Penalty, you must use the associated multiplier. Multiplier values can be found in the corresponding tables.

Mission Clear pts.

Mission	Mission Clear pts.
1	500
2	1500
3	2000
4	2000
5	1500
6	2500
7	2500
8	2000
9	1500
10	2500
11	2500
12	1000
13	2000
14	1500
15	3000
16	3000
17	2500
18	1500
19	3500
20	1000

Difficulty mode Multiplier

Difficulty Level	W
Human	x 0.85
Devil Hunter	x 1.0
Son of Sparda	x 1.8
Dante Must Die!	x 3.0

Clear Time Multiplier

Rank	X
S	x 3.0
A	x 2.5
B	x 2.0
C	x 1.5
D	x 1.0

Orbs Found Multiplier

Rank	Y
S	x 2.0
A	x 1.75
B	x 1.5
C	x 1.25
D	x 1.0

Bonus & Penalty Multipliers

Type	Name	Multiplier for Z
Bonus	No Damage	x 1.5
	No Item	x 1.2
Penalty	Gold Orb Used	x 0.7
	Continue Used	x 0.8
	Enemy Level Down	x 0.8

Let's say, for example, that you finished Mission 03 with a Clear Time Rank of A, 10153 Stylish pts., an Orbs Found Rank of B, received the No Item Bonus, the Continue Used Penalty and were playing in Son of Sparda mode. In that case, the formula yields:

> **Devil Hunter Rank =**
> **(2000 + 10153 pts.) x 1.8 x 2.5 x 1.5**
> **x (1.2 x 0.8) = 78751 pts.**

Once the Devil Hunter Rank has been calculated, it will be ranked according to the Mission and difficulty level. In the example above, 78751 pts. in Son of Sparda would yield an A rank.

Proud Soul

It's finally time to calculate the total amount of Proud Souls you've earned:

> **Proud Souls =**
> **Devil Hunter Rank x 0.03**

The example from the previous section would yield a score of 78751 x 0.03 = 2362 Proud Souls.

In earlier sections, it was stated that you can also get Proud Souls when leaving the game via the Pause Menu or the Continue Screen. In that case, the Proud Souls are calculated as described here, but with the Mission Clear pts. set to zero and the Clear Time Multiplier set to 1.0.

Best of luck with your adventure, demon hunter, and may you see tons of high scores along the way.

Opponents

You are faced with a host of demons from the underworld. Each comes with its own strengths and weaknesses. In this chapter, we disclose all the information you need, not only to confront these beasts but also to take them down with style!

02

About This Chapter

As described in detail in the Game System chapter, there are adjustments for each difficulty level. The numerical values you find in this chapter are based on the Devil Hunter difficulty (Normal), which is the base value. For other difficulty levels, please refer to the Game System chapter for the modifiers needed to adjust these values.

Definitions

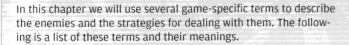

In this chapter we will use several game-specific terms to describe the enemies and the strategies for dealing with them. The following is a list of these terms and their meanings.

DT
Devil Trigger.

DT Time
In the DMD difficulty level, enemies can use Devil Trigger. This entry is the amount of time it takes for the enemy to activate DT after it appears on screen.

HP
Hit Points, this is the amount of Health that an enemy has or that will be taken from you if you are hit by an attack. For reference, each "bar" or "cell" in your Health Meter is worth 1000 points.

Difficulty Levels

Abbreviation	Level
H	Human (Easy)
DH	Devil Hunter (Normal)
SoS	Son of Sparda (Hard)
DMD	Dante Must Die (Very Hard)

Holy Water Sensitivity

Vulnerability & Damage	H	DH	SoS	DMD
0.40	8000	4000	2000	800

The number in the first column is the percentage of a Holy Water's power that will affect the enemy. In this example it's 40%. The next four columns show the numerical damage per difficulty level based on the enemy's vulnerability.

Attack Data

Attack	Damage	Range	DT Increase	Level
Horizontal Slash	800	Short	240	3

Attack
The name of the attack the enemy uses.

Damage
How much HP this attack will take from you.

Range
Short-range attacks require the enemy to be near you, while long-range attacks can reach you from across the room.

DT Increase
This is the amount of energy you receive for your DT Gauge if you are hit by the specified attack. The value is 30% (0.3) of the power of the attack. For reference, one "cell" of your DT Meter is worth 1000 points.

Level
The attack's Level number. Attacks above Level 3 will break your guard if you hold a block in Royal Guard.

Special Defence Data

Status	Short Range	Long Range	Buster
Guarding	0.3	0.3	0.3

Some enemies, but not all, are naturally resistant to your attacks, or employ defensive manoeuvres. This grants them special defence modifiers.

Status
This describes the enemy's action.

Short Range
This is a multiplier that adjusts the damage value of sword attacks used on the enemy.

Long Range
This is a multiplier that adjusts the damage value of gun attacks used on the enemy.

Buster
This is a multiplier that adjusts the damage value of Nero's Buster attacks.

Example: Nero's Red Queen Combo D has an attack power of 170 for the first hit. The Guarding adjustment is 0.3, giving us 170 x 0.3 = 51 in total damage.

Versus Devil Bringer

	Ground	Airborne	Hold
Buster	Yes	Yes	Yes
Snatch	Pull Enemy	Pull Enemy	

This chart describes an enemy's vulnerability to Nero's Devil Bringer. It should be noted that activating Devil Trigger not only increases the power of a Buster attack but also changes the animation. The changes typically add one or more extra moves to the animation.

Buster Ground
The enemy can be grabbed from the ground.

Buster Airborne
The enemy can be grabbed while airborne. For larger enemies (Berial, for example) this can apply when just Nero is airborne.

Buster Hold
Once you've got the Aegis Shield, you're able to "hold" some enemies and use them as a shield against other enemy attacks. This entry lets you know if it's possible to do this.

Snatch Ground
If you use Snatch, what will happen? If Snatch isn't blocked, there are two possible outcomes: Snatch pulls the enemy to Nero, or Snatch pulls Nero to the enemy.

Snatch Airborne
Same as the ground entry, but applies to the enemy being airborne.

Snatch Hold
The Aegis Shield does not affect the Snatch manoeuvre.

> **Pro Tip!**
> When you execute a special Buster attack with DT activated, you can still fire your gun while the attack is in progress to deal extra damage.

Common Boss Strategies

Certain strategies are unique to each character and are applicable to all enemies. Common Boss strategies are of particular interest. These are strategies that you can, and should, use on every Boss in the game.

Snatch
A Boss is too big and too heavy to be pulled to Nero with Snatch. Instead, Nero will be pulled to the Boss. This allows you to get close to the Boss quickly and use your melée attacks. When you're airborne, you can stay in the air by using Snatch repeatedly to circle the Boss as you attack.

Weak Spot
You can damage nearly every Boss anywhere on its body. However, each Boss has a particular weak spot where your attacks will do extra damage. You should always find and target the weak spot.

Unconscious or Dizzy
If you strip enough HP from Bosses in a short period of time, they become Unconscious or Dizzy and will be unable to move for a short period of time. When this happens, they're particularly vulnerable. When fighting them, always open the encounter with your most damaging attacks. These will make their HP fall so quickly that they become unconscious.

Buster
Every Boss has a weakness to Buster when Dizzy or Unconscious. Using Buster at this time on the right part of the Boss's body will trigger a special attack, complete with special animation and massive damage. However, if you use Buster before the Boss is stunned, then the Boss will often counter with its own special attack!

Devil Trigger
As Nero, you should always try to ensure you have at least three bars of DT gauge at the ready during Boss fights so that, once the boss is knocked unconscious, you can use the DT version of the special Buster attacks to really take advantage of the situation.

Real Impact
Dante doesn't have the benefit of Buster to trigger special attacks, but he does have Gilgamesh, the most potent melée weapon in the game. The most powerful attack available using Gilgamesh is Real Impact, although it's slow and can be interrupted by an enemy strike. The best time to use it is when a Boss is Unconscious or Dizzy.

Scarecrow (Arm)
600 HP

Holy Water Sensitivity

Vulnerability & Damage		H	DH	SoS	DMD
	0.60	12000	6000	3000	1200

Description

First Appearance: Mission 02. A veritable grunt amongst the demons. Slow, and not very cunning or skilful, it comes in packs of two or more. Its weapon is a large sword, which is attached to its arm and can be used to block your attacks.

 DT Time 45 seconds

Attack Data

Attack	Damage	Range	DT Increase	Level
Horizontal Slash	800	Short	240	2
Vertical Slash	800	Short	240	2
Spin, 1st rotation	600	Short	180	2
Spin, 2nd rotation	600	Short	180	2
Hold Escape	300	Short	90	2

Special Defence Data

Status	Short Range	Long Range	Buster
Guarding	0.3	0.3	0.3

Versus Devil Bringer

	Ground	Airborne	Hold
Buster	Yes	Yes	Yes
Snatch	Pull Enemy	Pull Enemy	

Strategy

The Scarecrow Arms are the most basic type of Demon and will very rarely attack the player at all at lower difficulty levels. When they do attack they are fairly slow, thus allowing you almost unlimited freedom with your combat. This is a great enemy to experiment on when you're learning the controls and Combat System.

Experimenting with a Scarecrow is fairly safe, so try Hold and other techniques if you wish.

Scarecrow (Leg)
900 HP

Holy Water Sensitivity

Vulnerability & Damage		H	DH	SoS	DMD
	0.60	12000	6000	3000	1200

Description

First Appearance: Mission 02. Almost identical to the Scarecrow (Arm), except that this demon has its blade attached to its leg. Comes in packs of two or more.

DT Time 45 seconds

Attack Data

Attack	Damage	Range	DT Increase	Level
Horizontal Slash	700	Short	210	2
Vertical Roll Slash	450	Short	135	2
Somersault	400	Long	120	2
Jump fall	1100	Long	330	2
Hold Escape	300	Short	90	2

Special Defence Data

Status	Short Range	Long Range	Buster
Guarding	0.3	0.3	0.3

Versus Devil Bringer

	Ground	Airborne	Hold
Buster	Yes	Yes	Yes
Snatch	Pull Enemy	Pull Enemy	

Strategy

The Scarecrow (Leg) is very similar to the Arm version and, on its own, is nothing more than a training dummy. Grouped with other enemies, however, it can sometimes get an attack in, unless you're keeping a careful eye on it. Its attacks,

The Scarecrow (Leg) has only three attacks, all of which are easily evaded.

other than the Vertical Roll Smash, are slow and easy to evade. The easiest way to keep these Demons under control is to just use Streak/Stinger continuously. As Nero, you can get one out of the way quickly with a Buster or two.

All types of Scarecrow have the same audio attack cues. They're never completely silent, but they will give out an obvious scream just before each of their attacks. At this point, two consecutive Jumps or Side Rolls will safely get you out of the way of their attacks. The usual best option is simply to attack them when you hear this cue, knocking them out of their attack, but this will not work in DMD mode if they are using their DT.

Mega Scarecrow

1500 HP

Holy Water Sensitivity

Vulnerability & Damage		H	DH	SoS	DMD
	0.60	12000	6000	3000	1200

Description

First Appearance: Mission 12. This is a huge, overstuffed version of the smaller Scarecrows. It's equipped with seven blades and has many more attacks in its arsenal. When you kill this beast, it doesn't go quietly but will instead launch a blade into the sky for one final attack as it dies. Make sure you avoid the falling blade when you dispatch these demons.

 DT Time 90 seconds

Attack Data

Attack	Damage	Range	DT Increase	Level
Dual Arm Slash	650	Short	195	2
Blade Throw (Spin-up)	300	Short	90	2
Blade Throw (Each Blade)	350	Short	105	2
Blade Throw (Finish Flex)	400	Short	120	2
Jump Bodyslam (Launch)	600	Short	180	2
Jump Bodyslam (Land)	1200	Short	360	3
Rolling Dash	1350	Short	405	3
Rolling Bounce	1350	Short	405	3
Hold Escape	450	Short	135	2
Rolling Counter	350	Short	105	3
Death Blade	1200	Short	360	3

Special Defence Data

Status	Short Range	Long Range	Buster
Normal	0.7	0.7	0.7
DT Active	0.2	0.2	0.2

Versus Devil Bringer

	Ground	Airborne	Hold
Buster	Yes	Yes	Yes
Snatch	Pull Enemy	Pull Enemy	

Strategy

These creatures are big, slow and easily stunned. When faced with one, hit it fast and hard. Stinger or Streak are great choices. These stun the Mega Scarecrow and allow you to follow up with even stronger attacks

When a Mega Scarecrow gets on all fours like this it will shortly begin one of its Rolling attacks.

When these beasts die, they have one last attack left!

such as Real Impact. When confronting one of these demons alongside a bunch of weaker Scarecrows, launch the beast into the air and kill it with an aerial combo well out of reach of the other enemies.

If you are combating other enemies while one of these beasts is around, try to keep a Charge Shot at the ready and then, before launching an attack, target the demon as soon as you hear the tell-tale shout it gives. Hitting it with a Charge Shot at any distance will disrupt any attack it tries.

Frost
1500 HP

Holy Water Sensitivity

Vulnerability & Damage		H	DH	SoS	DMD
	0.60	12000	6000	3000	1200

Description

First Appearance: Mission 03. This ferocious beast has claws made of ice and a shield of ice on its right arm. The ice shield is the source of its power. If intact, it can deploy magical, ice-based attacks.

 DT Time 75 seconds

Attack Data

Attack	Damage	Range	DT Increase	Level
Claw Attack	400	Short	120	2
Claw Slam	500	Short	150	2
Jump Claw	800	Short	240	2
Frost High Time	800	Short	240	2
Lariat	900	Short	270	2
Somersault Dash	1000	Long	300	2
Frost Helm Breaker	900	Short	270	2
Claw Shot	200	Long	60	2

Attack	Damage	Range	DT Increase	Level
Spread Claw Shot	600	Long	180	2
Ice Wave	1000	Long	300	2
Jump Freeze	1500	Short	450	2
Ice Shard Spread	1000	Long	300	2
Shard Explosion	700	Long	210	2

Versus Devil Bringer

	Ground	Airborne	Hold
Buster	Yes	Yes	Yes
Snatch	Pull Enemy	Pull Enemy	

Strategy

Using the Buster throw on Frosts can be a good way to attack other enemies.

You can break the ice shield on its right arm with your attacks. When its shield is damaged or its HP is low, the Frost will encase itself in a cocoon of healing ice. The ice restores the shield and will add 500 HP to the Frost. You can break the ice cocoon by inflicting 600 points of damage to it. This stops the healing process and boosts your Style Rank. Use Snatch frequently to interrupt its attacks and keep it stunned. Buster is also a good choice for launching a damaging throw. Be aware, however, that the Frost can break free from Snatch and Buster - nearly always on higher difficulty levels.

Destroy the healing ice quickly!

After a successful Snatch, follow up with sword strikes. You can either use Streak/Stinger to knock the Frost away, or reset its position with another Snatch and then continue attacking from there. Keeping a Frost knocked over is a good idea when there are other threats in the area, and you'll need to take Frosts out before focusing on other opponents, as they don't have any real attack cues to rely on when your attention is not on them. If a Frost is some distance away it's very likely that it will use an Ice Shard attack, especially if you see it get airborne. If it's nearer, and decides to jump above you, it will almost certainly use the Jump Freeze, so be sure to Jump or Side Roll out of the way.

Assault

1000 HP

Holy Water Sensitivity

Vulnerability & Damage		H	DH	SoS	DMD
	0.60	12000	6000	3000	1200

Description

First appearance: Mission 08. This small reptilian demon is fast and very skilled. It comes in packs of two or more and can quickly overwhelm you. The Assault carries a shield to completely block your frontal attacks (including Snatch and Buster). It also wears a mask that reduces the damage of your attacks by 50%.

 DT Time 60 seconds

Attack Data

Attack	Damage	Range	DT Increase	Level
Submerge	900	Short	270	3
Eruption	900	Short	270	3
Claw Slash	350	Short	105	2
Scratch	350	Short	105	2
Claw High Time	700	Short	210	3
Claw Helm Breaker	800	Short	240	2
Lariat	900	Short	270	2
Jump Scratch	800	Short	240	2
Drill Dash	750	Short	225	2
Dash Stab	1300	Short	390	3
Jumping Dash Stab	2500	Short	750	3
Claw Missile	300	Long	90	2
Howling	150	Short	45	2
Howling Finisher	1500	Short	450	3

Special Defence Data

Status	Short Range	Long Range	Buster
Attacked from behind	2.0	2.0	1.0

Versus Devil Bringer

	Ground	Airborne	Hold
Buster	Yes	Yes	Yes
Snatch	Pull Enemy	Pull Enemy	

Strategy

Be careful with crowd control when up against these beasts. They can quickly surround you and tear you to pieces. You can get behind them and attack them in the back, where you'll deal double damage. When they have their shield up to block, attack strongly. This will shatter the shield and stun them. Buster is also a great option for a multiple-hit throw, but be careful with Buster when others are close by, as the throw animation is a long one and you have no defence while it's happening. After you break the shield, you can launch further attacks to smash the mask they wear. Once this is wrecked, they'll begin using the Howling attack.

Chimera Assaults are lethal and highly unpredictable...

...Dante can use Pandora or Stingers to keep them knocked over.

If you keep close to Assaults they will rarely use the Claw Missile attack. With Nero, a Level 3 Charge shot, followed by a Buster throw, deals a lot of damage. With Dante, use Sword Master's Dance Macabre and, before the "Homerun" strike, switch to Gilgamesh. And then, while the Assault is stunned, use Real Impact. The Assaults are another enemy that gives no attack cues at all, and some of their attacks are very fast. For this reason you'll need to keep them knocked over as much as possible. For this you can use Streak (Nero) or Pandora (Dante). If you can keep multiple Assaults on the ground and bunch them up, you should be able to land heavy attacks on all of them en bloc, using Real Impact or Exceeded Streaks.

Attacking from the back is the only way to deal full damage to an Assault.

Blitz
2500 + 1500 HP

Holy Water Sensitivity

Vulnerability & Damage		H	DH	SoS	DMD
	0.50	10000	5000	2500	1000

Description

First Appearance: Mission 15.

Electric Charge HP	1000
Charge Off HP	2500
Overcharge HP	1500

This massive demon covers itself with an electric field. When the field is on, you can't damage the beast with melée attacks. If you try, you'll get a nasty electric shock (Electric Counter).

DT Time 150 seconds

Attack Data*

Attack	Damage	Range	DT Increase	Level
Claw Strike	800	Short	240	3
Claw Strike (Off)	600	Short	180	2
Blitz High Time	1000	Short	300	3
Blitz High Time (Off)	800	Short	240	2
Jump Claw	1200	Short	360	3
Jump Claw (Off)	1000	Short	300	2
Somersault Dash	1500	Long	450	3
Somersault Dash (Off)	1200	Long	360	2
Blitz Helm Breaker	1200	Short	360	3
Blitz Helm Breaker (Off)	1000	Short	300	2
Lightning Blast (Series)	150	Long	45	2
Lightning Bolt Swing	1500	Long	450	3
Eruption	2000	Short	600	3
Electric Counter	500	Short	150	2
Kamikaze (Grab)	1000	Short	300	4
Kamikaze (Hold)	110	Short	33	0
Kamikaze (Finish)	1200	Short	360	4
Destruct Explosion	2000	Short	600	3

* Off denotes whether the protective electrical field is on of off.

Versus Devil Bringer

	Ground	Airborne	Hold
Buster	Yes	No	No
Snatch	Pull Nero	Pull Nero	

Strategy

03_34
03_35

Begin by using your guns to inflict 1000 damage on the field, in order to disrupt the electrical charge and shut if off. When the field is down it will regenerate in 15 seconds. If you do enough damage to Blitz, he'll go into overcharge mode and self-destruct in 30 seconds. During that time he'll try to grab you and take you with him (Kamikaze).

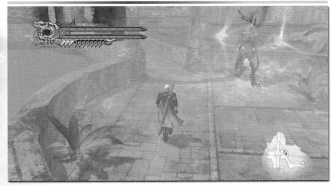

After teleporting, Blitz will sometimes raise his hands like this...

... which will be followed quickly by his lightning blast attack.

With Dante you can use a combination of Royal Guard and Gilgamesh to remove Blitz's lightning quickly and safely. Use basic Gilgamesh strikes on Blitz (or a Full House if you have time), and then hold **B**|**◎** as soon as the attack connects. This will cause you to instantly Royal Block the lightning spark the Blitz emits, allowing you to damage the Blitz's shield without receiving any damage in return.

While Blitz is teleporting around, use Side Rolls and don't get too close. If you Roll just as he stops teleporting you'll be able to avoid his direct attacks. If he comes out of the teleports with a Lightning Blast, you'll have enough time to use another Side Roll to evade it. If, after this, Blitz keeps his hands up in the same position, he'll go into Lightning Blot Swings, which must be dodged in the same way. You can do all of this while holding Charge Shots and releasing them between Blitz's attacks.

As soon as the field is down, move in fast and dish out your heaviest attacks. A combination of DT and Gilgamesh with Dante is ideal. For Nero, use Buster with Devil Trigger to launch a special attack (during which you must make sure you use Summoned Swords). Once his initial HP is gone and he overcharges, keep on the move and continue to use your guns. If you're quick off the mark, you can destroy him before he self-destructs, netting yourself a huge Style bonus. Interestingly enough, Blitz is blind and so will attack anything in the area, including other enemies!

Strike Blitz's lightning shield with Rebellion or Gilgamesh...

...and then instantly Royal Block his lightning spark to quickly remove the shield.

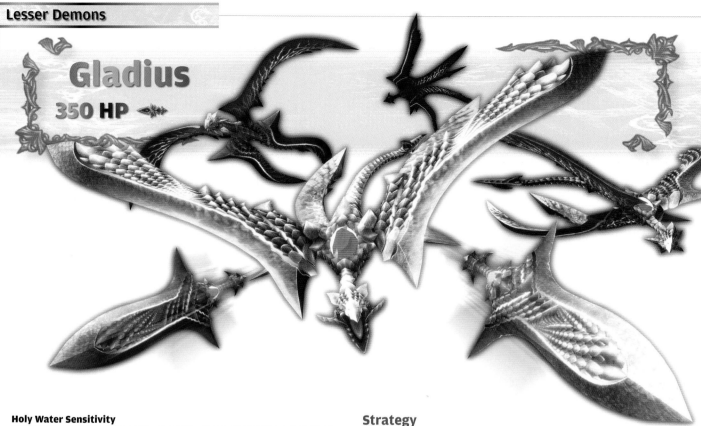

Gladius
350 HP

Holy Water Sensitivity

Vulnerability & Damage		H	DH	SoS	DMD
	0.60	12000	6000	3000	1200

Description

First Appearance: Mission 06. These winged beasts have two forms. In their winged form, they appear as bird-like demons. During their attack mode, or during a recovery mode, they take on the form of a sword.

 DT Time 45 seconds

Attack Data

Attack	Damage	Range	DT Increase	Level
Dash Stab	500	Short	150	2
High Slash	500	Short	150	2

Versus Devil Bringer

	Ground	Airborne	Hold
Buster	Yes	Yes	Yes
Snatch	Pull Enemy	Pull Enemy	

Strategy

You can use your guns to knock Gladius out of the sky, or Nero can use Snatch to pluck them from the air. The instant they fall to the ground they revert to sword form and, with Nero, you can use Buster to deploy a special throw, or simply run to the incapacitated beast and finish it with a combo.

When they use the Dash Stab attack, you can fend it off with your own well-timed melée attacks. In the course of this, when they glow yellow, they incur four times the normal amount of damage, so it pays to attack them quickly at this point, if you're close enough. From further away, if you see them glow yellow and spin for a second or two, look out for a quick flash of light followed by a metallic ring. These occur just before they launch themselves towards you, buying you time to get ready with a Deflect or an evade.

Against a big group of Gladius, Dante can make things easy by using Lucifer. Simply summon a full set of blades and then execute the Climax command. Any contact with the pins will kill a Gladius instantly!

Knock the Gladius into sword form and let them have it with a Buster throw.

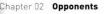

Cutlass
900 HP

Holy Water Sensitivity

Vulnerability & Damage		H	DH	SoS	DMD
	0.60	12000	6000	3000	1200

Description

First Appearance: Mission 06. These fish-like demons can "swim" through solid matter as if it were water. In a pack they're tough cookies. Single one out, and the fight becomes much more manageable.

 DT Time 60 seconds

Attack Data

Attack	Damage	Range	DT Increase	Level
Eruption	400	Short	120	2
Fin Somersault	500	Short	150	3
Fin Dash	300	Short	90	2

Versus Devil Bringer

	Ground	Airborne	Hold
Buster	Yes	Yes	Yes
Snatch	Pull Both	Pull Both	

Strategy

03_36　You have to get Cutlasses out of the ground to deal damage. With Nero, use Blue Rose on the dorsal fin repeatedly, so that it stutters under the impact of the damage. Then use Snatch to

Snatch can pull this beast from the air.

pull Nero to the fin. Once there, use Buster to rip the beast out of the ground. You can also use Snatch to pull a Cutlass from the air when it jumps from the ground to attack you. A Charge Shot with Dante will have the same effect. Charge Shots with Nero at Level 2 or above can be used to rip a Cutlass instantly from the ground.

As Dante, you can use your guns on the dorsal fin to slow it down, and then use Stinger to get close. When you are near the demon, use an uppercut attack, such as Prop or High Time, to prise the Cutlass from the ground. Once it's exposed, lay into it with your best moves.

Once a Cutlass is down, another one will attempt to come to its aid with an attack...

...time a powerful attack at this point to take out both of them at once.

Cutlasses never operate alone, so, when you land one of them, one of the others will try to help it. You can take advantage of this by killing both of them at once. Simply knock a Cutlass down and keep it near you. Another Cutlass will then either warp directly underneath you or use its Somersault attack to try and hit you. By using Nero's Shuffle or Dante's Real Impact, you'll catch it just as it is about to strike and kill its fallen friend into the bargain. Instantly.

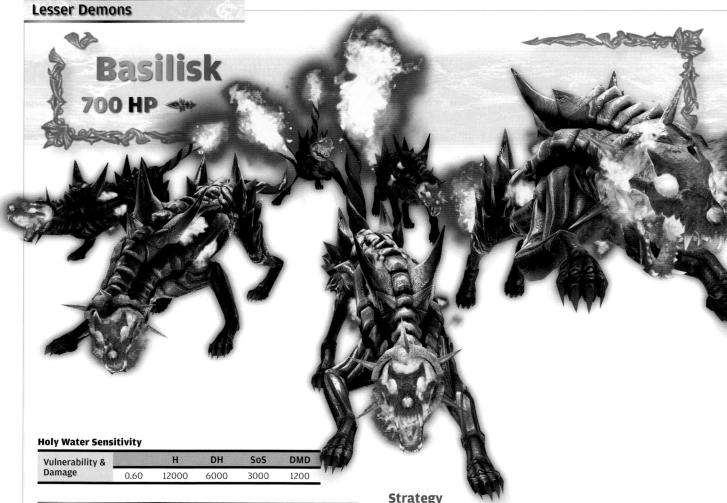

Basilisk
700 HP

Holy Water Sensitivity

Vulnerability & Damage		H	DH	SoS	DMD
	0.60	12000	6000	3000	1200

Description

First Appearance: Mission 16. These dog-like beasts have heads of flame. They can fire these flaming skulls at you and then regenerate them it to do it all over again.

 DT Time 45 seconds

Attack Data

Attack	Damage	Range	DT Increase	Level
Flaming Skull	400	Long	120	2
Jump Flaming Skull	500	Long	150	2

Versus Devil Bringer

	Ground	Airborne	Hold
Buster	Yes	Yes	Yes
Snatch	Pull Enemy	Pull Enemy	

Strategy

Nero can use Buster to launch a special cannon-blast attack on these demon dogs. Dante should use Stinger to close the gap and then hit them hard to eliminate them. They will try to keep their distance so that they can fire a flaming skull at you, so be vigilant and watch for the flash of light that signals the attack, buying you just enough time to dodge it. When you're close, they can side-step your attacks, so be careful about how you attack them.

Nero can take advantage of Snatch to jump well above these demons and then bring one of them up to him. At this point, you can use Buster to fire the dog's head at another Basilisk below. Doing this repeatedly will ensure your safety when you're dealing with a large pack of them.

Use Buster to create you own Basilisk cannon!

Chimera Seed / Chimera
350 HP

Holy Water Sensitivity

Vulnerability & Damage		H	DH	SoS	DMD
	0.60	12000	6000	3000	1200

Description

First Appearance: Mission 07. These are the children of Echidna. In Seed form, they are quite harmless, but when they're around a Scarecrow (Arm, Leg, and Mega) or an Assault, things change. The Seeds are parasitic and will take possession of these enemies, making them faster and far more deadly. They also share the HP of the host demon they colonise, although they can attack independently of it.

 DT Time 30 seconds

Attack Data

Attack	Damage	Range	DT Increase	Level
Parasitic Jump	550	Short	165	2
Tentacle Swipe	400	Short	120	2

Versus Devil Bringer

	Ground	Airborne	Hold
Buster	Yes	Yes	Yes
Snatch	Pull Enemy	Pull Enemy	

Strategy

When they are in Seed form, use Buster with Nero to unleash a one-hit kill. With Dante, just lay into them with strong attacks. When they take over a Scarecrow (Arm or Leg) or an Assault, use your guns to put them to sleep and then deal with the host. During possession the Chimera share the HP of the host, so, although you've incapacitated them with your guns, they're not actually dead, just unconscious, and will be revived shortly. Using their tentacles, they attack independently of the host.

Buster instantly dispatches the Chimera Seed.

It should be noted that the Seeds can't possess a Mega Scarecrow, but they will try if one is in the area. When this happens, the Mega Scarecrow will turn on the Seed and fight it.

Mephisto
1200 HP

Holy Water Sensitivity

Vulnerability & Damage		H	DH	SoS	DMD
	0.60	12000	6000	3000	1200

Description

First Appearance: Mission 05. These creatures are covered with a magical dark cloth. This cloth is the source of their power. Rip the cloth away and expose the inner insect-like demon.

 DT Time 45 seconds

Attack Data

Attack	Damage	Range	DT Increase	Level
Point Attack	800	Short	240	2
Spin Slash	750	Short	225	2
Gyro Wind-up	100	Short	30	2
Gyro Dash	500	Short	150	2
Gyro Finish	700	Short	210	2
Dash Swipe	1250	Short	375	3
Cloth Renew	500	Short	150	2

Special Defence Data

Status	Short Range	Long Range	Buster
Normal (flying)	0.25	0.5	0.0
Deflected (flying)	2.25	0.5	0.0
Change to Insect	0.5	0.5	0.5
Insect	1.2	1.0	1.0
DT Normal (flying)	0.5	0.5	0.0
DT Insect	1.2	1.0	1.0

Versus Devil Bringer

	Ground	Airborne	Hold
Buster	Yes	Yes	Yes*
Snatch	Pull Enemy	Pull Enemy	

* Insect form only.

Strategy

When the Mephisto's cloak is intact, use an up-close Level 3 Charge shot to peel it away instantly. You can also use repeated deployments of Snatch or Buster to rip away the cloth. With Dante, use Pandora. This will expose the extremely vulnerable insect demon beneath. If you tear the cloth away when the Mephisto is above a spot where it can't fall, it will immediately regenerate the cloth. There must be a landing spot on solid ground the insect can fall to.

A Level 3 Charge Shot easily removes the cloth of a Mephisto!

Once they are in insect form, you have 10 seconds before their dark cloak regenerates. Unleash your best attacks when the insect is exposed. Buster, especially with Devil Trigger, is ideal.

While the cloak remains around the Mephisto, you can actually deal full damage by deflecting its Point attack. This is easy to do, as the Mephisto telegraphs it by spinning round while its claw glows brightly. A Charge Shot is a good option for this, but you can just as easily wait until the claw is stuck in the ground and then strike it with your sword. This stuns the creature for a period of time, during which it will incur maximum damage from all attacks. This vulnerable time is based on the attacks you land, so try to use a damaging combo that finishes with a very powerful strike.

Look for the Mephisto's finger to glow while it spins around, to signal the Point attack...

...dodge the attack and then strike the claw to stun the Mephisto...

...allowing you deal full damage with regular attacks.

Faust
3000 HP

Holy Water Sensitivity

Vulnerability & Damage		H	DH	SoS	DMD
	0.50	10000	5000	2500	1000

Description

First Appearance:
Mission 10. Just like a Mephisto, but with more tricks up its sleeve.

DT Time 150 seconds

Attack Data

Attack	Damage	Range	DT Increase	Level
Dual Pierce 1st	700	Short	210	2
Dual Pierce 2nd	800	Short	240	2
Spin Slash	850	Short	255	2
Claw Slash 1st	600	Short	180	2
Claw Slash 2nd	600	Short	180	2
Dual Uppercut	1400	Short	420	3
Deflect Counter	750	Short	225	2
Summoned Piercers	450	Short	135	2
Summoned Dash Piercers	450	Short	135	2
Cloth Renew	500	Short	150	2

Special Defence Data

Status	Short Range	Long Range	Buster
Normal (flying)	0.25	0.5	0.0
Deflected (flying)	2.25	0.5	0.0
Change to Insect	0.5	0.5	0.5
Insect	1.2	1.0	1.0
DT Normal (flying)	0.5	0.5	0.0
DT Insect	1.2	1.0	1.0

Versus Devil Bringer

	Ground	Airborne	Hold
Buster	Yes	Yes	Yes*
Snatch	Pull Enemy	Pull Enemy	

* Insect form only.

Strategy

03_37 Faust can be handled in the same way as Mephisto, but a little more cautiously. His cloth is more resilient and is worth more damage when ripped away, so Charge Shots are essential. The Faust also uses other attacks, so it only rarely uses Dual Pierce. Dual Pierce has a much shorter version of the Mephisto's Point's visual cue, so, if Faust does use it, you can still deflect the attack to stun Faust. With so many other potential attacks at the Faust's disposal, however, you'd do better to focus on removing the cloak than to rely on it using this single attack.

Rip away the Faust's cloth to make it vulnerable.

If the Faust uses Summoned Piercer it can make dodging a lot harder, especially in cramped spaces.

On higher difficulties the Faust will hold its claws out in front of it and summon a set of six thin, red Piercers to accompany its attacks. This means that, while you circle round the Faust, dodging its attacks, you need to use a series of Side Rolls to ensure that you also dodge the Summoned Piercer attacks that follow its normal attacks. Even more essential, then, to use Charged Shots to remove the cloak, as other methods, like Snatch and Pandora, will leave you vulnerable for a little too long.

Bianco Angelo

1100 HP

Holy Water Sensitivity

Vulnerability & Damage		H	DH	SoS	DMD
	0.60	12000	6000	3000	1200

Description

First Appearance: Mission 03. These armoured beasts carry shields that can withstand 900 damage points before shattering. They carry lances to stab you with, and can fly and dash at will.

DT Time 60 seconds

Attack Data

Attack	Damage	Range	DT Increase	Level
Shield Bash	500	Short	150	2
Lance Stab	700	Short	210	2
Lance Stab (air)	700	Short	210	2
Stabbing Dash	1000	Short	300	3
Stabbing Dash (air)	1000	Short	300	3
Backhand	300	Short	90	2
Shield Backhand	600	Short	180	2

Versus Devil Bringer

	Ground	Airborne	Hold
Buster	Yes	Yes	No
Snatch	Pull Nero	Pull Nero	

Strategy

Buster does exceptional damage to their shields, but this prompts them to counter immediately with a shield bash and lance stab. Since you know this is coming, make frequent use of Buster, and then Side Roll, to get behind them and deal massive damage. They are weak against attacks from the back, since their shield is at the front, so the use of Exceeded Red Queen strikes on a Bianco's back

can very quickly finish it off. You can trigger a special Buster attack from the front when the shield is down, or from behind when it is up, or with good timing, as they launch an attack against you. With Dante, you can use Yamato to eliminate the Bianco's shield quickly. A couple of Yamato slashes, followed by strikes from Rebellion or Gilgamesh, then Yamato again, will break through their defence quickly.

Use Buster once the Bianco's shield has been shattered.

While in the air, it's possible to knock them to the ground with a Charge Shot or well-timed strike from Red Queen. Use Snatch to get behind them, where you can deal damage easily. Dante's Dance Macabre can interrupt their attacks effortlessly and deal massive, unhindered damage. When using Dance Macabre, switch to Gilgamesh before the last strike and then use Real Impact to inflict mega damage.

Alto Angelo
3000 HP

Holy Water Sensitivity

Vulnerability & Damage	H	DH	SoS	DMD
0.80	16000	8000	4000	1600

Description

First Appearance: Mission 09. This demon is an enhanced version of the Bianco Angelo. He's faster and stronger and can command the Biancos to launch special attacks. His shield can withstand 700 damage points before shattering.

DT Time 120 seconds

Lesser Demons

Attack Data

Attack	Damage	Range	DT Increase	Level
Bare Backhand	300	Short	90	2
Shield Bash	500	Short	150	2
Shield Backhand	600	Short	180	2
Sword Slash 1st	300	Short	90	2
Sword Slash 2nd	300	Short	90	2
Sword Slash 3rd	300	Short	90	2
Exceed Slash 1st	700	Short	210	3
Exceed Slash 2nd	700	Short	210	3
Exceed Slash 3rd	700	Short	210	3
Exceed Slash 4th	800	Short	240	3
Mid-Air Slash 1st	700	Short	210	3
Mid-Air Slash 2nd	700	Short	210	3
Energy Ball	1200	Short	450	3
Troop Stab	2000	Short	600	4

Versus Devil Bringer

	Ground	Airborne	Hold
Buster	Yes	Yes	No
Snatch	Pull Nero	Pull Nero	

Strategy

You can deal with Alto Angelos in much the same way as you would a Bianco. Get behind them, where it's easy to deal damage, use Buster to weaken the shield and, when the shield is down, use Buster for a special attack. Most notable here is the Altos' special energy attack. When they call the Biancos to them for the Energy Ball attack, you can reflect the attack with a Charge Shot or Red Queen strike, killing every single one of them and netting SSS style in one fell swoop.

When paired with Biancos, they also have the ability to command the Biancos to make a suicide strike. They will do this more often at high difficulties, so all you have to do is avoid the Biancos' charge and watch as they destroy themselves.

Use a Charge Shot to deflect the Energy Ball and kill them all with style.

Fault

200 HP

Holy Water Sensitivity

Vulnerability & Damage	H	DH	SoS	DMD
N/A	Immune	Immune	Immune	Immune

Description

First Appearance: Mission 14. These odd little demons have only one goal in life and that is to grab you and pull you down to a secluded pit filled with other demons. Once in the pit, you have to kill everything in the area in order to escape. This adds time, and possibly damage, to your Mission. Faults have low HP and not a single attack, but you would be well advised to avoid their trap! When they appear, it's not hard to kill them and put them out of your misery.

Kill a Fault quickly for some peace of mind.

Bosses

These are the biggest and baddest enemies in the game. You'll need to be especially Stylish if you wish to get past these monstrous demons. In DMD mode, all Bosses (except Dante) will activate DT when they have 20% or less of their HP left. Every Boss has 10 bars in its Health Meter, which means they will DT when they are down to two bars or less. You can also calculate the HP value of each bar by dividing their total HP by 10.

Berial
10000 HP

Holy Water Sensitivity

Vulnerability & Damage		H	DH	SoS	DMD
	0.40	6000	3000	1500	600

Description

First Appearance: Mission 02. This massive Centaur-like demon enters our world via a Hellgate. He is cloaked in fire and carries a huge flaming sword. At first he's rather slow on the attack, but as the fight progresses and he loses HP, he turns up the heat. Be prepared for Berial to get far more aggressive toward the end of the battle.

Attack Data

Attack	Damage	Range	DT Increase	Level
Sword Foreslash	1000	Short	300	3
Sword Backslash	800	Short	240	3
Jump Foreslash	800	Short	240	4
Jump Backslash	1100	Short	330	4
Howling	700	Short	210	4
Right-Hand Uppercut	800	Short	240	3
Sword Slam	1200	Short	360	3
Dash Slam	700	Short	210	3
Front Stomp	1000	Short	300	3
Rear Stomp	1000	Short	300	3
Front Dash Stomp	700	Long	210	3
Hyper Dash	1700	Long	510	4
Magma	500	Long	150	10
Nova Blast (core)	1800	Short	540	4
Nova Blast (splash)	1200	Long	360	4

Versus Devil Bringer

	Ground	Airborne	Hold
Buster	Yes	Yes	No
Snatch	Pull Nero	Pull Nero	

Strategy

🖥 | 03_38   Nearly all Berial's attacks can be interrupted with Buster, but he will immediately counter with a Stomp, which can be quickly evaded, giving a boost to your DT gauge. You can damage Berial anywhere on his body but his weak spot is his head, where your attacks deal 20% more damage. As Nero, use Snatch constantly to pull yourself to his head and launch your attacks. As Dante, use Air Hike to get close. Berial has three modes of action, all based on his HP level.

Berial's Action Modes

Mode	HP Level
Normal	10000 - 7001
Aggravated	7000 - 4001
Enraged	4000 - 1

Berial will always use the Nova Blast attack when he changes modes. Nova Blast has two damage values. One is for when you're caught at ground zero of the blast (core) and the other for when you're at a distance from the attack and are hit by the waves radiating from the core (splash). With each mode he gets faster and also employs more attacks. If you do enough damage to Berial in a short period of time you can extinguish the flames covering his body. After you've dampened the flames, Berial is vulnerable to a special Buster attack.

Three Buster attacks can be triggered. Firstly, by using Buster on his head when he's standing. Secondly, by using Buster on his body while he's standing. Thirdly, by using Buster anywhere on him when he's been knocked down. While Berial's flames are extinguished, you can knock him down by dealing a specific amount of damage before the flames regenerate. The following tables detail the damage required to extinguish his flames ("Flame-out"), the knockdown damage required during a Flame-out and how much time it takes for Berial to regenerate the flames ("Flame-on").

When the flames are out, jump up to Berial's head..

...and use Buster for a powerful throw.

Dante can use a jumping Royal Block to make avoiding the Nova Blast damage easier.

Dante Must Die!

03_39   As Nero, use Snatch and Roulette, while constantly holding down a Charge Shot. Release the Charge Shot on Berial's Head as soon as it reaches level 3, which has the advantage of stopping most of Berial's attacks in their tracks. You should aim to keep as much height as possible to help avoid attacks, and use Calibur to get closer to Berial when needed.

This will remove the flames quickly, especially if you Exceed the Roulettes. Dante can easily remove Berial's Flame by attacking his head with Full House. Use Jump Canceling to stay in the air and perform quick repetitions of Full House without touching the ground. Try to stay as high as possible to avoid most of Berial's attacks. There are fairly large gaps between his attacks, so once you have dodged one you'll often have time to use Real Impact on his side before he can do anything about it, and then continue with Full House at the peak of the attack.

When Berial uses Nova Blast it's important to avoid it with Nero's Shuffle, or with a jumping Royal Block (with Dante). When the flames have gone, use Nero's DT to hack away at Berial and follow up with a DT Buster to his head and another to his fallen body. Dante in this situation can simply use DT Real Impact a couple of times, which should leave Berial all but dead.

You can use Buster to stop Berial's attacks...

...which cause him to rear up and stomp the ground...

If you need to boost your DT gauge quickly during the fight, you can attempt to Buster Berial (or use sword attacks on his hind legs with Dante) when his flame is still on. This causes him to use the Stomp attack, which you can easily avoid by using Shuffle (or a jump with Dante), even while holding a Charge Shot. Repeating this keeps you safe while quickly building your DT gauge up. Don't use an Exceed Shuffle, however, as this will allow Berial to hit you as you recover.

...so use Shuffle to evade the attack get your DT gauge up.

Flame-out & Flame-on Parameters

Mode	Total Damage For Flame-out	Knockdown Damage	Flame-on vs Nero	Flame-on vs Dante
Normal	2000 in 40 seconds	1000	6.66 seconds	0.666 seconds
Aggravated	3500 in 20 seconds	1200	3 seconds	0.666 seconds
Enraged	2000 in 40 seconds	800	1 seconds	0.666 seconds

Bael / Dagon
10000 HP

Holy Water Sensitivity

Vulnerability & Damage		H	DH	SoS	DMD
	0.30	6000	3000	1500	600

Description

Bael's First Appearance: Mission 04.
Dagon's First Appearance: Mission 15. Bael and Dagon are identical in all aspects except colour. Bael is light-coloured, with blue Rusalka's on his tentacles, while Dagon is darker and has red Rusalkas. Both of these demon toads can hide in the shadows while manipulating the Rusalkas to attack you. When they're visible, they'll often try to eat you or flatten you with a Body-slam attack.

Attack Data

Attack	Damage	Range	DT Increase	Level
Rusalka				
Right Uppercut	1000	Short	300	2
Left Uppercut	1000	Short	300	2
Spin Slash	500	Short	150	2
Jump Spin Slash	600	Short	180	2
Embrace	0	Short	0	3
Bael / Dagon				
Tentacle Swipe	700	Short	210	2
Tentacle Slap	1000	Short	300	2
Jump Tentacle Slap	700	Short	210	2
Devour	1000	Short	450	2
Chew	300	Short	90	0
Jump Bodyslam	1200	Short	360	2
Ice Rain	600	Long	180	2
Ice Wave	1200	Long	360	2
Stomp	700	Short	210	2

Versus Devil Bringer

	Ground	Airborne	Hold
Buster	Yes	No	No
Snatch	Pull Nero	Pull Nero	

Strategy

🖥 | 03_40 When these beasts hide in the shadows, you have the Rusalkas to contend with. When you've dealt sufficient damage to the Rusalkas, Bael/Dagon will emerge. Because the Rusalkas and Bael/Dagon share HP, all damage you do to the Rusalkas counts as damage to the main body. If a Rusalka embraces you, you'll end up frozen and Bael/ Dagon will immediately appear to Devour you. If you are ever frozen or eaten, use Devil Trigger (if you have it) right away in order to break free. Dagon is far more aggressive than Bael, and will use the Devour attack much more frequently.

Bael's ice breath will freeze you...

...so use Devil Trigger to break free.

If you do damage a Rusalka enough, she'll lose consciousness. This is indicated by her growing dark and then falling to the ground. You can make this happen quickly by hitting a Rusalka with Red Queen and then firing a Level 3 Charge Shot at her. The Rusalkas dodge all gunfire, except when they're going through damage animation, so precede your shot with a sword strike.

When a Rusalka is unconscious, you're unable to inflict any more damage. So use Buster on her to pull Bael/Dagon immediately from the shadows. He'll be stunned for a moment, so attack him quickly. These beasts will also emerge from the shadows if a Rusalka freezes you or if you deal a Rusalka 1000 damage points.

You can damage a Bael/Dagon anywhere on its body, but the face is the weak spot. Its back is covered with ice, but the amount of ice shrinks as a result of the damage from your attacks. When all the ice is gone, the creature loses consciousness. When this happens, use Buster quickly to launch a special attack on its tongue. Occasionally, these beasts will fall down while you are attacking them, so, when you see them lose their footing and fall, deploy Buster quickly in another special attack.

Use Buster on an unconscious Rusalka...

...this will pull Bael/Dagon from the shadows.

When Bael/Dagon is unconscious, use Buster on the exposed tongue...

...for an amazingly powerful throw.

When Bael/Dagon is down to 40% (3 bars) of his HP, he will become Enraged. In this state he moves faster, uses the Devour attack more frequently and no longer disappears into the shadows. These demons also have a Guard mode which involves their covering themselves with ice. During a Guard, you can't damage them, but you can attack the Rusalkas to release Green Orbs.

Dante Must Die!

03_41   A single Red Queen strike against the Rusalkas will not usually not manage to faze them enough for Nero's Charge Shot to hit, so use Streak instead, watching for the reel-back animation as your cue to release your Charge Shot. Also, remember that you can stop the Rusalka's attacks dead in their tracks with a well-timed Buster. Dante should use Gilgamesh's Kick 13 to keep the Rusalkas occupied, but he can't use Buster to drag Dagon back into the fight, so you should focus on just one Rusalka until it falls unconscious, and then move on to the next.

Nero can use Exceeded Streaks to approach Bael's head. From there you can follow up with Exceeded Red Queen strikes, while holding a Charge Shot and dodging his attacks with side rolls. Staying at Bael's side is the safest option, as none of his attacks can reach you there, but it's worth aiming for his head when releasing your Charge Shots. Dodging the Ice Wave attack to either side will allow you to land a Charge Shot on Bael's tongue as he recovers, which will hurt him badly.

Dante can simply dodge Dagon's attacks close up and then follow with a Real impact while the beast recovers

As soon as the Rusalkas reappear, and you've dragged Bael back into the fight, use your DT to launch some Red Queen Combo Cs, along with summoned swords, to inflict enough damage to get Bael unconscious, ready for the DT Buster attacks.

Echidna
13000 HP

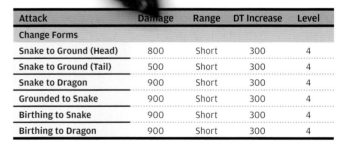

Holy Water Sensitivity

Vulnerability & Damage		H	DH	SoS	DMD
	0.40	8000	4000	2000	800

Description

Echidna's Forms

Form	Description
Dragon	Female body is not visible. She flies and uses diving attacks.
Snake	Female body is visible with tail of dragon.
Birthing	Plants legs in ground and produces Chimera Seeds via her Seed Tube.
Grounded	Buries Dragon tail in ground and only female body is visible.

First Appearance: Mission 07. Echidna is a formidable adversary bringing many variations and possibilities to the fight. She has 4 forms that she assumes during battle, and which she augments when she becomes Enraged. If you are near Echidna when she changes forms, you can be damaged by the process. Echidna will become Enraged when you kill her children (the Chimera Seeds) and when her HP falls to 3900 or less (~2.5 bars). When Echidna is Enraged, she moves more quickly and will fire Chimera Seeds at you. She also exposes her female body while she is in Dragon form.

Attack Data

Attack	Damage	Range	DT Increase	Level
Hair Swing (1st)	300	Short	90	2
Hair Swing (2nd)	500	Short	150	3
Tail Swipe	1300	Short	600	4
Tentacle Stab	300	Short	150	2
Tentacle Slam	500	Short	240	3
Tentacle Swing	400	Short	180	3
Flower Snap	800	Short	300	4
Dragon Dive	1000	Short	300	4
Dragon Bite	500	Short	300	4
Seed Throw	200	Long	90	2

Attack	Damage	Range	DT Increase	Level
Change Forms				
Snake to Ground (Head)	800	Short	300	4
Snake to Ground (Tail)	500	Short	300	4
Snake to Dragon	900	Short	300	4
Grounded to Snake	900	Short	300	4
Birthing to Snake	900	Short	300	4
Birthing to Dragon	900	Short	300	4

Versus Devil Bringer

	Ground	Airborne	Hold
Buster	Yes	Yes	No
Snatch	Pull Nero	Pull Nero	

Strategy

03_42 When she is in Snake form, run to her and jump up to attack her exposed female body. As Nero, use Snatch to keep yourself close to her

When she is in Birthing form, move in quickly for a Buster attack.

02

for your attacks. With Dante, Air Hike to her and use Aerial Rave. When she falls unconscious in Snake form, use Buster to activate a special attack. During this attack, you'll notice Nero is working the Exceed handle of Red Queen. This is your cue to rapidly tap the Exceed Trigger repeatedly to inflict rapid-fire extra damage on Echidna! This also applies to her Enraged Snake form.

When she dives at you in Dragon form, you have several options. As Nero, you can evade her or use a Charge Shot to stop her in her tracks. You can also use a well-timed High Roller or Shuffle to phase through her. When Echidna is in Enraged Dragon mode, you can execute a carefully timed Buster to grab her and perform the special Exceed attack. As Dante, you can either evade or use Pandora's Epidemic to stop her. It is possible to perform Royal Guard to Royal Block the attack

...At the start of the battle Echidna will come at you in dragon form...

...which is the perfect time for a Royal Release to strip away half of her health in one hit.

or to execute a Royal Release during the attack. A Royal Release inflicts a huge amount of damage.

When she is in Birthing form, use Buster on the Seed Tube for a special attack. During the Buster manoeuvre, tap the Buster button rapidly to land more strikes and inflict more damage. You can climb up top to damage her female body but you'll need Air Hike to get there. While you're on top, watch out for her Hair Swing attack and Flower Snap attack.

When she is in Grounded form, she'll make tentacles rise out of the ground and attack you. Avoid them when they appear and go directly to her female body to attack her. If she falls unconscious during this form, use Buster with Nero or Real Impact with Dante.

When Echidna is Enraged, she will throw Chimera Seeds at you. You can destroy these with your guns or you can deflect them back at her with your sword. Deflecting them back is a good way to cause damage whilst simultaneously boosting your Style Rank.

Dante Must Die!

🖳 | 03_43 Echidna will spend a lot more time in Grounded form on DMD, presenting a perfect opportunity to hack away at her with Exceeded Red Queen combos, preferably in DT if your gauge is high enough. Her tentacles will rarely be in a position where they can hit you, and even those that are can be avoided with Shuffle. The Hair Swing is a greater threat and must be jumped to avoid both hits. Dante can use Rebellion's Dance Macabre on her in Grounded form to cause substantial damage while retaining the ability to dodge attacks. Using your DT here is also a good idea to gain a considerable early lead in the fight, and will usually knock her unconscious for further DT punishment.

As usual you should be holding a Charge Shot at the ready to deal extra damage and to stop the more deadly attacks cold. This is important when dealing with Echidna's Snake and Dragon forms, especially when you use aerial combos against her in Snake form, as stopping the Hair Swing is very important. Dante can use Pandora's Epidemic to knock Echidna away when she's attacking in Dragon form.

Using the DT versions of the special Buster throws is essential once you have knocked her unconscious or when she flies straight at you in Dragon from. Dante can again use Full House cancelled repeatedly into Enemy Step to safely damage Echidna when she is in Snake form. If she enters Birthing mode, using Pin-Up to release the full complement of 15 Lucifer Blades and then Air Hiking and directing them into her upper body will deal substantial damage. This move can be repeated twice if detonated as quickly as possible with Ecstasy.

When she is in Grounded form, Dante can use DT Dance Macabre while she is unconscious for staggering damage.

Agnus
10000 HP

Holy Water Sensitivity

Vulnerability & Damage		H	DH	SoS	DMD
	0.30	6000	3000	1500	600

Description

First Appearance: Mission 06. Agnus hides behind a glass barrier in his secret laboratory. You must destroy the barrier to reach him.

Attack Data

Attack	Damage	Range	DT Increase	Level
Electric Turret	1500	Long	450	4

Versus Devil Bringer

	Ground	Airborne	Hold
Buster	No	No	No
Snatch	N/A	N/A	

Strategy

This fight isn't really against Agnus but against the room he is in. You have to destroy the barrier that Agnus is hiding behind. You can use your weapons to do this, although they can only cause very little damage. Instead, use the Gladius that are flying about the room. You can use Snatch or Blue Rose to knock a Gladius out of the sky easily. Once it falls, it converts to sword form and sticks in the ground. Use Buster to grab the sword and throw it at the barrier. This does much more damage than your weapons!

Pro Tip!

If you watch Agnus behind the barrier, his actions will telegraph the Gladius attacks!

When the electrical turret in the centre of the room begins firing, stand on top of it to avoid damage. You can also jump into the air and use Snatch or Blue Rose on a Gladius to remain suspended in the air until the electrical attack below is over. The length of time for the electrical attack varies according to the difficulty level.

Use Buster to throw the sword Gladius at the barrier.

Duration of Electrical Attack

Difficulty	Duration
Human	1 second
Devil Hunter	2 seconds
Son of Sparda	3 seconds
Dante Must Die	4 seconds

Angelo Agnus
12000 HP

Holy Water Sensitivity

Vulnerability & Damage		H	DH	SoS	DMD
	0.25	5000	2500	1250	500

Description

First Appearance: Mission 09. This is Agnus's demon form. He may come across as a nerdish researcher, but he is actually a formidable opponent. He uses 1 or 2 swords at a time and a magic Fireball Cannon, and can summon Gladius, Basilisk and Cutlass to fight alongside him. He also has two ways to steal your HP for himself.

Attack Data

Attack	Damage	Range	DT Increase	Level
Single Sword Slash-1	600	Short	180	3
Single Sword Slash-2	500	Short	150	3
Dual Sword Slash-1	600	Short	180	3
Dual Sword Slash-2	800	Short	240	3
Fireball Cannon	500	Long	150	3
Cutlass Spin (Wind-up)	400	Short	120	3
Cutlass Spin (Throw)	500	Long	150	4
Cutlass Somersault (Into Ground)	500	Short	150	2
Cutlass Somersault (From Ground)	800	Short	240	4
Weak Absorb (Grab)	1000	Long	300	4
Weak Absorb (Absorbing)	25	Short	7.5	0
Weak Absorb (Throw)	500	Short	150	4
Strong Absorb	2500	Long	750	4

Versus Devil Bringer

	Ground	Airborne	Hold
Buster	No	Yes	No
Snatch	Pull Nero	Pull Nero	

Strategy

📺 | 03_44   As Nero, use Snatch and Buster to pull the Gladius from the air and throw them at Agnus. You can also use Snatch to pull yourself to Agnus and unleash your melee attacks. As Dante, you can often use Real Impact when he is stationary. With Sword Master, jump towards him and use Aerial Rave, or attack him from the ground.

When he tries the Weak Absorb, you can either evade as he dashes towards you, use a Charge Shot to stop him or interrupt him by attacking him with your sword. If he grabs you with the attack, activate Devil Trigger to break free. When he begins using the Strong Absorb attack, attack him quickly to make him stop.

When Angelo Agnus is dizzy, use Buster for a devastating special attack.

You can obtain White Orbs by destroying the enemies he summons, so using Devil Trigger is often a good idea. Once you deal enough damage to Agnus, he becomes dizzy. When this happens, use Buster with Nero or Real Impact with Dante. When he summons the Fireball Cannon or the Cutlass, evade his attacks to avoid damage.

📺 | 03_45   Using the usual combination of Roulette and level 3 Charge Shots works very well against DMD Agnus. Combine this with early use of DT and rendering Agnus unconscious shouldn't take long at all. Dante can simply run towards Agnus when the battle begins and use DT Real Impact up to three or four times in a row to gain a substantial early lead. When Agnus summons the Gladius swords around him, attacking him from the side with an air combo such as Roulette will deal good damage while also destroying all of the swords. This keeps your DT Gauge full, allowing you to use it very freely.

Nero's Roulette can be used to knock Agnus out of most of his attacks.

Dante can gain an early lead using Real Impact before Agnus gets going.

Once you've hacked at him for a while and gained a good lead, Agnus will usually move to the centre of the room to begin the Strong Absorb. You'll need to land a quick series of attacks to take him out of it: Roulette is perfect for this with Nero. Dante can use mid-air Lucifer strikes here instead, which have the advantage of inflicting extra damage when the blades explode.

Using an Air Hike followed by Blue Rose shots will enable you to stay high enough to evade the Cutlass Spin attacks that Agnus uses late in the fight. Dante can use Lucifer in the air during the Cutlass Spins and then, once the attack has finished, direct all of the Blades into Agnus' body. This causes extra damage, which may be necessary to finish Agnus off safely if he uses his DT.

Angelo Credo
10000 HP

Holy Water Sensitivity

Vulnerability & Damage		H	DH	SoS	DMD
	0.25	5000	2500	1250	500

Description

First Appearance: Mission 08. This is the demon form of Credo, Kyrie's brother and General in command of the Holy Knights of the Order of the Sword. He is very skilled with his sword and carries a shield with a magical Aura for defence. He blocks and counters at an alarming rate, and he also has long-range magical attacks to round out his close-range arsenal. He is truly a foe to be reckoned with.

Attack Data

Attack	Damage	Range	DT Increase	Level
Sword Combo 1st	500	Short	150	3
Sword Combo 2nd	400	Short	120	3
Sword Combo 3rd	400	Short	120	3
Angelo Helm Breaker	600	Short	180	4
Counter Slash	600	Short	180	4
Shield Bash	700	Short	210	4
Angelo High Time	400	Short	120	4
Angelo Stinger	800	Short	240	4
Angelic Slash	800	Short	240	4
Javelin Throw	800	Long	240	4
Phantom Spear Shot	300	Long	90	2
Phantom Spear Ring	100	Long	30	2

Versus Devil Bringer

	Ground	Airborne	Hold
Buster	Yes	Yes	No
Snatch	Pull Nero	Pull Nero	

Strategy

03_46   Credo has a 3-part sword combo attack, which he can end with Angelo Helm Breaker to make it a 4-part combo. He can also start the combo with move 2 and then end it with Angelo Helm Breaker for a 3-part combo. He will often follow Angelo High Time with Angelo Helm Breaker. While Credo can use these moves effectively for his counterattacks, he also has dedicated counterattacks that you will have to contend with. Counter Slash is only used as a counter and Shield Bash is only used when you attempt a Snatch.

After his counterattack, there is a short window of opportunity when he is vulnerable to attack. You can land up to 3 strikes during this time before he blocks or evades. Buster is also a great choice. A typical and effective string of moves for attacking Angelo Credo is Streak, Evade, Streak, Buster. Credo will block your initial Streak attack and will then launch his own counterattack. Evade his counter, then immediately use Streak again. This stuns Credo and leaves him open to further attacks. While he is stunned, it is a perfect time to use Buster!

Strike Credo's shield to provoke a response...

...once he retaliates, dodge the attack...

...and launch him for a combo as he is recovering

The Shield Bash counter can actually be exploited to your benefit. When you attempt a Snatch, Credo immediately executes this move in which he dashes towards you and hits you with his shield. You can easily evade this with a Side Roll, which will put you behind him. Now quickly use Streak to hit him from behind for immediate damage!

The shield Angelo Credo carries is enchanted with a magical aura. It can sustain a set amount of damage before the Aura is shattered. When the shield starts glowing red, it is close to losing its Aura. When this happens, you have 12 seconds before the Aura regen-

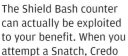
Using Buster when the shield's Aura is down leads to a devastating attack.

erates. While the Aura is down, Credo can't block, providing the perfect opportunity to use Buster for a special attack. You can use Buster from the ground or in the air, with or without Devil Trigger activated. Each of these 4 scenarios has its own slightly different animation and damage values.

Once Credo's HP has fallen to 30% (3 bars) or less, he becomes Enraged and his attack pattern changes: he becomes faster and uses more devastating attacks than earlier in the fight. Just before this happens, Credo will fall to his knees in exhaustion. At this point, the Aura on his shield is reduced to half strength and Credo is open to attack. Quickly run to him for a Buster attack when this happens.

Once at a distance, Credo will likely throw a javelin...

...use Buster to catch the javelin and throw it back at Credo...

...which leaves him stunned and open to attack.

Credo will occasionally move to the far side of the combat area and use a long-range attack. When he is not Enraged, he will throw a large javelin. Once he becomes Enraged, he also adds two Phantom Spear attacks to the javelin throw. You can either evade the Javelin or, if your timing is good, catch it with Buster and throw it back at Credo! This impales Credo and leaves him open to further attacks. When he uses the Phantom Spears, you can evade or use Red Queen to knock the spears from the air. When he throws the javelin, watch for the flash of light over his right shoulder and start the Buster manoeuvre as soon as you see it.

Pro Tip!
You do not have to be facing Credo to catch the javelin. You can catch it even if your back is to him!

Dante Must Die!

03_47 You will need to be patient in this fight to remove Credo's shield reliably. Use Shuffle or side rolls to avoid his attacks and then take any opportunity to launch Credo with High Roller, including after you have caught his Javelin Throw. Don't use the Exceed or DT versions of the High Roller to launch Credo, as it will probably enable him to escape any aerial combo you attempt. Try to keep all your aerial combos short to prevent Credo tech rolling away. With Nero a single Red Queen strike followed by a mid-air Buster is sufficient, as you are only relying on the Buster to damage the shield.

Once you have landed enough Busters, the shield will eventually fall and you are free to use the DT Buster for the real bulk of your damage in this fight.

Dante vs Credo (in Bloody Palace mode)

Dante is not as reliant on dodging Credo's attacks as Nero. You can instead use repeated Full House kicks to simply beat your way through his attacks and, once this happens, you can follow up with Gilgamesh's Kick 13 to launch him. Once Credo is in the air, use Full House again to bring him to the ground near you and continue with another Kick 13, which Credo will partially block. At this point Credo is certain to attack and if you dodge well, you'll be able to land Kick 13 again to repeat the process. Once the shield is gone, use DT Dance Macabre as many times as possible to destroy Credo's health.

The Savior
7750 HP

Holy Water Sensitivity

Vulnerability & Damage		H	DH	SoS	DMD
	0.15	3000	1500	750	300

Description

First Appearance: Mission 11. This statuesque behemoth was brought forth by Sanctus and the Order of the Sword. Sanctus preaches that The Savior holds the key to the world's salvation. You face The Savior 3 times in the game. There is little to do in the first and last encounter, but Mission 18 is completely devoted to battling this ultimate demon.

Attack Data

Attack	Damage	Range	DT Increase	Level
Mission 11				
Right Hand Punch	2000	Short	600	4
Mission 18				
Right Hand Swat	800	Short	240	4
Left Hand Swat	800	Short	240	4
Arm Slam	1300	Short	390	4
Arm Chop	1200	Short	360	4
Dual Arm Smash	1300	Short	390	4
Elbow Smash	1200	Short	360	4
Axe Kick	1400	Short	420	4
Roundhouse Kick	1200	Short	360	4
Final Flash (stream)	200	Short	60	4
Final Flash (finish)	600	Short	180	4
Platform Destruction	1300	Short	390	4
Platform Debris*	500	Short	150	4
Quad Energy Ball	300	Long	90	2
Triple Cannon Shot	500	Long	150	4
Cannon Shot Explosion	100	Short	30	2
Mission 20				
Right Hand Punch	1500	Short	450	4
Left Hand Punch	2000	Short	600	4

* Debris triggered after Platform Destruction

Versus Devil Bringer

	Ground	Airborne	Hold
Buster	Yes	No	No
Snatch	N/A	N/A	

Strategy

 03_48 In Mission 11, you primarily fight Sanctus. Towards the end of the fight, Sanctus will retreat into The Savior who will then attack you with a right-handed punch. Use Buster to deflect this punch and knock Sanctus to the ground.

The last encounter in Mission 20 is much the same as the first. The Savior will throw a right-handed punch and then a left-handed punch. You must deflect both of these with Buster. Once you have done so, use Buster a final time on The Savior's head.

Mission 18 is a more complex battle consisting of 2 parts. In part 1, you must destroy 8 Cores that are located on various spots on The Savior's body. In part 2, you must destroy the Main Core on The Savior's chest. The Main Core has a Health Meter in part 2; none of the Cores in part 1 do.

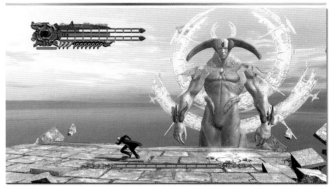

A Health Meter appears for the Main Core during part 2 of the fight.

The entire battle will take place on small platforms located high above the Castle Town of Fortuna. You must make your way around the platforms using Jump Pads. There is no set path or order for this fight so you can choose how you wish to handle it. The basic rule of movement is always to move to the right. You can move to the left, but occasionally The Savior will destroy a platform in that direction, which can lead to you landing on a dead-end platform without a Jump Pad (a Jump Pad will deactivate if its corresponding platform has been destroyed).

During part 2, you start on a series of small platforms that require you to move to the right. Once you have passed all of these, you land on a central platform with others to the right or left. The final battle now begins and the Main Core's Health Meter is displayed.

Suggested Preparation for part 1

Item	Description	Status
Style	Trickster	Fully levelled
Melee Weapon	Gilgamesh	Kick 13 acquired
Gun	Shotgun	Standard
Ability	Air Hike	Standard

Part 1 Core HP

Core Location	HP Value	Core Location	HP Value
Left Leg	150	Left Shoulder	250
Right Leg	150	Right Wrist	250
Back	250	Right Shoulder	250
Left Wrist	250	Forehead	200

In part 1, you should select the Trickster style for its Dash and Sky Star abilities, which make evading enemy attacks much easier. The Shotgun is used for destroying the Cores, since some of them are out of your melee weapons' range. Adding Air Hike is beneficial to evasion and also help you gain altitude for rapid shotgun fire. You can fire four blasts with your shotgun during an Air Hike before you come back down to the ground. The power and speed of Gilgamesh's Kick 13 quickly activates the Emblem Switches, saving you valuable time.

Use the Laser Turrets and Pulse Cannons to your advantage.

During part 1, there are Laser Turrets and Pulse Cannons on some of the platforms, which are activated by attacking the Emblem Switch attached to each of them. Use a Laser Turret to paralyse one of The Savior's arms. Use a Pulse Cannon to knock The Savior unconscious for 90 seconds.

When you start the fight, concentrate on taking out the Cores on his legs and back. Use a Pulse Cannon to knock him unconscious, then take the right Jump Pad in front of you to reach the leg and back platforms. Again, move to the right and break each Core you come to.

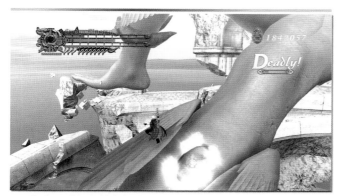

The Shotgun is invaluable for breaking the Cores.

When you have destroyed the first 3 cores, concentrate on the arms. Use a Laser Turret to paralyse an arm during his arm attacks, and climb on the arms to reach the cores. You can also reach the forehead core from the shoulder of either arm. During part 1, there are regular enemies that you'll encounter on the platforms. In particular you should watch out for the Faults: as in previous Missions, the Fault will drag you down into a pit filled with enemies that you must defeat before you can be released.

Suggested Preparation for part 2

Item	Description	Status
Style	Trickster	Fully levelled
Melee Weapon	Gilgamesh	Kick 13 acquired
Gun	Pandora	Fully levelled
Ability	Air Hike	Standard

 Main Core HP: 6000

03_49 The only change suggested for part 2 is to swap the shotgun with a fully levelled Pandora. When Pandora is completely levelled up, you gain the Revenge attack which is highly beneficial in part 2 of this fight. You'll also want to use Gilgamesh to attack the Main Core when the time arrives.

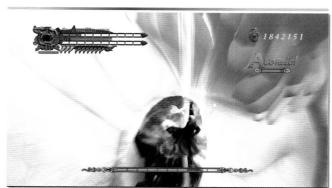

Real Impact is ideal for taking out the Main Core.

During this part of the battle, evade The Savior's attacks as before. Move from platform to platform and when he pauses, use Pandora's Revenge to knock him unconscious. Once he is down, use the Jump Pad to reach the Main Core. You don't get much time with the Main Core, so you'll have to use your fastest and most powerful attacks when the opportunity arises. Activating Devil Trigger and using Real Impact or Kick 13 are excellent choices.

Sanctus
15000 HP

Holy Water Sensitivity

Vulnerability & Damage	H	DH	SoS	DMD
0.25	5000	2500	1250	500

Description

First Appearance: Mission 11. He is the leader of the Order of the Sword. Having ascended, he possesses great demonic powers and seeks to bring The Savior to life. The Halo on his back is the source of his power and he protects himself with a magic shield.

Attack Data

Attack	Damage	Range	DT Increase	Level
Shield Blast	500	Short	150	2
Lightning Blast	800	Short	240	1
Lightning Rain*	800	Short	240	2
Fireball Blast	200	Long	60	2
Flame Wave	1200	Long	360	0
Missile Strike	300	Long	90	4
Savior Strike	2000	Short	600	4

* This attack covers a wide area.

Versus Devil Bringer

	Ground	Airborne	Hold
Buster	Yes	Yes	No
Snatch	Pull Both	Pull Both	

Strategy

03_50 To deal damage to Sanctus, you must first break his shield and then destroy the Halo on his back. Use Snatch repeatedly to get close and stay airborne. Attack the shield with Red Queen;

You must shatter the shield surrounding Sanctus before you can damage him.

Roulette Spin is a great attack for this. Once the shield is down, you have only a short time before it regenerates. Use Snatch again to move closer and strike him once with Red Queen to break the Halo before the shield comes back. When the shield regenerates, it does so with an explosive blast, so stay clear of Sanctus when the shield is reforming.

With the Halo gone, he will fall to the ground and be powerless. It is then possible to use Snatch on him to pull him towards you. You have a short time before he regenerates the Halo. You can attack him with melee attacks during this time, but make sure to use Buster with Devil Trigger activated before the Halo is regenerated. Using Buster triggers a special and very damaging attack. You can increase the damage by rapidly tapping the Buster button while the attack is in progress.

Break the Halo on Sanctus's back to knock him to the ground.

Sanctus has two Missile Pods in front of him. These will charge and fire at you occasionally. Although you can't destroy them, you can deactivate them by shooting them with Blue Rose. You can also use Snatch on them to pull yourself closer to Sanctus. When Sanctus uses the Fireball Blast attack, you can use Blue Rose repeatedly to shoot the fireballs out of the air!

When Sanctus is down to 30% (3 bars) of his HP or less, he will retreat into The Savior. When he does this, The Savior will lash out with a strong right-handed punch. Use Buster to deflect this punch. Not only does this negate the attack, but it also knocks Sanctus from The Savior without his shield or Halo so that he is immediately vulnerable to your attacks.

Deflecting The Savior's attack will expose Sanctus instantly.

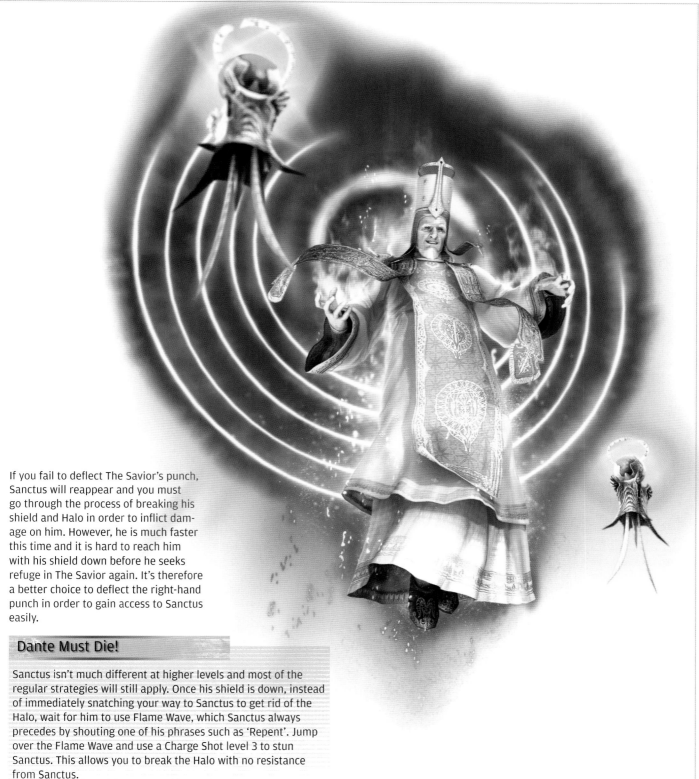

If you fail to deflect The Savior's punch, Sanctus will reappear and you must go through the process of breaking his shield and Halo in order to inflict damage on him. However, he is much faster this time and it is hard to reach him with his shield down before he seeks refuge in The Savior again. It's therefore a better choice to deflect the right-hand punch in order to gain access to Sanctus easily.

Dante Must Die!

Sanctus isn't much different at higher levels and most of the regular strategies will still apply. Once his shield is down, instead of immediately snatching your way to Sanctus to get rid of the Halo, wait for him to use Flame Wave, which Sanctus always precedes by shouting one of his phrases such as 'Repent'. Jump over the Flame Wave and use a Charge Shot level 3 to stun Sanctus. This allows you to break the Halo with no resistance from Sanctus.

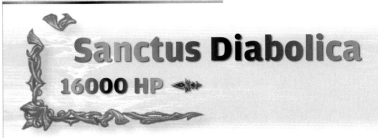

Sanctus Diabolica
16000 HP

Holy Water Sensitivity

Vulnerability & Damage	H	DH	SoS	DMD
0.25	5000	2500	1250	500

Description

First Appearance: Mission 20. The early part of this fight is identical to the Mission 11 encounter. However, as Sanctus loses HP, he ups the game by adding special attacks with the Sword of Sparda.

Attack Data

Attack	Damage	Range	DT Increase	Level
Shield Blast	500	Short	150	2
Lightning Blast	800	Short	240	1
Lightning Rain*	800	Short	240	2
Fireball Blast	200	Long	60	2
Flame Wave	1200	Long	360	0
Missile Strike	300	Long	90	4
Sparda Slash 1st	1200	Short	360	2
Sparda Slash 2nd	1500	Short	450	2
Sparda Stinger	2500	Long	750	2
Sparda Stinger (Turn)	500	Short	150	2

* This attack covers a wide area.

Versus Devil Bringer

	Ground	Airborne	Hold
Buster	Yes	Yes	No
Snatch	Pull Both	Pull Both	

Strategy

🖥 | 03_51

Once Sanctus shouts 'Burn!', stand directly underneath him to avoid his fireballs, and land a Charge Shot.

Early in the fight, follow the same strategy used on Sanctus in Mission 11 but with one difference: this time, when you break the shield, he will block your attacks with the Sword of Sparda. In order to hit him, you must use Buster to break his guard, and then hit him with Red Queen to break the Halo.

Once his health begins to fall, he will teleport to the ground to slash at you with his sword. You can either evade this attack or use Buster to deflect it and stun him. Once he is stunned, you are free to attack him and use Buster. As before, activate Devil Trigger with Buster to deal more damage.

Use Buster to deflect his Sparda attacks...

When Sanctus's HP is very low, he will begin using Sparda Stinger. This is a very damaging attack but is easily deflected with Buster. As Sanctus dashes forward with the attack, use Buster to deflect it and trigger a special counterattack of your own!

...for a very cool throw animation.

Also new to this round is his ability to call forth several Missile Pods to surround you. Once they have encircled you, they will fire within 1 second. Use Snatch to pull yourself out of the ring of Missile Pods before they fire. You can also use Air Hike to escape them. When Sanctus uses the Fireball Blast, you can evade or shoot the fireballs down with Blue Rose as in the previous encounter.

Dante Must Die!

DMD Sanctus Diabolica will move much faster than on lower difficulties, making it hard to keep up with him. He will telegraph his Fireball Blast by focusing energy and emitting a roar. When this happens, standing directly underneath him will enable you to avoid the attack easily and will also shorten the attack so that you can go back on the offensive sooner.

When Sanctus brings the sword up to his chest and then lowers it, he will either shout 'I sentence you to death' to signal the Lightning Rain attack or simply go straight into Lightning Blast, which is your cue to jump up and attack him. If his shield is down, this will be a superb opportunity to use Roulette to remove the Halo and stun Sanctus. If you are too far away, a jumping Charge Shot can be used to stop either attack. The subsequent explosion from the Shot will then stop Sanctus in his tracks briefly, allowing time to remove the Halo with melee attacks.

Dante
3000 / 7000 HP

Holy Water Sensitivity

Vulnerability & Damage		H	DH	SoS	DMD
	0.25	5000	2500	1250	500

Description

First Appearance: Mission 01.
Mission 1 HP: 3000.
Mission 10 HP: 7000.

Dante the demon hunter, the owner of Devil May Cry and Son of Sparda, is the hero of the previous games and the co-star of this game. Unfortunately, he is also a Boss that you must face to prove yourself worthy. When you face Dante, he can use any of the attacks in his arsenal and any of the four Styles he employs. Please refer to the Combat System chapter for full details of all Dante's attacks and damage values.

Versus Devil Bringer

	Ground	Airborne	Hold
Buster	Yes	Yes	No
Snatch	Pull Enemy	Pull Enemy	

Strategy

03_52

In Mission 01, Dante holds back slightly. All you need do is stay close and attack with Red Queen. When he attacks, use a well-timed Side Roll to avoid damage. When you stun him with your attacks, use Buster for a grab and throw attack.

The encounter in Mission 10 is far more advanced. Dante pulls out all the stops, so you'll need to be very defensive and time your attacks appropriately. During this encounter, Dante will use all 4 styles available to him. He uses Helm Breaker a lot, no matter which style is employed. When he uses this attack, Side Roll away, and then jump into the air and counter with Split. You can also jump into the air and use Snatch to interrupt this attack.

Snatch and Buster are essential to deal Damage to Dante...

...but Dante can escape your Buster, leading to a series of weapon clashes.

If you have good timing, you can use Buster as he approaches with a sword strike. When he walks up to you, use Buster to interrupt his move just as he unleashes his attack (not Helm Breaker) and throw him to the ground. When he uses his guns to shoot at you, jump into the air near him and use Snatch to pull him up to you, and then immediately use Buster for a powerful throw. In fact, you can use Snatch at almost any time to pull Dante to you and then use Buster quickly for a throw. Be careful with this move though, as Dante can occasionally break free and counter with Helm Breaker.

Shoot at Dante from this range to open him up to Snatch and other attacks.

When he uses Trickster style, you can often hit him with Blue Rose during a dash. This is a great time to use a Charge Shot. However, this is the only case where Blue Rose is an effective tactic. When Dante switches to Royal Guard, he means to block your attacks. Now is the perfect time to use Buster for a damaging slam and throw manoeuvre.

Dante is also very susceptible to your Devil Trigger, which greatly enhances your Buster throw. If you find yourself the facing the brunt of one of Dante's ruthless Million Stab attacks (or any other multiple hit attack), activate Devil Trigger to interrupt him. When you do so, immediately strike him twice and then use Buster for a throw.

Dante Must Die!

▢ | 03_53   Hitting Dante with regular attacks can be very difficult and first requires you to evade one of his attacks or Snatch him. A critical factor in this battle is the knowledge that using Blue Rose will make Dante respond with shots from Ebony & Ivory when he's not at very close range. If you do this whilst approaching Dante, you can quickly land a Snatch (or a Buster if you are close enough) while Dante is shooting. It's possible simply to walk towards him shooting and then Buster him as soon as you are within range. You can then repeat this when he gets up again but remember not to approach too close, to ensure that he starts shooting.

Once you have Dante open, use a series of three slashes...

...and then quickly use Snatch to allow you to repeat this combo...

...eventually finishing with a DT Buster.

From further away you can shoot Dante and then Snatch him out of his responding fire. A successful Snatch can be instantly followed up with a Buster, but Dante will always spring free of your grab and commence a long sequence of weapon clashes with Nero. If you win this sequence outright, Dante will be pushed back and lose a significant amount of health. However, it's more likely that you will end up right next to Dante with either you or him at a considerable advantage. The slightly random nature of this scenario means you're better off simply striking Dante with Red Queen after a Snatch. You can land the first 3 slashes of Combo A (preferably using Exceed) and then Snatch again quickly after the third hit connects. You can repeat this three times and Dante will then escape during the fourth set of slashes. For this reason it is best to enter DT after the third set of strikes and use DT Buster to finish the combo. Immediately exit DT and then repeat the whole process from the start.

Dante vs Dante (in Bloody Palace mode)

Your shadowy opponent in this battle is of course Dante himself, with access to all of his abilities. Unlike Nero's confrontation with him, Dante can be fought here without the need to be overly defensive, as he will not always evade your attempts to initiate an attack with Stinger 2 from a distance. Once Stinger has knocked him down, you can quickly follow up with Million Stabs or Slash Dimension F. Using Stinger followed by Slash Dimension F repeatedly will usually cause Dante to respond by entering Royal Guard. If this happens you can fire a few shots at him from afar and then fire again while you are above him. This will make him use the Royal Release below you, after which he will usually revert to a different Style.

Using Royal Guard against Dante is a good idea, as his attack animations should be very familiar to you, making them relatively easy to Royal Block. If Dante evades your Stinger you should have little difficulty in Royal Blocking his response. Once this happens, follow up with one or two slashes from Rebellion and then switch to Gilgamesh for a couple of basic strikes followed

Use Stinger to attack from a distance...

...and if Dante evades it, you can deal with his counter attacks with Royal Block or Royal Release.

by a Kick 13 to launch him. You can use Full House in the air to bring Dante to the ground and then use Gilgamesh's Shock to hit Dante while he's getting back up. Doing this a few times will also build up the Royal Gauge enough for a powerful Royal Release next time Dante evades your Stinger and counters with an attack of his own. If you have DT Gauge to spare, you can simply use DT Real Impact to blast through the opposing Dante's attacks. Repeating this can very quickly reduce his health and finish the fight.

Chapter 03

Combat System

As with the previous installments of the Devil May Cry series, this game offers the player near limitless and fully customizable combat maneuvers. Between the two heroes of Nero and Dante, you have at your disposal a demon arm, 4 long range weapons, 5 melee weapons, and a staggering list of abilities and moves that can all be woven together with insane style. This chapter will explore every aspect of combat in Devil May Cry 4 so that you are fully prepared to face the demon hordes that seek to destroy you.

The Basics

Combos and Attack Chains

In Devil May Cry 4, your attacks are extremely varied, not just a single hit. Whilst you can throw a single slash, or fire a single shot, the combat engine has far more to it. Your most basic moves are pre-set "Combos" that have multiple parts or hits. These Combos require multiple and often varied lengths of button press. The beauty of the system is that you are not committed to performing all strikes of a pre-set Combo sequence; you can interrupt these sequences at any time with jumps, evades or special moves at almost any point. This freedom in Combat allows you to customize your playing style and create your own personalised combos. During Combat, you will often string together several Combos, partial Combos, or gun manoeuvres. String these varied moves together to form an "attack sequence" or "attack chain". The length of the sequence is dependent only upon the enemy's health and your desire.

During Combat, you will often string together several Combos, partial Combos, or gun manoeuvres. String these varied moves together to form an "attack sequence" or "attack chain". The length of the sequence is dependent only upon the enemy's health and your desire.

Lock On

From the very start of the game, Lock-On is a vital aspect of combat. Hold **RB** | **R1** to bring up a target marker that will appear over the enemy closest to your character's position.
When you are locked on to an enemy, regardless of which direction you move the Left Stick, the character will always face the currently targeted enemy.

The circular marker indicates a Lock-On and the enemy's health level.

The circular target marker which appears when you lock on also doubles as the enemy's Health Meter, allowing you to see how much life your opponent has left. As you damage the enemy, the Lock-On target marker will dwindle in size. Once the marker is completely gone, so is the enemy.

Lock-On has one other important aspect to it. It's used as the primer for inputting commands for special attacks. Certain attacks in the game require **RB** | **R1** to be held down (activate Lock-On) in order for you to input other commands to execute the attack. For example, to execute High Roller you must hold **RB** | **R1**, then pull back on the Left Analog while also tapping **Y** | **△**. There are many special commands in the game that require Lock-On to be active. We'll discuss them all in this chapter.

Direction Change

If you aren't locked on to an enemy, you can change the direction of attack during the execution of a Combo or attack sequence. Upon executing a manoeuvre in a sequence, push the Left Stick in any direction and your character will turn that way and strike, using the next move in the sequence.

Defensive Manoeuvres

Side Roll

While holding **RB** | **R1** to execute a Lock-On press the Left Stick sideways in relation to the direction your character is facing and press **A** | **✕**. This command will execute a Side Roll allowing you to zip out of the way of an incoming attack quickly.

Enemy Attack Cues

Upon starting stage 2 you will be faced with a group of three Arm Scarecrows. Dispatch two of these enemies, leaving the third one unharmed. Now you are free to learn evading skills using the remaining enemy as a test dummy.

Lock-On to this enemy by holding **RB** | **R1** and listen to the sound it makes before it strikes you with it's weapon. The sound emitted by the Scarecrow is your cue to evade. This enemy uses an audio cue to signpost an imminent attack, so you can anticipate an attack even if it's coming from off-screen. The lesson to learn here is that as soon as you see or hear a cue from an enemy, evade immediately using a side roll or jump. Once you have mastered anticipating a single enemy's movements it might be a good idea to restart the mission and do the exercise again with all three enemies alive and active. Try to get used to the way you can still evade the attacks of other enemies while still holding Lock-On to target a single enemy in front.

Jumping

With Lock-On held down, the direction Nero faces while jumping will always be towards the targeted enemy. Push the Left Stick forwards or backwards + **Ⓐ** | **Ⓧ** to perform a front flip or back flip respectively, while a sideways jump is replaced by the Side Roll. The only jump animation completely unaffected by Lock-On is the standard straight-up jump, performed by pushing **Ⓐ** | **Ⓧ** alone. This simple jump is extremely useful as an evade and as a means to pursue an enemy blasted upwards by one of Nero's attacks.

Tight Evade

Executing an evasion just before an enemy attack hits is called a Tight Evade. The window of opportunity to score a Tight Evade is very narrow. Not only are Tight Evades completely safe in terms of getting out of the way of incoming danger, but they will also increase your Stylish Points and Devil Trigger gauge (covered later).

Evade conditions

Situation (Nero & Dante)	CP Value	CP Timer	DT Increase	Comment
Tight Evade (> 5 frames & ≤ 20 frames) *1	150	0	350	Use Side Roll or Jump*2
Tight Evade (≤ 5 frames) *1	250	0	800	Use Side Roll or Jump*2

*1 A frame is equivalent to 0.016 seconds.
*2 Table Hopper is different from Side Roll.

Deflect

If you launch an attack just as an enemy is launching its own, the two attacks will clash. This situation is known as a Deflection. With good timing, you can deflect the attacks of just about every enemy you come across in the game.

Air Royal Block

By performing a simple jump just as an enemy's attack would hit you, you can increase the window of opportunity for a Royal Block. Just jump as an attack nears you, then perform the block to Royal Block the attack easily.

Offensive Manoeuvres

Long Range Attacks

Nero's long-range weapon is Blue Rose. Blue Rose is capable of targeting enemies from a great distance. Its power, however, is too low for it to be useful as a primary method of attack. Blue Rose is complementary to Nero's sword attacks. For example, gunfire can hold an enemy aloft after it has been blasted upwards by a sword slash.

Use Blue Rose to juggle an enemy in the air with ease.

Melee Attacks

Pressing **Ⓨ** | **△** button repeatedly will launch sword strikes with Red Queen. If you hold **RB** | **R1** to Lock-On to an enemy, all sword attacks will be directed towards that enemy.

Special Attacks

Special attacks use a combination of the Left Stick directional commands and button presses. For these to be executed, Lock-On must be activated. Since Lock-On causes your character to face the targeted enemy, the Left Stick directional commands change according to the orientation of your character.

For example, if Nero has targeted an enemy on the left-hand side of the screen, then "Front" on the Left Stick is to the left, since that is the direction Nero Faces. Conversely, if Nero were facing the camera (the TV screen), then "Front" would be down on the Left Stick.

Crowd Control

When you are Locked-On to a specific enemy, you are still open to attack from other enemies in the area. By releasing Lock-On during an attack sequence, you can change direction using the Left Stick and deliver attacks to enemies who are trying to hit you from behind or from the side. You can stop the attacks of most minor enemies in the game completely, simply by turning and striking them.

Streak can be used to push groups of enemies around, or knock them over.

As you deal damage to the enemy, you will be graded on how Stylish you are. In the upper right-hand corner of the screen is the Stylish Gauge. Each move you make is judged, rated, and added to this meter. There are seven style levels that can be displayed.

Combat Ranks

D	Deadly!
C	Carnage!
B	Brutal!
A	A comic!
S	Smokin'!
SS	Smokin' Style!!
SSS	Smokin' Sick Style!!!

There is also an E Rank, which is not displayed. This means that you must first be Stylish enough to get past E Rank before the Stylish Gauge is displayed. Below the letter rank is the Stylish Gauge bar. To increase your rank from one level to the next, you have to fill the gauge of each rank with "CP" or "Combat Points" (not to be confused with "Stylish Points", which are different and are discussed in the Game System Chapter).

The SSS Rank is the highest and most coveted combat rank you can achieve.

Every move in the game has a certain CP value associated with it. Each time you perform a move, that CP amount is added to the gauge. But there is a catch. After a move has been performed once, a timer is activated, and you must wait until that timer expires before using the same move again. If you use the same one too soon, or repeatedly, in a sequence, then you don't get CP for it.

Each rank has a set value of CP required to fill the Style Gauge and move you up to the next Rank. Further, as time passes the gauge will become slowly depleted. Each rank depletes itself at a different rate. The higher your Style, the faster the gauge will fall, so you must add more CP to the gauge quickly in order to maintain

your rank. Devil May Cry 4 runs at 60 frames of animation per second. The Style Gauge updates every frame that passes.

Style Gauge Values

Rank	Gauge CP Value	Depletion Rate
E	500	0.5 - frame
D	700	1.0 - frame
C	900	1.2 - frame
B	1000	1.5 - frame
A	1500	2.0 - frame
S	750	2.5 - frame
SS	1250	3.0 - frame
SSS	1250	3.5 - frame

The table shows that you must acquire at least 501 CP before you can exit the E Rank category and move up to D Rank and display the Stylish Gauge on screen. The time in seconds for a frame is given as 1 / 60 = 0.016. That is 16 thousandths of a second per frame. To find how much time you have per rank before the gauge is fully depleted, divide the Gauge CP Value by the frame depletion rate, then multiply that by 0.016. Let's look at the B Rank.

$$B \text{ Rank} = 1000 / 1.5 = 666$$

It will take 666 frames to completely deplete a full B Rank Style Gauge. This equates to 666 * 0.016 = 10.65 seconds.

If you are hit or otherwise damaged during combat, the Style Gauge immediately drops two full ranks per hit! Furthermore, S, SS, and SSS ranks are all treated as 1 gauge with respect to damage. So if you have an S Rank, or an SS, or an SSS and get hit, you immediately fall to B Rank.

As mentioned before, in order to receive CP, you must perform an action. Each attack that you land on an enemy has a CP value associated with it. If you haven't used that attack more than once within the specified time limit, then that CP value is added to the gauge. The CP value for each attack for both Nero and Dante is listed later in this chapter.

Alongside normal combat, there are special bonuses for certain moves that you can perform in the game. The following tables list all of these bonuses. The CP Timer value is given in frames. This is the number of frames that must pass before you can use the manoeuvre again, if you want the CP Value to be counted. For example, a Taunt has a CP Timer value of 600 frames. At 60 frames per second, you can see that you must wait 10 seconds after a Taunt before the next Taunt is counted.

The tables also show the amount of "DT" or "Devil Trigger" energy you receive for these manoeuvres. Devil Trigger and its gauge are discussed later in this chapter.

Defensive Manoeuvres

Case	CP Value	CP Timer	DT Increase
Both Nero and Dante			
Taunt	*	600	*
Tight Evade (> 5 frames & ≤ 20 frames)	150	0	350
Tight Evade (≤ 5 frames)	250	0	800
Enemy Step	150	150	350
Nero Only			
Table Hopper (> 5 & ≤ 7 frames)	150	0	350
Table Hopper (≤ 5 frames)	250	0	800
Evade with Shuffle (> 5 frames & ≤ 20 frames)	150	0	350
Evade with Shuffle (≤ 5 frames)	250	0	800
Block attack with Aegis Shield	150	60	350
Dante Only			
Block	150	60	350
Just Block	350	0	1000
Guard Release	200	60	500
Just Release	500	60	1000
Flipper	300	0	500
Mustang	300	200	500
Evade with Dash	150	0	350
Evade with Sky Star	150	0	350
Evade with Air Trick	150	0	350
Sheath Yamato	400	0	1000

* Varies based on your current Stylish Rank.

Nero's Exceed can give your Style a big boost if your timing is good enough...

...while Dante can use powerful attacks such as Real Impact for the same purpose.

Special Combat Situations

Case	CP Value	CP Timer	DT Increase
Alto Angelo: Deflect Energy Ball	2000	60	2000
Alto Angelo: Destroy Shield	1000	60	1000
Angelo Credo: Destroy a Phantom Spear	200	0	300
Angelo Credo: Catch Javelin with Buster	1000	60	1000
Angelo Credo: Destroy Javelin	1000	60	1000
Angelo Credo: Deflect a Sword strike	1000	60	1000
Angelo Credo: Break Shield Aura	1000	60	1000
Assault: Destroy Shield	350	0	500
Assault: Destroy Mask	500	0	500
Bael & Dagon: Use Buster on Unconscious Rusalka	500	0	1000
Berial: Evade Magma with Buster	350	300	1000
Berial: Evade Hyper Dash with Buster	300	200	1000
Berial: Attack Lower Body after Buster Throw	300	200	1000
Bianco Angelo: Destroy Shield	800	0	500
Blitz: Destroy Before Blitz before Destruct Explosion	4000	0	3000
Dante (enemy): Deflect a Sword strike	350	0	750
Echidna: Stop Dragon Dive	1500	0	1000
Echidna: Destroy a Seed Throw	500	0	1000
Echidna: Deflect a Seed Throw	500	0	1000
Faust: Deflect Dual Pierce	400	60	750
Faust: Deflect Summon Piercers	150	60	300
Frost: Destroy Healing Ice	1200	0	1000
Mega Scarecrow: Deflect Rolling Dash	650	60	1000
Mephisto: Deflect Point Attack	400	0	750
Sanctus (M20): Deflect a Sparda Attack with Buster	1000	60	1000
Sanctus (M20): Use Snatch on a Missile Pod	200	0	100
Savior (M11): Deflect Savior Strike with Buster	1000	60	1000
Savior (M18): Destroy A Core	700	0	500
Savior (M18): Cause Damage Animation	500	0	500
Savior (M18): Knock Unconscious	1000	0	500
Savior (M18): Destroy Quad Energy Ball	150	0	50

About Nero

Abilities

Nero Ability List

Skill Name	Base Cost	Description	Controller Input
Table Hopper	150	Enhanced evasion	[RB] | [R1] + Left Stick + Ⓐ | ⓧ
Table Hopper 2	500	Enhanced evasion level 2	[RB] | [R1] + Left Stick + Ⓐ | ⓧ
Table Hopper 3	1000	Enhanced evasion level 3	[RB] | [R1] + Left Stick + Ⓐ | ⓧ
Speed	300	Increase running speed	Continue holding the Left Stick in any direction
MAX-Act	5000	Instantly charge 3 Exceed Lamps	Pull the [LT] | [L2] trigger with perfect timing on an Exceed Zone.
Get More Orbs	2000	Increases the range of Orbs drawn towards Nero	Automated effect
Enemy Step	5000	Use an enemy as a platform to jump from	When above or next to an enemy, press Ⓐ | ⓧ to jump
Air Hike	2000	Double jump	Press Ⓐ | ⓧ in mid-air to execute an additional jump

Table Hopper

This skill enhances your Side Roll evasion technique and has three levels of upgrade. This ability also has a unique timing feature that will enhance how the evasion looks, as well as how much it contributes to your Devil Trigger Gauge.

Table Hopper Conditions

Manoeuvre	CP Value	CP Timer	DT Increase
Evade less than 5 Frames*	250	0	800
Evade > 5 & ≤ 7 frames*	150	0	350
Evade more than 7 Frames*	0	0	0

* A frame is equivalent to 0.016 seconds.

As you can see, to achieve these bonuses you require split-second, perfect timing. Evading in fewer than 5 frames equates to completing the manoeuvre 0.08 seconds before the enemy attack strikes you. No easy matter. But you aren't lacking tools to help you accomplish this. Each enemy has unique audio and visual cues that signal their attacks. Learn these cues, and you'll be able to anticipate and evade the attack.

Upgrading the Table Hopper ability increases the number of successive dodges that can be performed after the initial Tight Evade. At Level 3, you're able to perform an additional 2 dodges after successfully executing the first one. This is a visually impressive display, in which you can zip around or away from an enemy with 3 Table Hoppers in succession. For example, just as a Scarecrow attack is about to strike, perform a Table Hopper to your left, then perform another immediately to the right, and a final Table Hopper to the right again. Not only do you boost your Style, but you're back in front of the unsuspecting enemy.

Speed

The Speed ability will increase Nero's running speed. The extra boost in speed will be activated after 10 running steps and will continue until you stop running, which happens when you return the Left Stick to neutral.

Rainbow

While executing Speed, aim Nero at an enemy and press [BACK] \| [SELECT] to deliver a stylish drop kick to knock down a hapless foe. This move deals the enemy a 180 damage points.

This odd little attack adds a bit of variety to your basic Speed manoeuvre.

Exceed Zones

Each and every sword slash Nero can perform has a certain "sweet spot" within its movement. If you pull the [LT] \| [L2] trigger at the right time, you'll be able to charge an Exceed Lamp instantly. This is enabled by the free ability Ex-Act. We'll refer to these spots as Exceed Zones. The location of each individual Exceed Zone is covered in Technical Data section of this chapter (page 137).

MAX-Act

This is an enhanced version of Ex-Act. As the name implies, it MAXes out your Exceed gauge by charging all three Exceed Lamps at once. As you might expect, it's a bit trickier to perform MAX-Act than Ex-Act. However, with persistence and practice, you can master MAX-Act and reap the rewards of this incredible ability.

Get More Orbs

This ability will increase the range from which Nero can absorb Red Orbs. Once you have this ability, any dropped or exposed Red orb on the screen will come flying to you, irrespective of distance. This comes in handy when there are lots of breakables in the area, as it allows you to use your guns to destroy the breakables and absorb the orbs from where you're standing.

Enemy Step

Enemy Step allows you to use an enemy's body as a stepping stone to jump from, regardless of whether it's on the ground, standing, or in the air. With Enemy Step, you can sustain height during aerial Combos, cancel aerial attack moves and increase the number of successive hits possible within an attack sequence.

Enemy Step properties

Situation	CP Value	CP Timer	DT Increase
Enemy Step Succeed	150	150	350

Air Hike

The magical field allows a double-jump.

Air Hike creates a platform of magical energy in mid-air, which Nero can use to execute an additional jump from. This double-jump allows you to reach higher platforms and ledges with ease, as well as safely evade enemy attacks. Be aware that the Kick Jump and Air Hike abilities cancel each other out!

You are only allowed two jumps before your feet must touch solid ground again. The first is a normal jump. The second can be either a Kick Jump or an Air Hike. It's up to you, but after you've executed one, you must touch the ground again before you can perform another Air Hike or Kick Jump. One exception is Enemy Step. Not only is Enemy Step a jump, but it also resets the jump count by one, allowing you to perform an additional Air Hike or Kick Jump.

Devil Bringer

Please refer to the Technical Data section of this chapter for damage data relating to Buster and Devil Buster.

Buster

Nero's demonic right arm gives him the ability to grab and throw enemies around like toys! The dramatic throws Nero performs are specific to each enemy type you face. During the throw animation, you're vulnerable to enemy attack. That's to say, while you throw one enemy with Buster, another enemy can easily strike you and cancel the throw.

When a Boss's defences are down, use Buster!

Buster is an extremely important technique when you are fighting a Boss. Bosses can have their defences breached, leaving them stunned and vulnerable to a Buster attack. Performing Buster in this situation will trigger an extremely powerful attack sequence, using the full power of the Devil Bringer. Even the toughest Bosses in the game will find themselves being thrown around like rag dolls, if you learn to recognize the precise moment their defences fail them.

Snatch

Against a lightweight enemy like a Scarecrow, this technique will grab the enemy and pull it to Nero's current position. Snatch can be performed from the ground or from the air, regardless of whether the enemy is on the ground or in the air. Snatch can be upgraded by purchasing the abilities Snatch 2 and Snatch 3. Each one increases the distance over which Snatch will work.

Hell Bound

The second function of the Snatch command occurs when the enemy you attempt to grab is too large or too heavily defended to be pulled to Nero's position. In this situation, the Snatch technique will instead drag Nero to the enemy. Hellbound is also used with stationary grapple points known as Grim Grips. Please refer to the Game System chapter for more information on Grim Grips.

Hold

Hold can be used to defend you against enemy attacks.

You gain this ability by acquiring the Aegis Shield in Mission 08. Hold is a defensive technique in which you start a Buster but, instead of tapping the button, you press and hold it. This causes Nero to hold the enemy in front of him as a shield to block incoming enemy attacks.

You can release an enemy at any time, or you can hold the enemy until it's killed by incoming attacks, or it performs a Hold Escape manoeuvre. Not all enemies can be held, and not all enemies employ a Hold Escape. You can still move, jump, fire Blue Rose and attack with Red Queen, while holding the enemy,

Blue Rose

Blue Rose Attack Data

Technique Name	Attack	CP Value	CP Timer	DT Increase
Normal Shot 1st (short range)*1	10	15	10	15
Normal Shot 2nd (short range)*1	20	15	10	30
Normal Shot 1st (middle range)*1	5	10	10	7
Normal Shot 2nd (middle range)*1	10	10	10	15
Normal Shot 1st (long range)*1	2	5	10	3
Normal Shot 2nd (long range)*1	4	5	10	6
Charge Shot Lv1 (short range)*1	200	200	100	300
Charge Shot Lv1 (middle range)*1	175	175	100	225
Charge Shot Lv1 (long range)*1	150	150	100	150
Charge Shot Lv2 (short range)*1	300	300	100	450
Charge Shot Lv2 (middle range)*1	250	275	100	375
Charge Shot Lv2 (long range)*1	200	250	100	300
Charge Shot Lv3 (short range)*1	400	400	100	600
Charge Shot Lv3 (middle range)*1	350	375	100	525
Charge Shot Lv3 (long range)*1	300	350	100	450
Special Damage				
Charge Shot Lv2 Knockback*2	80	130	250	0
Charge Shot Lv3 Knockback*2	80	130	250	0
Charge Shot Lv3 Bomb (explosion)	400	400	100	0
Charge Shot Lv3 Bomb (splash)	100	175	250	0

*1 Short distance: 0-4m; middle distance: 4m-8m; long distance: 8m and more
*2 The shot can knock an enemy away. If it hits another enemy, it deals damage.

Normal Shot

Repeated taps of ⊗ | ⊡ will fire a volley of shots from Blue Rose. Although not very powerful, the standard shot has many uses and features that are helpful when you're creating stylish combos and breaking down enemy defences.

Use a volley of shots from Blue Rose to juggle an enemy in the air.

Charge Shot

As soon as you've acquired this ability, hold ⊗ | ⊡ down to begin charging the Charge Shot. Nero will channel power from his Devil Bringer into the Blue Rose to increase its destructive power. A charge is signified by a flash on Nero's right arm. There are 3 levels of power for the Charge Shot that can be purchased. To reach each level, simply hold ⊗ | ⊡ down for the required amount of time. When a charge level is reached, you will see Nero's right arm flash as the power grows.

At Level 1, a Charge Shot will push a small enemy away from Nero. If Nero is airborne, the recoil will push him backwards as well. A Level 2 Shot has the same actions as a Level 1, but will also set the enemy on fire, dealing extra damage. If the flaming enemy touches another enemy, then it will be damaged by the demonic flames.

The Level 3 Charge Shot does what the previous levels do, but it also infuses the enemy with an energy bomb that will explode after 3 seconds. The explosion does massive damage to the enemy, and the "splash" (radiating waves of energy) of the blast will damage any foes nearby.

The explosion from a Level 3 Charge Shot is very damaging indeed.

03

Red Queen

Red Queen Command List

Technique Name	Controller Input
Combo A	(Y) | (△) (Y) | (△) (Y) | (△) (Y) | (△)
Combo B	(Y) | (△) pause then (Y) | (△) repeatedly
Combo C	(Y) | (△) (Y) | (△) pause (Y) | (△) (Y) | (△) (Y) | (△) (Y) | (△) (Y) | (△)
Combo D	(Y) | (△) (Y) | (△) (Y) | (△) pause (Y) | (△)
Aerial Combo	In mid-air (Y) | (△) (Y) | (△) (Y) | (△)
Roulette Spin	In mid-air (Y) | (△) (Y) | (△) pause (Y) | (△)
High Roller	Lock-On + Left Stick back + (Y) | (△)
Rising High Roller	Lock-On + Left Stick back + hold (Y) | (△)
Streak	Lock-On + Left Stick forward + (Y) | (△)
Shuffle	Lock-on + Left Stick back then forward + (Y) | (△)
Split	In mid-air Lock-On + Left Stick forward + (Y) | (△)
Calibur	In mid-air Lock-on + Left Stick back then forward + (Y) | (△)

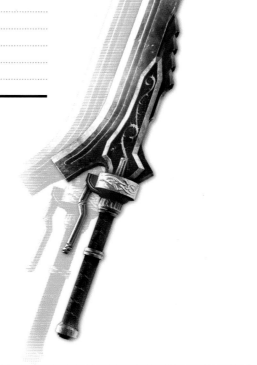

Red Queen Attack Data

Technique Name	Attack	CP Value	CP Timer	DT Increase
Combo A (1st hit)	80	130	250	120
Combo A (2nd hit)	60	130	250	90
Combo A (3rd hit)	40	130	250	60
Combo A (4th hit)	100	170	250	150
Combo B (1st hit)	80	130	250	120
Combo B (2nd hit)	100	130	250	150
Combo B (3rd hit)	80	130	250	120
Combo B (4th hit)	60	130	250	90
Combo B (trigger loop 1)*	28	130	5	42
Combo B (trigger loop 2)*	28	130	5	42
Combo B (11th hit – dual1)	100	130	250	150
Combo B (12th hit – dual2)	140	170	250	210
Combo C (1st hit)	80	130	250	120
Combo C (2nd hit)	60	130	250	90
Combo C (3rd hit – dual1)	40	90	250	60
Combo C (4th hit – dual2)	40	90	250	60
Combo C (5th hit)	60	90	250	90
Combo C (6th hit)	40	90	250	60
Combo C (7th hit)	100	130	250	150
Combo D (1st hit)	80	130	250	120
Combo D (2nd hit)	60	130	250	90
Combo D (3rd hit)	40	130	250	60
Combo D (4th hit)	170	170	250	255
Combo D (splash)	170	340	250	255
Aerial Combo (1st hit)	100	130	150	150
Aerial Combo (2nd hit)	80	130	150	120
Aerial Combo (3rd hit)	120	170	150	180

Technique Name	Attack	CP Value	CP Timer	DT Increase
Roulette Spin (1st hit)	100	130	150	150
Roulette Spin (2nd hit)	80	130	150	120
Roulette Spin (1st rotation)	90	65	150	135
Roulette Spin (2nd rotation)	90	65	150	135
Roulette Spin (3rd rotation)	90	65	150	135
High Roller	90	200	150	135
High Roller (rising)	90	200	150	135
Streak	120	200	150	180
Shuffle	150	250	150	225
Split (while falling)	40	50	150	60
Split (while landing)	60	150	150	90
Calibur (1st hit)	120	250	150	180
Calibur (2nd hit)	60	500	150	90

* Three hits are possible in the trigger loop

Red Queen Combo A

This basic sword combo is a series of three slashes followed by a final downwards slam. With this basic string, it is possible to make Nero change direction, tag special moves on to the combo, or jump out of any of the four sword slashes with ease. Flashy it may not be, but this combo allows you to attack quickly in any direction and won't limit your special move or evading options. Combos B, C, & D each build upon a strike from this Combo. Combo B uses the first strike and then becomes unique. Combo C uses the first two strikes, and Combo D the first three.

Red Queen Combo B

This is a vicious barrage of sword strikes, more akin to bludgeoning the enemy with a blunt club than slashing with a sharp blade! Once you've thrown the first opening slash, pause for half a second, and then tap the button again to initiate the combo. Once it's started, quickly tap **Y** | **△** repeatedly until the combo is over. It's possible to score 10 massive hits with this manoeuvre!

Red Queen Combo C

Combo C is a versatile 7-hit flurry of slashes which allows you to change the direction of attack easily, or flow into special moves throughout. The more precise, radial slashes of Combo C are in complete contrast to the violent, high-risk sword-bashing of Combo B.

Red Queen Combo D

Classing this string as a whole new combo is stretching the truth a little. Red Queen Combo D is simply Combo A with a more powerful finishing strike.

High Roller

If there's one technique that truly defines the Devil May Cry series, it's the ability to launch an enemy skywards and hold it in mid-air with a hail of gunfire. High Roller is Nero's standard launch technique. It will launch an enemy into the air from a standing position. Having launched it, the most basic Aerial Combo to deploy would be to Lock-On to the enemy and attack it with a barrage of gunfire.

Rising High Roller

You can employ this variation of the technique by holding down **Y** | **△** during the execution of High Roller launcher. Nero will take the move a step further by launching himself upwards with the enemy. As soon as they both reach the apex of the jump, Nero will be in the perfect position to do additional damage to his adversary.

Rising High Roller is a great way of launching an enemy for aerial combat.

Aerial Combo

The Aerial Combo is a 3-hit sword manoeuvre performed while in the air. After launching an enemy, tap **Y** | **△** three times to deliver a 3-hit sword combo. The 3rd strike of this combo will send the enemy crashing to the ground.

Streak

Nero quickly dashes forward and delivers a powerful sword strike with an attack range that is wide enough to mow down a whole group of enemies! This is a highly effective technique for closing the gap between you and a distant enemy and dealing good damage at the same time.

Split

If Nero is airborne, this diving sword attack will immediately send him plummeting towards the Earth to deliver a strong, vertical sword slash. Split is a very versatile manoeuvre. The sword will not only damage, and possibly knock down, any ground-based opponent, but it will actually slice an airborne foe downwards out of an Aerial Combo.

Roulette Spin

This mid-air strike allows you to gain height during an Aerial Combo. Upon proper execution of this manoeuvre, Nero will fly upwards in a whirlwind of strikes, taking the enemy with him.

Roulette Spin may be flashy, but it can push the enemy out of melée range.

Calibur

Calibur is great for finishing off an Aerial Combo with style, or simply for moving Nero quickly from one mid-air position to another. If you hit an airborne enemy with Calibur, the enemy will be pushed away from Nero. You're free to perform any other attack before or after Calibur, but you can't deploy Calibur itself more than once per jump.

Shuffle

The first part of this move is a backwards feint, which allows Nero to back away safely from an incoming attack. The second part is a huge uppercut, which is very useful as a launcher. The feint motion will actually make Nero invulnerable for a short time. Timing the execution of Shuffle as a Tight Evade will produce an invincible evade and counter-attack all in one move.

Pro Tip!
Executing Shuffle as a Tight Evade will boost the attack power of the counter attack with a 1.5 modifier.

Exceed

Exceed Upgrades

Ability	Base Cost	Remark
Exceed Level 2	500	Applies up to 2 Exceed Lamps to a special attack
Exceed Level 3	1000	Applies up to 3 Exceed Lamps to a special attack

Basic charging

Nero's Exceed System is a fuel-injection mechanism for Red Queen. Squeeze the [LT] | [L2] button as if you're revving a motorcycle and the Exceed Gauge at the top left-hand corner of the screen will fill up. Each time the gauge fills completely, you will gain one Exceed Lamp (indicated by a lit lamp above the gauge).

A maximum of three Exceed Lamps can be stored via this charging method. The purpose of an Exceed Lamp is to add extra speed and attacking power to sword attacks. Any sword attack can be injected with Exceed, re-gardless of whether it's a basic combo slash, aerial slash, or special move. Basic attacks, when executed, will use one Exceed lamp. The following tables show the damage values for the enhanced Exceed Basic attacks.

You can charge the Exceed Gauge manually at any time.

Exceed Basic Attacks

Name	Attack	CP Value	CP Timer	DT Increase
Combo A (1st hit)	100	130	250	150
Combo A (2nd hit)	75	130	250	112
Combo A (3rd hit)	50	130	250	75
Combo A (4th hit)	125	170	250	187
Combo B (1st hit)	100	130	250	150
Combo B (2nd hit)	125	130	250	187
Combo B (3rd hit)	100	130	250	150
Combo B (4th hit)	75	130	250	112
Combo B (trigger loop 1)*	35	130	5	52
Combo B (trigger loop 2)*	35	130	5	52
Combo B (11th hit – dual1)	125	130	250	187
Combo B (12th hit – dual1)	175	170	250	262
Combo C (1st hit)	100	130	250	150
Combo C (2nd hit)	75	130	250	112
Combo C (3rd hit – dual1)	50	90	250	75

* Three hits are possible in the trigger loop

Name	Attack	CP Value	CP Timer	DT Increase
Combo C (4th hit – dual2)	50	90	250	75
Combo C (5th hit)	75	90	250	112
Combo C (6th hit)	50	90	250	75
Combo C (7th hit)	125	130	250	187
Combo D (1st hit)	100	130	250	150
Combo D (2nd hit)	75	130	250	112
Combo D (3rd hit)	50	130	250	75
Combo D (4th hit)	212	170	250	318
Combo D (splash)	212	340	250	318
Aerial Combo (1st hit)	125	130	150	187
Aerial Combo (2nd hit)	100	130	150	150
Aerial Combo (3rd hit)	150	170	150	225
Roulette Spin (1st hit)	125	130	150	187
Roulette Spin (2nd hit)	100	130	150	150
Roulette Spin (1st rotation)	112	65	150	168
Roulette Spin (2nd rotation)	112	65	150	168
Roulette Spin (3rd rotation)	112	65	150	168

EX-Act

With this technique, you can fill 1 Exceed lamp instantly. All that's required is good timing. Each individual sword attack, whether standard combo slash or powerful special move, has its own specific Exceed Zone, where a perfectly timed press of [LT] | [L2] will immediately gain you 1 Exceed Lamp. You get only one chance per slash to press [LT] | [L2] in that particular move's Exceed Zone. If you miss, you forfeit the opportunity to EX-Act until the next sword slash.

Time it just right and you can gain a full Exceed Lamp with one trigger pull.

Exceed Zones are unique for each Red Queen attack. Learning each of Exceed Zones for every single slash is a daunting task, but one that will handsomely reward the player in Stylish and power-ful combat.

Please refer to the Technical Data section at the end of this chapter for a listing of all Exceed Zones (page 137).

Exceed the Exceed!

Exceed special moves also have their own Exceed Zones. This means that you can have an Exceed Lamp charged immediately after you unleash an Exceed move. Learn these zones so that you can maintain this high level of destructive power constantly from one move to the next. Again, refer to the Technical Data section at the end of this chapter for a full listing of Exceed Zones.

MAX-Act

If you time the ⟪LT⟫ | ⟪L2⟫ trigger press perfectly within an Exceed Zone, you'll immediately charge three Exceed Lamps. With MAX-Act equipped, you have the ability to max-out the Exceed gauge instantly with a single pull of ⟪LT⟫ | ⟪L2⟫.

MAX-Act Exceed Zones are much smaller and earlier than the Ex-Act Zones. As such, MAX-Act is not nearly as forgiving. Each MAX-Act Zone lies 3-5 frames prior to the corresponding Ex-Act Zone. While the Ex-Act Zone is 3-5 frames wide, the MAX-Act Zone is only 1-2 frames wide. It's tight, but is worth the effort.

Exceed Special Attacks

Exceed's injection system enables you to change the way special attacks work and look, and how much damage they can do. There are three Exceed Lamps, which means there are three levels of Exceed that can be applied to these special attacks. The deployment of an Exceed Special Attack will automatically use every Lamp available.

EX High Roller

Level 1 of Exceed adds a flame effect and increases the move's attack power. Another small change this technique undergoes, when Exceed is applied, is a slight delay to Nero's movement as he recoils from the attack. When the uppercut strike ends, Red Queen will continue to swing over Nero's head and bash the ground behind him, which will delay Nero's ability to initiate another attack.

Exceed Level 2 for this attack is the same as Level 1, but with the addition of a second uppercut. Exceed Level 3 gives you get a demon-destroying total of 3 fiery uppercuts.

EX Rising High Roller

Level 1 of this attack is similar to a standard Rising High Roller, with the addition of the fiery explosion. Level 2 adds a second rotation and strike as Nero rises, thereby increasing the attack's damage and height. Level 3 adds a third rotation, providing

The height you gain from EX Rising High Roller (Lv 3) is great for exploration.

even more damage and height. The height gained with Ex High Roller Level 3 can actually be used to reach some of the game's otherwise inaccessible locations.

EX Streak

Exceed changes this attack so that you can hold it in place before launching it. As you execute the command, hold down ⟪Y⟫ | ⟪△⟫. Nero will then hold a ready stance, during which you can rev Exceed to power up the Exceed gauge even further; all the way up to Level 3, if time permits. Each Exceed Lamp charged will add one extra rotation to the spinning strike Nero performs after the dash.

Double Down

When you charge Split with Exceed, it changes from a diving sword slash into a violent downward stab with an explosive finish. Each level of Exceed increases the size of the finishing ground explosion. The explosion can damage nearby enemies with its splash.

The Double Down explosion is good for Crowd Control.

EX Calibur

Charging Calibur with Exceed adds a fiery explosion to the attack. The higher the level of Exceed, the more fire you produce during the finishing sword swing that follows the explosion.

EX Shuffle

When Shuffle is charged with Exceed, you add an additional opening slash that precedes the finishing uppercut. You also, of course, add a fiery explosion to the attack. The higher the level of Exceed, the more fire you produce with the attack's sword swings.

Exceed Special Attacks

Attack Name	Power	CP Value	CP Timer	DT Increase
EX High Roller Lv1 (1st hit)	135	300	150	202
EX High Roller Lv1 (sword carry over)	67	600	150	100
EX Rising High Roller Lv1	135	300	150	202
EX High Roller Lv2 (1st hit)	90	200	150	135
EX High Roller Lv2 (2nd hit)	135	300	150	202
EX High Roller Lv2 (sword carry over)	67	600	150	100
EX Rising High Roller Lv2 (1st hit)	135	300	150	202

Attack Name	Power	CP Value	CP Timer	DT Increase
EX Rising High Roller Lv2 (2nd hit)	90	200	150	135
EX High Roller Lv3 (1st hit)	90	200	150	135
EX High Roller Lv3 (2nd hit)	90	200	150	135
EX High Roller Lv3 (3rd hit)	135	300	150	202
EX High Roller Lv3 (sword carry over)	67	600	150	100
EX Rising High Roller Lv3 (1st hit)	135	300	150	202
EX Rising High Roller Lv3 (2nd hit)	90		5	135
EX Rising High Roller Lv3 (3rd hit)	90	200	150	135
Ex Streak Lv1	180	300	150	270
Ex Streak Lv2 (1st hit)	120	200	5	180
Ex Streak Lv2 (2nd hit)	180	300	150	270
Ex Streak Lv3 (1st hit)	120	200	5	180
Ex Streak Lv3 (2nd hit)	120	200	5	180
Ex Streak Lv3 (3rd hit)	180	300	150	270
Ex Shuffle Lv1 (1st hit)	30	50	5	45
Ex Shuffle Lv1 (2nd hit)	30	50	5	45
Ex Shuffle Lv1 (3rd hit)	135	250	150	202
Ex Shuffle Lv2 (1st hit)	60	100	5	90
Ex Shuffle Lv2 (2nd hit)	60	100	5	90
Ex Shuffle Lv2 (3rd hit)	60	100	5	90
Ex Shuffle Lv2 (4th hit)	135	250	150	202

Attack Name	Power	CP Value	CP Timer	DT Increase
Ex Shuffle Lv3 (1st hit)	78	125	5	117
Ex Shuffle Lv3 (2nd hit)	78	125	5	117
Ex Shuffle Lv3 (3rd hit)	78	125	5	117
Ex Shuffle Lv3 (4th hit)	78	125	5	117
Ex Shuffle Lv3 (5th hit)	135	250	150	202
Double Down Lv1 (while falling)	60	100	150	90
Double Down Lv1 (landing)	90	200	150	135
Double Down Lv2 (while falling)	60	100	150	90
Double Down Lv2 (landing)	190	400	150	285
Double Down Lv3 (while falling)	60	100	150	90
Double Down Lv3 (landing)	290	600	150	435
Ex Calibur Lv1 (1st hit)	60	100	150	90
Ex Calibur Lv1 (2nd hit)	120	250	150	180
Ex Calibur Lv2 (1st hit)	90	100	5	135
Ex Calibur Lv2 (2nd hit)	90	100	5	135
Ex Calibur Lv2 (3rd hit)	120	350	150	180
Ex Calibur Lv3 (1st hit)	100	100	5	150
Ex Calibur Lv3 (2nd hit)	100	100	5	150
Ex Calibur Lv3 (3rd hit)	100	100	5	150
Ex Calibur Lv3 (4th hit)	120	450	150	180

Devil Trigger

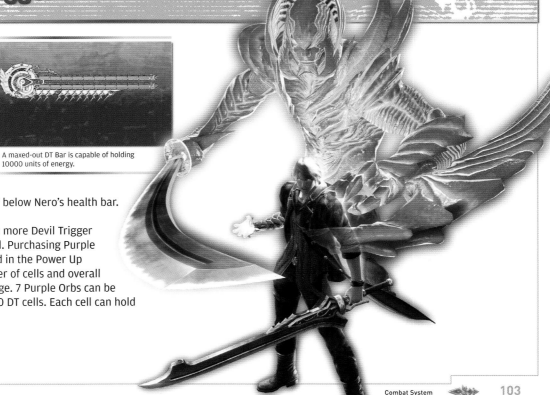

Nero's Devil Trigger is available when his demonic powers are awakened after his encounter with Agnus in Mission 6. Initially, you will only be able to enter this mode for a short time. The duration of Devil Trigger is determined by the length of the Devil Trigger

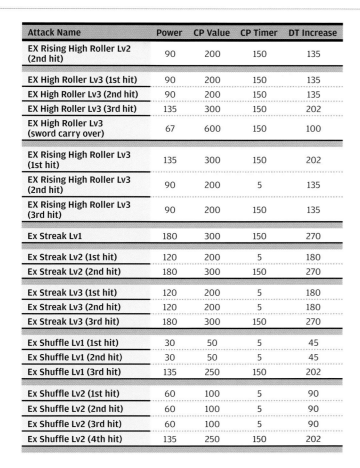

A maxed-out DT Bar is capable of holding 10000 units of energy.

Gauge, a row of glowing "cells" below Nero's health bar.

The longer the row of cells, the more Devil Trigger (DT) energy the gauge can hold. Purchasing Purple Orbs from the Item shop, found in the Power Up Menus, will increase the number of cells and overall length of the Devil Trigger Gauge. 7 Purple Orbs can be purchased for a maximum of 10 DT cells. Each cell can hold 1000 units of DT energy.

Devil Trigger Items

Item Name	Item Type	Item Effect	Remark
Purple Orb	Upgrade Item	Increases Devil Trigger gauge	Buy at shop
Devil Star S	Stock Item	Recover 5000 Devil Trigger Gauge	Buy at shop – find in-game
Devil Star L	Stock Item	Full recovery of Devil Trigger Gauge	Buy at shop – find in-game

The Devil Trigger gauge fills with DT energy when you take damage, damage enemies, successfully dodge attacks or Taunt the enemy. For detailed information on the amount of DT Increase contained in each manoeuvre, please refer to the attack data tables in this chapter and the enemy data tables in the Opponents chapter.

Activation and Consumption

You can press LB | L1 to immediately activate Nero's Devil Trigger, provided you have three or more full DT Gauge cells. On activation, an explosive burst of energy will damage any nearby enemies, and Nero's overall speed and attacking power will increase for however long Devil Trigger lasts. You can deactivate Devil Trigger at any time by pressing LB | L1 while it is active.

Activating Devil Trigger consumes 1500 units of DT energy (1.5 cells). After the initial explosive activation, there is a 3-second period where no DT is consumed. When the 3 seconds are up, the Devil Trigger gauge will drain at a rate of 11 DT units per frame. That's 660 units per second, which equates to little more than half a cell per second. This means Devil Trigger can remain active for 15.87 seconds (without the Trigger Heart enhancement).

Trigger Heart

Purchasing the Trigger Heart item from the Power Up shop will reduce DT consumption to 8.5 DT units per frame, extending the amount of time Nero can remain in Devil Trigger mode. This equates to 510 DT units per second, which is a half cell exactly for each second that passes. This means that, with Trigger Heart, Devil Trigger can remain active for 19.66 seconds (assuming a full 10 cells of DT energy).

Health Boost

When Devil Trigger is activated, Nero will recover 3.3 points of health per frame. So, not only does Devil Trigger increase Nero's attacking power, but it can also be used to recover health while he fights. The amount recovered equates to 198 health units per second. Not much, but it's free. You can regain one full health cell for every 5 seconds DT is active.

Yamato Abilities

Technique Name	Base Cost	Remark
Trigger Heart	2000	Reduces DT Gauge consumption.
Maximum Bet	5000	Strongest long-range attack for Nero.
Showdown	5000	Strongest combo attack for Nero.

Yamato Command List

Technique Name	Controller input
Maximum Bet	Lock-On + Left Stick back + ⓨ	△ and Ⓑ	◎
Maximum Bet Charged	Lock-On + Left Stick back + hold ⓨ	△ and Ⓑ	◎
Showdown	Lock-On + Left Stick forward + ⓨ	△ and Ⓑ	◎
Summoned Swords	Repeatedly Tap ⓧ	▣
Summoned Swords Charge 1	Hold ⓧ	▣ until Devil Bringer energy peaks once
Summoned Swords Charge 2	Hold ⓧ	▣ until Devil Bringer energy peaks twice
Summoned Swords Charge 3	Hold ⓧ	▣ until Devil Bringer energy peaks three times (max)

Yamato

Yamato originally belonged to Dante's brother Vergil. With Devil Trigger activated, Yamato is wielded by a demonic form that appears behind Nero. This apparition acts like an additional sword arm and, in this state, Nero is actually attacking with two swords at once.

As Nero attacks, with DT active, the demon follows suit.

The demon-wielding Yamato will mimic Nero's movements, effectively doubling the number of strikes dealt out by each attack. Not only is every strike doubled, but each strike the demon lands does the same damage as Nero's attack. For example, Combo A has 4 hits for a total of 280 in damage. With DT active, the demon strikes raise this to an 8-hit attack worth 560 in damage.

As you can see, this means that Nero's attacks don't increase in power but, instead, the demon joins him and attacks with the same manoeuvre, dealing the same damage Nero has inflicted. This effectively doubles the attack damage, as long as the demon's attacks hit the enemy.

Blue Rose acts a little differently. With Blue Rose, the demon throws a blade with every shot fired. Additionally, the number of Summoned Swords the demon uses increases with each level of your Charge Shot. The Summoned Swords have a fixed damage value, as shown in the following table.

Summoned Swords

Blue Rose acts a little differently. With Blue Rose, the demon throws a Summoned Sword with every shot fired. Additionally, the number of Summoned Swords the demon uses per shot increases with each level of your Charge Shot. You don't have to be firing a shot, however to use Summoned Swords. They can be used at any time, independently of any other attacks or animations, so it's a good idea to use them at all times in DT, including during strikes and Busters. The Summoned Swords have a fixed damage value, as shown in the following table.

Nero Devil Trigger Attack Data

Technique Name	Attack	CP Value	CP Timer	DT Increase
Trigger Burst (ground – short range)	150	300	150	0
Trigger Burst (ground – long range)	100	200	150	0
Trigger Burst (midair – short range)	125	300	150	0
Trigger Burst (midair – long range)	75	200	150	0
Showdown (1st hit)	250	200	150	0
Showdown (2nd hit)	250	200	150	0
Showdown (3rd hit)	250	200	150	0
Showdown (4th hit)	250	200	150	0
Showdown (5th hit)	250	200	150	0
Showdown (6th hit)	250	200	150	0
Showdown (7th hit)	1000	550	150	0
Maximum Bet (normal)	250	250	150	0
Maximum Bet (charged)	500	500	150	0
Maximum Bet Shockwave (normal)	250	500	150	0
Maximum Bet Shockwave (charged)	100	70	10	0
Summoned Swords	30	20	10	0

Summoned Swords Used

Blue Rose	Blades
Normal Shot	1
Charge Shot Level 1	2
Charge Shot Level 2	4
Charge Shot Level 3	6

Maximum Bet

Nero and the demonic spirit will combine forces to deliver a powerful dual slash, forming an X-shaped blast of energy that surges forwards in a powerful projectile attack. The attack range extends to the full distance of the area. The energy blast will move on forwards, through enemies, until it reaches a wall or area boundary. This powerful attack has no problem mowing down enemies a great distance away.

The attack can be charged by holding the buttons down for two seconds. Releasing them produces an even larger and more powerful energy blast, but which moves more slowly.

Showdown

Showdown is a massive combo sequence in which Nero and his demon spirit join forces to deliver a rapid-fire series of sword slashes. This attack takes a while to execute (3-second start-up time), so it's advisable to use this attack only when an enemy or group of enemies have been knocked down first or have been otherwise disabled. If you land the opening strike, the rest of the combo will follow automatically. If you miss the opening strike, you'll remain stuck in a 2-second finishing animation as a penalty.

> **Pro Tip!**
> If you are experimenting with combat and are interested in seeing this massive combo work, you can trigger it by landing the first strike on any breakable, such as a barrel, chair, etc.

> **Pro Tip!**
> Take advantage of the start-up time of this combo by firing Blue Rose to unleash Summoned Swords!

Devil Buster

Please refer to the Technical Data section of this chapter for damage data relating to DT Buster.

When Devil Trigger is activated, throwing moves become much more powerful and acquire completely new animations. The Devil Buster is extremely useful during Boss battles and, as you work on revealing a Boss's weakness against it, you'll also be building up DT energy.

When the opportunity arrives to grab the Boss with Buster, enter Devil Trigger just before. This greatly increases the power of the special Buster move, as well as changing the animation of the attack. The spectacular attacks the Buster technique triggers against Bosses are Nero's best weapons against them, so always look for the opportunity to use Buster with Devil Trigger during these encounters.

Devil Snatch

With Devil Trigger active, you're no longer limited to grabbing only one enemy at a time. If you're faced with a group of enemies bunched together, use Snatch against them to cause the whole pack to be pulled over in one go. Having Snatched the whole pack, you have the perfect opportunity to deliver a massive attack, using Showdown, for example.

Devil Hold

Hold will be performed by the demon himself. While holding an enemy, it will not join Nero in combat. You are, however, still free to fire Summoned Swords and move, evade and attack with the Red Queen, all while the demon keeps a firm grip on the hapless enemy.

The demon will hold your prey for you!

About Dante

Abilities

Dante Ability List

Skill Name	Base Cost	Controller Input	Description
Speed	300	Continue holding the Left Stick in any direction	After 10 steps, Dante starts running.
Get More Orbs	2000	Constant automated effect	Red Orbs are drawn to Dante from anywhere on screen.
Enemy Step	5000	When above or beside as enemy press Ⓐ | ⊗	Use an enemy as a platform to jump from.
Air Hike	2000	Press Ⓐ | ⊗ after a jump	Double jump.

Ebony & Ivory

Ebony & Ivory Upgrades

Technique name	Base cost	Remark
Charge Shot	150	Duration of firepower increase: 1 second
Charge Shot 2	500	Duration of firepower increase: 2 seconds
Charge Shot 3	1000	Duration of firepower increase: 3 seconds

Ebony & Ivory Attack Data

Technique name	Attack	CP Value	CP Timer	DT Increase
Normal Shot (short distance)	10	20	10	7.5
Normal Shot (middle distance)	5	15	10	3.75
Normal Shot (long distance)	2	10	10	1.5
Charged Shot (short distance)	15	20	10	11.25
Charged Shot (middle distance)	8	15	10	6
Charged Shot (long distance)	4	10	10	3

Short distance: 0-4m, middle distance: 4m-8m, long distance: 8m and more

Normal Shot

Dante's standard gun attack lacks power, but this is more than made up for with speed and range. With his trusty Ebony & Ivory, Dante is capable of rapid fire from the outset. These guns aren't great as a primary means of attack, but they're very useful for juggling enemies after they've been launched into the air.

Charge Shot

Charge Shot adds extra attack power to Ebony & Ivory for a set period of time, which increases with the charge level. If you hold ⊗ \| ▣ down, Dante's guns will glow. When they flash, the charge is complete.

When you see the flash, the guns are charged!

Coyote-A

Coyote-A Upgrades

Technique Name	Base cost	Remark
Charge Shot	150	Duration of firepower increase: 1 second
Charge Shot 2	500	Duration of firepower increase: 2 seconds
Charge Shot 3	1000	Duration of firepower increase: 3 seconds

Normal Shot

One Coyote-A shotgun blast consists of 10 pellets – a main pellet, which is the central round, and 9 "spread" pellets, which fan out over a distance. The closer you are to an enemy when you fire, the more spread pellets will hit, thereby increasing the damage of each blast.

Charge Shot

This upgrade allows Dante to channel demonic energy directly into Coyote-A, which increases its destructive power. Hold ❌ | ⬜ down until you see the energy flash in the shotgun. This shows that the charge is complete. The duration of the charge is fixed by the level of the Charge Shot you have acquired.

Coyote-A Attack Data

Technique Name	Attack	CP Value	CP Timer	DT Increase
Normal Shot (main: short distance)	15	25	150	11.25
Normal Shot (main: middle distance)	10	15	150	7.5
Normal Shot (main: long distance)	5	10	150	3.75
Normal Shot (spread: short distance)	15	25	150	11.25
Normal Shot (spread: middle distance)	10	15	150	7.5
Normal Shot (spread: long distance)	5	10	150	3.75
Charged Shot (main: short distance)	20	25	150	15
Charged Shot (main: middle distance)	15	25	150	11.25
Charged Shot (main: long distance)	10	15	150	7.5
Charged Shot (spread: short distance)	20	25	150	15
Charged Shot (spread: middle distance)	15	25	150	11.25
Charged Shot (spread: long distance)	10	15	150	7.5

Short distance: 0-2m, middle distance: 2m-4m, long distance: 4m and more

Pandora

Available after defeating Dagon in Mission 15

Pandora Upgrades

Technique Name	Base cost
PF124: Hatred	500
PF398: Revenge	1000

Disaster Gauge

The Disaster Gauge is the small, purple energy bar situated below Dante's Health Gauge. As you fire at enemies, using normal attacks from Pandora's various forms, this gauge will build up. The amount of Disaster Gauge charge accumulated varies between each attack type. The purpose of the Disaster Gauge is to store energy ready for when you need to unleash Pandora's full power with Gunslinger Style (described later in this chapter).

Pandora Attack Data

Technique name	Attack	CP Value	CP Timer	DT Increase
PF013: Epidemic (Missile)	50	150	150	37.5
PF013: Epidemic (Explosion)	150	150	150	112.5
PF124: Hatred (Missile)	100	200	150	75
PF124: Hatred (Explosion)	250	150	150	187.5
PF398: Revenge (Transform Blow)	180	400	150	250
PF398: Revenge (Wave Cannon)	450	400	150	337.5
PF262: Jealousy (short distance)	10	30	150	7.5
PF262: Jealousy (middle distance)	5	20	150	3.75
PF262: Jealousy (long distance)	2	15	150	1.5
DT PF262: Jealousy (short distance)	20	30	150	15
DT PF262: Jealousy (middle distance)	10	30	150	7.5
DT PF262: Jealousy (long distance)	4	20	150	3

Short distance: 0-2m, middle distance: 2m-4m, long distance: 4m and more

PF013: Epidemic

The basic ❌ | ⬜ Pandora attack will transform the box into a bow gun that fires 2 missiles. These explode 3.5 metres in front of Dante if they fail to hit a target. The resulting shockwave from the blast will damage all enemies within its blast radius. Best regarded as a mid-range attack, Epidemic can be aimed up and down vertically with the Left Stick while ❌ | ⬜ is held down and Lock-On is inactive.

The bow gun offers two missiles.

PF124: Hatred

This transformation of Pandora turns Epidemic into a bazooka. This new form fires 3 missiles, like Epidemic, but with a greatly extended range. As with Epidemic, you can aim Hatred vertically with the Left Stick while holding ❌ | ⬜ with Lock-On inactive.

The bazooka's capacity is three missiles.

PF398: Revenge

The final transformation in this sequence turns Hatred into a massive laser cannon. The range of the laser blast is the full area. The blast will travel forwards, through enemies, and won't stop until it hits a wall or area boundary. When Revenge is taking shape, you can actually damage an

The laser cannon does away with missiles all together.

enemy with the final placement of its transformation (transform blow). Revenge can also be aimed vertically with the Left Stick while holding ❌ | ⬜ with Lock-On inactive.

PF262: Jealousy

Pressing ❌ | ⬜ in mid-air will transform Pandora into a Gatling Gun. This can be used to rain down a hail of lead on a hapless enemy.

Jealousy is a rapid-fire machine-gun that's useful for filling the Disaster Gauge.

Rebellion

Rebellion Upgrades

Technique Name	Base Cost
Stinger	150
Stinger 2	700
Round trip	1000

Rebellion Command List

Technique Name	Controller Input
Rebellion Combo A	🅨 | 🅐 🅨 | 🅐 🅨 | 🅐
Rebellion Combo B	🅨 | 🅐 pause 🅨 | 🅐 🅨 | 🅐
Helm Breaker	🅨 | 🅐 in mid-air
High Time	Lock-On + Left Stick back + 🅨 | 🅐
Rising High Time	Lock-On + Left Stick back + hold 🅨 | 🅐
Stinger	Lock-On + Left Stick forward + 🅨 | 🅐
Million Stab	Hold or rapidly tap 🅨 | 🅐 during Stinger
Round Trip	Hold 🅨 | 🅐 until Rebellion glows, then release

Rebellion Attack Data

Technique name	Attack	CP Value	CP Timer	DT Increase
Combo A (1st hit)	100	130	300	75
Combo A (2nd hit)	80	130	300	60
Combo A (3rd hit)	130	170	300	97.5
Combo B (1st hit)	100	130	300	75
Combo B (2nd hit)	40	80	300	30
Combo B (3rd hit)	40	80	300	30
Combo B (4th hit)	60	100	300	45
Combo B (Million Stab)*1	15	25	300	11.25
Combo B (Million Stab Finish)	160	150	300	120
Helm Breaker (from height Lv1)	60	150	150	45
Helm Breaker (from height Lv2)	130	200	150	97.5
Helm Breaker (from height Lv3)	200	350	150	150
Helm Breaker (final shockwave – all levels)	70	80	150	52.5
High time & Rising High Time	120	200	200	90
Stinger	140	150	200	105
Million Stab*2	15	25	300	11.25
Million Stab Finish	160	150	300	120
Round Trip*3	50	40	0	37.5

*1 There are 22 possible hits during Combo B's Million Stab.
*2 There are 24 possible hits during the stand-alone version of Million Stab.
*3 There are 17 possible hits during Round Trip.

Rebellion Combo A

This simple 3-hit combo flows easily into other movements like evades, jumps or special attacks. The third and final sword slash of this combo string will knock lighter enemies away from Dante, so the first two slashes are those that prove the most useful when stringing together custom combos.

Rebellion Combo B

This Combo opens with the first slash of Combo A, and then adds a stylish 3-hit burst, which Dante finishes off with Million Stab. A rather effective combo, easily able to hold enemies in place as they feel the full brunt of this whirlwind attack. To increase the number of high-speed stabs, tap 🅨 \| 🅐 rapidly until the attack has finished.

Helm Breaker

The Helm Breaker is a powerful, vertical sword strike which can rip an enemy out of the air or pulverise an enemy on the ground. As it connects with the ground, Rebellion generates a small but damaging shockwave. Helm Breaker's attack power varies, depending on the height from which it is executed.

Helm Breaker Height Levels

Level 1	The height of an Enemy Step (of a small, fallen enemy).
Level 2	The height of a single jump.
Level 3	The height of a double jump (Air Hike).

High Time

High Time is a powerful uppercut, which will send an enemy into the air while Dante remains on the ground. After executing this attack, you can add further damage with gunfire or by jumping up to the airborne enemy and engaging in aerial combat.

Use High Time to get your opponent into the air.

Rising High Time

Continuing to hold after executing High Time will cause Dante to fly upwards instantly with the enemy. This is a perfect way of setting up an enemy for an aerial attack.

Stinger

Stinger is a high-powered, dashing sword stab, which will blast most foes out of the way with ease. This is a very straightforward attack (literally!) in which Dante rushes forwards and uses Rebellion to deliver a massive forward stab. You can upgrade this move to Stinger 2, which increases the distance Dante can cover with the dash of this attack.

Million Stab

After you've begun a Stinger, release the Left Stick (before you strike the enemy) so that it returns to the neutral position. Next, press and hold to begin the Million Stab manoeuvre. To increase the number of high-speed stabs, tap rapidly until the attack has finished.

Million Stab is great for tying up an enemy while doing damage.

Round Trip

Hold down the 🅨 | △ button until you see a flash of energy from Rebellion, and then release 🅨 | △ to make Dante throw the sword at the enemy. Rebellion will fly towards the unfortunate beast and spin violently around it while unleashing a massive 17-hit attack. When the attack is over, Rebellion will automatically return to Dante. To call Rebellion back early, simply press 🅨 | △. You can add more damage to this attack by firing your guns while Rebellion is doing its work, or you can change to a different melée weapon and join the ongoing attack. Insane!

Gilgamesh

Available after defeating Echidna in Mission 13

Gilgamesh Upgrades

Technique Name	Base Cost
Kick 13	500
Flush	1000

Gilgamesh Command List

Technique Name	Controller Input
Gilgamesh Combo A	🅨 | △ 🅨 | △ 🅨 | △ 🅨 | △
Gilgamesh Combo B	🅨 | △ 🅨 | △ pause 🅨 | △ 🅨 | △
Full House	🅨 | △ in mid-air
Draw	Lock-On + Left Stick back + 🅨 | △
Straight	🅨 | △ during Draw
Kick 13	Lock-On + Left Stick forward + 🅨 | △
Flush	Ⓐ | ⊗

Charging

Gilgamesh differs from the other Devil Arms in Dante's arsenal in that you can charge each attack individually during an attack sequence simply by holding down the button. Applying a charge to an attack will boost its attacking power.

As you're holding 🅨 | △ down, you'll notice that the booster effects on Dante's arms or legs begin to activate. When you see a burst of energy, this signals that a charge level has been completed. There are two Charge Levels for each attack: a Level 1 attack (normal), a Level 2 attack (1 charge), and a Level 3 attack (2 charges).

Just Charge

While you're charging a Gilgamesh attack, release 🅨 | △ just as the charge is complete, and you will increase the attack power of the strike to 1.5 times the normal value. This is known as a Just Charge, and it's a very powerful, albeit tricky, technique.

The flash of a standard Charge is much dimmer....

Once you've got into a rhythm and can recognize or "feel" the length of time a charge takes to complete, you'll flow naturally into Just Charging a Gilgamesh attack. You'll be aware that you've succeeded, because the resulting flash of a Just Charge is brighter than that of a normal Charge.

....than the flash of a Just Charge!

Just Charge Condition

Situation	Attack	CP Value	CP Timer	DT Increase
Release the button < 5 frames after charge is complete	1.5x attacking power	200	0	500

A frame is equivalent to 0.016 seconds.

Gilgamesh Combo A

This 4-hit combo consists of two punches and a high kick, and it ends with a powerful axe kick, which is capable of flooring enemies on contact. As discussed earlier, each of the 4 strikes of this combo can be charged up to two levels.

Gilgamesh Combo B

After the familiar pair of punches from Combo A, pause for half a second before pressing the button again. This will lead to a fast, rapid-fire kick sequence, which Dante will finish off with a spinning 2-hit kick manoeuvre. As with many Gilgamesh attacks, you can charge each attack in this sequence.

Gilgamesh Attack Data

Technique Name	Attack	CP Value	CP Timer	DT Increase
Combo A (1st hit – Lv1)	130	150	300	97.5
Combo A (1st hit – Lv2)	260	225	300	195
Combo A (1st hit – Lv3)	520	450	300	390
Combo A (2nd hit – Lv1)	120	150	300	90
Combo A (2nd hit – Lv2)	240	225	300	180
Combo A (2nd hit – Lv3)	480	450	300	360
Combo A (3rd hit – Lv1)	170	150	300	127.5
Combo A (3rd hit – Lv2)	340	250	300	255
Combo A (3rd hit – Lv3)	680	450	300	510
Combo A (4th hit – Lv1)	210	250	300	157.5
Combo A (4th hit – Lv2)	420	350	300	315
Combo A (4th hit – Lv3)	840	550	300	630
Combo B (1st hit – Lv1)	130	150	300	97.5
Combo B (1st hit – Lv2)	260	225	300	195
Combo B (1st hit – Lv3)	520	450	300	390
Combo B (2nd hit – Lv1)	120	150	300	90
Combo B (2nd hit – Lv2)	240	225	300	180
Combo B (2nd hit – Lv3)	480	450	300	360
Combo B (3rd hit – Lv1)	35	45	300	26.25
Combo B (3rd hit – Lv2)	70	70	300	52.5
Combo B (3rd hit – Lv3)	140	135	300	105
Combo B (4th hit – Lv1)	130	120	300	97.5
Combo B (4th hit – Lv2)	260	170	300	195
Combo B (4th hit – Lv3)	520	250	300	390
Combo B (5th hit – Lv1)	160	150	300	120
Combo B (5th hit – Lv2)	320	200	300	240
Combo B (5th hit – Lv3)	640	300	300	480
Full House	200	180	150	150
Straight (Lv 1)	250	250	200	187.5
Straight (Lv 2)	500	350	200	375
Straight (Lv 3)	1000	550	200	750
Kick 13 (1st hit)	110	40	200	82.5
Kick 13 (2nd hit)	80	50	200	60
Kick 13 (3rd hit)	100	55	200	75
Kick 13 (4th hit)	80	65	200	60
Kick 13 (5th hit)	150	150	200	112.5
Flush	70	40	0	52.5

Full House

Full House is executed during a jump. If you press **Y** | **△** in mid-air, Dante will perform a powerful diving kick, which will blast through anything in its path. This technique can be used against enemies who are airborne or on the ground. Since the angle of Full House is locked, make sure you check your spacing in relation to your target. If you execute this manoeuvre while you're close or directly above an enemy, you will sail straight past your target. Conversely, if you're too far away, the attack will land short of the enemy's position.

Watch your position, or Full House will miss your target.

Draw

This fast, backwards dash is used to dodge an incoming attack. If you perform this technique the moment an enemy attack is about to strike you, Dante will feint backwards, clear of danger.

Straight

After executing Draw, tap **Y** | **△** quickly to counter-attack immediately with a huge, straight punch. If you hold **Y** | **△** after Draw, you can charge this attack.

Kick 13

Kick 13 is a rapid 5-hit kick combo, capable of launching an opponent into the air. This is a quick attack, a great technique to string together with other Gilgamesh combos so that you can move the action smoothly into the air.

Flush

Dante's body acquires a flame element which adds attacking power to jumps. Since the attack power is low, enemies will not be fazed by this attack. It won't deflect incoming attacks, nor can it launch, knock away or juggle. It does, however, have enough attacking power to break an enemy's guard if it's blocking.

 ## Lucifer

Available after defeating Berial in Mission 16

Lucifer Upgrades

Technique Name	Base Cost
Pin-Up	500

Lucifer Command List

Technique Name	Controller Input
Lucifer Combo A	**Y** | **△** **Y** | **△** **Y** | **△** **Y** | **△** **Y** | **△**
Lucifer Combo B	**Y** | **△**, (pause) **Y** | **△**
Lucifer Combo C	**Y** | **△**, (pause) **Y** | **△**, (pause) **Y** | **△**
Lucifer Combo D	**Y** | **Y** | **△** pause **Y** | **△**
Lucifer Combo E	**Y** | **△** **Y** | **△** **Y** | **△** **Y** | **△** pause **Y** | **△**
Splash	**Y** | **△** in mid-air
Ecstasy	Lock-On + Left Stick back + **Y** | **△**
Pin-Up	Lock-On + Left Stick forward + **Y** | **△**

Lucifer Blade Casting

Although any of Dante's Styles can be used when attacking with Lucifer, the number of blades you're allowed to summon at any one time is determined by your current Sword Master Style level.

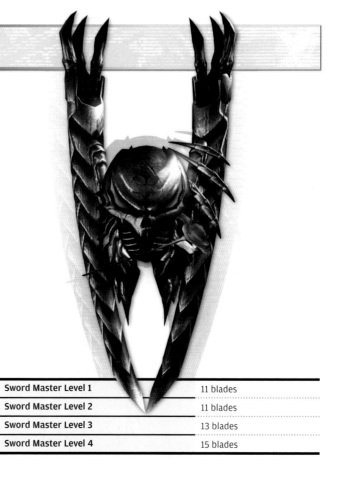

Sword Master Level 1	11 blades
Sword Master Level 2	11 blades
Sword Master Level 3	13 blades
Sword Master Level 4	15 blades

Lucifer Attack Data

Technique Name	Attack	CP Value	CP Timer	DT increase
Combo A (1st)	30	75	300	22.5
Combo A (2nd)	30	75	300	22.5
Combo A (3rd)	30	75	300	22.5
Combo A (4th)	20	50	300	15
Combo A (5th)	20	50	300	15
Combo B (1st)	30	75	300	22.5
Combo B (2nd)	20	50	300	15
Combo B (3rd)	150	250	300	112.5
Combo C (1st)	30	75	300	22.5
Combo C (2nd)	20	50	300	15
Combo C (3rd)	150	250	300	112.5
Combo C (stab loop)*	10	25	300	7.5
Combo C (finish)	50	100	300	37.5
Combo D (1st)	30	75	300	22.5
Combo D (2nd)	30	75	300	22.5
Combo D (3rd)	-	-	-	-
Combo E (1st)	30	75	300	22.5
Combo E (2nd)	30	75	300	22.5
Combo E (3rd)	30	75	300	22.5
Combo E (4th)	20	50	300	15
Combo E (stab loop)*	10	25	300	7.5
Combo E (finish)	50	100	300	37.5
Splash (1st)	30	80	150	22.5
Splash (2nd)	30	80	150	22.5
Ecstasy (Rose)	100	200	200	75
Pinup	-	-	-	-
Enemy Contacts Loose Blade	0	15	0	0
Blade Explosion	70	50	0	52.5
Climax Blade Explosion	150	150	0	112.5

* There are 6 hits possible during this stab loop.

Blade Detonation Conditions

The blades summoned and thrown by Lucifer will detonate, dealing explosive damage, after a fixed period of time. The amount of time prior to detonation is affected by various conditions that arise in combat.

Case 1: Loose blade detonation.
A blade will automatically explode five seconds after hanging in mid-air (not having struck an enemy).

Case 2: Embedded blade detonation.
Once a blade embeds itself in an enemy, it will explode after 10 seconds.

Case 3: Exploding via Ecstasy.
The Ecstasy command will immediately detonate all blades in the order in which they were thrown. This applies to both loose and embedded blades.

Case 4: Blade position reset.
When the Lucifer Sword Master techniques of Discipline, Climax, and Bondage are used to reposition any loose blades, this will reset the detonation timer of all blades to 2 seconds. Each repositioning resets the timer to 2 seconds, so it's possible to keep loose blades "alive" indefinitely with repeated repositions.

Case 5: Exploding via Climax.
The Climax command will draw all loose blades to Dante, encircling him and exploding within 2 seconds. After Climax has been executed, these blades can't be repositioned.

Lucifer Combo A

Lucifer Combo A is a continuous repetition of four strikes. Three blades are released at each repetition, one during the second strike and two during the fourth. If the Lucifer Combo A is being used against an enemy at close range, the blades will stick in its body and await detonation. Alternatively, if there's no enemy within range, the blades will simply float in the place where the strike occurred.

Lucifer Combo B

Combo B is a method for dealing purely physical damage with Lucifer. No blades are thrown during this combo variation. Instead, Dante will use Lucifer's blade sheaths to deal damage. This attack consists of a single strike, followed by a pair of slashes from the sheaths on Dante's back. Despite being slow, it's actually quite versatile, as you can change direction at will between strikes. However, the strikes can't be rushed. You must wait for Dante to face the front after each spin in order for this combo to be executed correctly. If you push 🅨 | Ⓐ too rapidly, Dante will revert to Combo A.

Lucifer Combo C

This combo has a very slow start, but all that changes when you reach the third press of 🅨 | Ⓐ. At that moment, Dante unleashes a very fast flurry of Lucifer strikes to finish off this sequence in style. Again, if you want Combo C to be executed correctly, you must wait for Dante to finish turning and face the front before each new press of 🅨 | Ⓐ.

Lucifer Combo D

Combo D sets up a defensive wall of blades behind Dante. When executed correctly, Dante will finish this Combo by turning to cast a row of four blades behind him. This technique is very useful if you want to set your blades in a circular formation when you're fighting a group of encroaching enemies.

Lucifer Combo E

This is a special, rapid-finishing attack you can add to the end of Lucifer Combo A. When this combo is over, Dante will unleash a 7-hit maelstrom, in the process of which four blades are produced.

Splash

Lucifer's aerial attack is a forward roll which releases four blades if front of Dante. This technique can be repeated many times from high jumps using the Air Hike or Enemy Step. It allows you to summon many blades in safety before returning to the ground below. Splash also works as a physical attack. The forward roll will use the sheaths to damage any enemy within range, which makes for some interesting Aerial Combos.

Ecstasy

The Ecstasy command will immediately trigger the detonation of all blades, regardless of whether they're embedded in an enemy or not. Blades will always explode in the order they were thrown in. During this manoeuvre, while triggering the detonation of all blades, Dante also throws a rose. If this rose hits an enemy, it will deal 100 in damage and launch the enemy forthwith into the air.

An enemy will be launched into the air instantly if hit by the rose.

Pin-Up

Pin-Up is a fast way of summoning blades. Each time Pin-Up is executed, Dante will throw a row of five blades into the air in front of him. A maximum of 15 blades is possible. As you increase the amount above 15, the earliest blades thrown will explode instantly. Any blade touched by an enemy will stick into its body.

Styles

Style Activation Commands

Style Name	Controller Input	Remark
Trickster	Directional Pad ↑	Changes **B** | ◎ function to specialised evasion techniques
Gunslinger	Directional Pad ←	Changes **B** | ◎ function to specialised gunplay techniques
Sword Master	Directional Pad →	Changes **B** | ◎ function to specialised melee techniques
Royal Guard	Directional Pad ↓	Changes **B** | ◎ function to specialised defence techniques
Dark Slayer	Directional Pad same direction as current style	Changes **B** | ◎ function to Yamato sword techniques

Trickster

Trickster Upgrades

Style Level	Base Cost
Trickster Level 2	300
Trickster Level 3	700
Trickster Level 4	5000

Tight Evade Conditions

Situation	CP Value	CP Timer	DT Increase
Tight Evade (> 5 frames & ≤ 20 frames)	150	0	350
Tight Evade (≤ 5 frames)	250	0	800

A frame is equivalent to 0.016 seconds.

Trickster Command List

Technique Name	Style Level	Controller Input
Dash	1	Left Stick + **B** | ◎
Mustang	2	Hold **B** | ◎ during dash
Flipper	2	Hit **B** | ◎ during a knockdown
Sky Star	3	Left Stick + **B** | ◎ while jumping
Air Trick	4	Lock-On + Left Stick forward + **B** | ◎

Trickster Evade Conditions

Technique Name	CP Value	CP Timer	DT Increase
Flipper	300	0	500
Mustang	250	0	500
Evade with Dash	150	0	350
Evade with Sky Star	150	0	350
Evade with Air Trick	150	0	350

Dash

A dash is no simple evasion! If you time the execution of a Dash just before any attack hits Dante, he'll sail out of the way or even straight through the incoming strike. Regardless of the type of strike coming your way, a well-timed Dash will guarantee your safety.

Mustang

If you continue to hold down **B** | **◎** during a Dash and you bump into an enemy, Dante will run up into the air using the enemy's body as a ramp.

Use Mustang to literally run over your enemy!

Sky Star

Sky Star has all the same invincible properties as Dash but you can perform the technique in mid-air. Just like the ground-based version, if you time the manoeuvre properly, Dante will glide straight through any attack unscathed.

Flipper

When Dante has been blasted off balance by a powerful attack, press **B** | **◎** to make him jump to his feet instantly. This requires good timing, as otherwise you'll have to go through the regular damage animation of regaining your feet. If you execute it properly, it means instant recovery.

Air Trick

The basic use of Air Trick is to quickly disappear and then reappear in front of a targeted enemy. This ability makes for some interesting combos. If an enemy is knocked away from Dante, remain locked on and perform Air Trick to instantly chase the enemy and resume your attack. Another feature making this a superb technique is that Dante is invincible when he disappears. If you time the execution of Air Trick so that the move activates just before an enemy attack connects, Dante will phase straight through the attack unharmed.

Gunslinger

Gunslinger Upgrades

Style Level	Base Cost
Gunslinger Level 2	300
Gunslinger Level 3	700
Gunslinger Level 4	5000

Gunslinger Command List

Weapon Name	Technique Name	Style Level	Controller input
Ebony & Ivory	Twosome Time	1	Left Stick + **B**	**◎**
	Rain Storm	2	**B**	**◎** in mid-air
	Honeycomb Fire	4	Rapidly tap **B**	**◎** during forwards Twosome Time
Coyote-A	Fireworks	1	**B**	**◎** while standing
	Fireworks Air	2	**B**	**◎** while jumping
	Backslide	3	Lock-On + Left Stick back + **B**	**◎**
	Gun Stinger	4	Lock-On + Left Stick forward + **B**	**◎**
Pandora	PF594: Argument	1	**B**	**◎** while standing or in mid-air
	PF422: Grief	3	Lock-On + Left Stick back + **B**	**◎**
	PF666: Omen	4	Lock-On + Left Stick forward + **B**	**◎**

Gunslinger Style Ebony & Ivory specific moves

Gunslinger Ebony & Ivory Attack Data

Technique Name	Attack	CP Value	CP Timer	DT Increase
Twosome Time (short distance)	15	20	10	11.25
Twosome Time (middle distance)	8	15	10	6
Twosome Time (long distance)	4	10	10	3
Rain Storm (short distance)	15	40	150	11.25
Rain Storm (middle distance)	15	30	150	11.25
Rain Storm (long distance)	15	20	150	11.25
Honeycomb Fire (short distance)	15	20	10	11.25
Honeycomb Fire (middle distance)	8	15	10	6
Honeycomb Fire (long distance)	4	10	10	3

Short distance: 0-4m, middle distance: 4m-8m, long distance: 8m and above

Twosome Time

This technique enables Dante to fire behind and to his sides while keeping one gun trained on the target ahead of him. While firing, move the Left Stick in the desired direction to make Dante fire one gun in that direction while he continues to train the other gun directly in front of himself.

Honeycomb Fire

During Twosome Time, if you push the Left Stick forward so that Dante aims both Ebony & Ivory ahead of him, rapidly tapping ⓑ | ◎ will trigger a new firing mode. Dante will quickly spin the guns in his hands and then unleash a torrent of rapid-fire shots at a much faster firing rate.

Rain Storm

Dante flips over in mid-air and rains down a storm of bullets by rapidly firing with Ebony & Ivory. Holding down ⓑ | ◎ will increase the duration of the spin, while tapping the button repeatedly will duplicate the whole motion many times during a single jump.

Rain Storm allows you to flood an enemy with a deluge of lead!

Gunslinger Style Coyote-A specific moves

Gunslinger Coyote-A Attack Data

Technique Name	Attack	CP Value	CP Timer	DT Increase
Gun Stinger (contact with shotgun)	50	100	150	37.5
Gun Stinger (main: short distance)	15	25	150	11.25
Gun Stinger (main: middle distance)	10	15	150	7.5
Gun Stinger (main: long distance)	5	10	150	3.75
Gun Stinger (spread: short distance)	15	25	150	11.25
Gun Stinger (spread: middle distance)	10	15	150	7.5
Gun Stinger (spread: long distance)	5	10	150	3.75
Back slide (main: short distance)	25	35	150	18.75
Back slide (main: middle distance)	15	25	150	11.25
Back slide (main: long distance)	10	15	150	7.5
Back slide (spread: short distance)	25	35	150	18.75
Back slide (spread: middle distance)	15	25	150	11.25
Back slide (spread: long distance)	10	15	150	7.5
Fireworks (main: short distance)	12	14	150	9
Fireworks (main: middle distance)	8	10	150	6
Fireworks (main: long distance)	4	6	150	3
Fireworks (spread: short distance)	12	14	150	9
Fireworks (spread: middle distance)	8	10	150	6
Fireworks (spread: long distance)	4	6	150	3

Short distance: 0-2m, middle distance: 2m-4m, long distance: 4m and above

Fireworks

Dante will rapidly flail the shotgun around his body like a pair of nunchucks to discharge 3 shots. This technique uses special ammunition that changes its pellet mixture randomly. Like other shotgun blasts, each shot consists of 10 pellets. However, with Fireworks, there is a 17.5% chance for each pellet to become a "main" pellet instead of a "spread" pellet.

The difference between a main and a spread pellet is not in the damage done, but the direction of travel. A main pellet leaves the muzzle in a straight line while a spread pellet leaves at an angle. This affects the number of pellets that actually strike an enemy in the path of the blast.

Fireworks Air

During a jump, pressing ❸ | ◎ will execute the Fireworks technique in mid-air.

Backslide

This stylish technique lets Dante fire off a quick shot directly behind him even if he is in the middle of a combo string. Backslide will make sure no other enemy can sneak up behind you for a cheap attack while you're busy with an enemy in front of you.

Gun Stinger

Very similar to the classic Rebellion attack, Gun Stinger is a rapid forward dash followed by a stab attack and shotgun blast. As such, it has two modes of damage: physical contact with the gun and the finishing blast. Note that the ending reload animation cannot be cancelled. While the execution of Gun Stinger is rapid, the slight delay at the end may leave you open to attack.

Gun Stinger works like Rebellion's Stinger with the added addition of a shotgun blast!

Gunslinger Style Pandora specific moves

Gunslinger Pandora Attack Data

Technique Name	Style Level	Attack	CP Value	CP Timer	DT Increase
PF594: Argument (Missile)	1	180	80	0	90
PF422: Grief	3	120	50	0	60
PF666: Omen	4	*	*	*	*
PF666: Omen (strike)	4	100	350	200	250
PF666: Omen (catch)	4	50	350	200	250

* See Omen entry further down for calculation of values.

Disaster Gauge

As you damage enemies with Pandora's regular attacks, you'll notice the small purple energy bar below Dante's health gauge start to fill. This gauge fills slightly when you inflict damage with Pandora. The energy stored in this gauge enables you to unleash the awesome power of Pandora's Gunslinger attacks. The maximum value of the Disaster Gauge increases with each level of the Gunslinger Style.

Disaster Gauge Capacity

Gunslinger	Capacity
Level 1	4000
Level 2	6000
Level 3	8000
Level 4	10000

PF594: Argument

The ultimate transformation for Pandora converts the box into a flying mobile missile launcher with Dante sitting safely in the cockpit. Pandora will drain 10 units of energy from the Disaster Gauge for each frame you spend flying in this form. That equates to 600 units per second, meaning you can fly for 16.6 seconds if you don't use any extra energy for attacks.

Ride Pandora's ultimate form for complete safety while dealing massive damage.

While in this form, pressing ✖ | ▢ will fire a single homing missile which will drain 500 units per shot. The most powerful attack for Argument is activated by pressing ❸ | ◎, which will cause Pandora to rain down a volley of devastating missiles. This attack is extremely powerful and can wipe out a whole group of enemies at once. This power comes at a steep cost, however, as the attack will drain a huge 4000 units of energy from the Disaster Gauge. Note that if you don't have 4000 units to begin with, you can't initiate this impressive attack.

PF422: Grief

This transformation code will change Pandora into a bladed boomerang. You can throw the boomerang at any time, regardless of the level of energy in your Disaster Gauge. However, this attack becomes much more interesting when you combine it with the gauge. If you hold down ❸ | ◎ once Pandora is thrown, the boomerang will continuously circle the targeted enemy, inflicting constant damage with each rotation. Doing this uses 22.5 units of energy per frame, which equates to 1350 units per second. This gives a 7.4 second continuous attack. Once the gauge has been depleted, Pandora will return to Dante.

Pro Tip!

During a continuous attack, you are free to change the currently targeted enemy by pressing Ⓛ | L3 to Lock-On to a different enemy and move the attack to them!

PF666: Omen

When Dante sets the box down and kicks it open, the overwhelming energy that pours out will damage all enemies in the same way as Holy Water. The strength of the attack is dictated by the amount of charge you have accumulated for the Disaster Gauge. Upon execution, your Disaster Gauge will be completely depleted.

This form is Pandora of like Holy Water on steroids!

Max Attack Values

Difficulty Level	Value
Human	2000
Devil Hunter	2000
Son of Sparda	1000
Dante Must Die!	400

Omen Attack Calculation

Disaster Gauge Value	Attack	CP Value	CP Timer	DT Increase
0-3999	0	0	0	0
4000-5999	Max Attack x (Disaster Gauge - 2000) / 10000	400	600	500
6000-7999	Max Attack x (Disaster Gauge - 2000) / 10000	500	600	700
8000-9999	Max Attack x (Disaster Gauge - 2000) / 10000	600	600	900
10000	Max Attack	800	600	1200

Omen attacks like Holy Water, but without the Item Penalty to your Mission Rank. The enemy's Holy Water resistances do not apply to Omen. Omen has the same blast radius of Holy Water, which is 100m. As an example of attack power, if you are playing on Devil Hunter (Normal) difficulty and you have 8500 in your Disaster Gauge, the attack is as follows:

Omen Attack Value	Max Attack x ([Disaster Gauge] - 2000) / 10000
Omen Attack Value	2000 x ([8500] - 2000) / 10000
Omen Attack Value	2000 x (6500) / 10000
Omen Attack Value	2000 x 0.65
Omen Attack Value	1300

Sword Master

Sword Master Upgrades

Style Level	Base Cost
Sword Master Level 2	300
Sword Master Level 3	700
Sword Master Level 4	5000

Prop

Prop is a great low-risk enemy launching technique which behaves in a similar way to High Time. Used against a lightweight enemy or an enemy which has had its defences broken, Prop will launch the creature into the air on contact.

Sword Master Style Rebellion specific moves

Sword Master Command List

Weapon Name	Technique Name	Style Level	Controller input
Rebellion	Prop	1	🅑 | ◎ while standing
	Shredder	1	🅑 | ◎ during Prop
	Aerial Rave	2	🅑 | ◎ 🅑 | ◎ 🅑 | ◎ in mid-air
	Drive	3	Lock-On + Left Stick back + 🅑 | ◎
	Quick Drive	3	🅑 | ◎ + 🅨 | Ⓐ
	Over Drive	3	Repeatedly tap 🅑 | ◎ during Drive
	Dance Macabre	4	Lock-On + Left Stick forward + repeatedly tap 🅑 | ◎
Gilgamesh	Shock	1	🅑 | ◎ while standing
	Shocking!	1	🅑 | ◎ in mid-air
	Beast Uppercut	2	Lock-On + Left Stick forward + 🅑 | ◎
	Rising Dragon	3	Lock-On + Left Stick forward + hold 🅑 | ◎ Lv 2
	Divine Dragon	3	Lock-On + Left Stick forward + hold 🅑 | ◎ Lv 3
	Real Impact	4	Lock-On + Left Stick back + 🅑 | ◎
Lucifer	Discipline	1	Left Stick + 🅑 | ◎
	Climax	2	Lock-On + Left Stick back + 🅑 | ◎
	Bondage	4	Lock-On + Left Stick forward + 🅑 | ◎

Sword Master Rebellion Attack Data

Technique Name	Style Level	Attack	CP Value	CP Timer	DT Increase
Prop*1	1	40	60	200	30
Shredder (2)*2	1	25	20	200	18.75
Aerial Rave (1st)	2	80	130	150	60
Aerial Rave (2nd)	2	70	100	150	52.5
Aerial Rave (3rd)	2	70	100	150	52.5
Aerial Rave (finish)	2	120	150	150	90
Drive (sword contact)	3	110	200	350	82.5
Over Drive 1st (sword contact)	3	60	150	350	45
Over Drive 2nd (sword contact)	3	90	200	350	67.5
Drive Blast Lv 1	3	250	400	350	187.5
Over Drive Blast 1st Lv 1	3	70	100	350	52.5
Over Drive Blast 2nd Lv 1	3	150	250	350	112.5
Drive Blast Lv 2	3	370	600	350	277.5
Over Drive Blast 1st Lv 2	3	120	150	350	90
Over Drive Blast 2nd Lv 2	3	200	400	350	150
Drive Blast Lv 3	3	720	900	350	540
Over Drive Blast 1st Lv 3	3	230	250	350	172.5
Over Drive Blast 2nd Lv 3	3	420	600	350	315
Quick Drive (sword contact)	3	100	200	350	82.5
Quick Drive (blast)	3	220	200	350	97.5
Dance Macabre (dash)	4	50	100	350	37.5
Dance Macabre (1st hit)	4	90	100	350	67.5
Dance Macabre (2nd hit)	4	70	100	350	52.5
Dance Macabre (3rd hit)	4	90	100	350	67.5
Dance Macabre (4th hit)	4	35	70	350	26.25
Dance Macabre (5th hit)	4	35	70	350	26.25
Dance Macabre (6th hit)	4	50	70	350	37.5
Dance Macabre (Million Stab)*3	4	10	25	350	7.5
Dance Macabre (Million Stab Finish)*4	4	140	100	350	105
Dance Macabre (7th hit)	4	100	100	350	75
Dance Macabre (8th hit)	4	90	100	350	67.5
Dance Macabre (9th hit)	4	100	150	350	75
Dance Macabre (Home Run)	4	500	600	350	375

*1 4 hits are possible during Prop.
*2 26 hits are possible during Shredder.
*3 9 hits are possible during the Million Stab of Dance Macabre.
*4 Hold **B** | ◎ when Million Stab starts. This will end Dance Macabre.

Shredder

Press and hold **B** | ◎ after Prop has connected and Dante will extend the attack into Shredder. The enemy will be held in place as Dante spins Rebellion like an aircraft propeller at ultra-high speed. Holding **B** | ◎ down will increase the duration of the Shredder attack.

Shredder can keep an enemy suspended in a painful predicament!

Aerial Rave

Aerial Rave is a rapid 4-hit Aerial Combo; the first three strikes will hold the enemy in place and the fourth strike knocks it away. You can perform this Combo any time in mid-air by pressing **B** | ◎ 4 times.

Drive

This attacks starts with Dante drawing back and preparing a massive sword uppercut that unleashes a hellish blast of energy. Once the attack is ready, Dante will perform the sword uppercut in the direction he is facing, which causes a blast of energy to burst forward. The blast's range extends across the whole area and will continue through enemies until it reaches a wall or room boundary.

But that's not all: you can charge this attack by two levels. If you hold down **B** | ◎ as this attack is winding up, Dante will hold the sword behind him until you release the button. Doing this builds up energy. When you see the second flash on the sword, the attack is fully charged to level 3.

Over Drive

Repeatedly tap **B** | ◎ when Drive is being performed to add 2 additional sword slashes. The Over Drive slashes will blast forward at the same charge level as the original Drive blast.

Quick Drive

Quick Drive is a quick and easy way of creating a combo using a version of the Drive technique. Pressing both **Y** | △ and **B** | ◎ together will execute a single sword slash which links straight into a less powerful version of the Drive attack.

Dance Macabre

After a small forward dash, this mighty combo sequence combines elements of Combo A, Combo B, Over Drive and High Time, concluding in a powerful attack similar to a baseball swing. This is a truly impressive show of stylish force that can level even the toughest of enemies. To increase the number of high-speed stabs (in the Million Stabs portion), rapidly tap **B** | ◎ until the attack has finished.

Sword Master Style Gilgamesh specific moves

Sword Master Gilgamesh Attack Data

Technique Name	Style Level	Attack	CP Value	CP Timer	DT Increase
Shock Lv 1	1	150	225	200	112.5
Shock Lv 2	1	300	315	200	225
Shock Lv 3	1	600	450	200	450
Shocking!	1	150	225	200	112.5
Beast Uppercut	2	230	250	200	172.5
Rising Dragon	3	460	350	200	345
Divine Dragon (multi-hit)*	3	125	100	200	93.75
Divine Dragon (finish)	3	500	200	200	375
Real Impact (opening)	4	0	300	350	0
Real Impact (rising)	4	500	200	350	375
Real Impact (finish)	4	1000	600	350	750

* There are 4 hits possible during the rise of Divine Dragon.

Shock

Dante punches the ground and unleashes a radial shock wave of concussive damage on all enemies within range. This is a great attack to scatter a crowd of enemies when you're surrounded. Since this attack damages everything around you in a circular blast, you don't need to be accurate when using it. As with regular Gilgamesh attacks, you can Charge and Just Charge this manoeuvre.

Shocking!

Shocking! is the aerial version of Shock. This mid-air variation of Shock cannot be Charged but it is still useful and a nice way to finish an aerial combo.

Beast Uppercut

This is a standard single-hit enemy launcher which behaves in a similar fashion to Rebellion's High Time. When used against a lightweight enemy or an enemy which has had its defences broken, Beast Uppercut will blast the targeted enemy skyward, into a position where you can continue the assault with gunfire or an aerial combo.

Rising Dragon

This is the Beast Uppercut after a single charge. It rises higher and does more damage, while taking the enemy into the air with Dante.

Divine Dragon

This is the Beast Uppercut with a double (max) charge. It rises even higher than Rising Dragon, has an added drill effect, and causes even more damage.

Real Impact

This is the strongest attack for Gilgamesh. In fact, it is the strongest attack of all the melee weapons in the game. This mighty power also has a substantial (slow!) start-up time, when you can be hit and interrupted by an enemy attack. Only use this monstrous manoeuvre when the enemy is stunned and there are no other hostiles nearby.

Real Impact is the most powerful melee attack in the game and deserves some love.

Lucifer Sword Master Style specific moves

Discipline

A single press of the Style Button will position all summoned blades into an offensive formation around Dante's body. The direction Dante is currently facing determines the orientation of the blades. After a brief moment the blades will then fire forwards. If you continue to hold down **B** | ◎, the blades will stay in formation around Dante until you release the button. You can move about the area when you do this, but even if you change directions, the blades will remain fixed and pointing in the original direction as when you first summoned them to you.

Climax

With a clap of Dante's hands, all loose blades fly into formation around his body in a porcupine-like protective measure. Should an enemy touch one of the blades, it will explode on contact. The blades will not move with Dante during this technique and will automatically detonate in 2 seconds. This is a good last-second manoeuvre to execute when you see an enemy charging in your direction.

Dante's Climax is explosive for encroaching enemies!

Bondage

This ability will command all loose blades to target and pierce the enemy you are currently locked on to. The blades will not track the enemy's movement, but will fire at the point where the enemy was at the moment Bondage was executed. When used against a fast-moving enemy, some or all of the blades may miss, so it is advisable to use this move against a foe that is currently immobile.

Royal Guard

Royal Guard Upgrades

Style Level	Base Cost
Royal Guard Level 2	300
Royal Guard Level 3	700
Royal Guard Level 4	5000

Royal Guard Command List

Technique Name	Style Level	Controller Input
Block	1	**B** | ◎ while standing
Air Block	2	**B** | ◎ while jumping
Royal Block	1	**B** | ◎
Release	1	Lock-On + Left Stick forward + **B** | ◎ while standing
Air Release	2	Lock-On + Left Stick forward + **B** | ◎ while jumping
Royal Release	1	Lock-On + Left Stick forward + **B** | ◎
Dreadnaught	4	Lock-On + Left Stick back + **B** | ◎ while standing

Royal Gauge

The Royal Gauge stores the accumulated attack power of all enemy strikes that you block using the Royal Guard techniques. When you successfully block an enemy attack, you absorb the full value of the attack as Royal Energy. For example, if you block a Frost's Jump Claw attack, which inflicts 800 units of damage, you will absorb 800 units of Royal Energy into the Royal Gauge.

Royal Guard Style	Royal Gauge Capacity
Level 1 & 2	10000 units
Level 3	20000 units
Level 4	30000 units

Defence Conditions

Situation	Effect	Remark
Block enemy attack up to level 2	Normal Block	Damage reduced to 1/4
Block enemy attack level 3 and above	Guard Break	Damage reduced by 1/2 but defence broken
Block 5 frames or less before any enemy attack	Royal Block	Incoming damage nullified, x2 attack power added to Royal Gauge, 10 frames invincibility.

Block

Against light attacks up to Level 2, hold **B** \| ◎ to enter a guard stance. During this guard, the damage of the attack will be reduced to 1/4 (x0.25) of its original value. If an enemy attacks at Level 3 or higher, this will shatter Dante's guard. Even though Dante's Guard is shattered, you can still enjoy enhanced defence and the power of the attack is reduced by 1/2 (x0.5). Please refer to the Opponents chapter for information on enemy attack levels.

If you block an incoming attack, damage is reduced to 1/4 the original value.

Air Block

This is a Block performed while Dante is airborne.

Royal Block

Royal Block is the real guts of the Royal Guard technique. This is a parry technique which completely negates damage from any incoming attack regardless of the attack level and adds x2 the attack power value to the Royal Gauge. The timing for a Royal Block is tight. You must perform the block within 5 frames of its striking you. No easy task, but well worth the effort.

With a Royal Block, all damage is completely negated!

Release

Successful Blocks and Royal Blocks store energy in the Royal Gauge. You can use this energy for an impressive attack by releasing it all at once. The more energy you have, the more powerful the attack.

Royal Release

Releasing the energy accumulated in the Royal Gauge just before an enemy attack strikes will significantly boost the destructive power of the Release. As you can see from the following table, the amount a Release is modified depends how well you timed it. When the execution of Release is timed perfectly, the attack animation will change slightly and rip through any enemy it connects with.

Release Conditions

Situation	Effect	Modifier
Release	Normal Release	0
Release 6 to 10 frames before enemy attack	Guard Release	100
Release 5 frames or less before enemy attack	Royal Release	350

Release Levels*

Royal Gauge Value	0	1-9999	10000-29999	30000
Normal Release	Level 1	Level 2	Level 3	Level 3
Guard Release	Level 2	Level 3	Level 3	Level 3
Royal Release	Level 4	Level 4	Level 4	Level 5

The "Level" of the attack determines the amount of CP and DT boost.

Release Attack Data

Technique Name	Attack	CP Value	CP Timer	DT Increase
Release (Lv 1)	*	0	300	0
Release (Lv 2)	*	200	300	150
Release (Lv 3)	*	300	300	500
Release (Lv 4)	*	150	300	250
Release (Lv 5)	*	400	300	750
Block succeed	-	150	60	350
Royal Block succeed	-	350	0	1000
Guard Release succeed	-	200	60	500
Royal Release succeed	-	500	60	1000

* Attack power is calculated based on the type of Release performed.

Release Damage Calculation

Release Attack Power = ([Royal Gauge Charge] x 0.08) + Modifier

With a full Royal Gauge at 30000 units, a Royal Release would have the following attack power.

The 2x modifier during Echidna's dive attack doubles a Royal Release's power.

Release Attack Power	([30000] x 0.08) + 350
Release Attack Power	(2400) + 350
Release Attack Power	2750

Bear in mind that certain enemies have damage modifiers applied to them. This can increase or decrease the final damage value of a Release. In cases where the modifier is increased, such as the 2x modifier during Echidna's Dragon Dive attack, a Just Release becomes the most powerful weapon in your arsenal, capable of inflicting 5500 points of damage or more!

Dreadnaught

Dreadnaught covers Dante in impenetrable armour. The duration of this invincible form is determined by the amount of energy you currently have accumulated in the Royal Gauge. On activation, the Dreadnaught will not drain the Royal Gauge for 3 seconds. After this time, depletion will resume at a rate of 35 points per frame until the gauge is empty. That's 2100 units per second, giving you 17.28 seconds with a full Royal Gauge.

Dreadnaught is a rough and ready suit of armour that makes you invincible.

Dark Slayer

Available after defeating Angelo Agnus in Mission 17

The Dark Slayer style is gained when Dante regains Yamato. This style only has one level and can't be upgraded. To activate this style, press the D-Pad in the same direction as the currently selected style. Do the same to deactivate Dark Slayer and revert to the previously selected style.

Dark Slayer Command List

Technique Name	Command
Slash Dimension F	Lock-On + Left Stick forward + 🅑 | ◎
Slash Dimension C	Lock-On + Left Stick back + 🅑 | ◎
Yamato Combo S	🅑 | ◎ 🅑 | ◎ 🅑 | ◎ while standing
Aerial Rave V	🅑 | ◎ 🅑 | ◎ in mid-air

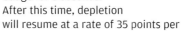

Yamato Attack Data

Technique name	Attack	CP Value	CP Timer	DT Increase
Sheath Hit	60	100	300	90
Sheath Slash	80	100	300	120
Drawing Slash	210	200	300	315
Aerial Rave V (1st attack, 1st hit)	50	80	150	75
Aerial Rave V (1st attack, 2nd hit)	60	80	150	90
Aerial Rave V (2nd)	110	150	150	165
Slash Dimension	350	300	200	525
Sheath sword (after attack)*	N/A	400	0	1000

* An enemy must be nearby to receive designated CP value.

Slash Dimension F

During this attack, Dante feints backwards into a stance ready to draw Yamato. When the sword is drawn, it projects a horizontal wall of magical sword slashes in the air far in front of Dante. This is a great move for damaging a whole group of enemies at a distance.

Slash Dimension C

This variation of Slash Dimension is the same as type F but is much closer to Dante.

Slash Dimension C can damage a whole pack of enemies at once.

Yamato Combo S

This combo consists of a pair of blunt strikes using Yamato's sheath followed by a final slash from the sword itself. The first 2 blunt strikes are not only very rapid, but will flow into any other striking attack perfectly. Another extremely useful aspect of Yamato is that Dante will not suffer any stun animation when he breaks a blocking enemy's defences using Yamato strikes.

Aerial Rave V

Aerial Rave V is a stylish trio of sword strikes which can be used to attack an enemy while in mid-air. This combo opens with Dante releasing an incredibly fast X-shaped energy blast by partially pulling Yamato from its sheath. This 2-hit blast holds the enemy in place for the final strike, when Dante fully draws Yamato for a horizontal strike which blasts the enemy away.

Devil Trigger

Activation and Consumption

Pressing **LB** | **L1** will immediately activate Dante's Devil Trigger as long as you have 3 or more DT Gauge cells filled. Unlike Nero, no damaging explosion is unleashed when Dante activates Devil Trigger. The maximum number of cells in Dante's Devil Trigger gauge is 10. Each cell is worth 1000 units of DT energy.

Activating Devil Trigger with Dante consumes 1500 units of energy. Upon activation, there is a 3-second period when no energy is consumed but after that time, the gauge depletes at a rate of 10 units per frame. This equates to 600 units per second, meaning that Devil Trigger can run for 17.16 seconds with a full Gauge (all 10 cells).

Trigger Heart reduces the consumption rate to 7.5 units per frame, which corresponds to 450 units per second. With Trigger Heart, Devil Trigger can run for 21.88 seconds with a full DT Gauge.

Strength Enhancement

Activating Devil Trigger increases Dante's overall speed and attacking power. In the Devil Trigger state, all of Dante's melee attacks gain a x1.5 attack power boost. Projectile attacks such as the Sword Master move, Drive, do not receive an attack boost.

Dante's long-range weapons become stronger as well: Ebony & Ivory's regular shot gains a 50% boost (x1.5) while the shotgun's regular blast is enhanced by 33% (x1.33). The special Gunslinger attacks for Ebony & Ivory and the shotgun all gain unique damage boosts. Please refer to the attack tables in the DT Gunslinger section that follows for the values of these DT-enhanced attacks.

Pandora's Jealousy is also boosted by 50%, but no other attacks from Pandora are affected. However, Pandora is transformed into its various forms much more quickly.

Speed Enhancement

Dante's overall speed increases when Devil Trigger is activated. All movements and actions receive a 10% speed boost. The only move not affected is Sword Master's Dance Macabre.

Defence Enhancement

Devil Trigger also improves Dante's defensive power so he sustains only 50% damage from all enemy attacks. The defensive effect of Devil Trigger allows Dante to withstand enemy attacks up to a Level 2 rating without going through damage animation. It is also possible to withstand up to three Level 3 rated attacks before Dante goes through damage animation.

Health Boost

While the Devil Trigger is activated Dante's health will regenerate at a rate of 3 points per frame, which equates to 180 Health points per second. You can regain a full health cell every 5.55 seconds that Devil Trigger is active.

Jump Enhancement

Devil Trigger enhances the Air Hike ability, allowing you to perform 2 Air Hikes per jump. This triple jump will allow you to sail away from even the largest enemy attacks or to reach the highest platforms with ease.

The jump enhancements offered by DT allow you to reach remote locations.

Weapon Specific DT Enhancements

Some special attacks also gain additional striking animations alongside the increase in speed and power. The special moves modified when Devil Trigger is active are detailed here.

Rebellion: DT Stinger

Stinger is powered up significantly while Devil Trigger is active. The sword thrust is modified into a devastating drill attack capable of ripping straight through an enemy. The range is also increased.

Technique Name	Attack	CP Value	CP Timer	DT Increase
DT Stinger (1st)	20	20	200	15
DT Stinger (2nd)	30	30	200	22.5
DT Stinger (3rd)	40	40	200	30
DT Stinger (4th)	50	50	200	37.5
DT Stinger (finish)	130	200	200	97.5

DT Stinger uses 1000 units of DT energy per activation.

Gilgamesh: DT Kick 13

With Devil Trigger active, Kick 13 is modified into a spectacular 13-hit combo which continues to strike the enemy even after it has been launched into the air.

Technique name	Attack	CP Value	CP Timer	DT Increase
DT kick 13 (1st & 2nd)	110	80	350	82.5
DT kick 13 (3rd, 5th, 7th, 9th)	20	35	350	15
DT kick 13 (4th, 6th, 8th, 10th)	40	55	350	30
DT kick 13 (11th)	150	100	350	112.5
DT kick 13 (12th)	110	80	350	82.5
DT kick 13 (13th)	180	200	350	135

DT Kick 13 uses 1000 units of DT energy per activation.

Lucifer: DT Pin-Up

DT Pin-Up allows Dante to summon 10 blades at once. Major destruction ensues once these blades are directed to a target and detonated.

Technique name	Attack	CP Value	CP Timer	DT Increase	Remarks
DT Pin-Up	0	0	0	0	Summon 10 blades at once.

DT Pin-Up uses 1000 units of DT energy per activation.

Style Specific DT Enhancements

DT Gunslinger Ebony & Ivory

Technique name	Attack	CP Value	CP Timer	DT Increase
DT Twosome Time (short distance)	20	20	10	15
DT Twosome Time (middle distance)	12	20	10	9
DT Twosome Time (long distance)	6	15	10	4.5
DT Rain Storm (short distance)	25	40	150	18.75
DT Rain Storm (middle distance)	25	40	150	18.75
DT Rain Storm (long distance)	25	30	150	18.75
DT Honeycomb Fire (short distance)	20	20	10	15
DT Honeycomb Fire (middle distance)	12	20	10	9
DT Honeycomb Fire (long distance)	6	15	10	4.5

Short distance: 0-4m, middle distance: 4m-8m, long distance: 8m and above

DT Gunslinger Coyote-A

Technique name	Attack	CP Value	CP Timer	DT Increase
DT Gun Stinger (main: short distance)	20	25	150	15
DT Gun Stinger (main: middle distance)	15	25	150	11.25
DT Gun Stinger (main: long distance)	10	15	150	7.5

Technique name	Attack	CP Value	CP Timer	DT Increase
DT Gun Stinger (spread: short distance)	20	25	150	15
DT Gun Stinger (spread: middle distance)	15	25	150	11.25
DT Gun Stinger (spread: long distance)	10	15	150	7.5
DT Backslide (main: short distance)	30	35	150	22.5
DT Backslide (main: middle distance)	25	35	150	18.75
DT Backslide (main: long distance)	15	25	150	11.25
DT Backslide (spread: short distance)	30	35	150	22.5
DT Backslide (spread: middle distance)	25	35	150	18.75
DT Backslide (spread: long distance)	15	25	150	11.25
DT Fireworks (main: short distance)	15	14	150	11.25
DT Fireworks (main: middle distance)	10	14	150	7.5
DT Fireworks (main: long distance)	5	10	150	3.75
DT Fireworks (spread: short distance)	15	14	150	11.25
DT Fireworks (spread: middle distance)	10	14	150	7.5
DT Fireworks (spread: long distance)	5	10	150	3.75

Short distance: 0-4m, middle distance: 4m-8m, long distance: 8m and above

DT Gunslinger Pandora

Technique name	Attack	CP Value	CP Timer	DT Increase
DT PF262: Jealousy (short distance)	20	30	150	15
DT PF262: Jealousy (middle distance)	10	30	150	7.5
DT PF262: Jealousy (long distance)	4	20	150	3

Short distance: 0-4m, middle distance: 4m-8m, long distance: 8m and above

Trickster

Trickster-specific evasive manoeuvres gain very useful boosts when Devil Trigger is active. The ground-based Dash can be performed continuously in any direction you like, while each of the Sky Star and Air Trick aerial evasion tactics are allowed twice per jump.

Royal Guard

The Royal Guard ability Block can be used against any attack (even a Boss attack) without a risk of Dante's guard being shattered. An attack defended with Block while Devil Trigger is active is reduced to 1/2 attack power while accumulating the full power in the Royal Guard Gauge. The Release technique also acquires a power boost of 20% (x1.2). With a full Royal Gauge, a successful Royal Release will inflict a massive 3300 points of damage.

Advanced Combat Techniques

Holding the Controller

Everything covered in this guide is tested and performed using the default Devil May Cry 4 controller configuration. As you explore the various mechanics we will cover, you may feel the need to re-configure the controller according to your taste to make it easier to execute the commands

To effectively use a technique like Enemy Step cancelling the transition from the jump button press to an attack button has to be a single fast and smooth motion. If you press each button individually with your thumb, you will find that you cannot possibly press and release each button fast enough to enable the Enemy Step techniques covered to work. Here are some tips to help you perform the more difficult command tricks using the default controller configuration.

Thumb Slide Ⓐ | ⊗ to Ⓑ | ◎

In order to execute an Enemy Step to cancel and repeat a Ⓑ | ◎ move, you need to slide your thumb from Ⓐ | ⊗ to Ⓑ | ◎. For example, Dante's Aerial Rave can be cancelled and instantly repeated by using Enemy Step after the 3rd strike connects. When the 3rd slash animation commences, relax your hand, then smoothly perform the slide from Ⓐ | ⊗ to Ⓑ | ◎ as soon as the 3rd sword slash of the sequence strikes the enemy. Instead of treating the sequence as 2 button presses, think of it as one smooth motion counting as a single command.

Thumb Slide Ⓨ | △ to Ⓐ | ⊗

When trying to cancel and repeat a Ⓨ | △ manoeuvre such as Full House with the Enemy Step, you'll need a fast transition from Ⓨ | △ to Ⓐ | ⊗. In order to achieve the fast, accurate button presses needed for this technique, slide the tip of your thumb from Ⓨ | △ to Ⓐ | ⊗ in one smooth motion. Be sure to use the very tip of your thumb if possible. If you slide your whole thumb down the surface of the controller, you may accidentally hit ⊗ | ▢ and Ⓑ | ◎ as well.

Thumb Roll Ⓐ | ⊗ to Ⓨ | △

Another transition which may prove useful in complementing the previously explained method is the Ⓐ | ⊗ to Ⓨ | △ thumb roll. Instead of sliding down from Ⓨ | △ to Ⓐ | ⊗, the process is reversed by pressing Ⓐ | ⊗ with the back of the thumb joint before curling the thumb forward to press Ⓨ | △. This method is useful when performing Enemy Step cancel techniques such as Rapid Calibur or Split Repeat, which require rhythmic rather than lightning-fast command execution.

Thumb Roll Ⓐ | ⊗ to ⊗ | ▢

Using the same thumb motion as the previous example, press Ⓐ | ⊗ with the back of the thumb joint before rolling the thumb forwards to hit ⊗ | ▢. This technique is very useful when executing Enemy Step gun techniques such as Extreme Jealousy, which involves repeatedly firing a gunshot while climbing an enemy's body with Enemy Step. As the transition from Ⓐ | ⊗ to ⊗ | ▢ is so smooth, you won't accidentally jump up past the enemy and break the combo.

Active Charged Shot

While holding ⊗ | ▢ with the left half of your thumb, roll your thumb over to the right to touch the Ⓨ | △ button when you want to throw a sword slash. This method allows you to keep the ⊗ | ▢ button held down while dealing out sword attacks. In order to jump using Ⓐ | ⊗, similar to the methods described previously, use the back of the thumb joint by rolling your thumb back slightly.

To ensure you don't lose height you must press the jump and attack buttons as quickly as possible...

...this allows you to cancel an Enemy Step into another attack while the jump animation is still beginning.

Mechanics

No Lock-On

If you do not lock on to an enemy, you are free to change direction with your attacks. This comes in handy when there are several foes rushing in to surround you and you need to turn quickly to hit each beast before it attacks you.

Input Buffering (Nero and Dante)

Inputting a command for a special attack during the animation frames of a preceding strike is called "buffering". By working ahead and buffering commands, you will ensure that the flow of execution from one move to the next is smooth and instant.

As Nero is firing Blue Rose, you can input buffer your next command!

Gun Interrupt (Nero and Dante)

Firing Nero's gun, the Blue Rose, or Dante's Ebony & Ivory is a quick and simple way of resetting any basic combo string in order to repeat it from the beginning. This comes in handy when a Combo string has a finishing move that knocks an enemy away but you want to keep the enemy close for repeated melee attacks. If the combo has 4 button presses and the 4th one knocks the enemy away, fire your gun once after the 3rd press so that the next press begins the combo again at button 1.

Snatch Interrupt (Nero)

Snatch can be used to reset a combo string in the same manner as gunfire. For example, during an Aerial Combo, if you perform the first two strikes and then quickly perform Snatch, you can then start the Aerial Combo again from the beginning.

Jump Cancelling (Nero and Dante)

The Enemy Step ability is not just for jumping over groups of enemies, in fact that's insignificant compared to the hell you can unleash by using it to cancel Aerial Combo moves! A jump during the animation of certain moves will cancel the action immediately, and during an Aerial Combo you can actually use the enemy's body currently being attacked as a platform to jump from. This will allow you to cancel and repeat moves which are usually only allowed once per jump. The small jump used for each cancel will also slow the rate of the character's decent during the combo.

Charged Shot Combos (Nero)

When you hold the ❌ | ⓪ button down to prepare for a Charge Shot, you are still free to move, attack and jump as normal. With this in mind, the Charge Shot becomes a valuable tool for stringing together interesting combos and for finishing off a sequence.

You can hold a Charge Shot while simultaneously striking with Red Queen.

Rapid Calibur (Nero)

Once you've got the hang of stopping the Calibur motion with a Jump Cancel you can use the move as a rapidly repeating strike. Against very large enemies (and bosses like Berial in particular) which are not knocked away by sword strikes, this technique is a very useful way of staying in the air while dealing decent damage. Jump up towards the enemy, Lock-On and perform Calibur. As soon as the strike connects, hit Ⓐ | ⊗ to cancel the motion with Enemy Step and then immediately perform Calibur again. If you quickly repeat this process over and over you will notice that Nero gains height on each repetition. Against a boss like Berial this technique can be used to strike at him while keeping well out of the way of his sword attacks.

Split repeat (Nero)

The Jump Cancelling technique can also be used to cancel the animation of other useful special moves. A Split (or Helm Breaker with Dante) is a great way to finish off an Aerial Combo, so how about making it hit twice? Notice how when Nero slashes the sword forwards during this attack, the enemy is still close enough to jump from. Quickly hit Ⓐ | ⊗ to jump when the Split connects, and then just after this jump executes, perform the command for Split again to strike again with the same move very quickly.

Rapid Full House (Dante)

This is Dante's primary equivalent to Split Repeat and Rapid Calibur. Compared to the individual sword slashes of an Aerial Rave, Full House is a powerful technique. After you have launched an enemy into the air with a Gilgamesh move such as Kick 13, jump straight up at the enemy. Start the process with the enemy still slightly above Dante; around half of Dante's height above is ideal. When in position press Ⓨ | ④ to throw a Full House, and as soon as the move connects tap Ⓐ | ⊗ and then Ⓨ | ④ again immediately. Making sure you cancel the Full House before the kick makes any movement through the enemy's body will ensure you can repeat the attack a few times over.

Extreme Jealousy

Tired of waiting such a long time for the Disaster Gauge to charge? Fret no more because with this technique you'll be able to have a full gauge charged in no time and in relative safety. An easy way to get this going is to launch an enemy with Rebellion's Rising High Time, and with Pandora selected, remain holding Lock-On and tap ❌ | ▢ when you are side by side with the enemy in mid-air. You'll notice that when Dante fires the Gatling Gun he'll lose height quite rapidly in relation to the enemy. Before you fall too far past the enemy's body press Ⓐ | ❌ to Enemy Step and then immediately press ❌ | ▢ again to resume fire. Once again Dante will fall slightly, so once again you must jump to regain the lost height and fire again. Repeating this process fast enough will actually hold Dante and his enemy in place in mid-air. This allows for an almost constant stream of fire with Jealousy, and will very quickly charge the Disaster Gauge.

Rapid Shotgun

Any time you have an enemy cornered without room to be knocked away, you can use jump cancelling to inflict a rapid barrage of close-range shotgun blasts. Whether you hold Lock-On or not doesn't matter, you just need to make sure that the enemy cannot be knocked backwards and that you are within Enemy Step range. Jump straight upwards and execute a shotgun blast while still low to the ground, as soon as the shot connects roll your thumb from Ⓐ | ❌ back to ❌ | ▢ in order to cancel and repeat the shotgun animation while taking a small leap upwards. This allows you to hover on the spot while dishing out a rapid series of lethal shotgun blasts.

Combo Techniques for Nero

In this section we'll look at building a large stylish combo using basic to advanced techniques with Nero.

High Roller

Tagging the command attack High Roller ([RB] | [R1] + Left Stick ⬅ + Ⓨ | Ⓐ) onto one of Nero's Red Queen Combos is the order of the day here. While you're free to simply open a combo with High Roller without any kind of lead-up to it, this guide will use the fact that you can tag command attacks onto the strikes of set combo strings whenever possible. Learning when and how command attacks flow without delay from the sword strikes of set combo strings will aid the player a great deal in the construction of personalised combos.

Red Queen Combo A 3-hit, High Roller.

Once the two opening slashes have met their mark, hold [RB] | [R1] to Lock-On as you press Ⓨ | Ⓐ again to activate the third slash. Now that Nero's direction is locked with Lock-On, input Left Stick ⬅ + Ⓨ | Ⓐ for a High Roller, which will launch the enemy into the air.

Air Juggle

After you've launched the enemy into the air with the High Roller command you are suddenly faced which even more possibilities. The iconic Devil May Cry action of stylishly holding an enemy up in the air with a hail of gunfire is easily achieved by simply firing the Blue Rose by repeatedly tapping ❌ | ▢ once the enemy has been lifted into the air.

In this situation where you have an enemy pinned into position by gunfire as it hangs in the air, you are free to move Nero should you need to get him out of the way in an incoming attack. It is possible to walk around while firing in order to keep away from danger as you shoot the airborne enemy, as you have the Lock-On button held down you are also free to use Nero's Side Roll should you need to abort and get out of the way.

Aerial Combo

High Roller, gunfire juggle, Aerial Combo.

Continuing on directly from launching an enemy into the air with High Roller, instead of simply firing at the launched enemy this time we will have Nero jump upwards after it. Launching an enemy into the air with High Roller will send it upwards to a height equal to Nero's single jump. Once you have launched an enemy into the air with High Roller, continue to hold Lock-On and fire off a few shots with the Blue Rose to steady the enemy and get your bearings. Once you're ready press Ⓐ | ❌ to execute a straight upwards jump, and once in the air and next to the enemy press Ⓨ | Ⓐ Ⓨ | Ⓐ Ⓨ | Ⓐ to execute Nero's Aerial Combo. The first two sword strikes will keep the enemy held in place until the third strike sends it crashing straight back down to the ground.

Launch the enemy with High Roller...

...and then jump up to leave you at the same height, ready for an aerial combo.

> **Aerial Combo 2-hit, gunshot, Aerial Combo 3-hit.**

The same rules apply to set combo strings in the air as they do on the ground; set strings may be interrupted and repeated by firing off a shot from the Blue Rose. The first two Strikes of Nero's Aerial Combo will keep the enemy held in front of him as the sword attacks are dealt out. The third strike however will knock the enemy straight back down to the ground immediately with a vertical strike. In order to eliminate this vertical strike you can fire a single shot with the Blue Rose after the second strike connects, this will reset the Aerial Combo back to the beginning and you can repeat the combo immediately thus increasing the number of successive mid-air sword strikes from three to five.

Time to Split

> **Red Queen Combo A 3-hit, jump, Split, Streak.**

Split can be used to knock away an enemy during a ground based combo sequence as well as taking the action from the air to the ground. Lock-On to the enemy with [RB] | [R1], and at this point you may want to keep the Lock-On held for the entire duration of the combo until you are comfortable with it. Once Lock-On is activated hit the [Y] | [△] button three times to perform the first three sword strikes of Red Queen Combo A, and when the third strike connects hit the [A] | [✕] button to jump. Now with Lock-On still activated, execute the command Left Stick ➡ + [Y] | [△] to perform Split, Nero will now dive down and deliver a vertical sword attack which will knock the enemy away. The trick here is that you continue holding Lock-On and the Left Stick ➡, and once the Spilt has done it's work hit [Y] | [△] again to rush at the enemy with Streak to deliver a final crushing blow.

> **Red Queen Combo A 3-hit, High Roller, Aerial Combo 2-hit, Split, Streak.**

💻 | **03_01** Here is an example of how Split can be used as a devastating way to drag the action out of the air and back to the ground, all within a smooth and stylish combo sequence. After three initial strikes with the Red Queen Combo A the enemy is launched skyward with Rising High Roller. Nero is now free to jump up after the enemy and deliver yet more pain with the first two strikes of the Aerial Combo, once the second strike hits home Split is executed and the enemy is dragged straight back down to the ground where an immediate Streak awaits.

Rising High Roller

> **R1 + Left Stick back + hold Y | △**

Here's where we take things to a higher level and deliver some stunning Aerial Combos! Holding the Y | △ button down while executing a High Roller will alter the move to it's rising variant. Instead of simply launching the enemy into the air Nero will actually fly upwards with it and end his upwards jump in a perfect position to deal an Aerial Combo. As Nero and the enemy end up much higher in the air compared to the standard version of the High Roller, the Aerial Combo itself can be much larger gives more time in the air to play around with different abilities before gravity takes it's toll.

Roulette Spin

> **In mid-air Y | △ Y | △ pause Y | △**

Roulette Spin really comes into play nicely when you start using the Rising High Roller to get that extra little bit of kick when launching an enemy skyward. As you have to leave a small delay within Roulette Spin's command execution you may find that you don't have enough time to complete the command if you simply jump upwards at the enemy. The Roulette Spin itself acts like an additional launcher but performed in mid-air; the enemy will be thrown upwards even higher than it initially was by the Rising High Roller.

> **Rising High Roller, Aerial Combo 2-hit, gunshot, Roulette Spin.**

💻 | **03_02** With the extra little bit of height gained by launching the enemy using the Rising High Roller this combo will demonstrate a simple way of adding extra hits leading into the Roulette Spin. To begin this combo, hold Lock-On and open with Rising High Roller to launch both you and the enemy into the air. Once Nero and the enemy are side-by-side continue with the Aerial Combo by pressing Y | △ Y | △. As we do not want to send the enemy back

down with the final slash of the Aerial Combo cancel the chain here with a single gunshot X | □. Immediately after the gunshot is fired the enter the Roulette Spin command Y | △ Y | △ (delay) Y | △ and Nero will perform a further two sword slashes followed by the upwards Roulette Spin to complete the sequence.

When you use two quick slashes in the air, try to exceed the second one...

...so the Roulette Spins benefit from a nice boost in damage.

Calibur

> **Red Queen Combo A 3-hit, Rising High Roller, Aerial Combo 2-hit, Calibur.**

This combo example using the Calibur within an Aerial Combo should get you started learning the Calibur's effect and how to execute the command smoothly. Open the combo by attacking an enemy with three strikes from Red Queen Combo A, and on the third strike hold RB | R1 to Lock-On and input the command for the Rising High Roller. Once you reach the peak of the jump and Nero is next to the enemy tap Y | △ twice to continue the combo with the first two strikes of Nero's Aerial Combo. During the second Aerial Combo strike, with Lock-On still held down input the Calibur command: Left Stick ← then Left Stick → + Y | △. After performing the two Aerial Combo strikes Nero will immediately launch himself into the Calibur technique and blast the enemy away from him.

Extended Aerial Combo

💻 | **03_03** Adding a tiny jump before the third slash of the Aerial Combo is a simple way to use Jump Cancelling to extend your aerial combos. After launching the enemy into the air with a Rising High Roller, start an Aerial Combo. Once the second Aerial Combo strike connects remain holding Lock-On and slide your thumb smoothly from A | X to B | ◎ and when the animation cancels and Snatch pulls the enemy back in, start the process again. You're aiming to jump out of the Aerial Combo animation when the second strike connects and then Snatch immediately. Even though the jump used to cancel the Aerial Combo animation is tiny you still gain a little height, so this sequence slows the rate of decent during an Aerial Combo very dramatically.

A second variation of this combo sequence would be to cancel the Aerial Combo animation on the first slash instead of the second. As Nero loses a little height during the second slash of the Aerial combo, eliminating it from the sequence will tip the balance so he'll actually gain height overall!

Aerial Extension from Calibur

03_04 Taking the extended Aerial Combo one step further here we add the Aerial special move Calibur into the mix. Launch an enemy and start the party with a pair of Aerial Combo slashes while holding Lock-On, and then during the second slash animation input the command for Calibur. As soon as Calibur connects hit **A** | **X** to jump in order to cancel the animation and then immediately execute Snatch. As soon as Nero Snatches the enemy start the process again with a pair of Aerial Combo slashes leading into another Calibur and so on. When cancelling the Calibur animation slide your thumb from **A** | **X** to **B** | **○** in one smooth motion, the aim is to make the jump so small that it's invisible.

After hitting with Calibur the enemy should be knocked away, ending your combo...

...but a really quick Snatch can bring it straight back to continue the fun.

The Devil Bringer

Nero is capable of the Devil Bringer technique whether he's on the ground or in mid-air. The Buster acts just like a gunshot does in relation to sword slashes, pressing **B** | **○** button while a sword animation is active will cause Nero to immediately switch into the Buster animation to follow up with a throwing move specific to which enemy type you are fighting.

> **Red Queen Combo A 3-hit, Buster.**

Here using the basic Red Queen Combo A again, this sequence illustrates how Buster will flow smoothly from set combo strings. Without Lock-On held tap **Y** | **△** **Y** | **△** **Y** | **△** to throw the first three slashes of Red Queen Combo A at an enemy. Once the third slash has connected tap **B** | **○** to immediately grab and throw the enemy with Buster.

> **Red Queen Combo A 3-hit, Rising High Roller,**
> **Aerial Combo 2-hit, Buster.**

In this example the basic Red Queen Combo A is used first, but bear in mind that you can use any Red Queen Combo to start things off or any cancelled and mixed up variations of these set strings. The first three strikes of the Red Queen Combo A are thrown at an enemy, and when the third strike connects hold Lock-On and input the command for Rising High Roller. Once in the air hit **Y** | **△** **Y** | **△** to perform the first two slashes of Nero's Aerial Combo. Once the second slash has connected exit Lock-On and then press **B** | **○**. Nero will now grab the enemy with the Devil Bringer and perform a throwing move specific to that enemy type. There is no correct time to release the Lock-On button; just do so at a time you are comfortable with.

Charge Shot Combos

It is possible to hold **X** | **○** button down to ready a Charge Shot while inputting other commands to perform a combo. A basic example of this would be to launch the enemy into the air with the Rising High Roller and continue the assault with all 3 hits of the Aerial Combo. When the third hit connects and knocks the enemy downwards immediately release the **X** | **○** button, and as the Charge Shot connects Nero will be thrown backwards. As soon as Nero lands execute the Streak to finish the combo.

An alternative to this is to launch the enemy, follow up with the three Aerial Combo slashes, and then instantly release a level 2 Charge Shot. This will launch the enemy upwards a little during the combo, allowing you to follow up with a buffered Calibur as a finisher, which is useful for knocking the enemy away.

Charge Shot Level 3

This time we'll use the maximum charge effect, the secondary explosion that occurs after Charge Shot level 3 will launch the enemy upwards on detonation. The next sequence will demonstrate a possible way this can be used to extend an aerial section of a combo.

> **Red Queen Combo C 6-hit, Rising High Roller, Aerial Combo 3-hit, Charge Shot level 3, Snatch, Rising High Roller, Aerial Combo 2-hit, jump, Aerial Combo 3-hit, Split, Enemy Step, Split, Streak.**

🖥 | **03_05** Start building the Charge Shot by holding ❌ | ⬜ but do not start the combo itself until the between the first and second flash of energy on Nero's arm. Keeping ❌ | ⬜ held down, Lock-On to your target and begin the sequence with six hits of Red Queen Combo C, and when the 6th sword strike has connected continue the combo with Rising High Roller.

Once you're in the air perform all three strikes of Nero's Aerial Combo, and when the third strike connects and sends the enemy to the ground, release the ❌ | ⬜ button. By the time you release ❌ | ⬜ you will have held it long enough to launch Charge Shot level 3, and when the shot connects Nero will recoil backwards and land on the ground, while at the same time the enemy will be launched back into the air by the Charge Shot. Leaving no gap at this point, remain holding Lock-On and Snatch the enemy as soon as you can move and immediately after that launch the enemy again with Rising High Roller.

When you reach the position for an aerial assault again perform the first two strikes of Nero's Aerial Combo and immediately jump using Enemy Step when the second strike connects. At the exact moment you jump the enemy will be launched upwards by the secondary explosion of the level 3 Charge Shot, as you have jumped at the same

A Level 3 Charge Shot will knock you back to the ground...

...but will stun the enemy just long enough to land an instant Snatch and continue the combo.

time you will both end up side by side again. From here perform all three hits of the Aerial Combo and follow the enemy down to the ground with Split. As soon as Split connects cancel the animation with Enemy Step and perform the Spilt again. This second Split will blast the enemy away from you, leaving you to finish the job with Streak.

As you can see, this combo sequence utilises a whole range of different play-mechanic manipulating techniques mixed together to make the whole thing flow seamlessly. As you master each element that makes up a combo like this the scope for creating even more outrageous combos increases.

Combo Techniques for Dante

In this section we'll look at building a large stylish combo using basic to advanced techniques with Dante. Dante doesn't have the Snatch or Buster abilities, so getting close to the enemy presents unique challenges if you knock the foe away from you.

Combo string to Command Attack

> **Rebellion Combo A 2-hits, Stinger.**

Lock-On to an enemy with ⟦RB⟧ | ⟦R1⟧, and press ❤ | 🔺 twice to execute two hits of Rebellion Combo A. As soon as the second strike connects finish the combo with Stinger (Left Stick ➡ + ❤ | 🔺). Inputting a command for a special move during the execution of another attack is known as buffering. By buffering in a command attack during the move that precedes it you will cancel the ending frames of the move and immediately execute the next attack. Less frames of animation mean faster execution and a smoother transition from one technique to the next.

The first hits of Rebellion Combo A can be used to start combos or lead into other attacks...

...such as a buffered Stinger.

> **Rebellion Combo A 2-hits,**
> **Helm Breaker, Stinger.**

This example demonstrates the way you can repeatedly perform a command attack during the animation of another command attack. Lock-On to an enemy and throw the first two hits of Rebellion Combo A, and as soon as the second strike connects jump up and hit **Y** | **△**. Ensure you press **Y** | **△** very soon after the jump executes, and try and time your button press to occur at the same time as the sound effect emitted shortly after Dante leaves the ground. This **Y** | **△** press during the jump will launch the Helm Breaker move which will strike the targeted enemy from above. As Dante performs this move hold the Left Stick ➡ and repeatedly tap **Y** | **△**. As soon as Dante is able to move after the Helm Breaker he will fly forward with a Stinger.

> **Rebellion Combo A 2-hit, gunshot, Rebellion**
> **Combo B 4-hit, Helm Breaker, Stinger, Million**
> **Stab.**

03_06 Here we'll step things up a little and add another buffered command attack into the mix, while applying the combo-extending Gun Interrupt technique. Lock-On to an enemy and perform the first two strikes of Rebellion Combo A, and as soon as the second strike connects cancel the combo chain with an Ebony & Ivory shot. Immediately after the shot is fired execute Rebellion Combo B, and after the input delay of the Combo B button sequence comes a spinning slash. When the last hit of the spinning slash connects, hit **A** | **✕** to jump, and then **Y** | **△** as you hear the jump sound effect. Helm Breaker will now be executed, and during this move keep holding the Left Stick ➡ and repeatedly tap **Y** | **△**. After the Helm Breaker Dante will launch forward into a Stinger, and as soon as you see the forwards dash of the Stinger release the Left Stick ➡ you've been holding and rapidly tap **Y** | **△** to flow straight into the Million Stab.

Sword Master/ Rebellion Aerial Rave

With Sword Master style selected and upgraded to Level 2 your basic aerial combo is the Aerial Rave with Rebellion. After launching an enemy into the air with Rising High Time, wait for Dante reach the top of the jump and hit **B** | **○** four times to execute the Aerial Rave. This aerial combo consists of three sword slashes, which will hold the enemy in place, before finishing the sequence with a fourth slash which knocks the enemy away from Dante.

Gunshot Aerial Rave Extension

Using the Gun Interrupt we can extend this combo by cancelling and repeating the Aerial Rave sequence before it reaches the fourth slash. After launching the enemy into the air start an Aerial Rave combo by tapping **B** | **◎**, and as soon as the third slash connects hit **X** | **▣** to fire a single Ebony & Ivory shot. This shot will reset the combo sequence, so immediately start tapping **B** | **◎** to perform an additional Aerial Rave. This will boost the Aerial Rave sword combo count from 4 hits to 7 hits.

Enemy Step Aerial Rave Extention

03_07 Jump Cancelling an aerial combo is a little different with Dante compared to what you may be used to with Nero. When you launch an enemy upwards with Rebellion's Rising High Time you will find that when you perform the Aerial Rave you will not be within range to Jump Cancel without losing height. Dante is ever so slightly out of range after the launcher, so you will have to correct your position in relation to the enemy. To achieve this, simply Enemy Step towards the enemy on the way up, at about 80% of the total height (just as Dante and the enemy are starting to draw level) after the launcher connects. As soon as this little jump commences and Dante is pushed very slightly towards the enemy, perform an Aerial Rave, and then you'll need to cancel the attack before the fourth strike knocks the enemy away. As soon as the third slash connects, press **A** | **⊗** to cancel the animation and then immediately perform an additional Aerial Rave. The key to this technique is to make sure the button presses occur in one smooth motion; the easiest way is to slide your thumb from **A** | **⊗** to **B** | **◎**.

To ensure you are lose enough to the enemy for a combo after launching wit Rising High Time...

...use an Enemy Step at this point on the way up.

Yamato Aerial Rave extension

03_08 Once you are comfortable with Jump Cancelling you can use it to float on the spot while dishing out the first slash of Aerial Rave V. Mixing this into your aerial combo will look fantastic! After launching an enemy, hit **B** | **◎** to execute a fast flick of a sword slash with Yamato. As soon as this slash connects hit **A** | **⊗** to cancel the animation, and then immediately press **B** | **◎** again to throw another slash. Once again speed is the most important thing to apply when performing this technique, the jump has to be absolutely tiny, so sliding your thumb over **A** | **⊗** to **B** | **◎** instead of pushing the buttons individually is essential.

Lucifer Rapid Splash

Another useful little move which works great when repeated is the Lucifer aerial combo move Splash. The situation explored here involves Splash being used as a fast combo attack to spice up a ground based combo. After a sequence of ground based strikes against a targeted enemy, lightly tap **A** | **⊗** to jump, and as soon as the jump commences immediately press **Y** | **△**. The Splash will now activate very close to the ground and strike the enemy in front of you. Splash carries Dante forwards, close enough to use the enemy as a platform, so on the second strike of Splash hit **A** | **⊗** to jump and cancel the animation before pressing **Y** | **△** again for another Splash.

Sword Master/Gilgamesh Shocking! Full House

After you have landed any number of Enemy Step cancelled Full House kicks finish the combo off in Shocking! style with a simple **B** | **◎** press. As long as you use the Enemy Step and cancel out of the final Full House you want to connect, Shocking! will always activate immediately.

Weapon Switching

Changing weapon mid-flow during a combo will allow you to seamlessly mix the attack chain of one weapon straight into the string of another weapon. A simple example of this is cycling through Dante's equipped weapons after completing part of the attack sequence of each. Executing two strikes of each weapon combo string before switching will ensure the enemy is not blasted away by the finishing strike of a string while keeping the striking rate constant. These repeating combo sequences are very useful against enemies who are weak against attacks from behind, as a constant stream of strikes will ensure the enemy cannot recover and counter.

With a full set of weapons you can still cycle through the list while performing a part of each weapon's attack string before switching. As there is an odd number of weapons in the cycle it's a good idea to get used to quickly tapping [RT] | [R2] twice to skip a weapon in the sequence. An easy way of getting used to skipping a weapon in the Weapon Switch sequence is to execute your [RT] | [R2] double-tap during a move with a long animation sequence. This is where Gilgamesh and Kick 13 come in very handy, by skipping past Lucifer as Kick 13 connects you can continue the combo smoothly by jumping after the enemy and scoring a Rebellion Aerial Rave.

Royal Guard Block Cancel

Instead of finishing Rebellion Combo A, cancel the second hit into a Block...

...and then start again with another Rebellion Combo A

03_09 When Royal Guard Style is selected you can instantly stop the flow of any combo string by simply pressing **B** | **◎** to Block. As Block is a very small animation it can be used to cancel and repeat ground-based combo strings quickly and easily. As an example of how this is useful, try cancelling and repeating Rebellion Combo A before it reaches the 3rd slash. This will prevent the enemy from being knocked away while you dish out a constant barrage of attacks. You are not limited to cancelling into the same combo chain again, you can for example cancel Rebellion Combo A into Rebellion Combo B and back again.

Style Switching

Switching Styles during combos can bring a wealth of new possibilities to your combat. A simple example of this would use the time it takes for Dante to complete the second sword slash of Rebellion Combo B to execute a style change. Start the combo off in Royal Guard with Rebellion Combo A, and on the second slash of this combo hit **B** | **◎** to cancel the animation with Block. Now immediately flow into Rebellion Combo B, and after the input delay hit **Y** | **△** to throw that long spinning 2nd slash, using the length of the animation here to your advantage to press the Directional Pad ← to switch into Sword Master. Launch the enemy into the air with Rising High Time and throw the first 3 strikes of the Aerial Rave, and as soon as the 3rd strike animation starts press the Directional Pad → to switch to Gunslinger and finish the combo off with **B** | **◎** Rain Storm.

Royal Guard to Sword Master

> **Royal Guard/Rebellion Combo A 2-hit, Block, Rebellion Combo B 4-hit (Sword Master), Prop, Shredder.**

Moving on from where we left off with the Block cancels, lets spice up the combo a little more by adding a move from a different style. First, with Royal Guard selected, throw the first two strikes of Rebellion Combo A, and cancel the animation with a Block. Now continue the combo with Rebellion Combo B. The second slash of this combo is a spinning slash with a long animation sequence, so use this time to press the Directional Pad → to switch over to Sword Master. With Sword Master now selected press **B** | **◎** to launch the enemy with Prop and follow this up with Shredder to complete the sequence.

Royal Guard to Sword Master to Gunslinger

> **Royal Guard/Rebellion Combo A 2-hit, Block, Rebellion Combo B 4-hit (Sword Master), Rising High Time, Aerial Rave 3-hit (Gunslinger), Rain Storm.**

03_10 Once again we will use the time it takes for Dante to complete the 2nd sword slash of Rebellion Combo B to execute a style change. As per the previous example start the combo off in Royal Guard with Rebellion Combo A, and on the second slash of this combo hit **B** | **◎** to cancel the animation with Block. Next, immediately flow into Rebellion Combo B, and after the input delay hit **Y** | **△** to throw that long spinning 2nd slash, again using the length of the animation here to your advantage to press the Directional Pad → to switch into Sword Master. Launch the enemy into the air with Rising High Time and throw the first three strikes of the Aerial Rave, and as soon as the 3rd strike animation starts press the Directional Pad ← to switch to Gunslinger and finish the combo off with **B** | **◎** Rain Storm.

As **Y** | **△** button attacks remain unchanged when you switch styles, you may want to take the combo a further step by finishing it off with a Helm Breaker after connecting the Rain Storm.

Dark Slayer and Yamato

> **Endless sequence of Rebellion Combo A 2-hit, Yamato Combo S 2-hit, Rebellion Combo A 2-hit...**

When Dark Slayer Style is selected Dante will gain a very effective 3-hit combo with the Japanese sword, not only does this combo offer incredible versatility it also causes Dante no recoil animation at all when a strike breaks an enemy's guard. The finishing strike of Yamato Combo S will usually knock the enemy away from Dante on impact but the two strikes preceding this finish are simply amazing for mixing up combos!

Using only the first two strikes of Yamato Combo S can lead to many combo possibilities...

...including an infinite loop with the first two hits of Rebellion Combo A.

After opening the sequence with the familiar Rebellion Combo A, cancel and start a completely different combo string simply by pressing **Ⓑ** | **◎** after the second strike of Rebellion Combo A. Press **Ⓑ** | **◎** once again to land the second strike of Yamato Combo S and then repeat the cycle again with Rebellion. As with all combos you are not limited to simply repeating the same chains over and over; you can mix and cancel into any attack string, in any order and with whichever weapon you like.

Aerial Rave Style Switch

Aerial Rave 3-hit, Enemy Step, Aerial Rave 3-hit, Enemy Step, Aerial Rave V 1-hit, Enemy Step, Aerial Rave V 1-hit, Enemy Step, Aerial Rave V 2-hit.

💻 | 03_11 Even in mid-air you can use the Style Switch to change the function of the **Ⓑ** | **◎** button. In this example we will explore mixing Rebellion Aerial Rave into Yamato Aerial Rave V by switching from Sword Master to Dark Slayer mid-combo. Launching the enemy into the air with Rebellion requires a slight adjustment to get into range for the Enemy Step; as was mentioned previously you must Enemy Step towards the enemy on the way up during the Rising High Time. Once you're in position, start the aerial combo with the first three strikes of Aerial Rave, Enemy Step cancel the combo on the third strike and then repeat the sequence again. As soon as the third slash animation starts for the second time, hit the Directional Pad ➡ to switch into Dark Slayer Style and immediately begin the thumb sliding **Ⓐ** | **Ⓧ** to **Ⓑ** | **◎** motion to repeat the first strike of Aerial Rave V twice before finishing the sequence with a complete Aerial Rave V.

Technical Data

Limited Invincibility

Certain moves have start-up frames of animation that impart limited invincibility. While these frames are playing, you are invulnerable to all damage.

Frames of Invincibility

Action	Time
Jump	20 frames from start
Back Jump	25 frames from start
Side Roll	20 frames from start
Stand Up	129 frames after knockdown
Use Holy Water	120 frames from use
Used Gold Orb	120 frames from use
Draw	10 frames at start, 10 frames for lower body only
Flush	20 frames from start
Real Impact (Rising)	15 frames from start, then 40 through Rising
Dash	25 frames from start
Flipper	25 frames from start
Mustang	20 frames from enemy contact
Sky Star	25 frames from start
Air Trick	22 frames from start
Royal Block	10 frames from successful Royal Block
Royal Release	30 frames from successful Royal Release
Dreadnaught	Length of Royal Gauge

Nero's Red Queen Exceed Zones

Exceed Zones are the parts of an attack where you can press the Exceed Trigger to charge 1 Exceed Lamp instantly. It should be noted that we use the point of impact as a visual reference, but you do not have to actually strike an enemy to charge a Lamp with Exceed. You can charge with Exceed at any time, even when no enemies are involved.

Exceed Zones Per Basic Attack

Attack	Exceed Zone
Combo A (1st hit)	Point of impact as Nero strikes the enemy.
Combo A (2nd hit)	Point of impact as Nero strikes the enemy.
Combo A (3rd hit)	Point of impact as Nero strikes the enemy.
Combo A (4th hit)	At the end of the slash when the sword strikes the ground.
Combo B (1st hit)	Point of impact as Nero strikes the enemy.
Combo B (2nd hit)	When the sword strikes the ground.

Attack	Exceed Zone
Combo B (3rd hit)	When the sword strikes the ground.
Combo B (4th hit)	When the sword strikes the ground.
Combo B (trigger loop 1)*	When the sword strikes the ground.
Combo B (trigger loop 2)*	When the sword strikes the ground.
Combo B (11th hit – dual1)	See 12th hit below.
Combo B (12th hit – dual2)	As Nero pulls the sword from the ground.
Combo C (1st hit)	Point of impact as Nero strikes the enemy.
Combo C (2nd hit)	Point of impact as Nero strikes the enemy.
Combo C (3rd hit – dual1)	See 4th hit below.
Combo C (4th hit – dual2)	Point of impact as Nero strikes the enemy.
Combo C (5th hit)	Point of impact as Nero strikes the enemy.
Combo C (6th hit)	Point of impact as Nero strikes the enemy.
Combo C (7th hit)	Just after impact as the sword drifts behind Nero's back.
Combo D (1st hit)	Point of impact as Nero strikes the enemy.
Combo D (2nd hit)	Point of impact as Nero strikes the enemy.
Combo D (3rd hit)	Point of impact as Nero strikes the enemy.
Combo D (4th hit)	At the end of the slash when the sword strikes the ground.
Combo D (splash)	See 4th hit above.
Aerial Combo (1st hit)	Point of impact as Nero strikes the enemy.
Aerial Combo (2nd hit)	Point of impact as Nero strikes the enemy.
Aerial Combo (3rd hit)	Point of impact as Nero strikes the enemy.
Roulette Spin (1st hit)	Point of impact as Nero strikes the enemy.
Roulette Spin (2nd hit)	Point of impact as Nero strikes the enemy.
Roulette Spin (1st rotation)	See 3rd rotation below.
Roulette Spin (2nd rotation)	See 3rd rotation below.
Roulette Spin (3rd rotation)	After impact as Red Queen swings back over Nero's head.
High Roller	After impact as Red Queen swings back over Nero's head.
High Roller (rising)	At the apex of the move as Red Queen swings back over Nero's head.
Streak	Right after impact as Nero swings Red Queen to the left.
Shuffle	Just after impact as the sword is travelling up and back away from the enemy.
Split	As the sword makes contact with the ground
Calibur	Just after impact as Nero brings Red Queen to the left.

* There are 3 hits possible in this trigger loop.

Nero's Special Attack Exceed Zones

Exceed Zones for Special Attacks are the parts of the attack where you can press the Exceed Trigger to charge 1 Exceed Lamp instantly.

Exceed Zones Per Special Attack

Attack	Exceed Zone
Ex High Roller	After impact as Nero starts the rotation of the finishing roll.
Ex Rising High Roller	After the apex of the move as Nero starts the rotation of the finishing roll.
Ex Streak	Just after impact as Nero swings Red Queen to his left.
Ex Shuffle	In the middle of the second sword slash.
Double Down	The moment the sword pierces the ground.
Ex Calibur	Once Nero's arm moves to the left after the explosive impact.

Nero's Buster Attack

Listed here are all the damage values for Nero's Buster attack per enemy.

Buster Attack Data

Enemy	Attack	CP Value	CP Timer	DT Increase
Scarecrow (Arm & Leg) ground	400	200	350	1200
Scarecrow (Arm & Leg) mid-air	400	200	350	1200
Mega Scarecrow – ground (1st)	400	200	350	1200
Mega Scarecrow- ground (2nd)	130	200	350	600
Mega Scarecrow – mid-air	450	200	350	1200
Frost – ground (impact wall)	50	50	350	0
Frost – ground (impact ground)	200	200	350	0
Frost – ground (throw)	300	200	350	1200
Frost – mid-air (impact wall)	50	50	350	0
Frost – mid-air (impact ground)	200	200	350	0
Frost – mid-air (throw)	300	200	350	1200
Frost – to healing ice	150	170	250	150
Assault – ground (impact ground)	40	100	350	300
Assault – ground (throw)	250	200	350	300
Assault – mid-air (impact ground)	40	100	350	300
Assault – mid-air (throw)	250	200	350	300
Assault – interrupt Dash attack	800	600	350	1500
Blitz – ground 1st	400	200	350	0

Enemy	Attack	CP Value	CP Timer	DT Increase
Blitz – ground 2nd	320	200	350	0
Blitz – ground 3rd	240	200	350	0
Blitz – ground 4th	160	200	350	0
Blitz – ground 5th & loop	80	50	350	0
Blitz – ground 6th & loop	80	50	350	0
Blitz – ground 7th	240	200	350	0
Blitz – ground 8th	800	200	350	2000
Blitz – mid-air 1st	400	200	350	0
Blitz – mid-air 2nd	320	200	350	0
Blitz – mid-air 3rd	240	200	350	0
Blitz – mid-air 4th	160	200	350	0
Blitz – mid-air 5th & loop	80	50	350	0
Blitz – mid-air 6th & loop	80	50	350	0
Blitz – mid-air 7th	240	200	350	0
Blitz – mid-air 8th	800	200	350	2000
Gladius – ground (impact anything)	200	200	350	1200
Gladius – mid-air (impact anything)	200	200	350	1200
Cutlass – ground	400	200	350	2000
Cutlass – mid-air	400	200	350	2000
Basilisk – ground	400	200	350	1200
Basilisk – mid-air	400	200	350	1200
Chimera Seed – ground	400	200	350	1200
Chimera Seed – mid-air	400	200	350	1200
Mephisto Insect – ground	300	200	350	1500
Mephisto Insect – mid-air	300	200	350	1500
Faust Insect – ground	400	200	350	1500
Faust Insect – mid-air	400	200	350	1500
Bianco Angelo – ground (stab)	100	200	350	300
Bianco Angelo – ground (twist)	50	100	350	300
Bianco Angelo – ground (explosion)	100	200	350	300
Bianco Angelo – ground (throw)	250	0	0	0
Bianco Angelo – to shield	300	170	250	450
Alto Angelo – ground 1st	800	200	350	1000
Alto Angelo – ground 2nd	200	300	350	1000
Alto Angelo – mid-air 1st	800	200	350	1000
Alto Angelo – mid-air 2nd	200	300	350	1000
Alto Angelo – to shield	300	170	250	450
Berial – Head	1500	600	350	1000
Berial – Legs 1st	200	200	350	500
Berial – Legs 2nd	400	600	350	500
Berial – ground throw 1st	200	200	350	500
Berial – ground throw 2nd	600	600	350	500
Bael & Dagon – Head (1st)	50	200	350	200
Bael & Dagon – Head (2nd)	300	200	350	200

Enemy	Attack	CP Value	CP Timer	DT Increase
Bael & Dagon – Head (3rd)	200	200	350	200
Bael & Dagon – Head (4th)	200	200	350	200
Bael & Dagon – Head (5th)	100	200	350	200
Bael & Dagon – Head (6th)	100	200	350	200
Bael & Dagon – Head (7th)	100	200	350	200
Bael & Dagon – Head (8th)	50	200	350	200
Bael & Dagon – Head (9th)	400	600	350	400
Bael & Dagon – Tail (1st)	500	200	350	1000
Bael & Dagon – Tail (2nd)	500	600	350	1000
Bael & Dagon – Rusalka - ground	400	200	300	1200
Bael & Dagon – Rusalka – mid-air	400	200	300	1200
Echidna Madam – Normal 1st*	40	200	350	400
Echidna Madam – Normal 2nd	70	200	350	400
Echidna Madam – Normal 3rd	60	200	350	400
Echidna Madam – Normal 4th	150	200	350	400
Echidna Madam – Normal 5th to 13th	20	50	350	0
Echidna Madam – Normal 14th	150	50	350	0
Echidna Madam – Normal 15th to 24th	20	50	350	0
Echidna Madam – Normal 25th	150	50	350	0
Echidna Madam – Normal 26th to 35th	20	50	350	0
Echidna Madam – Normal 36th	350	600	350	800
Echidna Madam – Exceed Trigger 1st	75	50	350	0
Echidna Madam – Exceed Trigger 2nd to 40th	10	50	350	0
Echidna Seed Tube – Normal 1st	100	200	350	0
Echidna Seed Tube – Normal 2nd	100	200	350	0
Echidna Seed Tube – Normal 3rd	100	200	350	0
Echidna Seed Tube – Normal 4th	100	200	350	0
Echidna Seed Tube - Normal 5th & loop	50	50	350	0
Echidna Seed Tube – Normal 6th & loop	50	50	350	0
Echidna Seed Tube – Normal 7th	100	200	350	0
Echidna Seed Tube – Normal 8th	350	200	350	1500
Echidna – when not vulnerable	100	130	350	150
Angelo Agnus (1st)	200	200	350	250
Angelo Agnus (2nd)	900	200	350	250
Angelo Agnus (3rd)	100	200	350	250
Angelo Agnus (4th)	100	200	350	250
Angelo Agnus (5th)	200	200	350	250

Enemy	Attack	CP Value	CP Timer	DT Increase
Angelo Agnus (6th)	500	600	350	250
Angelo Credo – ground (1st)	700	200	350	0
Angelo Credo – ground (2nd)	200	200	350	0
Angelo Credo – ground (3rd)	200	200	350	0
Angelo Credo – ground (4th)	200	200	350	0
Angelo Credo – ground (5th)	700	600	350	1500
Angelo Credo – mid-air (1st)	700	200	350	0
Angelo Credo – mid-air (2nd)	200	200	350	0
Angelo Credo – mid-air (3rd)	200	200	350	0
Angelo Credo – mid-air (4th)	200	200	350	0
Angelo Credo – mid-air (5th)	700	600	350	1500
Angelo Credo – to shield	300	170	250	450
Sanctus – ground 1st	180	200	350	0
Sanctus – ground 2nd	180	200	350	0
Sanctus – ground 3rd	90	200	350	0
Sanctus – ground 4th	90	200	350	0
Sanctus – ground 5th	70	200	350	0
Sanctus – ground 6th	70	200	350	0
Sanctus – ground 7th & loop	100	50	350	0
Sanctus – ground 8th & loop	100	50	350	0
Sanctus – ground 9th	90	200	350	0
Sanctus – ground 10th	180	600	350	1500
Sanctus – mid-air 1st	180	200	350	0
Sanctus – mid-air 2nd	180	200	350	0
Sanctus – mid-air 3rd	180	200	350	0
Sanctus – mid-air 4th	90	200	350	0
Sanctus – mid-air 5th	90	200	350	0
Sanctus – mid-air 6th	70	200	350	0
Sanctus – mid-air 7th	70	200	350	0
Sanctus – mid-air 8th & loop	100	50	350	0
Sanctus – mid-air 9th & loop	100	50	350	0
Sanctus – mid-air 10th	90	200	350	0
Sanctus – mid-air 11th	180	600	350	1500
Sanctus – interrupt Sparda slash	300	200	350	0
Sanctus – interrupt Sparda Stinger	1300	600	350	1500
Dante – ground	500	600	350	1200
Dante – mid-air	500	600	350	1200
Dante – clash (throw away)	750	600	350	1200
Battle Statue – ground	400	200	350	0
Battle Statue – mid-air	400	200	350	0

* Echidna "Madam" is the exposed female body of Echidna.

Nero's DT Buster Attack

Listed here are all the damage values for Nero's Devil Trigger enhanced Buster attack per enemy.

DT Buster Attack

Enemy	Attack	CP Value	CP Timer	DT Increase
Scarecrow (Arm & Leg) – ground 1st	200	200	350	0
Scarecrow (Arm & Leg) – ground 2nd	200	200	350	0
Scarecrow (Arm & Leg) – ground 3rd	600	200	350	0
Scarecrow (Arm & Leg) – mid-air	600	200	350	0
Mega Scarecrow – ground (1st)	200	200	350	0
Mega Scarecrow – ground (2nd)	200	200	350	0
Mega Scarecrow – ground (3rd)	130	200	350	0
Mega Scarecrow – mid-air	700	200	350	0
Frost – ground (impact wall)	50	50	350	0
Frost – ground (impact ground)	200	200	350	0
Frost – ground (throw)	300	200	350	0
Frost – mid-air (impact wall)	50	50	350	0
Frost – mid-air (impact ground)	200	200	350	0
Frost – mid-air (throw)	300	200	350	0
Frost – to healing ice	150	170	250	150
Assault – ground (impact ground)	40	100	350	0
Assault – ground (throw)	250	200	350	0
Assault – mid-air (impact ground)	40	100	350	0
Assault – mid-air (throw)	250	200	350	0
Assault – interrupt Dash attack	800	600	350	1500
Blitz – ground 1st	400	200	350	0
Blitz – ground 2nd	320	200	350	0
Blitz – ground 3rd	240	200	350	0
Blitz – ground 4th	160	200	350	0
Blitz – ground 5th	80	50	350	0
Blitz – ground 6th	80	50	350	0
Blitz – ground 7th	80	50	350	0
Blitz – ground 8th	80	50	350	0
Blitz – ground 9th & loop	80	50	350	0
Blitz – ground 10th & loop	80	50	350	0
Blitz – ground 11th	240	200	350	0
Blitz – ground 12th	800	200	350	0
Blitz – mid-air 1st	400	200	350	0
Blitz – mid-air 2nd	320	200	350	0
Blitz – mid-air 3rd	240	200	350	0
Blitz – mid-air 4th	160	200	350	0
Blitz – mid-air 5th	80	50	350	0
Blitz – mid-air 6th	80	50	350	0
Blitz – mid-air 7th	80	50	350	0
Blitz – mid-air 8th	80	50	350	0
Blitz – mid-air 9th & loop	80	50	350	0
Blitz – mid-air 10th & loop	80	50	350	0
Blitz – mid-air 11th	240	200	350	0

Enemy	Attack	CP Value	CP Timer	DT Increase
Blitz – mid-air 12th	800	200	350	0
Gladius – ground (impact anything)	200	200	350	0
Gladius – mid-air (impact anything)	200	200	350	0
Cutlass – ground	400	200	350	0
Cutlass – mid-air	400	200	350	0
Basilisk – ground	400	200	350	0
Basilisk – mid-air	400	200	350	0
Chimera Seed – ground	400	200	350	0
Chimera Seed – mid-air	400	200	350	0
Mephisto Insect – ground 1st	120	200	350	0
Mephisto Insect – ground 2nd	120	200	350	0
Mephisto Insect – ground 3rd	400	200	350	0
Mephisto Insect – mid-air	400	200	350	0
Faust Insect – ground 1st	200	200	350	0
Faust Insect – ground 2nd	200	200	350	0
Faust Insect – ground 3rd	600	200	350	0
Faust Insect – mid-air	600	200	350	0
Bianco Angelo – ground (stab)	100	200	350	0
Bianco Angelo – ground (twist)	50	100	350	0
Bianco Angelo – ground (explosion)	100	200	350	0
Bianco Angelo – ground (throw)	500	0	0	0
Bianco Angelo – to shield	300	170	250	450
Alto Angelo – ground 1st	250	200	350	0
Alto Angelo – ground 2nd	250	200	350	0
Alto Angelo – ground 3rd	1000	300	350	0
Alto Angelo – mid-air 1st	250	200	350	0
Alto Angelo – mid-air 2nd	250	200	350	0
Alto Angelo – mid-air 3rd	1000	300	350	0
Alto Angelo – to shield	300	170	250	450
Berial – Head (Yamato strike)	100	50	350	0
Berial – Head (throw down)	1550	600	350	0
Berial – Legs (toss up)	200	200	350	0
Berial – Legs (Yamato strike)	50	50	350	0
Berial – Legs (throw)	400	600	350	0
Berial – Fallen (toss up)	300	200	350	0
Berial – Fallen (Yamato strike)	50	50	350	0
Berial – Fallen (throw)	600	600	350	0
Bael & Dagon – Head (1st)	50	200	350	0
Bael & Dagon – Head (2nd)	350	200	350	0
Bael & Dagon – Head (3rd)	200	200	350	0
Bael & Dagon – Head (4th)	100	200	350	0
Bael & Dagon – Head (5th)	200	200	350	0
Bael & Dagon – Head (6th)	100	200	350	0
Bael & Dagon – Head (7th)	100	200	350	0
Bael & Dagon – Head (8th)	50	200	350	0
Bael & Dagon – Head (9th)	100	200	350	0
Bael & Dagon – Head (10th)	50	200	350	0
Bael & Dagon – Head (11th)	100	200	350	0
Bael & Dagon – Head (12th)	50	200	350	0
Bael & Dagon – Head (13th)	50	200	350	0
Bael & Dagon – Head (14th)	500	600	350	0

03

Enemy	Attack	CP Value	CP Timer	DT Increase
Bael & Dagon – Tail (1st)	500	200	350	0
Bael & Dagon – Tail (2nd)	500	200	350	0
Bael & Dagon – Tail (3rd)	500	600	350	0
Bael & Dagon – Rusalka – ground	600	200	350	0
Bael & Dagon – Rusalka – mid-air	600	200	350	0
Echidna Madam – Normal 1st*	40	200	350	0
Echidna Madam – Normal 2nd	70	200	350	0
Echidna Madam – Normal 3rd	60	200	350	0
Echidna Madam – Normal 4th	150	200	350	0
Echidna Madam – Normal 5th to 13th	20	50	350	0
Echidna Madam – Normal 14th	150	200	350	0
Echidna Madam – Normal 15th to 24th	20	50	350	0
Echidna Madam – Normal 25th	150	200	350	0
Echidna Madam – Normal 26th to 35th	20	50	350	0
Echidna Madam – Normal 36th	150	200	350	0
Echidna Madam – Normal 37th to 46th	20	50	350	0
Echidna Madam – Normal 47th	350	600	350	0
Echidna Madam – Exceed Trigger 1st	75	50	350	0
Echidna Madam – Exceed Trigger 2nd to 55th	10	50	350	0
Echidna Seed Tube – Normal 1st	100	200	350	0
Echidna Seed Tube – Normal 2nd	100	200	350	0
Echidna Seed Tube – Normal 3rd	100	200	350	0
Echidna Seed Tube – Normal 4th	100	200	350	0
Echidna Seed Tube – Normal 5th	50	50	350	0
Echidna Seed Tube – Normal 6th	50	50	350	0
Echidna Seed Tube – Normal 7th	50	50	350	0
Echidna Seed Tube – Normal 8th	50	50	350	0
Echidna Seed Tube – Normal 9th & loop	50	50	350	0
Echidna Seed Tube – Normal 10th & loop	50	50	350	0
Echidna Seed Tube – Normal 17th	100	200	350	0
Echidna Seed Tube – Normal 18th	350	200	350	0
Echidna – when not vulnerable	100	130	350	150
Angelo Agnus (1st)	200	200	350	0
Angelo Agnus (2nd)	1200	200	350	0
Angelo Agnus (3rd)	100	200	350	0
Angelo Agnus (4th)	100	200	350	0
Angelo Agnus (5th)	100	200	350	0

Enemy	Attack	CP Value	CP Timer	DT Increase
Angelo Agnus (6th)	100	200	350	0
Angelo Agnus (7th)	300	200	350	0
Angelo Agnus (8th)	700	600	350	0
Angelo Credo – ground (1st)	700	200	350	0
Angelo Credo – ground (2nd)	200	200	350	0
Angelo Credo – ground (3rd)	200	200	350	0
Angelo Credo – ground (4th)	200	200	350	0
Angelo Credo – ground (5th)	700	200	350	0
Angelo Credo – ground (6th)	1000	600	350	0
Angelo Credo – mid-air (1st)	700	200	350	0
Angelo Credo – mid-air (2nd)	200	200	350	0
Angelo Credo – mid-air (3rd)	200	200	350	0
Angelo Credo – mid-air (4th)	200	200	350	0
Angelo Credo – mid-air (5th)	700	200	350	0
Angelo Credo – mid-air (6th)	1000	600	350	0
Angelo Credo – to shield	300	170	250	450
Sanctus – ground 1st	180	200	350	0
Sanctus – ground 2nd	180	200	350	0
Sanctus – ground 3rd	90	200	350	0
Sanctus – ground 4th	90	200	350	0
Sanctus – ground 5th	70	200	350	0
Sanctus – ground 6th	70	200	350	0
Sanctus – ground 7th & loop	100	50	350	0
Sanctus – ground 8th & loop	100	50	350	0
Sanctus – ground 9th & loop	100	50	350	0
Sanctus – ground 10th & loop	100	50	350	0
Sanctus – ground 11th & loop	100	50	350	0
Sanctus – ground 12th & loop	100	50	350	0
Sanctus – ground 13th	90	200	350	0
Sanctus – ground 14th	180	600	350	1500
Sanctus – mid-air 1st	180	200	350	0
Sanctus – mid-air 2nd	180	200	350	0
Sanctus – mid-air 3rd	180	200	350	0
Sanctus – mid-air 4th	90	200	350	0
Sanctus – mid-air 5th	90	200	350	0
Sanctus – mid-air 6th	70	200	350	0
Sanctus – mid-air 7th	70	200	350	0
Sanctus – mid-air 8th & loop	100	50	350	0
Sanctus – mid-air 9th & loop	100	50	350	0
Sanctus – mid-air 10th & loop	100	50	350	0
Sanctus – mid-air 11th & loop	100	50	350	0
Sanctus – mid-air 12th & loop	100	50	350	0
Sanctus – mid-air 13th & loop	100	50	350	0
Sanctus – mid-air 14th	90	200	350	0
Sanctus – mid-air 15th	180	600	350	1500
Sanctus – interrupt Sparda slash	300	200	350	0
Sanctus – interrupt Sparda Stinger	1833	600	350	0
Dante normal – ground (1st)	150	200	350	0
Dante normal – ground (2nd)	150	200	350	0
Dante normal – ground (3rd)	600	600	350	0
Dante normal – mid-air	850	200	350	0
Dante Battle – ground (throw away)	750	600	350	0
Battle Statue – ground 1st	200	200	350	0
Battle Statue – ground 2nd	600	200	350	0
Battle Statue – mid-air	600	200	350	0

* Echidna "Madam" is the exposed female body of Echidna.

Chapter 04

Walkthrough

Like previous installments, this game is combat-intensive and filled with enemies who seek to destroy you. There are numerous items to be found and a multitude of upgrades to be purchased. During this adventure, you'll control a new combatant named Nero, as well as Dante, the familiar demon slayer from the previous games. There is much to see and do in Devil May Cry 4, and this walkthrough will ensure you don't miss a thing as you complete the game with Smokin' Sick Style.

Elements Of The Walkthrough

Walkthrough Example Page

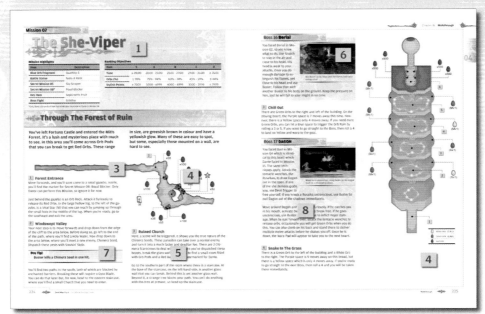

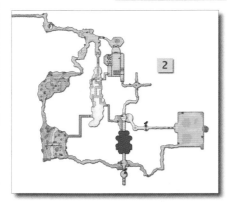

1 Mission Heading

This heading details the mission entry that follows. It lists the mission number, mission name, and then looks at its highlights, ranking parameters, and full walkthrough.

2 Overview Maps

These large maps show the entire area of a mission and the fastest route through it, as indicated by a solid line. You can see at a glance how large the area is and where you should go next.

3 Sub-Area Maps

These are smaller, detailed maps that will show the sub-areas of the mission. On these you'll find icons for all things of interest, such as the location of Items, Orb Drops, Point Icons, and more.

4 Map Icons

These are various map icons that you'll see displayed on our exclusive maps.

White Orb (S,M,L)	Orb Pods
Green Orb (S,M,L)	Continuum Pad
Red Orb	Jump Pad
Gold Orb	Teleport Pad
Vital Star M	Elevator
Vital Star S	Teleport Mist
Vital Star L	
Devil Star S	Divinity Statue
Devil Star M	
Holy Water	Evil Legacy
Blue Orb Fragment	Anima Mercury
Battle Statue	Rusalka Corpse
Secret Mission	Wing Talisman
Emblem Switch	Aegis Shield
Gyro Blade	Key of Cronus
Orb Rock	Sephirothic Fruit

5 Point Icon Text Entry

This numbered text entry corresponds to the numbered icon on the Sub-Area Map. The points on the map show you the route through the Sub-Area. By following the Point numbers on the map, you'll find it easy to work out where to go next, and the text fully describes what to do at each location. This allows you to either read the walkthrough from start to finish, or quickly find your location in a Mission to get a quick tip.

6 Screenshots

The walkthrough uses screenshots taken directly from the game. These are used to enhance the text and show you particular points of interest. This gives you a superior picture of your objectives in a Mission.

7 Extra Box

An Extra Box offers you a special hint, tip, or insight, concerning the area you are in.

8 Boss Box

A Boss Box is a short entry that will offer you tips on how to defeat a Boss. We offer only brief tips in the walkthrough, so that you have the option of tackling the Boss on your own. When you want more information on a Boss (or any enemy), you can refer to the Opponents chapter, which has complete details and strategies for every adversary in the game.

Mission Ranking

Devil May Cry 4 comprises 20 Missions. Each Mission has a specific goal and challenges. At the end of a Mission, you are given a Mission Clear screen and a "Devil Hunter Rank". The ranking you receive is based on the number of "Devil Points" you acquire for the Mission.

In addition, the number of Proud Souls (your "currency" for purchasing upgrades) you receive is based on your Total Devil Points. You receive 3% of your Devil Points as Proud Souls. So, if you achieve 1,000 Devil Points during a Mission, you'll receive 30 Proud Souls. It should be noted that, unlike in previous Devil May Cry games, there is no special bonus in the game for S Ranking a Mission. However, you do unlock an online "achievement".

As was explained in the Game System chapter, Devil Points are calculated using a formula which takes into account several factors and multipliers. The Mission Clear screen shows the various multipliers: Time, Stylish Points, Orbs Found, and your Bonus or Penalty. You have the chance of 2 Bonuses during a Mission: 'do not use an Item' and 'do not receive any damage'. Not using an Item is typically far easier to achieve than not taking damage, thus the bonus for No Damage is substantial. There are also penalties for having to use a 'Continue' during a Mission, Enemy Handicap (if you had to continue the Mission 3 or more times), using a Gold Orb, and using a special unlockable character for the Mission.

Because of the various bonuses, you're not required to achieve an S Rank in all three sub-categories of Time, Stylish Points, and Orbs Found to S Rank the entire Mission. There are basic minimums you can achieve which, when all are factored into the Mission Ranking formula, enable you to obtain the coveted S Rank.

In this walkthrough, we give S Ranking Tips for each Mission at the end of each Mission's entry. These tips, like the walkthrough itself, will be based on the Normal (Devil Hunter) difficulty level. At each

The Mission Clear screen details how well you performed in the Mission.

different difficulty level, the requirements for S Ranking the Mission change, and so your approach may change as well. Also, the S Ranking Tips will assume that you have already completed the game at least once and have the required upgrades, as described.

It should be noted that the individual Ranking categories of Time, Orbs, and Stylish Points are based on a range of numbers. The value you achieve in a Mission will fall within one of these ranges, thereby earning you that rank. Of particular interest is the Stylish Point range. Since Stylish Points are included in the Mission Ranking formula as a numerical value and not a percentage multiplier, like Time and Orbs, the actual value you achieve is more important than the Rank range the value falls into.

For example, in a Mission, you could end up needing 5445 Stylish Points to get the S Rank for the Mission but, if you achieve one point less (5444), then you'll not get the S Rank. The S Ranking Tips will give you the exact value you need for the scenarios we describe.

Ranking Requirements per Difficulty Level

The following tables show the base number required for you to receive the Rank listed. If your score is below that base number, then your rank is the one below. For example, Mission 07, on the Son of Sparda difficulty level, requires a time of 40:00 for a C Rank. If you score 40:01 (one second greater) then your Rank will be D.

Orb Requirements: All Missions, All Difficulty

	C	B	A	S
Orbs (%)*	45%	60%	75%	95%

*Missions 18 and 20 do not have set Orbs. An automatic 100% is given.

Stylish Point Requirements

Mission	Human & Devil Hunter				Son of Sparda and DMD			
	C	B	A	S	C	B	A	S
1	315	330	410	500	315	330	410	500
2	3000	4000	5000	6500	3600	4900	6750	9250
3	3000	5500	7500	10000	3000	5500	7500	10000
4	3000	4500	5500	6500	4000	5000	7500	9250
5	2500	3500	4500	6000	3100	4400	5750	7750
6	5000	7500	10000	12500	5000	7500	10000	12500
7	3000	4000	5000	7000	3000	4000	5000	7000
8	2500	3500	4500	6500	2500	3500	4500	6500
9	4000	6000	8000	10000	5500	8000	10750	13750
10	4000	6000	8000	10000	4300	6500	8700	11000
11	5000	7500	9500	11500	5000	7500	9500	11500
12	3000	4000	5000	7000	3000	4000	5000	7000
13	3000	4000	5000	7000	3400	4650	5900	8250
14	2000	3000	4000	6000	2450	3700	5000	7400
15	5000	7500	9500	11500	5250	7900	10000	12250
16	4500	6500	8000	10000	4700	6850	8450	10650
17	6500	9500	13000	17000	6500	9500	13000	17000
18	2000	3000	4000	5000	2000	3000	4000	5000
19	5000	7000	9500	12500	7250	10500	14250	20000
20	3500	4000	4500	5500	3500	4000	4500	5500

Time Requirements

Mission	Human				Devil Hunter			
	C	B	A	S	C	B	A	S
1	2:15	1:30	1:05	0:45	3:00	2:00	1:30	1:00
2	18:30	15:00	13:00	11:00	25:00	20:00	17:30	15:00
3	26:00	18:30	15:30	13:30	35:00	25:00	21:00	18:00
4	26:00	18:30	15:30	13:30	35:00	25:00	21:00	18:00
5	16:30	13:00	10:30	9:00	22:00	17:30	14:00	12:00
6	30:00	22:30	18:30	16:30	40:00	30:00	25:00	22:00
7	26:00	20:00	17:00	15:00	35:00	27:00	23:00	20:00
8	18:30	15:00	13:00	11:00	25:00	20:00	17:30	15:00
9	17:30	13:30	11:00	9:30	23:30	18:00	15:00	13:00
10	26:00	20:00	17:00	15:00	35:00	27:00	23:00	20:00
11	18:30	15:00	13:00	11:00	25:00	20:00	17:30	15:00
12	12:30	10:30	9:00	7:30	17:00	14:30	12:00	10:00
13	26:00	18:30	15:30	13:30	35:00	25:00	21:00	18:00
14	26:00	18:30	15:30	13:30	35:00	25:00	21:00	18:00
15	33:30	26:00	23:00	21:00	45:00	35:00	31:00	28:00
16	30:00	24:30	21:00	18:30	40:00	33:00	28:00	25:00
17	26:00	18:30	15:30	13:30	35:00	25:00	21:00	18:00
18	12:30	10:30	9:00	7:30	17:00	14:30	12:00	10:00
19	37:00	30:00	25:30	22:30	50:00	40:00	34:00	30:00
20	9:30	6:00	3:45	2:30	13:00	8:00	5:00	3:15

Time Requirements

Mission	Son of Sparda				Dante Must Die			
	C	B	A	S	C	B	A	S
1	3:30	2:15	1:45	1:15	4:15	2:45	2:00	1:25
2	34:30	28:00	25:00	21:00	42:00	34:00	30:00	26:00
3	40:00	28:00	24:00	20:00	50:00	35:00	30:00	25:00
4	50:00	30:00	24:00	21:00	60:00	45:00	38:00	33:00
5	30:00	25:00	21:00	18:00	38:00	30:00	25:00	21:30
6	45:00	35:00	28:00	25:00	55:00	42:00	35:00	30:00
7	40:00	30:00	26:00	23:00	50:00	38:00	32:00	28:00
8	28:00	23:00	20:00	17:00	35:00	28:00	24:00	21:00
9	40:00	32:00	26:00	23:00	50:00	40:00	32:00	28:00
10	43:00	34:00	29:00	25:00	53:00	41:00	35:00	30:00
11	28:00	23:00	20:00	17:00	35:00	28:00	24:00	21:00
12	20:00	16:30	13:30	11:30	24:00	20:00	17:00	14:00
13	45:00	32:00	27:00	23:00	55:00	40:00	33:00	29:00
14	45:00	33:00	28:00	24:00	55:00	40:00	33:00	29:00
15	55:00	42:00	38:00	34:00	65:00	50:00	46:00	41:00
16	48:00	40:00	34:00	30:00	58:00	48:00	41:00	37:00
17	40:00	29:00	24:00	21:00	50:00	35:00	29:00	25:00
18	20:00	16:30	13:30	11:30	24:00	20:00	17:00	14:00
19	80:00	66:00	55:00	50:00	100:00	80:00	68:00	60:00
20	15:00	9:00	5:30	3:45	18:00	11:00	7:00	4:30

Devil Hunter Point Requirements

Mission	Human				Devil Hunter			
	C	B	A	S	C	B	A	S
1	1020	1870	3060	5100	1200	2200	3600	6000
2	4250	10200	20400	42500	5000	12000	24000	50000
3	5100	13600	25500	55250	6000	16000	30000	65000
4	5100	12750	25500	42500	6000	15000	30000	50000
5	4250	10625	22950	34000	5000	12500	27000	40000
6	8500	17000	42500	68000	10000	20000	50000	80000
7	5100	13600	25500	42500	6000	16000	30000	50000
8	5100	11050	22100	42500	6000	13000	26000	50000
9	6375	15300	29750	51000	7500	18000	35000	60000
10	8500	18700	34000	59500	10000	22000	40000	70000
11	8500	21250	42500	68000	10000	25000	50000	80000
12	5100	10625	21250	38250	6000	12500	25000	45000
13	6800	14875	25500	42500	8000	17500	30000	50000
14	4250	10200	19125	36125	5000	12000	22500	42500
15	10200	21250	34000	59500	12000	25000	40000	70000
16	8500	21250	34000	59500	10000	25000	40000	70000
17	11050	25500	55250	85000	13000	30000	65000	100000
18	5100	10200	18700	32300	6000	12000	22000	38000
19	10625	22950	42500	76500	12500	27000	50000	90000
20	5100	10625	17000	28050	6000	12500	20000	33000

Devil Hunter Point Requirements

Mission	Son of Sparda				Dante Must Die			
	C	B	A	S	C	B	A	S
1	2160	3960	6480	10800	3600	6600	10800	18000
2	13500	31500	63000	108000	22500	52500	105000	180000
3	10800	28800	54000	117000	18000	48000	90000	195000
4	16200	32400	68400	117000	27000	54000	114000	195000
5	13500	27000	50400	90000	22500	45000	84000	150000
6	18000	36000	90000	144000	30000	60000	150000	240000
7	10800	28800	54000	90000	18000	48000	90000	150000
8	10800	23400	46800	90000	18000	39000	78000	150000
9	21600	45000	90000	153000	36000	75000	150000	255000
10	18000	45000	81000	135000	30000	75000	135000	225000
11	18000	45000	90000	144000	30000	75000	150000	240000
12	10800	22500	45000	81000	18000	37500	75000	135000
13	15300	31500	54000	99000	25500	52500	90000	165000
14	9900	24300	45000	90000	16500	40500	75000	150000
15	23400	49500	90000	153000	39000	82500	150000	255000
16	21600	47700	76500	135000	36000	79500	127500	225000
17	23400	54000	117000	180000	39000	90000	195000	300000
18	10800	21600	39600	68400	18000	36000	66000	114000
19	31500	63000	126000	225000	52500	105000	210000	375000
20	10800	22500	36000	59400	18000	37500	60000	99000

Upgrade Styles

As you're playing through the game, you'll acquire Proud Souls that you can use to upgrade your abilities. A quick glance at the Power Up menus shows you there is much to choose from. Each purchase increases the price of the remaining upgrades making each additional upgrade more expensive. In light of this, you need to make smart choices in order to ensure success. Here are some upgrade recommendations tailored to individual playing styles.

Playing Style

Style	Description
Survivalist	I just want to get through the game alive.
Explorer	I have to find every item and secret.
SSS Stylist	I'm going to kill every beast with Smokin' Sick Style!
Chronologist	I'm going as fast as I can for a Time Attack.
S-Ranker	I'm out to S-Rank every Mission.
DMD Purist	I will conquer the hardest levels of Hell!
Budgeteer	I want the most upgrades for the lowest price.

Survivalists want to get through the game as easily as possible. The desire is to see the story to the end regardless of Style Ranks. Explorers want to take their time to discover every little thing hidden in the game. Rank isn't important, nor is time as long as every secret is uncovered.

SSS Stylists have just one thing in mind, and that is Stylish Combat. These players aren't happy unless SSS is consistently being displayed while they are destroying their opponents. An S-Ranker is the player that wants to see that lovely red S displayed on every Mission Results screen. The DMD Purist is one that thrives on difficulty and combat, while also craving an S-Rank for making it through the toughest challenges Devil May Cry 4 has to offer. Finally, for the frugally minded, we offer Budgeteer for all those who want to pick the cheapest upgrades first regardless of use or playing style.

You'll notice that each style relies on a core set of skills to accomplish the task. These are the skills you should acquire first, to achieve the goals of the selected play-style. Any upgrades chosen after that are up to you. Be aware that no matter which upgrades you pick, the total cost is always the same.

Proud Soul Requirement for all Upgrades

Character	Total
Nero	290450
Dante	290400

Getting a Refund

Unlike previous games in the Devil May Cry series, buying an upgrade is not permanent. You can use the Power Up menus before a mission, or a Divinity Statue within a mission, at any time to refund an upgrade. A refund returns 100% of the orbs you paid for the ability. There is no penalty for getting a refund other than losing the use of that ability. You can then use the refunded orbs to purchase a different ability, or you can buy back the refunded ability.

Since buying an ability increases the cost of every other ability on offer, you should remember that you will have to pay more to buy back a refunded ability, if you buy others first. Making use of the refund system allows you to change playing styles on the fly. So you can easily switch from a Survivalist, to an Explorer, and then back to being a Survivalist or even to an SSS-Stylist, all during the course of the same mission!

Upgrade Recommendations

The core skills needed for each playing style are listed here. As mentioned, any skills other than those listed are extra and up to you. You'll notice that Nero's Yamato upgrades aren't recommended, at least not for the core skills. Those techniques, while powerful, are slow to execute. That means you're more likely to be hit by the enemy when you try to use them. You'll also notice that Nero's Charge Shot to Level 3 is recommended in some cases. This is because it is invaluable in destroying a Mephisto quickly, as well as knocking down larger enemies for quick damage.

Dante's Gunslinger is recommended for exploration, as it allows you to use Pandora's Argument to fly to locations that are harder to reach. Also, quickly switching between Sword Master and Gunslinger is an easy way to vary your attacks and boost your Style Rank in combat. Royal Guard is reserved for the DMD Purists as it is an advanced style, but once mastered, is truly devastating to the enemy, even Bosses.

You'll notice combat is not considered in the Explorer style. This style of play is basically used once you have cleared an area of enemies and now want to find a hard to reach secret. All the abilities of the Explorer playing style enhance your movements, allowing you to go further, higher, and faster than normal.

Survivalist

Nero		Dante	
Skill Name	Cost*	Skill Name	Cost*
Streak	50	Stinger	150
Streak 2	600	Stinger 2	800
Air Hike	2150	Trickster Lv2	450
Snatch 2	500	Trickster Lv3	900
Snatch 3	1250	Trickster Lv4	5250
Charge Shot	350	Air Hike	2300
Charge Shot 2	700	Sword Master Lv2	650
Charge Shot 3	1500	Sword Master Lv3	1100
Red Queen Combo B	750	Sword Master Lv4	5450
Red Queen Combo C	1000	Trigger Heart	2500
Trigger Heart	2800	Round Trip	1600
		Kick 13	1200
Total	11650	Total	22350

Explorer

Nero		Dante	
Skill Name	Cost*	Skill Name	Cost*
Streak	50	Stinger	150
Streak 2	600	Stinger 2	800
Air Hike	2150	Trickster Lv2	450
Calibur	700	Trickster Lv3	900
Exceed 2	750	Trickster Lv4	5250
Exceed 3	1300	Gunslinger Lv2	600
Speed	700	Gunslinger Lv3	1050
		Gunslinger Lv4	5400
		Air Hike	2450
		Trigger Heart	2500
		Speed	900
Total	6250	Total	20450

SSS Stylist

Nero		Dante	
Skill Name	Cost*	Skill Name	Cost*
Streak	50	Stinger	150
Streak 2	600	Stinger 2	800
Split	200	Sword Master Lv2	450
Roulette Spin	700	Sword Master Lv3	900
Red Queen Combo B	400	Sword Master Lv4	5250
Red Queen Combo C	600	Air Hike	2300
Table Hopper	550	Gunslinger Lv2	650
Air Hike	2500	Gunslinger Lv3	7400
Exceed 2	1100	Gunslinger Lv4	5450
Exceed 3	1700	Round Trip	1500
Shuffle	1100	Kick 13	1100
Snatch 2	1300	Trigger Heart	2700
Table Hopper 2	1750	Enemy Step	5800
Snatch 3	2500	PF124: Hatred	1400
Table Hopper 3	2750	PF398: Revenge	2000
Trigger Heart	4000		
Enemy Step	8000		
Calibur	4500		
Total	34300	Total	37850

Chronologist

Nero		Dante	
Skill Name	Cost*	Skill Name	Cost*
Streak	50	Stinger	150
Streak 2	600	Stinger 2	800
Split	200	Round Trip	1150
Red Queen Combo C	500	Sword Master Lv2	500
Air Hike	2250	Sword Master Lv3	950
Speed	600	Sword Master Lv4	5300
Roulette Spin	900	Air Hike	2350
Snatch 2	800	Kick 13	900
Snatch 3	1600	Trigger Heart	2450
Trigger Heart	2700	Speed	800
Charge Shot	850	Gunslinger Lv2	900
Charge Shot 2	1300	Gunslinger Lv3	1400
Charge Shot 3	2250	Gunslinger Lv4	5800
Exceed 2	2000	PF124: Hatred	1400
Exceed 3	2750	PF398: Revenge	2000
Total	19350	Total	26850

* This cost reflects the price increase applied when you buy a new skill.

S-Ranker

Nero		Dante	
Skill Name	Cost*	**Skill Name**	Cost*
Streak	50	Stinger	150
Streak 2	600	Stinger 2	800
Split	200	Sword Master Lv2	450
Roulette Spin	700	Sword Master Lv3	900
Red Queen Combo C	550	Sword Master Lv4	1250
Red Queen Combo B	450	Air Hike	2300
Snatch 2	700	Gunslinger Lv2	650
Air Hike	2500	Gunslinger Lv3	7400
Snatch 3	1600	Gunslinger Lv4	1450
Exceed 2	1200	Kick 13	1000
Exceed 3	1800	Round Trip	1600
Shuffle	1300	Trigger Heart	2700
Trigger Heart	3250	PF124: Hatred	1300
Table Hopper	1650	PF398: Revenge	1900
Table Hopper 2	2250		
Table Hopper 3	3000		
Calibur	3500		
Total	**25300**	**Total**	**23850**

DMD Purist

Nero		Dante	
Skill Name	Cost*	**Skill Name**	Cost*
Streak	50	Stinger	150
Streak 2	600	Stinger 2	800
Air Hike	2150	Air Hike	2150
Split	250	Sword Master Lv2	500
Red Queen Combo C	550	Sword Master Lv3	950
Roulette Spin	800	Sword Master Lv4	5300
Table Hopper	550	Trigger Heart	2350
Exceed 2	1000	Kick 13	900
Exceed 3	1600	Royal Guard Lv2	750
Snatch 2	1000	Royal Guard Lv3	1200
Trigger Heart	2800	Royal Guard Lv4	5600
Table Hopper 2	1500	Gunslinger Lv2	1000
Snatch 3	2250	Gunslinger Lv3	1500
Shuffle	1800	Gunslinger Lv4	5900
Table Hopper 3	2750	Enemy Step	6000
Charge Shot	2050		
Charge Shot 2	3300		
Charge Shot 3	5000		
Red Queen Combo B	5150		
Calibur	8000		
Total	**43150**	**Total**	**35050**

Budgeteer

Nero		Dante	
Skill Name	Cost*	**Skill Name**	Cost*
Streak	50	Stinger	150
Split	150	E&I Charge Shot	250
Charge Shot	200	Shotgun Charge Shot	300
Combo B	350	Speed	500
Table Hopper	400	Trickster Lv2	550
Combo C	600	Sword Master Lv2	600
Shuffle	700	Gunslinger Lv2	650
Charge Shot 2	800	Royal Guard Lv2	700
Snatch 2	900	Kick 13	950
Speed	1000	Pinup	1000
Roulette Spin	1300	E&I Charge Shot 2	1100
Exceed 2	1500	Shotgun Charge Shot 2	1200
Streak 2	1750	PF124: Hatred	1300
Calibur	2000	Stinger 2	1600
Table Hopper 2	2250	Trickster Lv3	1700
Exceed 3	3000	Sword Master Lv3	1800
Charge Shot 3	4000	Gunslinger Lv3	1900
Snatch 3	5000	Royal Guard Lv3	2000
Table Hopper 3	6000	Round Trip	2400
Air Hike	9500	Flush	2500
Trigger Heart	12000	E&I Charge Shot 3	2750
Get More Orbs	17000	Shotgun Charge Shot 3	3000
Max Act	25000	PF398: Revenge	4000
Maximum Bet	35000	Air Hike	6000
Showdown	55000	Trigger Heart	7000
Enemy Step	105000	Get More Orbs	9500
		Trickster Lv4	15000
		Sword Master Lv4	25000
		Gunslinger Lv4	35000
		Royal Guard Lv4	55000
		Enemy Step	105000
Total	**290450**	**Total**	**290400**

* This cost reflects the price increase applied when you buy a new skill.

Birds Of A Feather

Mission Highlights

Item	Description
Boss Fight	Dante

Ranking Objectives

Item	S	A	B	C	D
Time	≤ 1:00	1:01 – 1:30	1:31 – 2:00	2:01 – 3:00	≥ 3:01
Orbs (%)	≥ 95%	75% – 94%	60% – 74%	45% – 59%	≤ 44%
Stylish Points	≥ 500	410 – 499	330 – 409	315 – 329	≤ 315

The Tutorial

This mission takes place in the one-room Opera House. In order to help you get acquainted with the controls and combat of Devil May Cry 4, Mission 01 begins with a Tutorial, during which you'll be introduced to various aspects of gameplay and be required to perform specific actions in order to advance to the next section of the Tutorial. For each section, you'll have limited control of Nero: i.e. only the specified movement or technique will be recognized.

During the Tutorial portion of this mission, you have infinite life and can't take damage. But once the Tutorial has been completed, you'll be given full control of Nero and will start the final Boss Fight with Dante himself.

Gunplay

The first aspect of gameplay you are introduced to is using Nero's gun, Blue Rose. The goal during this part of the Tutorial is to keep your distance from Dante and use Blue Rose to deal damage. You must hurt Dante 5 times in order to get past this section. A counter displayed at the bottom centre portion of the screen shows your progress. At the start it reads 0/5. Each shot that causes Dante damage will increment this counter until you have caused Dante damage 5/5 times.

You need to be aware that Dante can absorb several shots from Blue Rose before actually taking damage. As you fire a barrage of bullets at him, he continues to walk towards you, apparently unharmed. Then, every 5th shot that hits him will suddenly cause him to stagger as a result of the damage. Once you have made this happen 5 times, you'll move on to the next part of the Tutorial.

Evasion

During this part of the Tutorial, your objective is to avoid Dante's bullets by jumping over them. As the stream of Dante's gunfire approaches you, jump to the left to avoid it. You must perform this action successfully 3 times. Once again, a counter will be displayed at the bottom of the screen to mark your progress.

After you have avoided Dante's fire with a simple jump, you must use a more advanced evasion technique called a "Side Roll". Wait for the gunfire to get close, and then execute a Side Roll just before it reaches you. You must do this 3 times in order to get through this part.

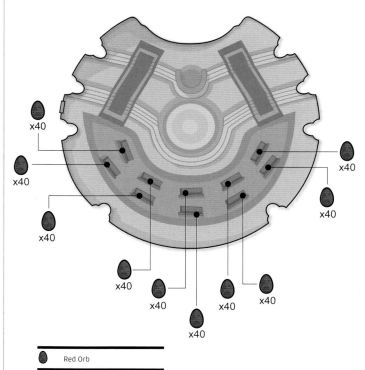

x40
x40
x40
x40
x40
x40
x40
x40
x40
x40
x40

Red Orb

Swordplay

Next, you learn about using your melée weapon, Red Queen. You must deal damage to Dante 3 times, using the basic 4 Slash Combo. Although Dante isn't nearly as offensive or defensive as he can be, he won't make this very easy for you. He will occasionally evade your attacks, as well as launching his own counter attacks.

You can deflect Dante's attack by clashing swords with him.

Once you've damaged Dante 3 times with Red Queen, you'll be challenged to attack him using a more advanced technique called "High Roller". It should be noted that, when you perform this move, you have two options for its execution. If you simply tap the button during this manoeuvre, Nero will perform the uppercut, but remain on the ground. If you press and hold the button during this manoeuvre, he will perform the uppercut but also follow the enemy into the air.

Unleashing Devil Bringer

Now that you've tried your hand at Blue Rose and Red Queen, it's time to discover the third aspect of Nero's arsenal, Devil Bringer. Nero's right arm is enhanced with demon power and can be used for grabbing and throwing enemies. For this Tutorial, you're required to use Devil Bringer to grab and throw Dante 3 times. This move is called "Buster".

Final Fight

Now that the Tutorial has taught you the basics, it's time to put it all together in your first real fight. You have full control of Nero, and you'll notice that the onscreen display changes to show your orb count, as well as your Health Meter and Stylish Gauge. From this point onwards, you'll sustain damage if you are hit with an attack. If your Health Meter is completely depleted, then it's Game Over.

Pro Tip!

As soon as the fight begins, you'll notice that all the benches have been replaced. Remember to break each of these during this fight.

Boss 01 **Dante**

The full strategy for this Boss is listed in the Opponents Chapter. Here are a few tips.

There is very little point using Blue Rose in this encounter. From a distance, Dante will use Ebony and Ivory to shoot your bullets out of the

Make frequent use of Buster to seriously damage Dante.

air so that you never hit him. If, in the heat of battle, you manage to land a shot with Blue Rose, it does such little damage that it isn't worth the effort. You should instead rely primarily on Red Queen and Buster.

Stay close to Dante so that he doesn't use his guns, and time your attacks so that your initial strike clashes with Dante's own attacks. This will negate his manoeuvre and briefly stun him, allowing you more time to deal damage. When Dante becomes stunned in this manner, this is your ideal opportunity to use Buster to throw him to the ground and deal heavy damage.

S Ranking Tips

Devil Points Required: **6,000**

No Damage S Rank Requirements

Criteria	Rank	Value
Time	B	2:00 or less
Stylish Points	B	334 or more
Orbs Found	A	75% to 94%
Bonus	-	No Item
Bonus	-	No Damage

This is one of the few Missions where it's very easy to get the No Damage Bonus. In order to achieve it, you don't need very high ranks in the other categories. If you can't get by without taking damage, then you'll have to increase your Time Rank to A (1:30 or less) and your Orb Rank to S. You'll also need to boost your Stylish points to 500 or more.

Getting an S Rank in Orbs is easily achievable if you keep the fight on the floor amongst the benches, so that your combat destroys them. If you break all the benches, you'll find 100% of the Orbs.

La Porte De L'Enfer

Mission Highlights

Item	Description
Blue Orb Fragment	Quantity: 1
Battle Statue	Nero: B Rank
Secret Mission 01	Annihilation (page 235)
Key Item	Evil Legacy
Boss Fight	Berial

Ranking Objectives

Item	S	A	B	C	D
Time	≤ 15:00	15:01 – 17:30	17:31 – 20:00	20:01 – 25:00	≥ 25:01
Orbs (%)	≥ 95%	75% – 94%	60% – 74%	45% – 59%	≤ 44%
Stylish Points	≥ 6500	5000 – 6499	4000 – 4999	3000 – 3999	≤ 2999

Head for Fortuna Castle

Before starting this Mission, go to the Power Up. Depending on how many Orbs you have to spend, your best bets for early upgrades are Red Queen's "Streak", "Split" and "Roulette Spin". When you've purchased the desired upgrades, save your game and then begin the Mission.

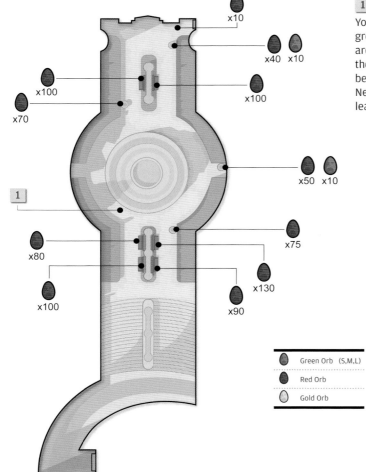

1 Opera House Plaza

You find yourself in a plaza outside the Opera House. You're greeted immediately by a new enemy, the Scarecrow Arm. There are three of these to deal with. After you have dispatched all the Scarecrows, be sure to walk around the Plaza and break the benches and rubbish bins to release the Red Orbs they contain. Next, head to the north-east corner, where you'll find a door that leads to the next area.

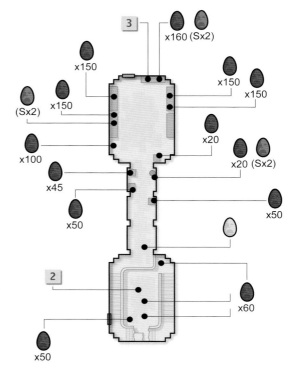

Green Orb (S,M,L)
Red Orb
Gold Orb

2 | Storehouse

In the northern wall, a few feet above the ground, is a small recessed alcove. Get directly below this alcove, and then perform a jump followed by a Kick Jump to reach it. In the alcove you'll find a Gold Orb.

Gold Orbs are used as a continue of sorts. Should you meet an untimely demise and have a Gold Orb in your possession, you can use it to get fully revitalised on the spot. For more information on Gold Orbs, please refer to the "Game System" chapter of this guide. Now that you have obtained the Gold Orb, take a few seconds more to go round the room smashing the barrels to get Red Orbs. When you've finished, go up the stairs and down the hallway you find at the top.

A well timed Kick Jump will allow you to reach the Gold Orb in this room.

3 | Required Fight

As soon as you enter this room, a Red Seal will rise. You are now confronted with your first sealed room. Many of the fights in DMC4 are not mandatory, but some are. The Red Seal will keep you locked in the current area until you have defeated every enemy within it. In this particular fight, you'll face three Scarecrows. When you've eliminated the enemy, head to the northern wall, where you'll find a door to leave by.

4 | Cathedral

After a brief scene, go forwards towards the camera, and then head left to find another door. Once through it you'll be in the Cathedral. As soon as you enter this area, move straight ahead to a gate that's blocking your way. Use a Kick Jump to jump high into the air to reach some cleverly hidden Red Orbs! Now head down the stairs to the lower sitting area. Approach the glowing column located in the centre of the wall and inspect it. By so doing, you'll acquire "Evil Legacy", which adds two new long-range abilities called "Snatch" and "Hellbound" to your Devil Bringer arm.

Inspect this column to receive Evil Legacy.

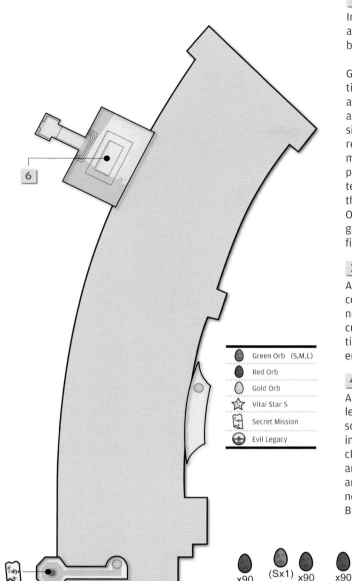

Green Orb (S,M,L)
Red Orb
Gold Orb
Vital Star S
Secret Mission
Evil Legacy

x90 (Sx1) x90 x90 x90

x100

x100

x200

Before continuing, note that the walls to the north and south are cells with locked gates. In these you'll find a Green Orb and a Vital Star (S). Since the cell doors are locked, you won't be able to get inside to reach the items, but you can use your new ability, Snatch, to get them.

Now that you've gathered these treasures, go and stand on the Continuum Pad to activate a Grim Grip above you. Use Hellbound to latch on to the Grim Grip and pull yourself up to the second-floor balcony. Head down the balcony to another Continuum Pad. Use Hellbound to reach the balcony on the far side. Head to the end of the balcony, where you'll find a door and a broken area, where the balcony has fallen away. Across this gap is a large Red Orb. Use Snatch to claim this prize, and then head out through the door.

5 Terrace / Business District

Move down the balcony to a Continuum Pad. Use Hellbound to vault over the mayhem in the streets below and reach the terrace on the far side. Once there, continue forwards and you'll trigger a Tutorial concerning Secret Missions. Secret Missions are a sort of mini-game where you must complete a certain task as specified by the Secret Mission.

You can recognize a Secret Mission by the beige-coloured parchments marking the location. These are inscribed with red symbols. When you find one, approach and inspect it to enter the Secret Mission. If you succeed in the Mission, you'll obtain the Blue Orb Fragment. When you've collected 4 fragments, you'll complete a whole Blue Orb, which will increase your Health Meter by one bar. If you fail, you'll be kicked out of the Mission with no prize, apart from any Red Orbs you might have obtained. There are 12 Secret Missions in all.

The Secret Mission in this area is Secret Mission 01: Annihilation. The locations of all Secret Missions, and detailed strategies for successfully completing each of them, are listed in the "Extras" chapter of this guide (page 235).

This beige and red marker marks the entry point of a Secret Mission.

Go forwards past the Secret Mission marker and find another Continuum Pad. Use it to cross to the far side, where a Red Seal will be activated. Here, you're required to dispatch two Scarecrows. When you've done this, go forwards and use the Continuum Pad to reach the next area.

6 Ambushed

Here, a Red Seal rises and you must destroy 5 Scarecrows. This is a great fight for boosting your Stylish Points. Vary your attacks. In particular, launch the Scarecrows and follow them up so that you can engage them in in-air combat, as well as using a Buster throw to the ground. As soon as the enemy has been dispatched, head through the door to the next area.

The Outskirts

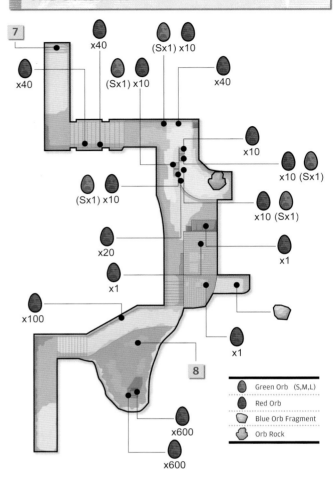

7 Residential Area

You find yourself on a small balcony overlooking an alley below. Walk forwards, fall down to the alley and then continue to a stairway on your left. You'll be confronted by 3 Scarecrows in the alley ahead. After defeating all three, it's time to explore this area for some fairly valuable treasure. Mid-way down the alley you'll find a large red stone. This is an Orb Rock. Attack it repeatedly with your sword, releasing Red Orbs with each strike. After your first strike you have just 9 seconds to attack the Orb Rock before it shatters.

Go back to the alley and walk a short distance forwards, and then go left to a little alcove. Here you'll find a small trail of Red Orbs. Follow the Orbs to another small alcove that contains a Blue Orb Fragment. Walk into the fragment to claim it, and then return to the alley.

8 A Recreational Climb

Outside the alley you'll come to a small, open area with a large tower. Use a Kick Jump on the side of the tower to reach the landing above. Once there, stay still for a second and you'll trigger an Orb Drop, which is a secret place in the environment that causes a large number of Red Orbs to fall from the sky. Orb Drops are scattered throughout the game.

In fact, there is another Orb Drop in this very area, on the roof of the tower landing directly above you. However, this one is much harder to get at and you'll need the Air Hike ability to reach it. Once you've acquired the Air Hike ability, you'll need to do a short jump forwards from the tower landing and then an Air Hike towards the tower. If you perform this move correctly, Nero will land on the roof of the tower and trigger the Orb Drop. When you're ready, follow the stairs to the southwest to reach the door into the next area.

There are two Orb Drops located on this tower!

🖵 | 03_54

When the Blue Seal is down, go to your left and then jump up to the small area above you. There, you'll find a door leading to a small balcony. Go to the end of this balcony and investigate the control panel there to trigger a scene. This lowers the drawbridge.

10 A Little Backtracking

Head back outside the Customs House, where you'll meet three more Scarecrows. After defeating them, go to the Continuum Pad and use it to cross back to the other side. Head back up the pier to a ramp on your left that leads to a large open area, where you are confronted by 7 Scarecrows. When you've eliminated the enemy, head to the north and across the newly lowered drawbridge, where you'll find a flight of stairs leading to a door and the next area.

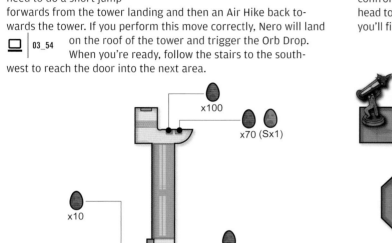

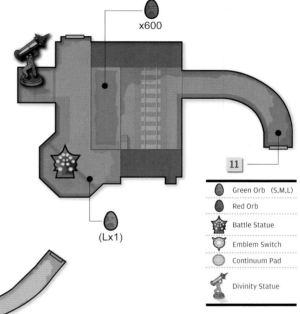

x600

x100

x70 (Sx1)

x10

x10

9

10

x100

x20

Green Orb (S,M,L)
Red Orb
Battle Statue
Emblem Switch
Continuum Pad
Divinity Statue

(Lx1)

11

11 First Mining Area

Head down the tunnel to the large room at the end. First, jump into the water canal, directly opposite the way in, and find 6 large Red Orbs. Then go to the southern end of the room, where you'll find two Grim Grips in a row that you'll need to use in order to reach the upper area.

Arriving in the upper area, go to your left, where you'll find a large Green Orb and your first Battle Statue. This statue will test your combat abilities and, if you are deemed worthy, you'll receive a Blue Orb Fragment. The objective is to attack the statue and

Unleash your Stylish manoeuvres on these statues to obtain a Blue Orb Fragment.

achieve a specific Stylish Rank. There are 8 Battle Statues in the game, each requiring a different Stylish Rank for you to succeed. The one you are in front of now requires a B Rank.

9 Port Caerula

Go forwards to the Continuum Pad and use it to reach the docks across the water. Once on the far side, go forwards to a door that leads into the Customs House. As soon as you are inside, a Red and Blue Seal rises. You are now up against three Scarecrows. Dispatch these creatures to lower the Red Seal. Make your way over to the eastern wall, where you'll find a large, blue, glowing pedestal. This is an Emblem Switch. You must use this in order to lower the Blue Seal. To operate the switch, attack it continuously with your sword.

After you have dealt with the Battle Statue, go to your right, where there is a "Divinity Statue". A Divinity Statue can be used during a Mission to buy Items and Upgrades. Simply approach the statue and inspect it to open the menus. Using a Divinity Statue is the same as using the Power Up option at the start of a new Mission. However, there is an extra advantage to having a Divinity Statue in a Mission.

In the upgrade menus you have the ability to obtain a refund of your upgrade purchases. You can select any ability you've purchased and have those Orbs refunded to you. Although you lose the ability, you regain the full amount of Orbs you originally used to purchase it. This comes in handy if you want to try a new skill for an upcoming fight, or a new ability for exploring the environment. As soon as you have finished with the Divinity Statue, continue to the right and find a door leading to the next area and a Boss Fight.

Boss 02 **Berial**

The full strategy for this Boss is listed in the Opponents Chapter. Here are a few tips.

Berial's weak spot is his head. Use Snatch repeatedly to pull yourself close to his head and attack him with Red Queen. When

When Berial's flames are extinguished, use Buster for a special attack.

you have done enough damage, Berial's flames will be extinguished and he'll be stunned. Use Snatch quickly to get to his head and then use Buster for a devastating attack that throws him to the ground. Follow up by approaching him on the ground and launching another Buster attack. Repeat this cycle as often as you need, until Berial falls before you. Go up the stairs to the north and continue forwards to a large tunnel. Enter the tunnel and the Mission will end.

S Ranking Tips

 Devil Points Required: **50,000**

Minimum S Rank Requirements

Criteria	Rank	Value
Time	S	15:00 or less
Stylish Points	A	5445 or more
Orbs Found	S	95% or more
Bonus	-	No Item

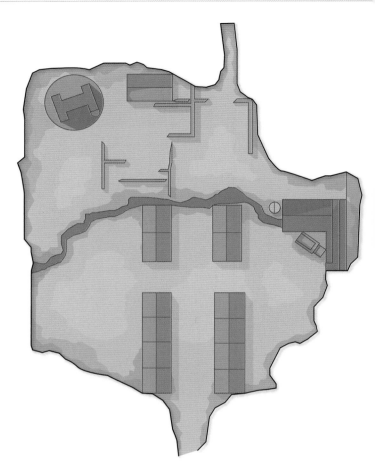

For this Rank you'll have to get S Ranks in both Time and Orbs. Time isn't hard and, if you're diligent, you'll get the Orbs easily. You must get both of the Orb Drops on the tower, just past the Orb Rock (Point 08 in the walkthrough), as well as destroying all the breakables. Refer to the map to see where all these valuable Orbs are to be found.

You need a lot of Stylish Points in this Mission, and there aren't many enemies to get them from. You'll need to taunt the Scarecrows quite a bit to raise your Stylish Ranking, so that each attack is worth more Stylish Points. The last fight at the Port of Caerula (Point 10 in the walkthrough) is a particularly good one in which to net Stylish Points. Seek out the Scarecrows one at a time and get them on their own. Taunt them as often as you can, and then destroy them. Avoid being hit, as this reduces your Stylish Rank by two levels for every hit.

When you fight Berial, attack him fast and hard to extinguish his flames quickly. As soon as you have done this, activate Devil Trigger and perform both Buster grabs to inflict massive damage and win Stylish Points.

Mission 03

The White Wing

Mission Highlights	
Item	Description
Blue Orb Fragment	Quantity: 2
Key Item	Quicksilver Anima

Ranking Objectives					
Item	S	A	B	C	D
Time	≤ 18:00	18:01 - 21:00	21:01 - 25:00	25:01 - 35:00	≥ 35:01
Orbs (%)	≥ 95%	75% - 94%	60% - 74%	45% - 59%	≤ 44%
Stylish Points	≥ 10000	7500 - 9999	5500 - 7499	3000 - 5499	≤ 2999

Search For Fortuna Castle

Now that you've got past Berial, it's time to press on forwards to Fortuna Castle. If possible, before starting the Mission, use the Power Up option to acquire upgrades. In particular, you'll want to go for Snatch 2 and Air Hike as soon as possible, as these manoeuvres make Stylish Points easier to get.

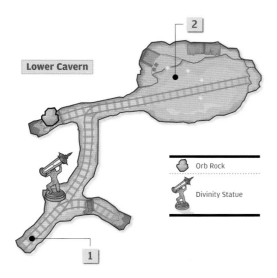

Lower Cavern

🪨 Orb Rock

Divinity Statue

1 Second Mining Area

This Mission starts in a small area where there is a Divinity Statue. Move forwards through the tunnel and you'll come to a "T" junction, where you can go either right or left. Your path takes you right, where you'll be up against 3 Scarecrows. Eliminate them, then backtrack to the left fork of the tunnel. At the end of the left-hand path you'll find a small, boarded-up alcove. Attack the boards to smash the obstacle and uncover an Orb Rock. When you're ready, head back down the tunnel to the next area.

Attack these stones quickly and release a host of Red Orbs.

2 New Heights

Go to the northern rear section of the room, where there is a small ledge to your left. Jump up on to the ledge and then up on to the small platform there. To your right, you'll see a Grim Grip. There are in fact 9 Grim Grips, all of which you'll need to reach the upper area of this mining shaft.

When you reach the top, there's time for a little exploration before you proceed any further. To your left you'll see several platforms. On one of these rests a large Red Orb. Go to your left across the platforms and drop down to get the Red Orb. Higher up in this shaft is a Blue Orb Fragment. There are actually two fragments here, but you can only acquire one of them in this Mission. You'll return here in a later Mission, when the second fragment will become available.

In order to obtain the fragment that is available in this Mission, you must have the Air Hike ability. It's quite expensive, and you probably won't have it when passing through here for the first time. However, if you have enough Proud Souls saved and invested in upgrades, you can use the Divinity Statue to refund all your Orbs, and you can then purchase Air Hike for this particular task.

🖵 | 03_55   When you've acquired Air Hike, go to your left and follow the platforms to the end. Arriving on the last platform, you'll see 2 Grim Grips to your right. This is a tricky course, and there are actually 3 more Grim Grips above you. Also above you is a hard-to-reach ledge that holds the Blue Orb Fragment.

Get on this platform to start your climb to the Blue Orb Fragment above.

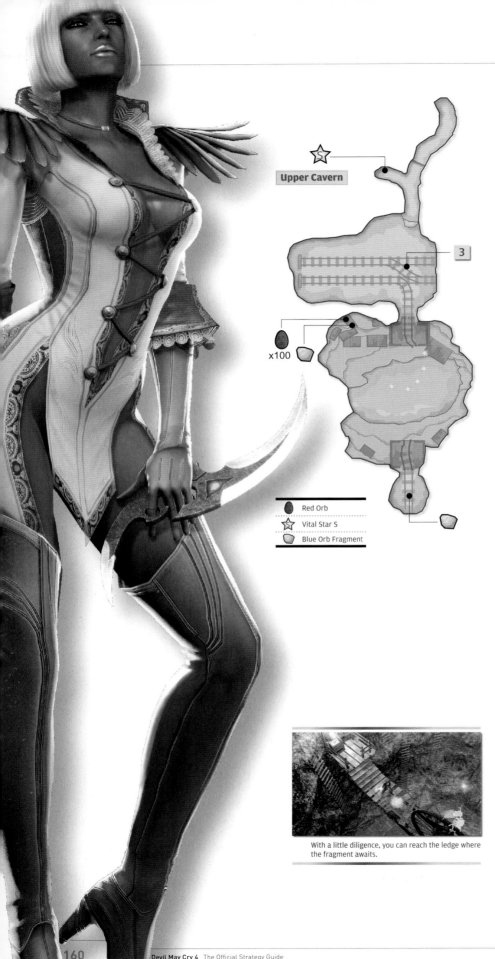

Upper Cavern

3

x100

Red Orb

Vital Star S

Blue Orb Fragment

To reach the fragment, Lock On to the first Grim Grip (remember to keep [RB] | [R1] held down during this entire process). Now, perform a single jump (not an Air Hike) straight up from the platform you're standing on. At the apex of the jump, use Hellbound to latch on to the first Grip. This will pull Nero towards it at an angle so that he's under the second Grip.

The timing here is critical, and you need to wait nearly a full second after getting past the first Grip. Once Nero starts to fall, quickly attach yourself to the second Grip. This will launch Nero upwards at a 45 degree angle, which gives him the height needed to reach the 3rd grip off-screen and above you. At the apex of the throw from the second Grip, you need to press up on the Left Analog Stick and then quickly tap **B** | **◎** to attach yourself to the 3rd Grip. After you've done this, continue forwards by latching on to the 4th, then 5th Grip.

When you've made it to the 5th Grip, you'll be thrown fairly high above it. Wait as this is happening and allow Nero to fall towards the platform that holds the Blue Orb Fragment. As soon as Nero has fallen low enough to be even with the ledge, activate Air Hike quickly, while also pulling the Left Analog Stick towards the ledge. With perfect timing, you'll Air Hike over the parapet and land squarely on the platform. Now walk carefully down the platform ledge and claim the Blue Orb Fragment. As soon as the fragment is yours, return to the main platform below and continue forwards though the opening into the next area.

Pro Tip!

When you are on a ledge, or some other area where you can walk off the edge, pressing and holding down [RB] | [R1] will stop Nero from inadvertently going over the side as you walk round.

With a little diligence, you can reach the ledge where the fragment awaits.

3 | A Little Company

In this area you'll be confronted by four Scarecrows. Dispatch them Stylishly, and then continue forwards through the opening in the northern wall. Once through the opening, turn quickly to your left, where you'll find a small alcove containing a Vital Star (S). Next, continue up the path to the north, until you find a wall blocking your way. Attack the wall to destroy it and open the path ahead of you.

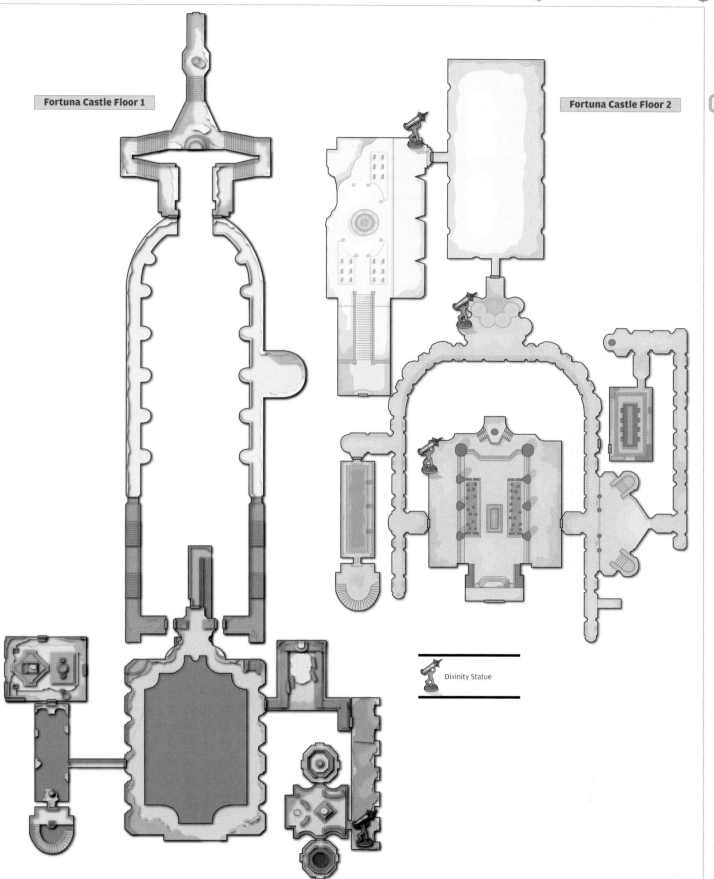

Fortuna Castle Floor 1

Fortuna Castle Floor 2

 Divinity Statue

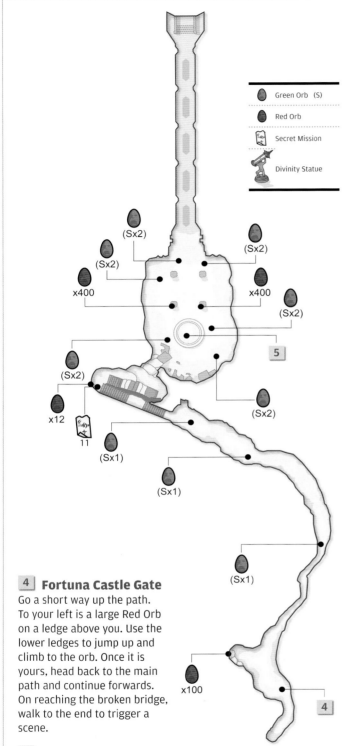

Green Orb (S)

Red Orb

Secret Mission

Divinity Statue

(Sx2)

(Sx2)

(Sx2)

(Sx2)

x400

x400

(Sx2)

5

(Sx2)

(Sx2)

x12

11

(Sx1)

(Sx1)

(Sx1)

x100

4

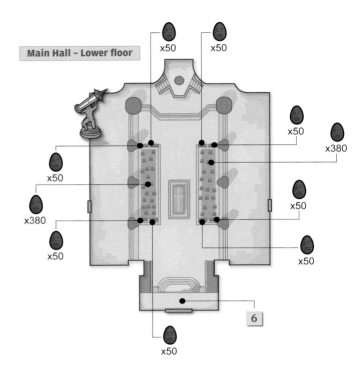

Main Hall – Lower floor

x50

x50

x50

x50

x380

x50

x380

x50

x50

x50

6

x50

4 Fortuna Castle Gate

Go a short way up the path. To your left is a large Red Orb on a ledge above you. Use the lower ledges to jump up and climb to the orb. Once it is yours, head back to the main path and continue forwards. On reaching the broken bridge, walk to the end to trigger a scene.

5 Frigid and Fearsome

When the scene is over, a Red Seal rises and you are faced with a new enemy, Frost. There are two Frosts here that you must eliminate, and they are fairly aggressive. When you've dealt with them, the Red Seal will fall. The exit is an archway leading to a bridge to the north. However, before you leave, there are two valuable Orb Drops for you to discover. As you face the archway, which is the exit, you'll see four large columns, two on the left and two on the right.

The columns furthest away from the exit have the Orb Drops. Use a Kick Jump to get on top of each column and you'll be showered with Red Orbs. Now, continue forwards through the archway and down the bridge to enter the Castle.

Get on top of the column to trigger the Orb Drop.

6 Grand Hall – First Floor

Move to the centre of the room where you'll find a large, rusted coffin imbued with a magical power. You can't do anything with it immediately. Go to the left-hand side of the Grand Hall where you'll find a Divinity Statue. To the left of the statue is a door which leads to the next area.

7 Large Hall

Here, you'll hear the battle music commence, which signals that there are enemies close by. In this large U-shaped hallway you'll find 8 Scarecrows. Take a little time out now to run the length of the hallway and exterminate them all. When you've finished, return to where you first entered the hallway. At the end of it, behind a magical obstacle, you'll find a "Gyro Blade".

You can't do anything with the Gyro Blade immediately, but near it is a large mirror on the western wall. Destroy this to reveal a small alcove holding two large Red Orbs. A little further up the hallway is another mirror that you can break, but there is nothing behind it. Now that you have discovered the mirror's secret, proceed a little further up the hallway to a smaller hallway leading to a door that takes you through to the next area.

04

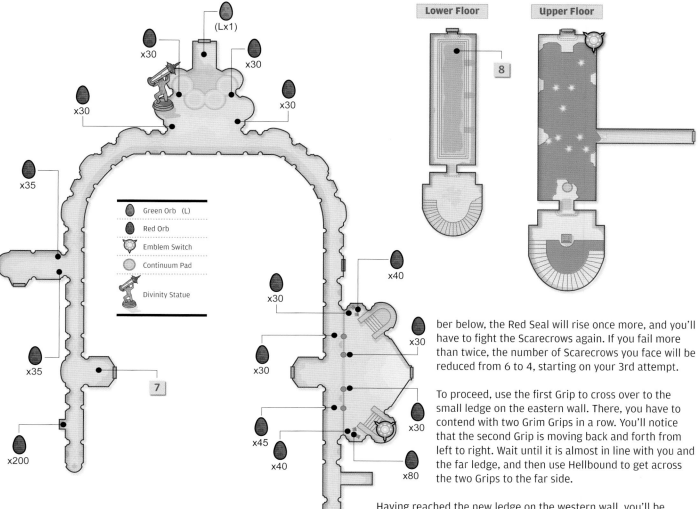

Lower Floor

8

Upper Floor

Green Orb (L)
Red Orb
Emblem Switch
Continuum Pad
Divinity Statue

(Lx1)

x30
x30
x30
x30
x35
x35
x200
7
x30
x30
x40
x30
x30
x30
x45
x40
x80

ber below, the Red Seal will rise once more, and you'll have to fight the Scarecrows again. If you fail more than twice, the number of Scarecrows you face will be reduced from 6 to 4, starting on your 3rd attempt.

To proceed, use the first Grip to cross over to the small ledge on the eastern wall. There, you have to contend with two Grim Grips in a row. You'll notice that the second Grip is moving back and forth from left to right. Wait until it is almost in line with you and the far ledge, and then use Hellbound to get across the two Grips to the far side.

Having reached the new ledge on the western wall, you'll be confronted by 3 Grips in a row. These disappear and reappear in a fixed pattern. As soon as the 3rd Grip has materialised, you have 3 seconds to cross all three Grips to the far side. This run is a little tricky and, to do it successfully, you have to be quick. As you cross, don't pause for very long or Nero will fall down below the Grip, changing the angle of the Hellbound manoeuvre. When this

happens, Nero will get thrown upwards, hitting the spikes in the ceiling above. This will damage him and knock him down into the chamber below, where you'll have to fight the Scarecrows once more.

Get past these Grips quickly to reach the far side.

8 **Torture Chamber**

03_56   As you arrive in this area a Red Seal will rise and you'll face another 8 Scarecrows. To lower the Red Seal, destroy the Scarecrows, and then go through the doorway at the southern end of the room. Take the stairs to the upper floor, where you'll find a rusted statue imbued with magical blue power. You can't do anything with it now, so go through the door directly opposite the statue.

You'll find a Continuum Pad here. Stand on the pad to activate the Grim Grip at the far end of the room and use Hellbound to cross over. Once on the far side, you're confronted with a kind of Grim Grip obstacle course, which you must negotiate. This time, however, the Grim Grips are not stationary. Some appear and disappear at set intervals, while others move back and forth on a fixed path.

If you fail during any part of this course and fall back down into the cham-

This Continuum Pad activates a distant Grim Grip.

When you've made it across to the far side, you'll face a set of two tricky Grips. The pattern of events here starts with the appearance of both Grips. The one on the left remains stationary during the whole cycle, but the one on the right will disappear and reappear 5 times. At the 5th time, both Grips will disappear briefly and then reappear to begin the cycle all over again. During each appearance, you have at least 1 second to get past the first Grip.

After passing these two Grips, you have one final set to negotiate. This time, you're faced with a Stationary Grip, then one that moves from left to right, and a final Grip on the last platform. Wait until the middle Grip is nearly in line with the far side, and then begin the Hellbound manoeuvre. With good timing, you'll reach the second Grip just as it gets in front of the third and final one. After you're thrown past the second Grip, quickly latch on to the 3rd one and make it to solid ground. Now proceed forwards and find the door into the next area.

9 Grand Hall – Second Floor

You'll notice that a blue shield surrounds this area, preventing you from jumping down to the first floor or even exploring the upper balcony. Your only option is to head to the north (left of Nero).

When you get near the large portrait of Sanctus, you'll notice a small Red Orb floating in mid-air in front of a large circular column. At the top, you can see a small ledge with a baluster and a large Red Orb. On that upper ledge there is also an Orb Drop. However, you can't reach it without Ex-High Roller (Level 3) and the Air Hike ability. If this is your first time through, it's unlikely that you'll have acquired these expensive abilities yet.

When you eventually acquire Ex-High Roller and Air Hike, charge your Exceed Gauge fully and face the column. Perform Ex-High Roller and, at the apex of the manoeuvre, execute Air Hike, while pressing the Left Analog Stick towards the upper ledge. Perform this correctly, and you'll go over the parapet and land on the ledge. Now stand in the middle of the small area and trigger the Orb Drop.

If you don't have the required abilities to reach the upper ledge, you can use a Kick Jump to get as high as possible, and then use a Snatch to grab the large Red Orb on the ledge. When you've finished gathering Orbs, move towards the portrait of Sanctus. You'll find a door to your left. Go through this to the next area.

Ex-High Roller (Level 3) gives you the height you need to reach the secret ledge.

	Vital Star S
	Battle Statue

10 Central Courtyard – Left Balcony

🖵 | 03_57 Go up the stairs to a long balcony situated above the Central Courtyard of the castle. Midway down the balcony, you'll be attacked by two Frosts. Deal with them Stylishly, and then go to the end of the balcony, where you'll find a door into the next area.

11 Foris Falls

Make your way down the stairs to the central area that lies in front of the waterfall. You can't get past the water at this time, but you can use a Kick Jump to get to the top of the pillar in the middle of the area. Once on top, jump up to obtain a Vital Star (S).

Now, take the stairs on the left up to the door. Along the way, you'll find a Battle Statue. This one is red. When you attack it you are told you can't interact with it. This is because Red Battle Statues are earmarked for Dante; Nero can only interact with blue statues. Go past the statue and take the door to the next area.

12 Central Courtyard – Right Balcony

You are now on the right-hand balcony of the Central Courtyard. As happened on the left-hand side, you are attacked by two Frosts. Deal with these beasts with Style and then continue forwards to the door and the next area.

Main Hall – Upper Floor

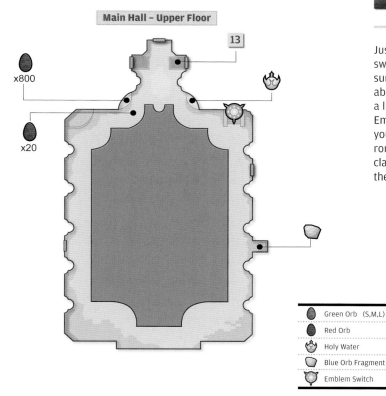

x800
x20

13

Behind the shattered mirror lies a Blue Orb Fragment

Just past the Holy Water you'll find an Emblem Switch. Attack the switch repeatedly to activate it and lower the blue shield that surrounds the Grand Hall. Once the shield is down, you can move about the hall freely. Before continuing with the Mission, explore a little and discover a valuable treasure. Head south from the Emblem Switch and ignore the door for now. Just past the door you'll find a large mirror on the wall. Attack and shatter this mirror to reveal a small alcove that holds a Blue Orb Fragment. After claiming the fragment, backtrack to the door and go through it to the next area.

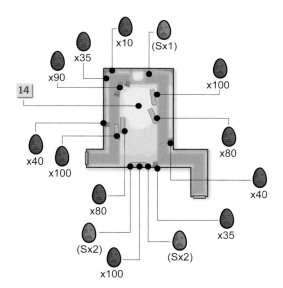

x10   (Sx1)
x35
x90
x100
14
x40
x100
x80
x40
x80
x35
(Sx2)   (Sx2)
x100

	Green Orb (S,M,L)
	Red Orb
	Holy Water
	Blue Orb Fragment
	Emblem Switch

13 Grand Hall – Second Floor

03_58   You're back on the second floor of the Grand Hall. This time you're on the eastern side of the blue shield. On this side there is an identical circular column with a

small ledge at the top with a Holy Water on it. The only way you can get on this ledge is by using Ex-High Roller (Level 3) and Air Hike. However, you can grab the Holy Water by using a Kick Jump and then a Snatch at the apex of your jump. Perform this manoeuvre correctly, and the Holy Water is yours.

A well timed Snatch will get you the hidden Holy Water.

14 Gallery

As you enter this room, a Red Seal will rise and you'll be attacked by 8 Scarecrows. After you've dispatched these beasts, the Red Seal will fall and you are free to exit via the door to the east.

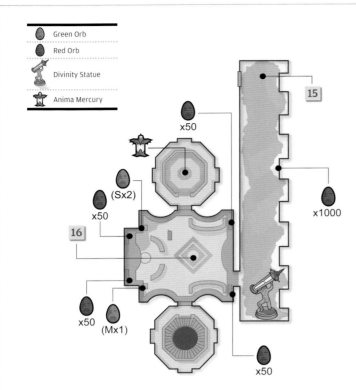

Legend:
- Green Orb
- Red Orb
- Divinity Statue
- Anima Mercury

x50
(Sx2)
x50
16
x50
(Mx1)
x50
15
x1000
x50

15 Outside the Library

After leaving the Gallery, you find yourself on a small balcony. On the left are large, ornate pillars. There is an Orb Drop on the 4th pillar from the south wall. However, to reach the Orb Drop you'll need the Air Hike ability.

If you have Air Hike, face the 4th column from the far (south) wall and jump up to the first small ledge. The Orb Drop is on the next small ledge above you. You'll notice that this ledge overhangs the one you're standing on, making a Kick Jump impossible. When you've finished, move forwards to the doorway to the south. You'll find a Divinity Statue there.

Use Air Hike to get to this secret Orb Drop.

16 Library Interior

After you go through the door to the Library, a magical barrier will bar the door and a scene will be triggered. When the scene is over, you're confronted by a new enemy, Bianco Angelo. You'll face 4 of these armoured demons.

When you've done away with the Bianco Angelos, work your way round the room, breaking the vases and benches to obtain Red Orbs. You'll find three benches on the second floor of the Library. Getting up there without Air Hike is tricky, but you can do it with a Kick Jump off the columns. After you've collected the Red Orbs, go into the circular room to the north. You'll notice on the map that there is another circular room to the south. You can't reach that room at present, so ignore it for now. It will come into play in a later Mission.

In the northern room, you'll find a glowing column. Go to the column and inspect it to gain the Key Item, Anima Mercury. This Item will enhance the Buster manoeuvre so that you can activate the Gyro Blades. As soon as you've obtained the Anima Mercury, the Mission is over.

S Ranking Tips

Devil Points Required **65,000**

Minimum S Rank Requirements

Criteria	Rank	Value
Time	S	18:00 or less
Stylish Points	A	7028 or more
Orbs Found	S	95% or more
Bonus	-	No Item

S Ranking time isn't hard, as long as you stay on the designated route and don't go into any rooms that aren't mandatory. Getting an S Rank on Orbs is going to require a little work. There are 4 hidden Orb Drops in this Mission, and you'll need Air Hike and Ex-High Roller (Level 3) to get them all. The hardest Orb Drop to obtain is in the Grand Hall on a high ledge to the left of the large portrait of Sanctus. This is the one that requires Ex-High Roller (Level 3). When you execute this manoeuvre, use Air Hike at the apex of the move to reach the ledge and trigger the Orb Drop.

There are plenty of enemies to fight, enabling you to gain your Stylish Points. The Torture Chamber and Gallery, in particular, are great fights in which to try high Style, as is the end-fight with the Bianco Angelos. Use Buster on the Angelos' shields and they will immediately counter. Deploy a Table Hopper at the last second to avoid damage, boosting your Style Rank, and then get behind them to attack. The use of Buster to finish off an Angelo is also good for your Stylish Points.

Mission 04

Cold-blooded

Mission Highlights

Item	Description
Secret Mission 02	Alley-Oop (Page 235)
Key Item	Rusalka Corpse
Boss Fight	Bael

Ranking Objectives

Item	S	A	B	C	D
Time	≤ 18:00	18:01 - 21:00	21:01 - 25:00	25:01 - 35:00	≥ 35:01
Orbs (%)	≥ 95%	75% - 94%	60% - 74%	45% - 59%	≤ 44%
Stylish Points	≥ 6500	5500 - 6499	4500 - 5499	3000 - 4499	≤ 2999

Gather The Four Gyro Blades

Now that the Anima Mercury is yours, you can activate the mysterious Gyro Blades. This new power will open paths that were previously barred to you. Is Nero ready for the new perils that lie ahead?

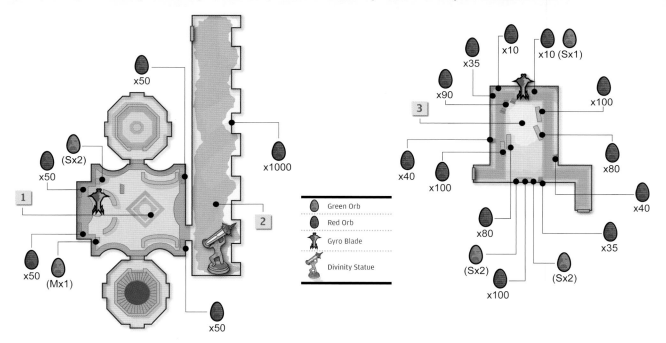

1 Library

You start this Mission in the Library, immediately where you left off in Mission 03. Get behind the Gyro Blade so that you're facing the doorway and the blue barrier. Use Buster to activate the Gyro Blade. As soon as it's active, hit it twice with Red Queen to power it up. Finally, use Buster again to launch the device. If your aim is true, the Gyro Blade will glide over to the doorway and destroy the barrier. If you miss, and the Gyro Blade ricochets round the room aimlessly, try again. It may help to only power up the Gyro Blade with one strike from Red Queen, or not at all, if you're having trouble.

2 Outside The Library

03_59 As before, you'll find the Divinity Statue here, together with the Orb Drop on the 4th column from the south wall. You'll need Air Hike to reach the Orb Drop. When you're ready, go towards the door and enter the next area.

3 Gallery

The moment you enter the Gallery, a Red Seal will rise, and you'll be up against 2 Scarecrows and 2 Frosts. Eliminate these beasts to lower the Seal. If you wish, you can make this fight extremely easy by using the Gyro Blade at the back of the room. Simply activate

Main Hall – Upper Floor

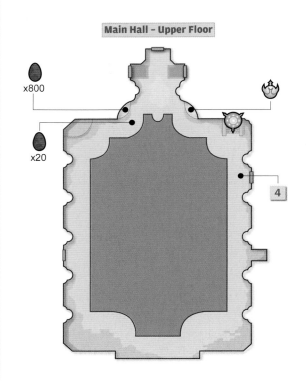

x800

x20

4

it, power it up, and then send it spinning into the enemy to deal major damage. Even a glancing blow will kill a Scarecrow instantly, and a full-on hit can kill a Frost. You won't gain much in the way of Stylish points by using the Gyro Blade, but it does make short work of the enemy.

You can use the Gyro Blade to destroy your adversaries.

4 Grand Hall

After you've left the Gallery, you'll find yourself back on the second floor of the Grand Hall. With the blue field now down, you can jump over the railing to reach the main floor below. Before doing this, remember that there is an Orb Drop on the ledge to the left of the portrait of Sanctus. As before, you'll need Ex-High Roller and Air Hike in order to reach it. Drop down to the first floor and go through the door on the eastern side of the room.

Main Hall – Lower Floor

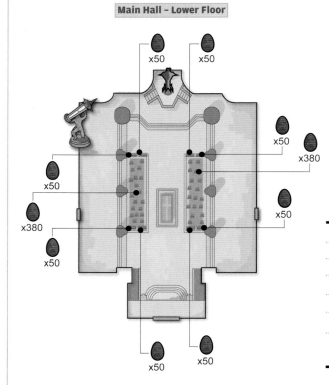

x50   x50

x50

x380

x50

x380

x50

x50   x50

6

x10 (Sx1)

x180

x50

x180

x50

5

x10 (Sx1)

02

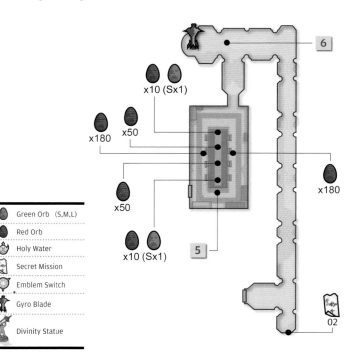	Green Orb (S,M,L)
	Red Orb
	Holy Water
	Secret Mission
	Emblem Switch
	Gyro Blade
	Divinity Statue

5 Dining Room

Head north a few paces and find a door on your right. Go through and enter the Dining Room. As soon as you are inside, a Red Seal rises and you are faced with two Bianco Angelos. Dispatch these monsters in the Stylish manner of your choosing, then exit.

6 Fire Trap

 03_60   You'll find a Gyro Blade here, which you should activate and push out into the eastern hallway. There is an active fireball trap in the hallway, but the Gyro Blade will stop the fireballs hitting you. Stay behind the Blade and push it forwards as you make your way to the source of the trap. When you are close enough, push the Gyro Blade into the trap mechanism. This destroys it and lowers the Blue Seal blocking the exit.

With the fireball trap disabled, you are free to inspect the wall where the trap once resided. There you'll find a beige parchment with red writing. This is your clue that Secret Mission 02: Alley-Oop is waiting for you. When you've finished, go through the door to the west and enter the next area.

Use the Gyro Blade to block the fireball.

7 Large Hall

Your entry into this area causes a Red Seal to rise and you'll have 8 Scarecrows to deal with. When they have been dispatched, go to the Emblem Switch and activate it in order to lower the gate. When it has been lowered, more Scarecrows will appear in the hallway. You can eliminate them either by hand, or by using the Gyro Blade you find in this room to make light work of them. In order to progress, you are required to move the Gyro Blade, but using it to kill the Scarecrows will not net you as many Stylish Points. As soon as you're ready, activate the Gyro Blade and push it into the hallway.

8 Get The Second Gyro Blade

Your goal is to push the Gyro Blade all the way round the U-shaped hallway to the far end and use it to destroy the magical barrier. When at the magical barrier, don't forget to also shatter the mirror on the wall to reveal the small alcove containing 2 large Red Orbs.

Map legend:

- Green Orb (S,M,L)
- Red Orb
- Emblem Switch
- Gyro Blade
- Divinity Statue

(Lx1)

x30 · x30 · x30 · x30 · x35 · x35 · x200 · x30 · x40 · x30 · x30 · x45 · x40 · x30 · x80

9 · 10 · 8 · 7

---

9 Solve the Gyro Puzzle

Now, in order to solve this puzzle, you must push both Gyro Blades back to the middle section of the hallway and place them on the Gyro Pads. As you begin this task, more Scarecrows will spawn. You can deal with them by hand, or use the Gyro Blade instead to make short work of them.

10 Solving The Puzzle

As soon as you have put both Blades on the vacant Gyro Pads, a scene is triggered and the blue barrier lowers itself. You now have access to the doorway and a large Green Orb. On the other side of the newly exposed door is a Boss Fight. There is a Divinity Statue in this area, which you might wish to use to prepare yourself for the upcoming encounter. When you're ready, head through the door to engage the Boss.

Boss 03 Bael

At first, you have to attack the tentacled wenches, the Rusalkas. If a Rusalka grabs you, Bael will immediately appear and try to eat you. When this happens, press ⓧ | ⓞ rapidly to break free from the Rusalka's ice casing. When you've done enough damage to the Rusalkas, Bael will emerge from the shadows. To damage him, you can attack him from all sides, but his face is the weak spot. You can also climb on his back from the side near his tail (Air Hike makes this easier). If Bael rushes towards you to eat you, quickly evade to the side to avoid the attack.

When Bael is unconscious, use Buster on his exposed tongue!

Use Snatch repeatedly to pull yourself close to Bael for your attacks. When you have done sufficient damage, Bael will fall unconscious and expose his tongue. Quickly use Buster to make a massive attack on his tongue. Bael will eventually retreat to the shadows, leaving you to contend with the Rusalkas once more. Keep up the sequence of first battling the Rusalkas, then Bael, until he is no more. When the fight is over, go through the exit door to the west, ending this Mission.

 Rusalka Corpse

S Ranking Tips

Devil Points Required: 50,000

Minimum S Rank Requirements

Criteria	Rank	Value
Time	S	18:00 or less
Stylish Points	B	4944 or more
Orbs Found	S	95% or more
Bonus	-	No Item

Aim for S Ranks on both Time and Orbs in this Mission. The Orbs will require you to break all the chairs and benches in the Grand Hall, as well as get the hard-to-reach Orb Drop on the high ledge to the left of Sanctus's Portrait. During the Boss fight with Bael, attack him furiously until you knock him out, then use Buster on his exposed tongue to inflict a lot of damage and boost your Stylish Points. When Bael moves away from you, this is a great opportunity for you to taunt him.

Mission 05

Trisagion

Mission Highlights

Item	Description
Secret Mission 03	Non-violent Resistance (page 236)
Secret Mission 10	Puppet Master (page 238)
Key Item	Wing Talisman

Ranking Objectives

Item	S	A	B	C	D
Time	≤ 12:00	12:01 – 14:00	14:01 – 17:30	17:31 – 22:00	≥ 22:01
Orbs (%)	≥ 95%	75% – 94%	60% – 74%	45% – 59%	≤ 44%
Stylish Points	≥ 6000	4500 – 5999	3500 – 4499	2500 – 3499	≤ 2499

Obtain The Wing Talisman

Each new Item grants Nero more power and opens more doors for him. However, he still hasn't enough to complete this journey. If he is to succeed, he must seek out and obtain the necessary tools.

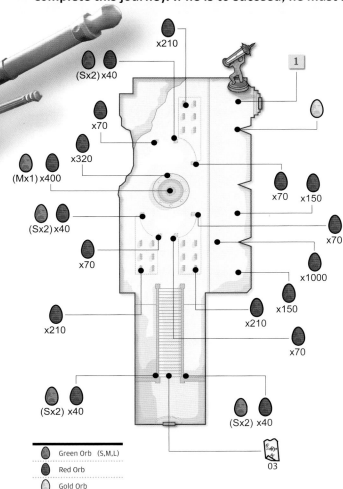

x210
(Sx2) x40
x70
x320
(Mx1) x400
(Sx2) x40
x70
x210
(Sx2) x40

x70 x150
x70
x1000
x150
x210
x70
(Sx2) x40
03

Green Orb (S,M,L)
Red Orb
Gold Orb
Secret Mission
Divinity Statue

1 Soldier's Graveyard

03_61 There is a Divinity Statue near the doorway you entered from. As you take a step forwards, a scene is triggered and you're introduced to a new enemy, Mephisto. There are two to deal with here. When you have dispatched these monstrosities, circulate in the area and do some exploration and orb collection.

> **Pro Tip!**
> Use Buster or Snatch to pull the dark cloth from the Mephisto and expose the inner demon.

First, destroy all the tombstones and statues in the area to obtain Red Orbs. After this, make your way to the eastern wall. Now that you have the Rusalka Corpse, Nero's right hand will glow whenever you are near a secret. The closer you are to the secret, the brighter his hand glows. These secrets include Secret Missions, Orb Drops, and Blue Orb Fragments.

Blue Rose can quickly destroy a row of multiple breakables.

As you approach the eastern wall, Nero's glowing hand indicates that there is something there. In fact, there are two Orb Drops on this wall. You'll find the first by jumping on to the small platform in the furthest alcove to the right as you face the wall. The next Orb Drop is in the next alcove on the left.

In the centre of this area, there is a large pedestal with a statue on top. You can break the statue to obtain Green and Red Orbs, and then you can stand on top of this pedestal to get a better view of two other secrets in this area. On the eastern wall, perched on top of the spires overhead, is a large Red Orb to your right and a Gold Orb to your left. Obtaining these Orbs is a little difficult and will require the abilities Calibur and Air Hike to reach them.

Using Calibur, you can reach the building spire.

As soon as you have these abilities, stand on top of the pedestal in the centre of this area and face the spire directly in front of you. Now do a double jump (jump once, then activate an Air Hike) and, at the apex of this jump, use Calibur to fly forwards and reach the spire ahead of you. Your aim has to be perfect, which is somewhat tricky. If you're slightly off-target, you'll fly past the spire and fall to the ground. With a little trial and error, you'll be able to reach the spire and Nero will then stand on it.

🖥 | 03_61 03_62 When you're ready, go for the large Red Orb. To obtain it, either double jump towards it and then perform a Snatch to grab it, or perform a short jump towards it and then trigger Calibur again to land on the spire so that you can then walk to the Red Orb. Now that it's yours, return to the centre spire and use Air Hike and Calibur to reach the spire on the left, where the Gold Orb sits.

Walk behind the stairs to find the marker for the Secret Mission.

Next, head towards the stairway situated in the northern area. To the left and right of the stairway are fence sections that you can destroy. Once past these fences you'll be able to walk behind the staircase and discover the marker for Secret Mission 03: Non-violent Resistance. When you're ready, go back to the staircase and climb up to the top, where you'll find a door leading to the next area.

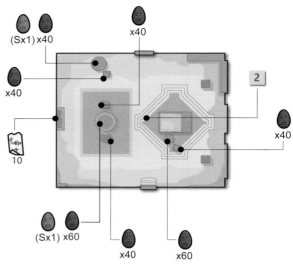

2 Master's Chamber

After entering this room you are confronted by 3 Bianco Angelos. There's no Red Seal this time, so you're free to leave the room without fighting, if you wish. However, dispatching these beasts is quite beneficial in terms of your Stylish Ranking. Not to mention that there is yet another Secret Mission located in this room.

Destroy the mirror above the fireplace to expose the Secret Mission marker.

As soon as you're rid of the Bianco Angelos, go to the fireplace situated in the eastern wall. Above it is a mirror that you can shatter. Once it's destroyed, you'll be able to access the small alcove that contains the marker for Secret Mission 10: Puppet Master. When you've finished in this room, leave through the southern door to reach the next area.

3 Torture Chamber

This area will be familiar to you. The last time you were here, you were down on the lower floors, but this time you're on the catwalk above. To the right is an Emblem Switch. Activate the switch to lower the gate and catwalk, forming a path for you across this chamber. Activate the Gyro Blade and then push it to the room on the far side and destroy the rusty statue. This will trigger a scene.

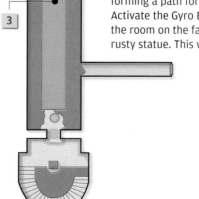

🟢	Green Orb (S,M,L)
🔴	Red Orb
📜	Secret Mission
⚙	Emblem Switch
🗡	Gyro Blade

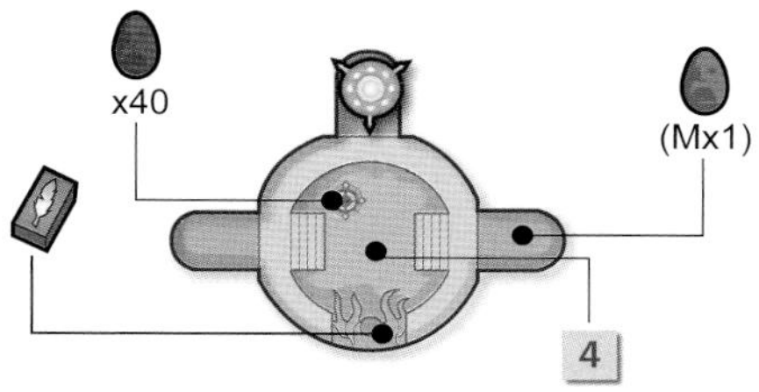
x40
(Mx1)
4

Ground Level

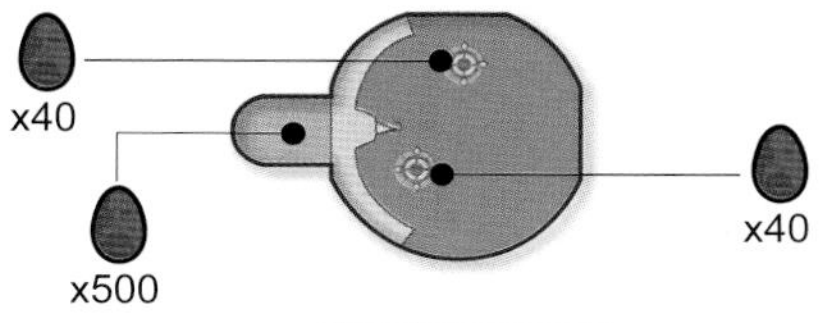
x40
x500
x40

1st Level

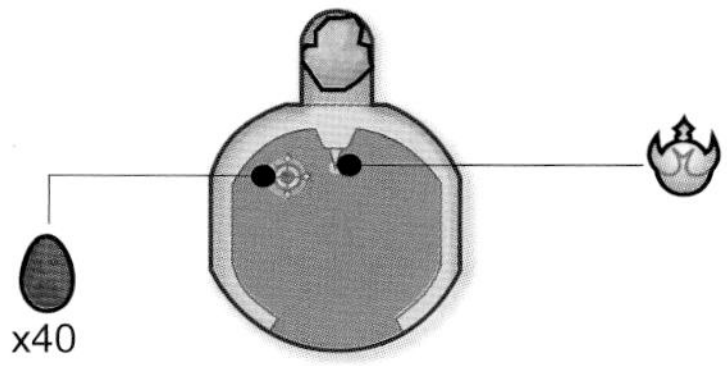
x40

2nd Level

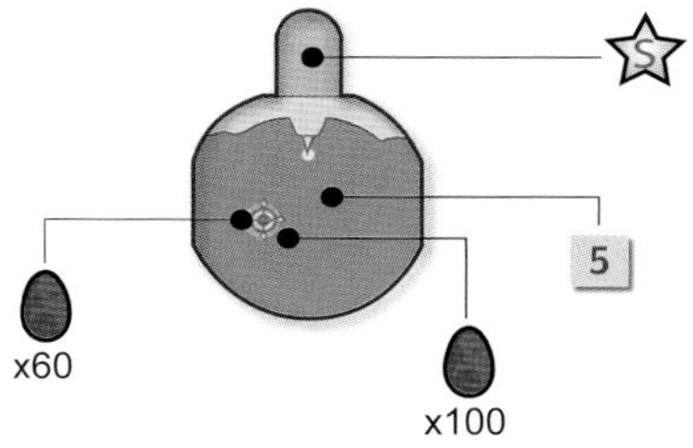
x60
x100
5

3rd Level

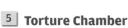

4 Spiral Well

When the scene is over, you'll find yourself falling down into the Spiral Well. At the bottom, you'll have to deal with two Mephistos. Eliminate these beasts and then inspect the glowing column to acquire the Key Item, Wing Talisman. This Item activates "Jump Pads" that will send Nero soaring into the sky.

In the northern cell you can see an Emblem Switch, but you can't reach it. There is nothing you can do with this switch at present, since it won't come into play until a later Mission. For now, approach the newly activated Jump Pad and jump on to it. This will shoot Nero up to a specified height. The objective here is to bounce from one Jump Pad to another so as to reach the top of the dreary well.

There are 5 Jump Pads in all. On the way up, there are Orbs suspended in mid-air, and there are three ledges that you can reach to find an Orb Drop, an Orb Rock and a Vital Star (S). You can reach the first ledge by using the 1st Jump Pad. The next ledge can be accessed from the 2nd Jump Pad and the final one from the 4th Jump pad. The Vital Star (S) is behind a gate, so use Snatch to claim it. When you're ready, use the Jump Pads to exit the area.

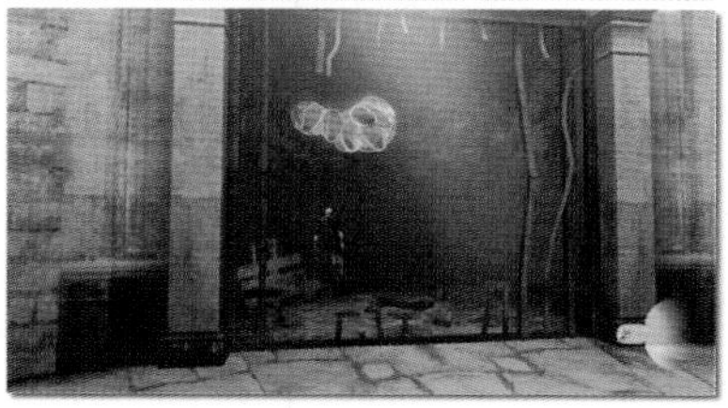

Take a detour during your jumps to claim this area's secrets.

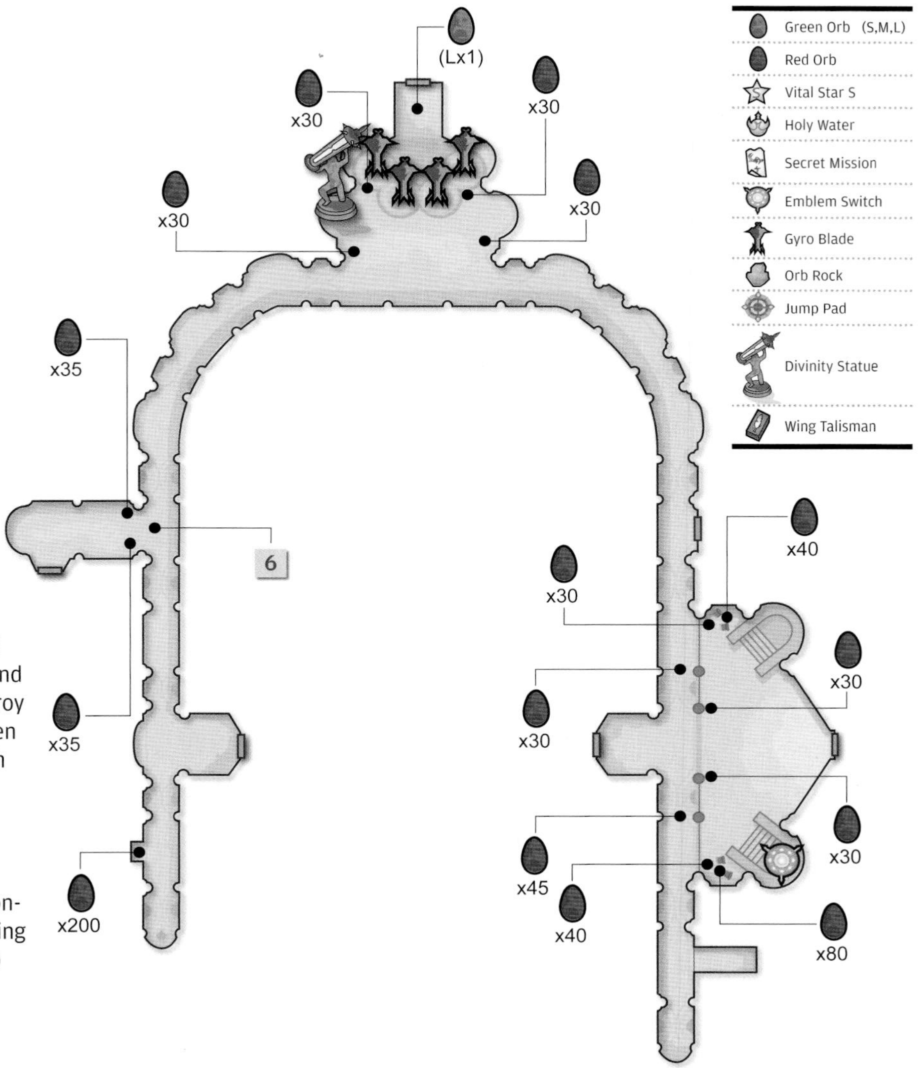
(Lx1)
x30
x30
x30
x30
x35
x35
6
x200
x40
x30
x30
x30
x30
x45
x40
x80
Green Orb (S,M,L)
Red Orb
Vital Star S
Holy Water
Secret Mission
Emblem Switch
Gyro Blade
Orb Rock
Jump Pad
Divinity Statue
Wing Talisman

5 Torture Chamber

You're now back on the lower floor of the Torture Chamber and, as before, a Red Seal will rise. This time, you face 6 Scarecrows and 2 Mephistos. Pull out all the stops and destroy these creatures with Smokin' Sick Style. Then head through the door to the north to reach the next area.

6 Large Hall

You've been in this hall a few times before. This time, you meet 3 Frosts. Take these monsters out and then exit the Large Hall by going through either of the two doors that lead to the Grand Hall.

Main Hall – Upper Floor

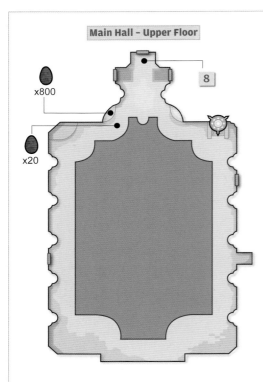

x800
x20
8

Main Hall – Lower Floor

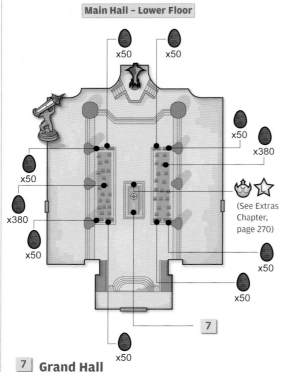

x50   x50
x50
x380
x50
x380
x50
x50
x50
x50
(See Extras Chapter, page 270)
7

7 Grand Hall

Once in the Grand Hall, you'll see that the Jump Pad beneath the coffin has been activated, now that you have the Wing Talisman. If you didn't break the coffin during Mission 04, use the Gyro Blade to do so now and expose the Jump Pad. Use the Jump Pad to reach the large chandelier that hangs above the Grand Hall. Inspect the central rod on the chandelier to trigger a scene.

8 Finding The Exit

When the scene is over, make your way forwards through the new opening. Follow the stairs down to a door. To the left of the door you'll see a glowing green object behind some bars. Use Snatch to claim the Vital Star (S) and then go through the door to the next area. Continue down the hallway in the Underground Laboratory to the next room, where a scene will be triggered, bringing the Mission to an end.

S Ranking Tips

Devil Points Required: **40,000**

Minimum S Rank Requirements

Criteria	Rank	Value
Time	S	12:00 or less
Stylish Points	B	4056 or more
Orbs Found	S	95% or more
Bonus	-	No Item

S Ranking this Mission has many options. To get an S Rank on Orbs will require a little bit of work. In the first area, where you fight the Mephistos, there are many breakables that need to be destroyed, so having the "Get More Orbs" ability is highly recommended. There is also a hard-to-reach Red Orb on a building spire high above the ground that, to obtain, will require Calibur and Air Hike. If you miss it, you'll be denied the S Rank on Orbs.

Doing all that work for Orbs will eat into your time. In this Mission it's actually quite easy to get the No Damage bonus. Couple this with the No Item Bonus, and you can S Rank the Mission with very few Stylish points.

No Damage Option

Criteria	Rank	Value
Time	S	12:00 or less
Stylish Points	C	2733 or more
Orbs Found	A	75% to 94%
Bonus	-	No Item
Bonus	-	No Damage

To use this option, you can run away from the fights against the Bianco Angelos in the Master's Chamber at Point 02 and also the last fight against the Frosts in the Large Hall at Point 06. You'll need to get all the Orbs in every other room, including the hard-to-reach Orb on the spire in the Soldier's Graveyard. Make sure you don't get hit as you run away from these fights!

To get past the Mephistos easily, use a Level 3 Charge shot to instantly knock the dark cloth from them. At Point 04, as you are falling into the Spiral Well, perform an Air Hike towards the west wall so that you land on the ledge where the Orb Drop is. Once there, trigger the Orb Drop and then charge Blue Rose to Level 3. With Blue Rose charged, fall down to the bottom and destroy the Mephistos.

Achieving the No Damage bonus in this Mission is fairly easy.

Mission 06

Resurrection

Mission Highlights

Item	Description
Blue Orb Fragment	Quantity: 2
Secret Mission 04	Tracking Treasure Down (page 236)
Key Item	Yamato – Devil Trigger
Boss Fight	Agnus

Ranking Objectives

Item	S	A	B	C	D
Time	≤ 22:00	22:01 – 25:00	25:01 – 30:00	30:01 – 40:00	≥ 40:01
Orbs (%)	≥ 95%	75% – 94%	60% – 74%	45% – 59%	≤ 44%
Stylish Points	≥ 12500	10000 – 12499	7500 – 9999	5000 – 7499	≤ 4999

Release Your True Power

There is more to Nero's demonic power than just his arm. Locked inside him is a great force, unknown to even Nero himself. To achieve his goals, Nero will need to find a way to unlock this mysterious power.

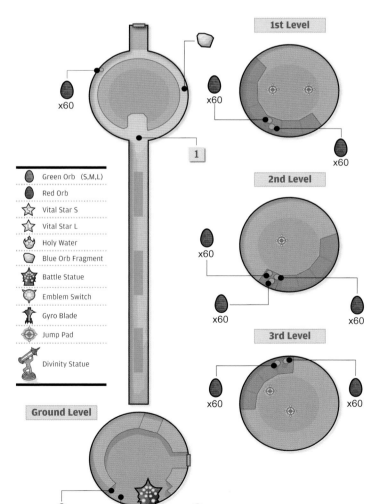

Green Orb (S,M,L)
Red Orb
Vital Star S
Vital Star L
Holy Water
Blue Orb Fragment
Battle Statue
Emblem Switch
Gyro Blade
Jump Pad
Divinity Statue

1 Underground Laboratory

When the Mission starts, you find yourself at the top of a deep shaft. The idea is to walk forwards and jump into the shaft to reach the bottom, but before doing so, walk to the left, around the upper ledge of the shaft, where you'll find a Blue Orb Fragment. It's now time to jump into the shaft, but you don't want to fall right to the bottom immediately. On your way down you can land on three ledges that have barrels you can break to get red Orbs.

Start by going to the right of the entrance, where you'll find a barrel. From there, walk to the edge and perform a short jump out into the shaft, and then immediately push back towards the wall to guide Nero in that direc-

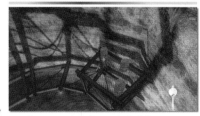

On your way down, jump on to the ledges to find breakable barrels.

tion, so that he falls on to the first ledge below. If you are a little off-target with the jump, using Air Hike just as you come to the ledge will ensure that you make it.

The next ledge is on the opposite side of the shaft. Use Streak to fly over to it from the ledge you're on. The final ledge is much easier to reach. It's directly below you, so jump towards it from where you've just broken the barrels and you'll land squarely on it. Now, allow yourself to fall all the way to the bottom of the shaft. There is a Red Battle Statue there, but only Dante can use it. Go through the door to the next area.

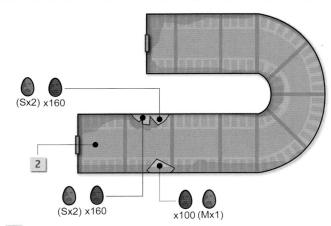

(Sx2) x160

2

(Sx2) x160   x100 (Mx1)

2 R&D Access

Walk forwards a short distance to trigger a scene and then a Red Seal will rise, locking you in battle with a new enemy, Cutlass. You are up against 3 of them here. In a pack they can be formidable. When they're all dead, the Red Seal will fall, and you are free to continue forwards to the end of the tunnel. Before leaving the area though, break any pieces of the gate that are lying around in the hallway to obtain more Red Orbs.

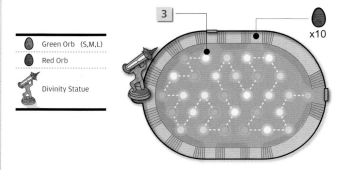

3

x10

	Green Orb (S,M,L)
	Red Orb
	Divinity Statue

3 Game Room

03_64   As soon as you enter this room, a scene will be triggered. When it's over, you'll notice that a Blue Seal has come up. The floor of the room is covered with illuminated circles, all joined together. In the first of these is a statue of Nero. Also on the floor is a large rotating die. To solve this puzzle, you must play the dice game, in which the objective is to move the statue of Nero to the far end, where the exit is.

If you walk around the room and inspect the blue panels between the staircases, you can find hints on what you need to do. The objective is to hit the die to make it "roll". The statue of Nero will move the number of times shown on the die. As you move it, you can land on one of 4 coloured spaces.

Game Space Action

Colour	Outcome	Action
White	Neutral	Nothing Happens.
Blue	Good	You are rewarded with Orbs or Chests.
Yellow	Neutral	Shift to a nearby yellow space, changing your route.
Red	Bad	An enemy fight or trap is triggered.

As you can see from the table, you need to land on Blue or Yellow spaces, if possible. White is also a good choice, but landing on Red means an enemy fight or a trap. There is a 66% chance that the Red space will trigger an enemy fight, and a 33% chance that it will spawn a laser trap. If you happen to trigger the lasers, you have to move about the room for 30 seconds to avoid being hit and taking damage. One good way of doing this is to use Streak. If you trigger an enemy fight, you have to kill them all before you can proceed.

Reading the clues given to you on the 3 panels scattered about the room, you'll find that knocking the die high into the air will yield a positive result, while using your Devil Bringer (Snatch or Buster) is less successful. The secret is to launch the die into the

Use High Roller to select your desired number.

air so that it goes higher than Nero. This means that using Devil Bringer or ground attacks will result in a random roll but, by using High Roller, you can actually select the number you want to come up.

It's easy to pick the number you want. Just watch the top number displayed on the die as it rotates, and when your desired number is displayed, use High Roller. The die rotation goes through the numbers in the following sequence: 1, 4, 2, 6, 3, 5. It's easier to actually start the High Roller manoeuvre on the number preceding the target number. For example, if you want to roll a 4, then start High Roller when you see the 1 appear.

There are 7 Blue spaces in total. If you wish to hit them all, you need to roll the following sequence: 1, 2, 5, 5, 1, 5, 4, 4 (to White), 3 (or greater). If you want to get through the dice game as quickly as possible, use the Yellow spaces by rolling the following sequence: 2, 6 (to Blue), 2, 1, 5 (or 6).

There is a 66% chance that you'll trigger the Orb Rain when you land on a Blue space and a 33% chance you'll trigger the 5 Chests. If the 5 Chests appear, you can break them to obtain Orbs and Items. Only 4 of the Chests are filled. If you break the empty one, all the remaining Chests will disappear. The mix of filled and empty Chests is random, so there's a bit of luck involved. Their contents are always as described in the following table.

Chest Contents

Chest Number	Contents
Chest 1	50 Red Orbs
Chest 2	100 Red Orbs
Chest 3	200 Red Orbs + Green & White Orbs
Chest 4	Stock Item: Random Gold Orb = 12.5% chance Holy Water = 12.5% chance Vital Star (M) = 25% chance Vital Star (S) = 50% chance

Moving using the Yellow spaces is bi-directional, so you can move backwards as well as forwards. If you land on a Yellow space, after previously passing the one it's connected to, you'll be sent back to the previous Yellow space. While doing this, you can revisit any

One of these chests is empty, but which one is anyone's guess!

Blue spaces you passed, if you wish. This gives you the power to visit the Blue spaces as often as you like. You don't get a bonus for doing this, but it does give you a chance to load up on stock items. The Red Orbs collected in this room don't count towards your Mission Ranking, but the time you spend in the room does! To leave this room go to the north.

Boss 04 Agnus

The full strategy for this Boss is listed in the Opponents Chapter. Here are a few tips.

The objective is to shatter the glass barrier Agnus hides behind. Your weapons can damage it, but not seriously. Use Snatch or Blue Rose to knock a Gladius out of the air. Once the Gladius is in "sword" form, use Buster to grab it. This throws the sword Gladius at the barrier, dealing substantial damage. When the lightning turret in the centre of the room begins to fire, stand on it to avoid damage. As soon as the barrier has gone, a scene triggers and you gain the Key Item, Yamato.

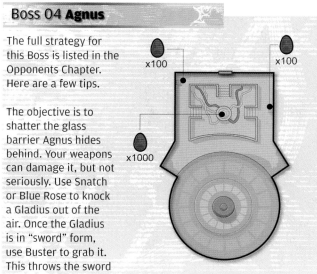

4 The Aftermath
With Yamato, you can now use Devil Trigger to enhance your attacks. Before leaving the room you're in, stand on the platform with the blue light in the middle of the room. This will trigger an Orb Drop, after which you can exit via the door to the north.

5 Foris Falls
A Blue Seal is locking you in this area. Go to the Emblem Switch in front of you and activate it to trigger a scene. The Blue Seal will then fall. Now, head up the stairs to the second level. A door here leads to the next area but, before you leave, you'll notice a broken section of railing directly opposite the door.

Approach this broken railing. You'll see a Blue Orb Fragment suspended in mid-air. The distance is too great for a normal jump, or even an Air Hike. The only way to get at this fragment is to use Streak 2 to fly over the edge of the platform and across to it. When you're near it, use Air Hike before you begin to fall and you'll nab

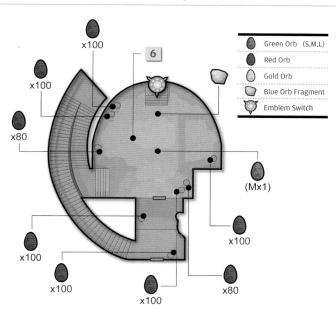

| Green Orb (S,M,L) |
| Red Orb |
| Gold Orb |
| Blue Orb Fragment |
| Emblem Switch |

this prize. Having claimed the fragment, go back to the door and proceed to the next area.

6 Angel Creation
Move down the hallway to the next room and a Red Seal will rise. You'll then face 3 Bianco Angelos. Dispatch them all and then go to the eastern side of the room, where you'll find 3 cages with test subjects locked inside. To the left of the centre cage you'll see the faint glow of the marker for Secret Mission 04: Tracking Treasure Down. When you're done, go to the western side of the room to the staircase.

You can find the Secret Mission marker to the left of this cage.

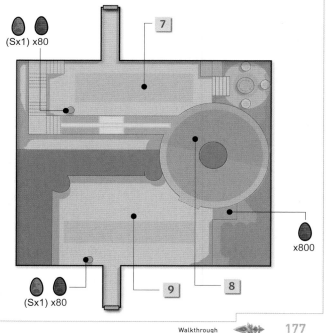

8 | Another Encounter

Climb the staircase to the upper level and move forwards to the end of the catwalk. When you get to the end, a Red Seal will rise and you must destroy 2 more Bianco Angelos. After this, move to the southern part of the platform and jump down to the area below. Next, go to the right and stand near the machinery you find there. This will trigger an Orb Drop.

9 | Armoured Resistance

Head for the centre of the room and a Red Seal will rise. During this fight you face 5 Bianco Angelos. Destroy them and then leave this area via the door to the south.

10 | Underground Laboratory

A gate is blocking your progress in this small room. To the right is an equipment console. Approach the console and inspect it to trigger a scene. When the scene is over, walk forwards and a Jump Pad will be activated. You'll notice that you're back in the shaft where you started the Mission. Use the Jump Pads to make your way to the top of the shaft. If you didn't break the barrels on the ledges here earlier, then here's your chance. When you get to the top of the shaft, head forwards to the exit.

11 | Grand Hall

Other than collecting all the Orbs in this room, there's nothing for you to do. When you're ready, take the door to the right or left of the portrait of Sanctus and leave the Grand Hall.

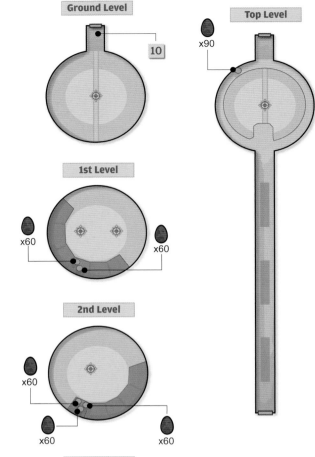

Legend	
Green Orb (S,M,L)	
Red Orb	
Vital Star S	
Holy Water	
Emblem Switch	
Gyro Blade	
Jump Pad	
Divinity Statue	

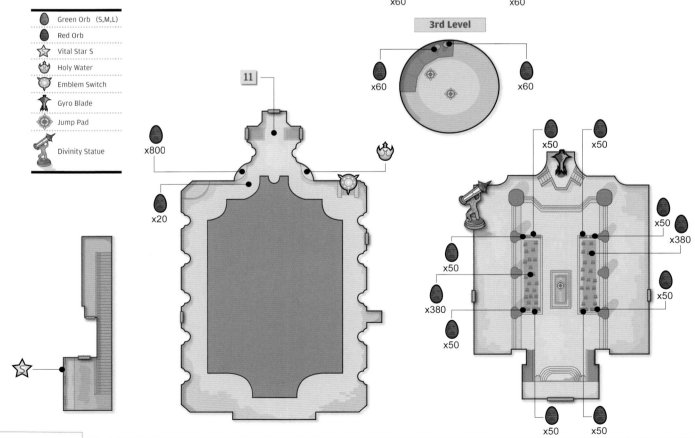

12 Central Courtyard

Make your way to the upper balcony and continue forwards. Half-way down you'll be attacked by 3 Frosts. You can run away from them, or dispatch them with Style. Continue forwards to the door at the far end.

13 Foris Falls

Make your way down to the waterfall and cross the newly extended bridge. When you arrive on the far side, a scene will be triggered. When it finishes, continue forwards through the tunnel to the far end and another scene will be triggered, thus ending the Mission.

S Ranking Tips

✦✦✦ Devil Points Required: **80,000**

Minimum S Rank Requirements

Criteria	Rank	Value
Time	S	22:00 or less
Stylish Points	B	8612 or more
Orbs Found	S	95% or more
Bonus	–	No Item

This Mission is fairly demanding. S Ranking Time and Orbs makes a great start, then you'll need at least 8612 in Stylish Points. To ensure a low time, use the Yellow spaces during the dice game in the Game Room at Point 03 to get past that area quickly. The fights with the Angelos and Frosts are great opportunities for boosting your Style. Destroying the Angelo's shield and the healing ice in which the Frost wraps itself will also boost your Style.

☆ Vital Star S

🏵 Battle Statue

The She-Viper

Mission Highlights

Item	Description
Blue Orb Fragment	Quantity: 1
Battle Statue	Nero: A Rank
Secret Mission 05	Sky Scraper (page 237)
Secret Mission 08*	Royal Blocker (page 238)
Key Item	Sephirothic Fruit
Boss Fight	Echidna

Ranking Objectives

Item	S	A	B	C	D
Time	≤ 20:00	20:01 – 23:00	23:01 – 27:00	27:01 – 35:00	≥ 35:01
Orbs (%)	≥ 95%	75% – 94%	60% – 74%	45% – 59%	≤ 44%
Stylish Points	≥ 7000	5000 – 6999	4000 – 4999	3000 – 3999	≤ 2999

* Only Dante can perform this Secret Mission. Available to Dante in Mission 14.

Through The Forest of Ruin

You've left Fortuna Castle and entered the Mitis Forest. It's a lush and mysterious place with much to see. In this area you'll come across Orb Pods that you can break to get Red Orbs. These range in size, are greenish brown in colour and have a yellowish glow. Many of these are easy to spot, but some, especially those mounted on a wall, are hard to see.

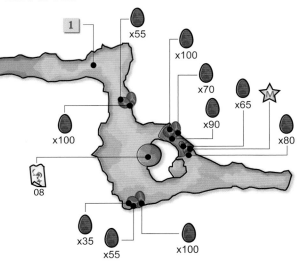

1 Forest Entrance

Move forwards, and you'll soon come to a small gazebo. Inside, you'll find the marker for Secret Mission 08: Royal Blocker. Only Dante can perform this Mission, so ignore it for now.

Just behind the gazebo is an Orb Rock. Attack it furiously to release its Red Orbs. In the large hollow log, to the left of the gazebo, is a Vital Star (M) that you can reach by jumping up through the small hole in the middle of the log. When you're ready, go to the southeast and exit the area.

2 Windswept Valley

Your next step is to move forwards and drop down from the edge of the cliff to the area below. Before doing so, go left to the end of the path, where you'll find a Holy Water. Now drop down to the area below, where you'll meet a new enemy, Chimera Seed. Dispatch these pests with Smokin' Style.

Pro Tip!
Buster kills a Chimera Seed in one hit.

You'll find two paths to the south, both of which are blocked by enchanted barriers. Breaking these will require a Gyro Blade. You can do that later but, for now, head to the eastern staircase, where you'll find a small Church that you need to enter.

3 Ruined Church

Here, a scene will be triggered. It shows you the true nature of the Chimera Seeds. These parasites can take over a normal enemy and turn it into a much faster and deadlier foe. There are 3 Chimera Scarecrows to deal with here. When you've dispatched these beasts, break the glass wall to the west to find a small room filled with Orb Pods and a Red Battle Statue, earmarked for Dante.

Go to the southern part of the room where there is a staircase. At the base of the staircase, on the left-hand side, is another glass wall that you can break. Behind this is yet another glass wall. Beyond it, a strange tree blocks your path. You can't do anything with this tree at present, so head up the staircase.

04

Jungle Area

Green Orb (S,M,L)
Red Orb
Vital Star M
Devil Star S
Holy Water
Secret Mission
Orb Rock
Orb Pods
Divinity Statue

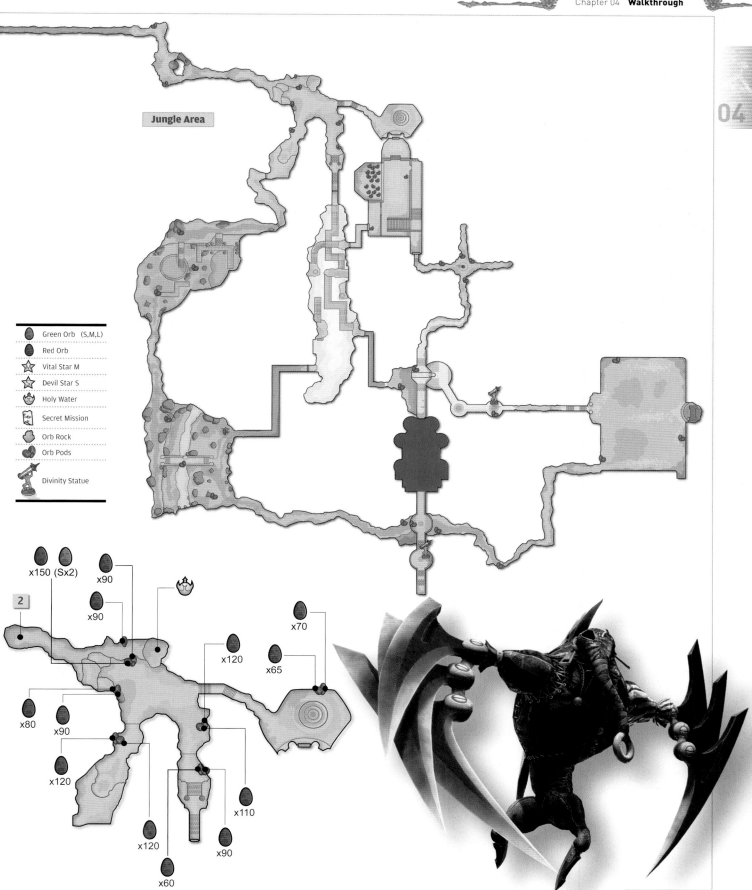

x150 (Sx2)
x90
x90

2

x70
x120
x65

x80
x90

x120

x110

x120
x90

x60

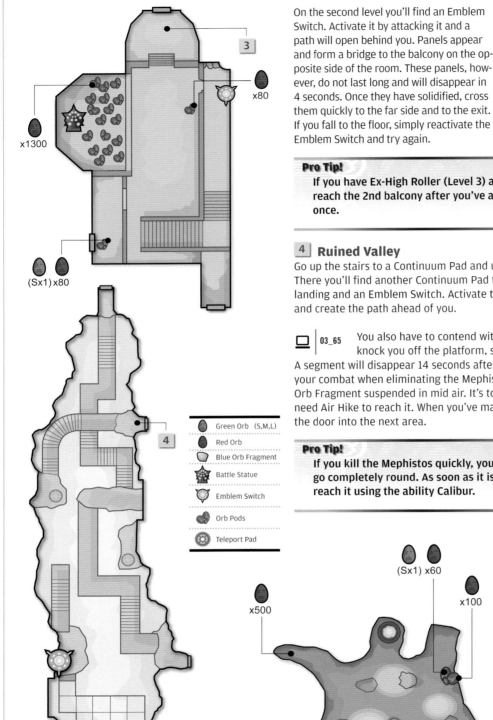

On the second level you'll find an Emblem Switch. Activate it by attacking it and a path will open behind you. Panels appear and form a bridge to the balcony on the opposite side of the room. These panels, however, do not last long and will disappear in 4 seconds. Once they have solidified, cross them quickly to the far side and to the exit. If you fall to the floor, simply reactivate the Emblem Switch and try again.

Break the glass wall to reach Orb Pods on the other side.

Pro Tip!
If you have Ex-High Roller (Level 3) and Air Hike, you can use them to reach the 2nd balcony after you've activated the Emblem Switch at least once.

4 Ruined Valley
Go up the stairs to a Continuum Pad and use Hellbound to cross to the other side. There you'll find another Continuum Pad that you need to use to reach the next landing and an Emblem Switch. Activate the Emblem Switch to trigger the panels and create the path ahead of you.

03_65 You also have to contend with two Mephistos here. These beasts can knock you off the platform, so it's advisable to dispatch them quickly. A segment will disappear 14 seconds after it has materialized, so be careful with your combat when eliminating the Mephistos. Along the path, you'll notice a Blue Orb Fragment suspended in mid air. It's too high for a standard jump, so you'll need Air Hike to reach it. When you've made it to the end of the path, go through the door into the next area.

Pro Tip!
If you kill the Mephistos quickly, you don't have to wait for the path to go completely round. As soon as it is directly opposite the door, you can reach it using the ability Calibur.

Green Orb (S,M,L)	
Red Orb	
Blue Orb Fragment	
Battle Statue	
Emblem Switch	
Orb Pods	
Teleport Pad	

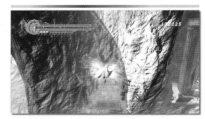

With the Mephistos out of the way, you can use Calibur as a shortcut!

If you fall off the platform, you'll land in a pit way below you, where you'll face a group of enemies. In the pit are also Orb Pods and an Orb Drop. If you fall into it, and you want 100% for your Orb Ranking, you'll need to collect the Orbs before leaving. If you don't fall in, you needn't worry about them.

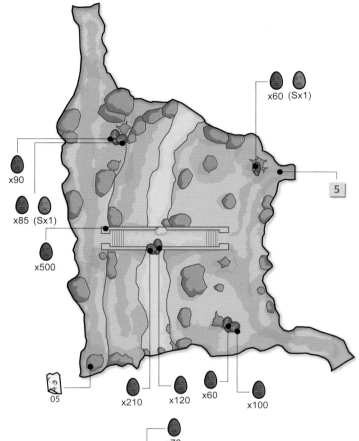

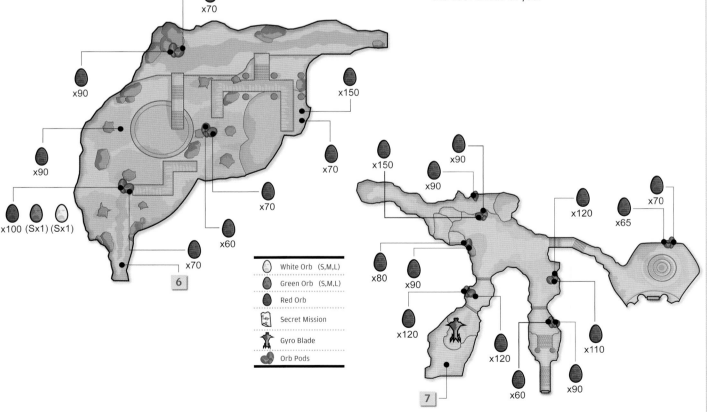

5 Lapis River

There are no enemies in this area, but there are several Orb Pods for you to destroy. In addition, in the far corner (check the map), there is a tree that has the familiar brown and red marker on its most southern side. That's the marker for Secret Mission 05: Sky Scraper. Once you've finished in this area, leave via the north-west corner.

6 Ancient Plaza

As you enter this area a Red Seal will rise and you'll encounter 5 Scarecrows and 6 Chimera Seeds. Concentrate on the Chimera Seeds first, and kill them before they can possess the Scarecrows. As soon as they are eliminated, take out the Scarecrows. The exit is to the south-west.

7 Windswept Valley

Activate the Gyro Blade here with Buster, and then power it up by striking it twice with Red Queen. Send the Buster flying forwards through the barrier and into the next area. There are 3 Scarecrows and Chimera Seeds to deal with here. You can rely on regular combat, or the Gyro Blade, to dispatch them with ease. When the enemy is gone, use the Gyro blade on the second barrier to open the way to the next area. With the barrier down, move forwards and through the door ahead of you.

	White Orb (S,M,L)
	Green Orb (S,M,L)
	Red Orb
	Secret Mission
	Gyro Blade
	Orb Pods

8 Ruined Valley

Go up the stairs to the catwalk and a scene will be triggered. You are now being chased by Echidna. The objective is to run quickly along the catwalk as she chases you. She will destroy the catwalk as she advances. You can't be knocked off the catwalk, but you can sustain damage if she hits you. When this happens, she will simply push you on to the next section of catwalk. As you move forwards, you'll encounter Orb Pods, which you'll need to break if you want 100% for your Orb Ranking. When you reach the end of the catwalk, Echidna leaves and the encounter with her is over for now. Continue forwards to the exit.

Move forwards quickly to avoid Echidna's attacks.

9 Forgotten Ruins

On entering this area you'll see a Battle Statue to your right. You need an A Rank to destroy it and release the Blue Orb Fragment it holds. When you've done this, continue up the path until you're confronted by 2 Scarecrows, 2 Chimera Seeds, and 2 Chimera Scarecrows. Destroy them all and then move on to the exit, which you'll find to the east.

x35

(Sx2)

x25

x25

(Sx2) x15

x15

| Green Orb   (S,M,L) |
| Red Orb |
| Blue Orb Fragment |
| Battle Statue |
| Emblem Switch |
| Orb Pods |
| Teleport Pad |
| Divinity Statue |

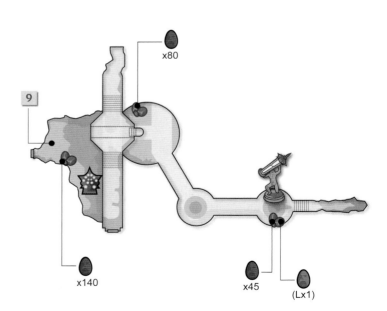

x80

x140

x45

(Lx1)

Boss 05 Echidna

The full strategy for this Boss is covered in the Opponents Chapter. Here are a few tips.

She has 4 forms, as listed in the following table. When she loses a certain number of Hit Points, she becomes enraged, in which she glows with anger and becomes much quicker and more powerful. She will also throw Chimera Seeds at you when Enraged.

Echidna's Forms

Form	Description
Dragon	Female body is not visible. She flies and uses diving attacks.
Snake	Female body, with Dragon's tail, is visible.
Birthing	Plants legs in ground and produces Chimera Seeds via her Seed Tube.
Grounded	Buries Dragon's tail in ground, leaving only female body visible.

There are Orb Pods in this area, which you'll need to break if you're aiming for 100% on Orbs for your Mission Rank. As for Echidna, use Snatch to get close to her female body when she is in Snake form and attack her. If you knock her female body unconscious, use Buster to launch a special attack and inflict substantial damage.

When she dives at you in Dragon form, either evade, or use a Charge shot to her open mouth, or unleash a well timed High Roller to phase through the attack. When she's in Enraged Dragon form, you can use Buster to

When Echidna goes unconscious, get close to her and use Buster for a special attack.

stop her dive attack as well. When she's in Birthing form, attack the Seed Tube with Buster. When she's on the ground, avoid the tentacles and attack her body. Again, if she loses consciousness, use Buster. Keep the pressure on her, and she'll soon fall. When you're ready, go to the south-west and inspect the Demon Tree here. It will wither, and you are then free to exit the area and end the Mission.

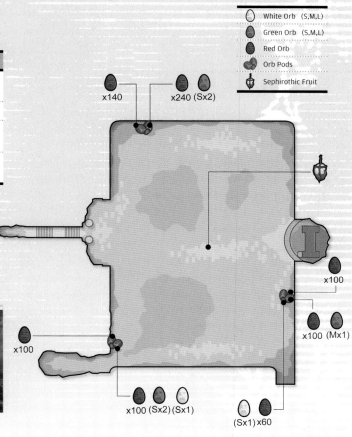

	White Orb (S,M,L)
	Green Orb (S,M,L)
	Red Orb
	Orb Pods
	Sephirothic Fruit

x140 x240 (Sx2)

x100

x100 (Mx1)

x100

x100 (Sx2)(Sx1)

(Sx1) x60

S Ranking Tips

✦ Devil Points Required: **50,000**

Minimum S Rank Requirements

Criteria	Rank	Value
Time	S	20:00 or less
Stylish Points	B	4445 or more
Orbs Found	S	95% or more
Bonus	–	No Item

This Mission is fairly forgiving when it comes to Stylish Points. Make sure you get S Ranks for both Time and Orbs. During the fight with Echidna, use a Charge shot when she dives in Dragon form. This will stop her in her tracks and boost your Style. If you also employ the many special Buster moves with her, you'll easily get the Stylish Points you need for this Mission.

Profession Of Faith

Mission Highlights

Item	Description
Blue Orb Fragment	Quantity: 2
Secret Mission 05	Sky Scraper (page 237)
Key Item	Aegis Shield
Boss Fight	Angelo Credo

Ranking Objectives

Item	S	A	B	C	D
Time	≤ 15:00	15:01 – 17:30	17:31 – 20:00	20:01 – 25:00	≥ 25:01
Orbs (%)	≥ 95%	75% – 94%	60% – 74%	45% – 59%	≤ 44%
Stylish Points	≥ 6500	4500 – 6499	3500 – 4499	2500 – 3499	≤ 2499

❋ Embrace the Light

Nero has defeated the Queen of the mysterious forest and claimed a new power. Now that he has the Sephirothic Fruit, he can access areas of the forest that were previously unreachable. Is Nero ready for the challenges that lie ahead?

1 Ancient Training Ground

Move up the path to an arched tunnel, where you'll find a Blue Fragment. You'll need Air Hike (the shape of the wall disallows a Kick Jump) to reach the fragment positioned behind the large Orb Pod that is attached to the ceiling. After leaving the tunnel you'll meet 2 Scarecrows and 2 Chimera Seeds. Dispatch the Seeds first, then kill the Scarecrows. Your exit is at the end of the path.

2 Lapis River

Directly in front of you is a Demon Tree. Inspect it, and the power of the Sephirothic Fruit causes it to wither. There are no enemies in this area, but there are plenty of Orb Pods waiting to be broken. And, if you didn't tackle it in the previous Mission, you'll find the marker for Secret Mission 05: Sky Scraper on the southern side of a tree in the south-west corner of this area. When you've completed this, look for the exit in the north-west corner.

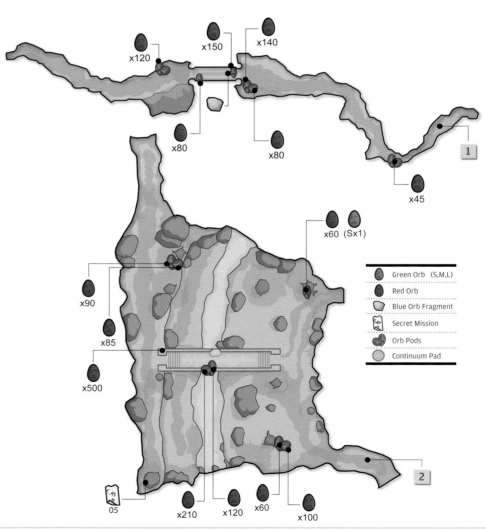

Legend:
- Green Orb (S,M,L)
- Red Orb
- Blue Orb Fragment
- Secret Mission
- Orb Pods
- Continuum Pad

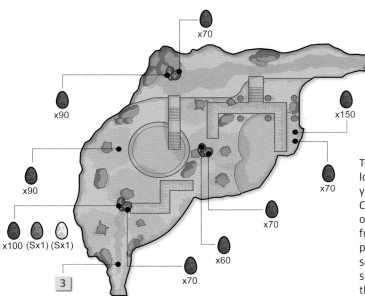

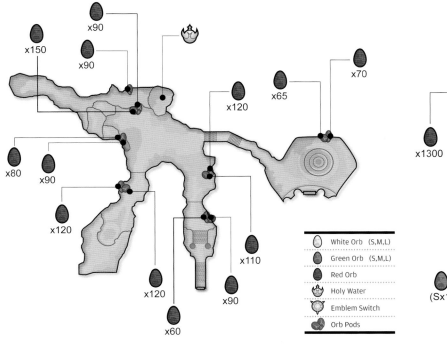

5 Lost Woods

03_66   Before you is a crossroads with four possible paths, in the centre of which stands a strange statue. Inspect it, and you are given a hint about light and darkness. This mysterious crossroads is a puzzle. To find the correct way out, you must follow the light. If you choose the wrong path, you'll be warped to a desolate area, "Hidden Pit", where you'll be forced to fight a group of enemies.

To find the correct path, look at the statue and you'll see a shadow. Currently, the shadow is on the side you entered from and where the hint plate is located; the light source is on the opposite side (see eastern path on the map).

Take note of where the shadow falls to find the source of the light.

Before you solve this puzzle completely and escape from the forest, it's actually to your advantage to go the wrong way once. In the Hidden Pit, there is a Blue Orb Fragment that you can claim if you have the Air Hike ability. The fragment is suspended in mid-air in the northern section of the Pit.

If you choose the wrong path, a second clue will light up on the statue standing in the centre of the crossroads. There are three clues altogether, suggesting that you should follow the light to get out of the place. You have to find the correct path three times. The right choices are: east, south, and north. If you don't change the camera angle, that equates to Straight, Right, and Left.

3 Ancient Plaza

Here, you are faced with a new enemy, Assault. There are 3 Assaults here. Take them out with Style. You'll find the exit in the south-west corner.

4 Ruined Church

As you enter the Church, a short scene will be triggered, after which you'll face 3 Scarecrows and 3 Assaults. Unleash your best sick and crazy moves on these beasts. When they're dead, break all the Orb Pods in the small western room that contains the Red Battle Statue. Next, approach the Demon Tree to the left of the staircase. Inspect the tree and it will wither, revealing a door that leads to the next area.

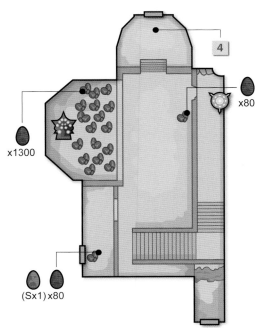

	Legend
○	White Orb (S,M,L)
●	Green Orb (S,M,L)
●	Red Orb
⚱	Holy Water
✦	Emblem Switch
●	Orb Pods

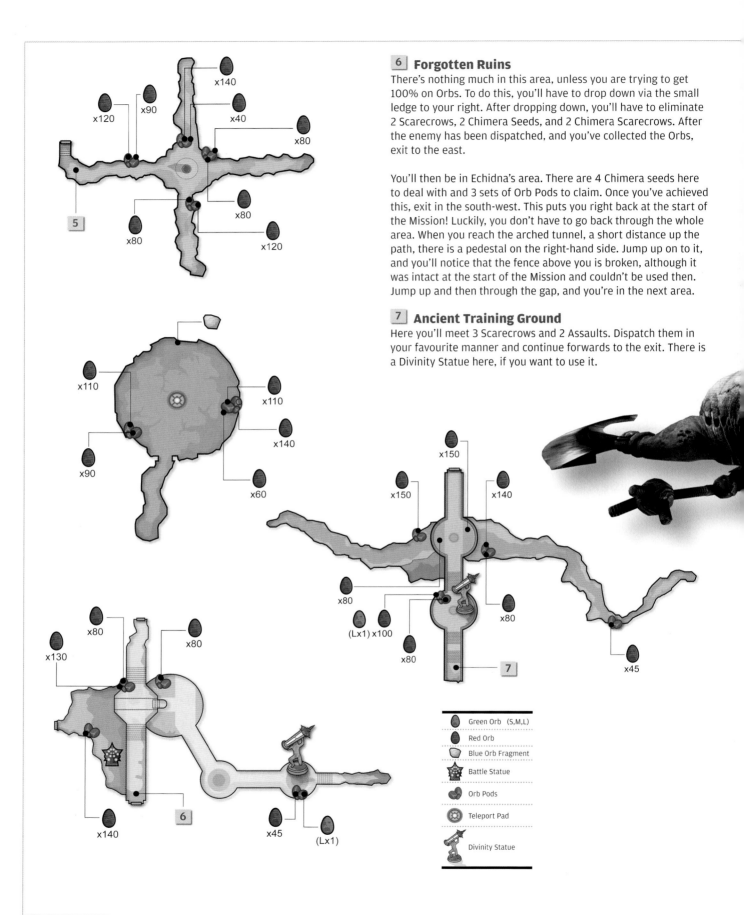

6 Forgotten Ruins

There's nothing much in this area, unless you are trying to get 100% on Orbs. To do this, you'll have to drop down via the small ledge to your right. After dropping down, you'll have to eliminate 2 Scarecrows, 2 Chimera Seeds, and 2 Chimera Scarecrows. After the enemy has been dispatched, and you've collected the Orbs, exit to the east.

You'll then be in Echidna's area. There are 4 Chimera seeds here to deal with and 3 sets of Orb Pods to claim. Once you've achieved this, exit in the south-west. This puts you right back at the start of the Mission! Luckily, you don't have to go back through the whole area. When you reach the arched tunnel, a short distance up the path, there is a pedestal on the right-hand side. Jump up on to it, and you'll notice that the fence above you is broken, although it was intact at the start of the Mission and couldn't be used then. Jump up and then through the gap, and you're in the next area.

7 Ancient Training Ground

Here you'll meet 3 Scarecrows and 2 Assaults. Dispatch them in your favourite manner and continue forwards to the exit. There is a Divinity Statue here, if you want to use it.

Legend:
- Green Orb (S,M,L)
- Red Orb
- Blue Orb Fragment
- Battle Statue
- Orb Pods
- Teleport Pad
- Divinity Statue

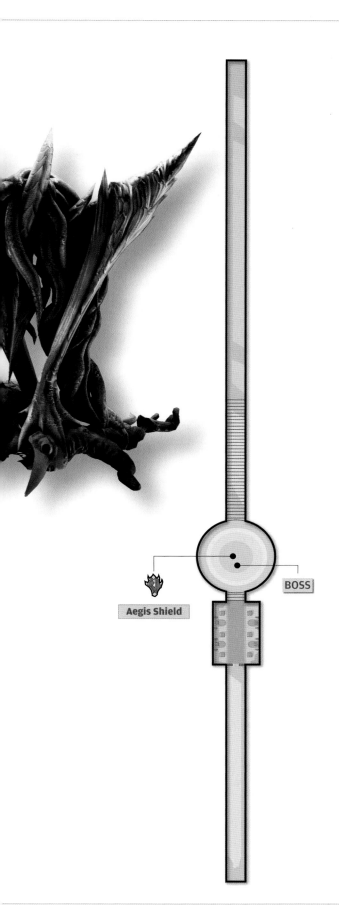

Boss 06 **Angelo Credo**

The full strategy for this Boss is listed in the Opponents Chapter. Here are a few tips.

Angelo frequently uses his shield to block your attacks. After a block, he often counters. Evade these and move quickly in for another strike. You can also get behind him with Snatch and let loose with a quick strike. Use Buster on his shield to weaken it. When it begins to glow red, the Aura on his shield almost disappears. If you completely destroy the Aura, you can then attack Credo freely, until

Use Buster to catch the javelin and throw it back at Credo.

the Aura regenerates itself. At this point, deploy Buster from the ground or air in a devastating manoeuvre. Activating Devil Trigger will enhance this attack and also change the animation.

When Credo moves away and throws a javelin at you, you can either evade it or use a well timed Buster to grab it and throw it back at him. If the javelin strikes, it will impale him and he'll become vulnerable to your attacks. Keep the pressure on Credo, using Buster when the shield Aura is down, and he will eventually succumb to your Stylish might. After the final battle scene, you'll acquire a new Key Item, Aegis Shield. Now that this is yours, exit to the south, ending this Mission.

S Ranking Tips

Devil Points Required: **50,000**

Minimum S Rank Requirements

Criteria	Rank	Value
Time	S	15:00 or less
Stylish Points	A	4945 or more
Orbs Found	S	95% or more
Bonus	–	No Item

The requirements here are similar to Mission 07, but more Stylish Points are needed. Again, get S Ranks for both Time and Orbs. During the fight with Angelo Credo, use Buster to grab the javelin he throws at you and throw it back at him to obtain a huge Style boost. In addition, you should try the many special Buster moves on him, once you've stripped the Aura from his shield. To make sure you get enough Orbs, drop to the lower area of the Forgotten Ruins at Point 07, and then go through Echidna's area to get back on track (make sure you break the Orb Pods in her area). If you run too slowly and get an A Rank in Time, you'll have to boost your Stylish Points to 6334.

Aegis Shield

BOSS

For You

Mission Highlights

Item	Description
Blue Orb Fragment	Quantity: 1
Battle Statue	Nero: S Rank
Key Item	Key of Cronus
Boss Fight	Angelo Agnus

Ranking Objectives

Item	S	A	B	C	D
Time	≤ 13:00	13:01 – 15:00	15:01 – 18:00	18:01 – 23:30	≥ 23:31
Orbs (%)	≥ 95%	75% – 94%	60% – 74%	45% – 59%	≤ 44%
Stylish Points	≥ 10000	8000 – 9999	6000 – 7999	4000 – 5999	≤ 3999

Find Kyrie

After the shocking turn of events in Mission 08, Nero finds himself in a desperate rush to locate Kyrie. What are Agnus and Sanctus planning? Nero must find out if he is to rescue the damsel in distress.

1 Gran Album Bridge

Move forwards to a small room where you'll find furniture to both right and left that you can break for Red Orbs. Continue down the path, where you'll face a new enemy, Alto Angelo. There are also 2 Bianco Angelos here. You should concentrate on the Bianco Angelos first, and then deal with Alto by himself. When they are all eliminated, continue forwards to the door and the next area.

2 Grand Hall

In this room, there is a Battle Statue to your left. You need an S Rank to free the Blue Orb Fragment it contains. Across from the Battle Statue (north-west corner) is Devil Star (S). Directly south of the Devil Star is a Red Orb Drop. The exit is the door to the south, past which there is a red Switch Pedestal. Inspect it to trigger a scene. After the scene is over, you'll know that you can't go that way, so head back to the previous room. A laser trap has been activated on the floor, and a door to the east has opened. Avoid the lasers and exit this room via the newly opened door.

3 Key Chamber

Inspect the column to receive the Key of Cronus.

💻 | 03_67 In this room a Red Seal rises. You have to defeat 1 Alto Angelo and 3 Bianco Angelos. As soon as you have dealt with the enemy, inspect the column you find in the southern part of the room. You'll receive the Key Item, Key, or Cronus, with which you can activate a Chrono Slicer to slow time down for a short period. Approach the newly risen Chrono Slicer in the middle of the room and activate it. With time slowed, you can easily get past the laser traps on the western door, which is your exit.

4 The Gauntlet

There is a small pit in the centre of this room. Stand in the middle of it to trigger an Orb Drop. In the northern area of the room, you'll find a Red Battle Statue (which is for Dante). Across from the Battle Statue to the south is an Emblem Switch. Activate it to lower an elevator.

5 Fight For A Ride

Once on the elevator, you are confronted by 4 Scarecrows. Defeat them, and the elevator will rise. During the elevator ride, you'll notice a Blue Orb Fragment just beyond the walls of the elevator. You'll be able to get that fragment in just a moment.

6 Step Carefully

Use Streak from this hard-to-see door to reach the fragment below.

Leave the elevator and use the Chrono Slicer to slow time down. Move past the lasers carefully to the next elevator. When you enter it, the door slams shut behind you and you are up against 3 Frosts. Defeat them and the elevator will finally move. When it arrives at its destination, the exit door to the north will open.

But don't leave yet. You've got the chance now to grab that Blue Orb Fragment you saw earlier. Inside the elevator you're in, there's another door to the south, hidden by the camera angle. Walk towards the camera to get it to spin and show you the door. Approach the door and then use Streak to fly over the edge. You'll fall on to a small area on the second level. Walk over past the elevator to see the Orb Fragment suspended in mid-air. Jump up to it to claim it, then fall back to the bottom and ride the elevators back up to where you left off.

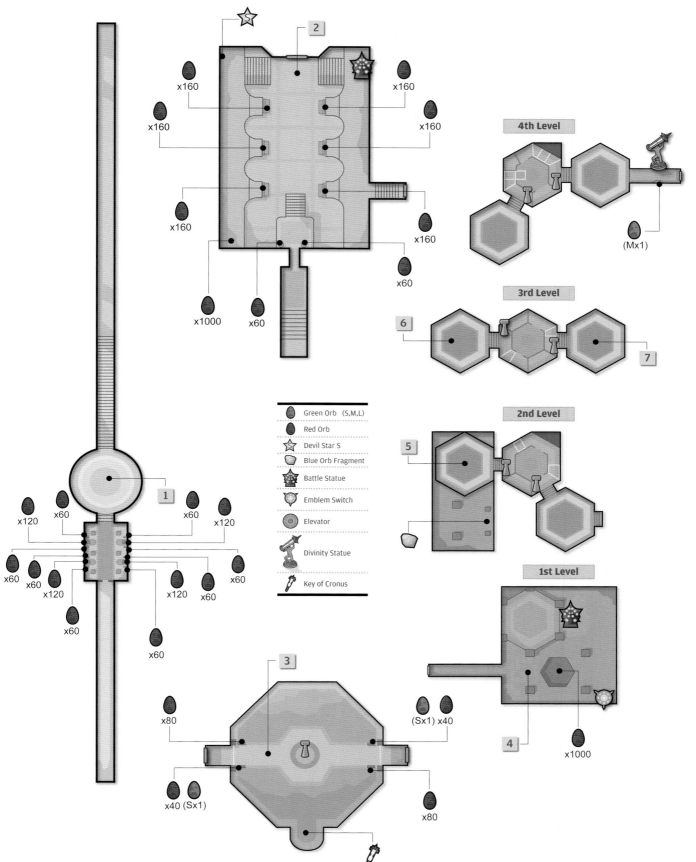

4th Level

(Mx1)

3rd Level

6

7

2nd Level

5

1st Level

4

x1000

x160

x160

x160

x160

2

x160

x160

x160

x60

x1000

x60

1

x120

x60

x60

x120

x60

x60

x120

x120

x60

x60

x60

x60

3

x80

(Sx1) x40

x40 (Sx1)

x80

Green Orb (S,M,L)

Red Orb

Devil Star S

Blue Orb Fragment

Battle Statue

Emblem Switch

Elevator

Divinity Statue

Key of Cronus

7 | One Last Ride

Now that you have the Blue Orb Fragment, enter the last elevator. As before, the door will slam shut and you need to fight. This time it's 5 Assaults. Annihilate these beasts, and then the elevator will take you to the upper level. Leave the elevator and you'll find a Green Orb and a Divinity Statue. When you're ready, continue forwards and up the stairs to the next area.

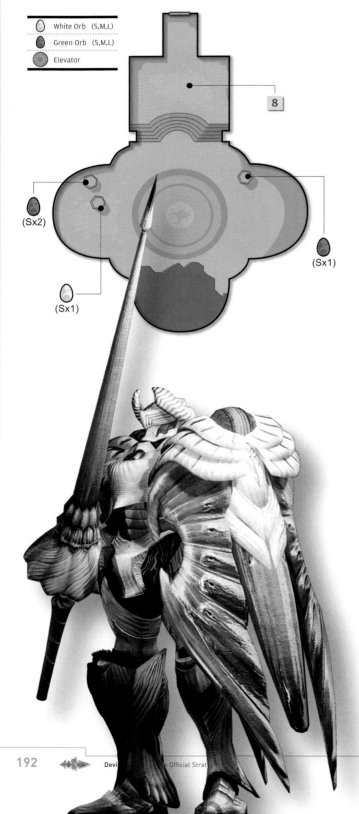

⬤ White Orb	(S,M,L)
⬤ Green Orb	(S,M,L)
⬤ Elevator	

8

(Sx2)

(Sx1)

(Sx1)

Boss 07 Angelo Agnus

You now come face-to-face with Agnus in his Demon form. He's a rather formidable opponent with many tricks up his sleeve. He can summon Gladius to fight with him, which is actually to your advantage. Snatch a Gladius from the air to make it revert to sword form, then use Buster to throw the Gladius sword at Agnus to inflict major damage. Whenever you destroy a Gladius, White Orbs are released, so you can use Devil Trigger fairly liberally in this fight.

When Agnus is Dizzy, approach him and use Buster.

Agnus will attempt to absorb your health for his own use. When he begins to do this, attack him quickly to stop the attack. If he does grab you, immediately activate Devil Trigger to break free and stop the drain. If you do enough damage to Agnus, he'll be stunned. When this happens, run up to him and use Buster in a special attack. You can enhance the animation and damage of this attack by activating Devil Trigger before you grab Agnus with Buster. As soon as Agnus has been defeated, a scene is triggered and the Mission is over.

S Ranking Tips

◆◆◆ Devil Points Required: **60,000**

Minimum S Rank Requirements

Criteria	Rank	Value
Time	S	13:00 or less
Stylish Points	B	6834 or more
Orbs Found	S	75% to 94%
Bonus	-	No Item

This Mission is fairly short, so S Ranking time shouldn't be a problem. If you do run a bit slow and A Rank your time, then increase your Stylish Points to 8501. It's actually fairly easy to accumulate a lot of Stylish Points in this Mission. When you fight the Alto and Bianco Angelos, reflect the energy ball they use. It will kill them all instantly and give you a huge Style boost. During the fight with Angelo Agnus, make use of the special Buster routines for Style boosts. Activate Devil Trigger repeatedly to gain more damage and Style.

Mission 10

Wrapped In Glory

Mission Highlights

Item	Description
Blue Orb Fragment	Quantity: 1
Secret Mission 06	Vermifuge (page 237)
Secret Mission 07	Free Running (page 237)
Boss Fight	Dante

Ranking Objectives

Item	S	A	B	C	D
Time	≤ 20:00	20:01 - 23:00	23:01 - 27:00	27:01 – 35:00	≥ 35:01
Orbs (%)	≥ 95%	75% - 94%	60% - 74%	45% - 59%	≤ 44%
Stylish Points	≥ 10000	8000 - 9999	6000 - 7999	4000 - 5999	≤ 3999

End the Ambitions of His Holiness

Sanctus himself has taken Kyrie away. Enraged at losing her when she was so close, Nero sets off to find her. Will he be in time to thwart Sanctus's evil plans?

1 The Gauntlet

There are some wire racks in this room that you can break to get Green and White Orbs. There's nothing else, so leave via the door to the north.

2 Locked In

In the hallway, you'll again find a Green Orb and Divinity Statue. Move forwards and enter the elevator to trigger a scene that introduces a new enemy, Faust. Accompanying Faust are 2 Mephistos. Destroy them all and the elevator doors will open. Exit to the west.

3 Lower The Seal

A Emblem Switch has risen. It can be deactivated by the Emblem Switch in the far room. Use the Chrono Slicer to slow time down and then move carefully past the lasers. Deactivate the Emblem Switch using the Emblem Switch. Now use the Chrono Slicer again and make your way to the newly exposed opening. Drop to the lower floor and quit this area via the door to the west.

(Sx2)

(Sx1)

(Sx1)

Legend	
White Orb (S,M,L)	
Green Orb (S,M,L)	
Red Orb	
Battle Statue	
Emblem Switch	
Elevator	
Divinity Statue	

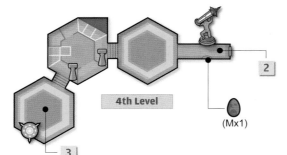

4th Level

(Mx1)

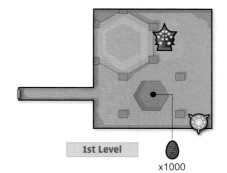

1st Level

x1000

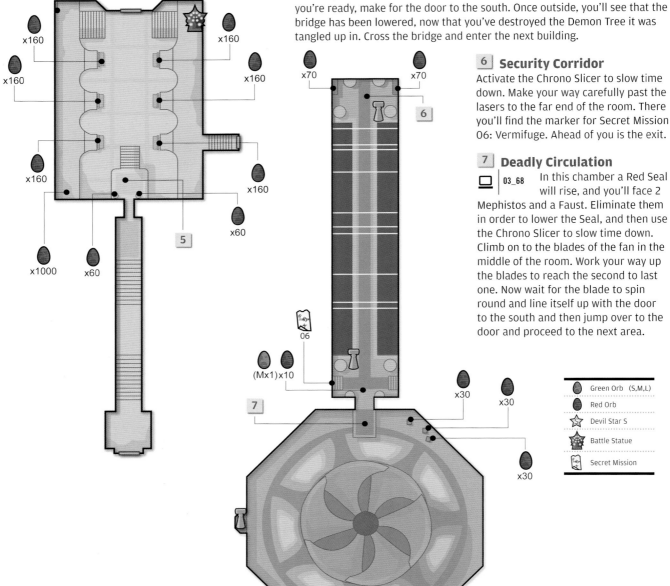

4 Key Chamber

In this room you are again attacked by 1 Alto Angelo and 3 Bianco Angelos. This time, however, you can use the Chrono Slicer to slow time down and win yourself a major advantage. This isn't a mandatory fight, so you can leave the room at any time. When you're ready, use the Chrono Slicer to slow time down and then go past the lasers guarding the eastern door.

Slow time down and tilt the odds in your favour!

5 Grand Hall

The laser trap on the floor of this room is still active. Don't forget about the Orb Drop, which can be found in the south-west corner of the room. When you're ready, make for the door to the south. Once outside, you'll see that the bridge has been lowered, now that you've destroyed the Demon Tree it was tangled up in. Cross the bridge and enter the next building.

6 Security Corridor

Activate the Chrono Slicer to slow time down. Make your way carefully past the lasers to the far end of the room. There you'll find the marker for Secret Mission 06: Vermifuge. Ahead of you is the exit.

7 Deadly Circulation

03_68 In this chamber a Red Seal will rise, and you'll face 2 Mephistos and a Faust. Eliminate them in order to lower the Seal, and then use the Chrono Slicer to slow time down. Climb on to the blades of the fan in the middle of the room. Work your way up the blades to reach the second to last one. Now wait for the blade to spin round and line itself up with the door to the south and then jump over to the door and proceed to the next area.

Green Orb (S,M,L)
Red Orb
Devil Star S
Battle Statue
Secret Mission

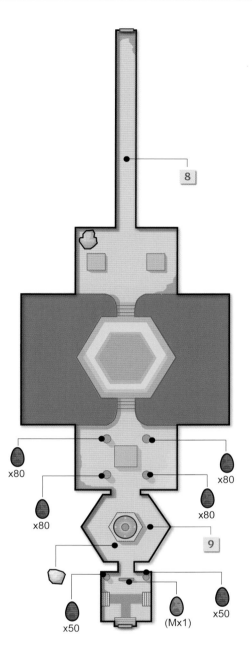

8

x80   x80

x80   x80

9

x50   (Mx1)   x50

9 A Little Higher

03_69 There is an elevator here, but don't use it yet. A Blue Orb Fragment is hidden on the second ledge of the elevator shaft. To get this fragment, you'll need Ex-High Roller and Air Hike. Charge Exceed to level 3. Stand on the elevator

Use Ex-High Roller and Air Hike to reach the ledges above the elevator.

next to the control column. Activate Ex-High Roller and, at the apex of your jump, do a short Air Hike to the ledge in front of you. Now Air Hike straight up, so that you can see the fragment. Face in that direction, then Air Hike towards it. As you approach it, use Snatch to grab it before you fall.

When you're ready, use the control column to activate the elevator and go up to the upper level. Move forwards from the elevator. Break the small gate blocking the door and enter the next room. The exit is to the south.

10 Meeting Room

In this room you'll be confronted by 2 Alto Angelos. After vanquishing these demons, head south to a smaller room. On the south-east wall you'll see the marker for Secret Mission 07: Free Running. When you're ready, take the door to the south.

White Orb (S,M,L)
Green Orb (S,M,L)
Blue Orb Fragment
Battle Statue
Secret Mission
Orb Rock
Elevator
Divinity Statue

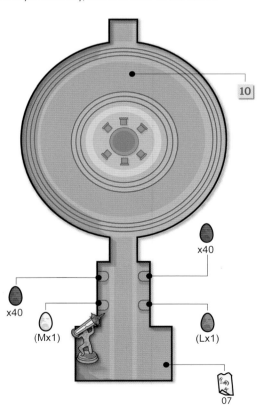

10

x40

x40

(Mx1)   (Lx1)

07

8 Experiment Disposal

You start off in a long hallway that leads to the next room, where there are 4 Bianco Angelos. If you don't move, they will come to you in the hallway. It's quite easy to defeat them in the hallway and, by challenging them there, you avoid the risk of inadvertently hitting the Orb Rock in the next room and starting its destruction timer while you're battling away. When the Angelos are dead, go into the next room, where you'll find the Orb Rock against the west wall. Head further south to the next room.

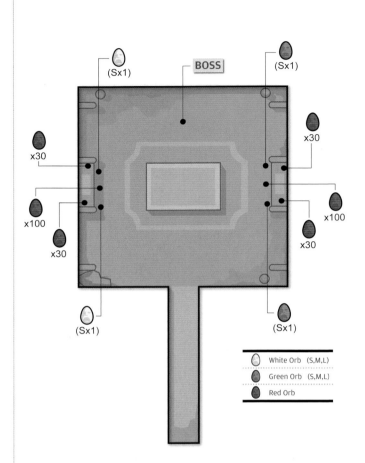

(Sx1)   BOSS   (Sx1)

x30

x30

x100

x100

x30

x30

(Sx1)   (Sx1)

	White Orb	(S,M,L)
	Green Orb	(S,M,L)
	Red Orb	

Boss 08 **Dante**

The full strategy for this Boss is listed in the Opponents Chapter. Here are a few tips.

Using Buster while Devil Trigger is active severely clobbers Dante!

Dante is very evasive and makes use of all of his available Styles. He deflects your attacks frequently and also evades your gunfire fairly often. However, he is very weak against your Devil Trigger. With Devil Trigger active, you can land most of your attacks as well as using Buster to deliver a devastating blow.

When Dante uses Royal Guard, don't bother attacking him but, instead, use Buster to launch a fast throw. When he uses Trickster, he's more vulnerable to gunfire than to the other Styles. When he commits to gunfire or Helm Breaker, jump above him and use Split. Remain very evasive and choose your attacks wisely. Once you've stripped Dante of all his health, the fight will end and a scene will be triggered, thus ending the Mission.

S Ranking Tips

Devil Points Required: **70,000**

Minimum S Rank Requirements

Criteria	Rank	Value
Time	S	20:00 or less
Stylish Points	B	7223 or more
Orbs Found	S	75% to 94%
Bonus	-	No Item

Aim for S Ranks in Time and Orbs. The Stylish Points may seem high, but you can easily amass the required 7223, and many more, well before you ever reach the Boss Fight with Dante. In particular, you can gain a lot of points in the Key Chamber at Point 02 when you fight the Angelos. Use the Chrono Slicer there to repeatedly slow time down, and then unleash your combos with Smokin' Sick Style.

The Bianco Angelos, who are confronting you at Point 06, offer another easy opportunity for you to get Stylish points. Eventually, at Point 08, the Alto Angelos are worth even more. To deal with these foes, first break their shield, then activate Devil Trigger and then use Buster for a special attack that gives a major boost to your Style. You can use Buster twice in succession, since the Alto will be stunned after the first Buster attack, while the second Buster usually destroys the armoured beast. So, by the time you get to the fight with Dante, you should have more than enough Stylish Points for the S Rank.

Mission 11

The Ninth Circle

Mission Highlights

Item	Description
Battle Statue	Nero: SSS Rank
Boss Fight	Sanctus & Savior

Ranking Objectives

Item	S	A	B	C	D
Time	≤ 15:00	15:01 – 17:30	17:31 – 20:00	20:01 – 25:00	≥ 25:01
Orbs (%)	≥ 95%	75% – 94%	60% – 74%	45% – 59%	≤ 44%
Stylish Points	≥ 11500	9500 – 11499	7500 – 9499	5000 – 7499	≤ 4999

Prevent The Birth Of A God

This Mission takes place in one large chamber. Your goal is to climb to the top and face Sanctus. You must stop him from bringing Savior to life. Only you can save our world.

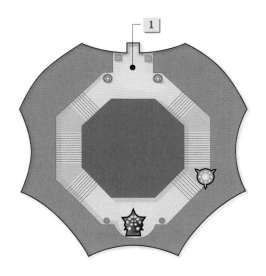

1 Advent Chamber

Go left up the stairs and, for now, go past the Emblem Switch. Just beyond the switch is a Battle Statue. You need a full SSS Ranking to destroy this statue, so pull out all the stops and claim the Blue Orb Fragment. When you've done this, backtrack to the Emblem Switch. Activating the switch will cause 4 Grim Grips to appear. Use Hellbound on the Grips to reach the 2nd floor above you.

2 Mephisto Fight

Walk forwards and a Red Seal will rise. You are faced with 2 Mephistos and 1 Faust. Conquer the beasts and then continue forwards to the elevator. Inspect the red control switch to activate it, and then ride it up to the next level.

3 Unlikely Partner

Here, a Warp Pad will appear that will warp you back to the main entrance. There's no need to go back there, but if you should fall during your climb, you can use the pad at the entrance to warp back to this spot. Go to your right, and you'll see a gate and plaque that you can read for a hint. The clue says that going alone is prohibited.

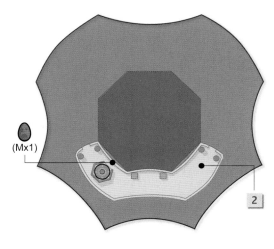

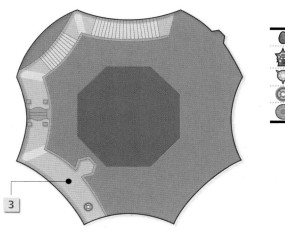

Green Orb (S,M,L)
Battle Statue
Emblem Switch
Teleport Pad
Elevator

The gate before you has two release pads. You must depress them both to lower the gate. Your partner in this is the Scarecrow on the opposite side. Use Snatch through the gate to pull him on to the opposite pad and then step on the one on your side. The

Use Snatch through the gate to pull the Scarecrow on to the pad.

gate will fall. Thank the Scarecrow for his help by dispatching him with Sick Style, and then continue onwards up the stairs to the next area.

🖥 | **03_70** As soon as you're ready, wait for the middle Grim Grip to reach its apex, and then start using Hellbound. You'll reach the 3rd Grip just as it nears its apex, landing you squarely on top of the wall. If you mistime this, you can use a Kick

There is a hidden Orb Drop here.

Jump against the far wall to get past it. As soon as you are on top of the far wall, walk away from the camera towards the back and stand there to trigger an Orb Drop.

6 An Emblem Switch

🖥 | **03_71** Drop down from the wall and you'll meet an Alto Angelo. Defeat him and then continue forwards past the Emblem Switch. On reaching the back wall, use Air Hike or a Kick Jump to get on the wall and then you'll see a large Red Orb suspended above you. To reach this Orb, Kick Jump off the wall to the left, turn in mid-air, then use Snatch to grab the Orb. Now return to the Emblem Switch and activate it. This reveals 7 Grim Grips that you must use in order to reach the next level.

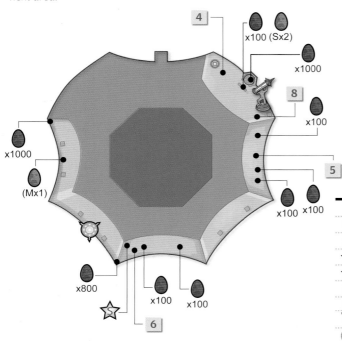

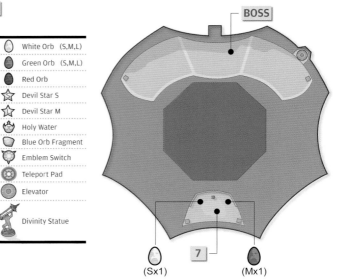

	White Orb (S,M,L)
	Green Orb (S,M,L)
	Red Orb
	Devil Star S
	Devil Star M
	Holy Water
	Blue Orb Fragment
	Emblem Switch
	Teleport Pad
	Elevator
	Divinity Statue

4 The Main Elevator

Here you'll find an empty elevator shaft and a Divinity Statue. Stand in the elevator shaft to trigger an Orb Drop. Next, go to your right past the Divinity Statue and drop to the lower area. Walk forwards to find a large Red Orb. While you are down below, position yourself beneath the Grim Grips above you, then jump up and use Hellbound to pull yourself up far enough to grab the Red Orbs that are suspended above each.

Now go back to the upper area and use Hellbound on the Grim Grips to reach the next level. You'll need to use a well timed Kick Jump off the far wall once you get past the second Grim Grip.

5 Get A Grip

Walk forwards and find 3 more Grim Grips, two of them moving. For now, drop down below them and a Red Seal will rise. You are up against 3 Bianco Angelos, so destroy these demons and use the Grim Grips above you to get the Red Orbs positioned near them. There is also a Devil Star (S) near the far wall of this area.

7 The Troops Attack

Walk forwards and inspect the red control switch. This will cause a Red Seal to rise, and a short scene shows you that an elevator has arrived on the previously empty shaft near the Divinity Statue you passed earlier. You'll now have to eliminate 1 Alto Angelo and 3 Bianco Angelos, after which the Red Seal will fall. Head to your left and backtrack to the newly lowered elevator.

8 | To The Final Level

As you arrive, a Warp Pad appears. It will warp you between here and the main entrance. You are also greeted by 3 Scarecrows, 2 Alto Angelos, 2 more Scarecrows, and then 2 Bianco Angelos, in that order. You don't have to fight them, but you can instead just ride the elevator up to the next level. Step on it when you're ready to go.

Boss 09 Sanctus & Savior

The full strategy for this Boss is listed in the Opponents Chapter. Here are a few tips.

Break his shield and Halo, and Sanctus will fall to the ground!

You must first break the shield surrounding Sanctus. Use Snatch to get close and stay close. Attack the shield with Red Queen until it shatters. Use Snatch to get close again and hit Sanctus to break the Halo on his back and knock him to the ground. When he's down, use Buster to launch a devastating attack before the Halo reforms.

When you've dealt enough damage, Sanctus will enter The Savior. The Savior will use a right-hand punch that you can deflect with Buster, which will immediately knock Sanctus out of The Savior and on to the ground. He won't have his shield or Halo, so is immediately vulnerable to a Buster attack. When you've defeated him, a scene will be triggered and the Mission ends.

S Ranking Tips

Devil Points Required: **80,000**

Minimum S Rank Requirements

Criteria	Rank	Value
Time	S	15:00 or less
Stylish Points	B	8612 or more
Orbs Found	S	75% to 94%
Bonus	-	No Item

Go for the S Ranks in Time and Orbs. For Orbs, make sure you trigger both Orb Drops. If you run a little slow on time, you'll have to increase your Stylish Points to 10834. If you S Rank your Time and Orbs, you can get more than enough Stylish Points from the enemy fights. The Bianco Angelos and Alto Angelos at Points 05, 06, and 07 offer huge opportunities for Style. Then, at Point 08, the multi-enemy fight is yet another perfect opportunity for you to rack up needed Points. When you fight Sanctus, make sure that, having broken his shield and Halo to inflict massive damage and gain a huge boost in Stylish Points, you use Buster with Devil Trigger activated.

A New Beginning

Mission Highlights

Item	Description
Battle Statue	Dante: B Rank
Secret Mission 06	Vermifuge (page 237)
Secret Mission 07	Free Running (page 237)
Key Item	Wing Talisman, Key of Cronus

Ranking Objectives

Item	S	A	B	C	D
Time	≤ 10:00	10:01 - 12:00	12:01 - 14:30	14:31 - 17:00	≥ 17:01
Orbs (%)	≥ 95%	75% - 94%	60% - 74%	45% - 59%	≤ 44%
Stylish Points	≥ 7000	5000 - 6999	4000 - 4999	3000 - 3999	≤ 2999

Player Change

This Mission starts with a brief screen introducing the change of player. You'll now be playing the game as Dante. The total sum of Proud Souls that Nero has collected so far is now available for Dante to use to upgrade his abilities. Dante also has all the Health Meter and Devil Trigger Gauge upgrades that Nero has. Finally, all Red Orbs and Items are also carried over for Dante to use. Before starting the Mission, you'll be taken to the Power Up Menu, where you can upgrade Dante's abilities. Notable upgrades that you should consider are: Stinger, Stinger 2, Air Hike, Speed, Sword Master to Level 4, and Trigger Heart.

1 Ascension Chamber

Here you're confronted by 8 Scarecrows. Eliminate them and then exit this room via the door to the north.

2 Meeting Room

Through the door, there is a Divinity Statue to your left and a marker for Secret Mission 07: Free Running to your right. Continue forwards to the main, circular room, where you confront a new enemy, Mega Scarecrow. There are 3 of these large beasts to contend with. Take them out and then exit to the north.

3 Experiment Disposal

03_72 Go to the elevator and inspect the control column to gain the Wing Talisman for Dante's use. Activate the panel and ride down to the lower level. If you weren't able to get the Blue Orb Fragment with Nero, Dante can obtain it with Air Hike. First, Air Hike up to the first upper ledge. Jump out from there, then Air Hike again to the ledge above. You can see the fragment now, so Air Hike over to it to make it yours.

Leave the elevator room and a scene will be triggered. Now that the Savior is gone, the building's self-destruct system has been activated. You have 10 minutes to escape from the building. Walk forwards and fall to the area below. A Gold Orb is lying on the ground in the north-east corner. Activate the Emblem Switch in the south-west to lower the elevator. When you board the elevator, the door slams shut and you face 3 Frosts that you must defeat before the elevator can go up.

Map Legend:

- White Orb (S,M,L)
- Green Orb (S,M,L)
- Red Orb

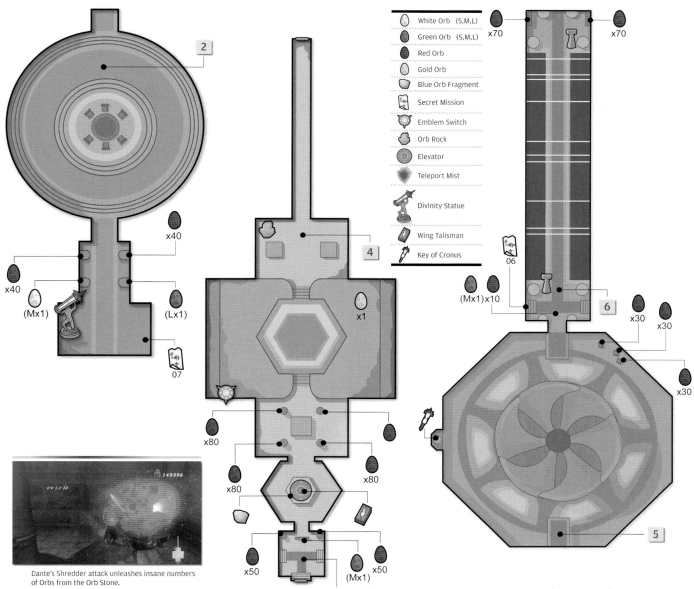

The legend/map includes:
- White Orb (S,M,L)
- Green Orb (S,M,L)
- Red Orb
- Gold Orb
- Blue Orb Fragment
- Secret Mission
- Emblem Switch
- Orb Rock
- Elevator
- Teleport Mist
- Divinity Statue
- Wing Talisman
- Key of Cronus

Dante's Shredder attack unleashes insane numbers of Orbs from the Orb Stone.

4 Bounty Of Orbs

When you reach the top of the shaft, quit the elevator and look for an Orb Stone to your left. Dante's Shredder with Sword Master is great for this. When you have finished with the Orb Stone, continue to the north and find a door into the next area.

5 Security Corridor

As soon as you come through the door, the ledge you are standing on falls to the ground below. A Red Seal rises, and you must dispatch 3 Mephistos. Dante's shotgun, "Coyote A", is the gun of choice for knocking the Mephistos out of the sky.

> **Pro Tip!**
> You can fire the shotgun more rapidly by jumping into the air first, and then tapping ⊗ | ⊡ as you fall.

After you've eliminated these demons, inspect the fan control module in the western wall and Dante will gain the Key of Cronus for his own use. When the fan stops, climb the blades to the top and leave this chamber via the door to the north.

6 Deadly Lasers

As you enter this room, you'll notice the marker for Secret Mission 06: Vermifuge. When you're ready, approach the Chrono Slicer and use it to slow time down. Now make your way carefully past the laser trap. As soon as you reach the far side of the room, break the benches to release Orbs, and then exit through the door.

7 Grand Hall

Cross the bridge over to the Grand Hall. In this room, a Red Seal will rise and you are confronted by 4 Bianco Angelos and 1 Alto Angelo. Try to keep the fight in the middle of the room so that you can also break the benches here for their Red Orbs. Take these demons out with Style. This is the last room of the timed run. Before you leave the building, take the door to the east.

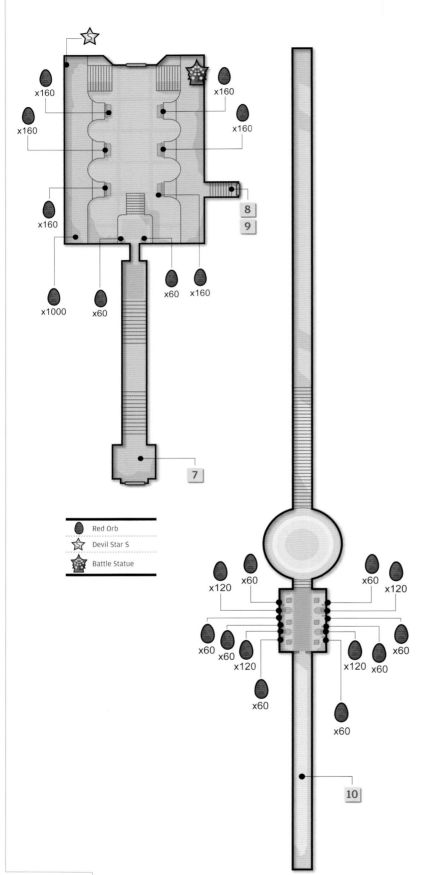

x160 x160 x160 x160 x160 x160 x60 x160 x1000 x60 x160

8
9

7

Red Orb
Devil Star S
Battle Statue

x120 x60 x60 x120
x60 x60 x120 x120 x60 x60

x60

x60

10

8 A Brief Detour

Proceed up the stairs to the first room, where you'll be attacked by a group of Gladius. Ignore them and use the Chrono Slicer to slow time down. Exit this room to the east.

9 Show Your Style

In spite of the time limit, make a detour to find this Battle Statue for Dante.

💻 03_73 Continue forwards and stand in the elevator pit in order to trigger the Orb Drop. Now go to the Battle Statue in the northern part of this room. To destroy this statue and claim the Blue Orb Fragment it holds, you need a B Rank. With that done, backtrack to the Grand Hall and take the door to the north to leave the building.

10 Gran Album Bridge

After a short scene, you're well out of the collapsing building and no longer hindered by a time limit. Follow the path ahead to the end and a scene will be triggered. When the scene is over, this Mission is complete.

S Ranking Tips

✦ Devil Points Required: **45,000**

Minimum S Rank Requirements

Criteria	Rank	Value
Time	S	10:00 or less
Stylish Points	A	5251 or more
Orbs Found	S	75% to 94%
Bonus	-	No Item

The S Rank time requirement for this Mission is a little tight, but it can be accomplished. Sword Master with Gilgamesh is a great choice. Switching quickly between Rebellion and Gilgamesh is a good technique, as Stinger can get you close to the enemy, while Gilgamesh can inflict heavy damage quickly. As you are unleashing your combos, switch between Sword Master and Gunslinger every so often, and use the shotgun for Fireworks and Gun Stinger to boost your Stylish Points.

Mission 13

The Devil Returns

Mission Highlights

Item	Description
Battle Statue	Dante: A Rank
Secret Mission 05*	Sky Scraper (page 237)
New Weapon	Gilgamesh
Boss Fight	Echidna

*Only Nero can complete this Secret Mission

Ranking Objectives

Item	S	A	B	C	D
Time	≤ 18:00	18:01 – 21:00	21:01 – 25:00	25:01 – 35:00	≥ 35:01
Orbs (%)	≥ 95%	75% – 94%	60% – 74%	45% – 59%	≤ 44%
Stylish Points	≥ 7000	5000 – 6999	4000 – 4999	3000 – 3999	≤ 2999

Destroy The Dragon

At the beginning of this Mission, you'll notice that the forest has changed since Nero was here. There are now spots of purple fog that will warp you to a different area in the forest. These fog patches have turned the forest into a veritable maze that Dante must now navigate until he reaches its end.

1 Ancient Training Ground

When the Mission starts, you'll notice a patch of purple fog behind you. This will warp you to the area below. If you want 100% for Red Orbs, go through the fog behind you, then move forwards along the path and break all the Orb Pods. When you reach the end of the path, there will be another patch of fog that will warp back to the Mission's starting point. As soon as you're ready, head north and go through the door to reach the next area.

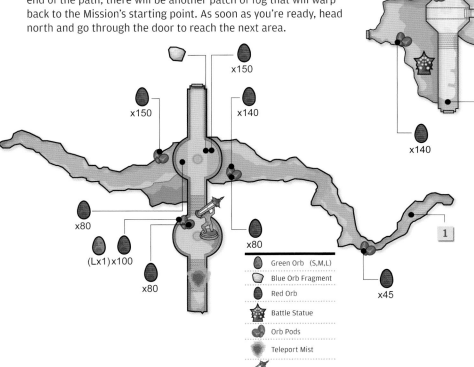

Green Orb (S,M,L)
Blue Orb Fragment
Red Orb
Battle Statue
Orb Pods
Teleport Mist
Divinity Statue

2 Forgotten Ruins

Make your way to the circular area near the centre of the path. Just ahead is a patch of fog that we don't advise you to cross. Instead, go to your right (east), where there is a small balcony. Approach it and jump over the edge to the ground below. Once there, you'll be attacked by 2 Scarecrows and 2 Chimera Seeds. Destroy them and then head up the path towards the south-east to the fog patch there and enter it.

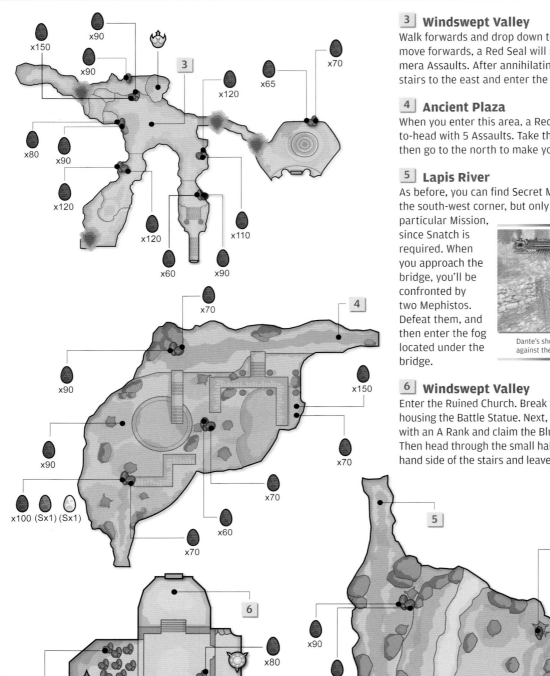

x150 x90

x90

3

x65 x70

x120

x80 x90

x120

x120 x110

x60 x90

3 Windswept Valley

Walk forwards and drop down to the area below. As you move forwards, a Red Seal will rise and you meet 3 Chimera Assaults. After annihilating these beasts, take the stairs to the east and enter the fog patch.

4 Ancient Plaza

When you enter this area, a Red Seal rises and you're head-to-head with 5 Assaults. Take these demons apart, and then go to the north to make your way out of this area.

5 Lapis River

As before, you can find Secret Mission 05: Sky Scraper in the south-west corner, but only Nero can complete this particular Mission, since Snatch is required. When you approach the bridge, you'll be confronted by two Mephistos. Defeat them, and then enter the fog located under the bridge.

Dante's shotgun is the weapon of choice against the Mephistos.

6 Windswept Valley

Enter the Ruined Church. Break the Orb Pods in the room housing the Battle Statue. Next, destroy the Battle Statue with an A Rank and claim the Blue Orb Fragment it holds. Then head through the small hallway at the base of the left-hand side of the stairs and leave through the door there.

x70

4

x90

x150

x90

x70

x100 (Sx1) (Sx1)

x70

x70

x60

x70

5

x60 (Sx1)

6

x80

x90

x85

x90

x1300

x500

05

(Sx1) x80

x210 x120 x60 x100

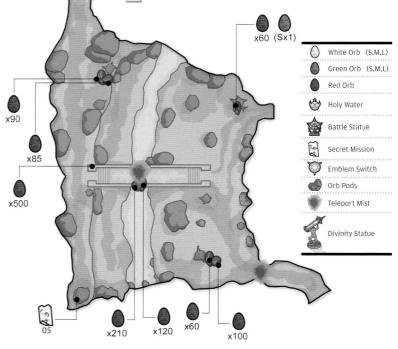

	White Orb	(S,M,L)
	Green Orb	(S,M,L)
	Red Orb	
	Holy Water	
	Battle Statue	
	Secret Mission	
	Emblem Switch	
	Orb Pods	
	Teleport Mist	
	Divinity Statue	

7 Lost Woods

03_74 As you move forwards, you're attacked by 2 Chimera Assaults. Vanquish these beasts and move to the crossroads at the centre of this area. You now face the forest's light puzzle. Approach the statue at the centre of the crossroads and note the shadow it casts on the ground. Your exit is on the opposite side, since that's where the light comes from. This time, there are four paths to take, in the following sequence: east, west, south, south. Assuming you don't change the camera angle, this equates to: Straight, Backwards, Right, Right. If you follow this route you'll warp to the next area.

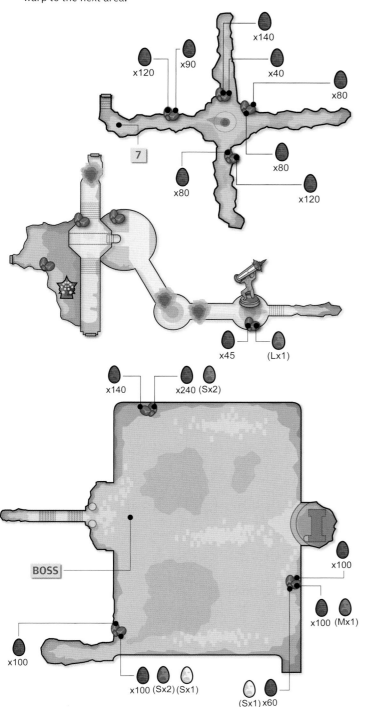

Boss 10 Echidna

Get on the leaves when she is in Birthing form to attack her directly.

The full strategy for this Boss is listed in the Opponents Chapter. Here are a few tips.

Sword Master is the Style of choice, due to its Aerial Rave attack. When Echidna is in Snake form (female body exposed), jump towards her and use the Aerial Rave attack. High Time is also a good opening choice, when you are on the ground in front of her. When she switches to Birthing form, either attack the Seed Tube with Aerial Rave, or use Air Hike to reach the upper level and attack her body directly.

As before, she will dive at you in Dragon form. You can either evade to avoid damage, or, as she approaches, use a properly timed High Time attack to phase through her. You can also switch to Royal Guard and use Royal Block to counter the Dragon attack. As soon as she has been vanquished, a scene will be triggered, and Dante will gain a new weapon, Gilgamesh. A brief tutorial will be displayed, explaining how to switch melée weapons. When you're ready, exit to the south-west and the Mission will end.

S Ranking Tips

Devil Points Required: 50,000

Minimum S Rank Requirements

Criteria	Rank	Value
Time	S	18:00 or less
Stylish Points	B	4945 or more
Orbs Found	S	75% to 94%
Bonus	-	No Item

This is a short Mission, so you'll have few opportunities to get your Stylish Points. The fight against the Assaults in the Ancient Plaza at Point 04 is a great time to rack up much needed points. Fight as Stylishly as possible against every enemy, and make sure to S Rank Time and Orbs. When you face Echidna, equip Pandora as your gun and Sword Master as your Style. Using Aerial Rave on her female body, followed by a switch to the Dark Slayer Style and its Aerial Rave, is a great way to rack up Stylish Points against her. When she dives at you in Dragon form, use Pandora's Epidemic to stop her in her tracks and boost your Stylish Points at the same time.

Forest of Ruin

Mission Highlights

Item	Description
Secret Mission 05*	Sky Scraper (page 237)
Secret Mission 08	Royal Blocker (page 238)

*Only Nero can complete this Secret Mission.

Ranking Objectives

Item	S	A	B	C	D
Time	≤ 18:00	18:01 – 21:00	21:01 – 25:00	25:01 – 35:00	≥ 35:01
Orbs (%)	≥ 95%	75% – 94%	60% – 74%	45% – 59%	≤ 44%
Stylish Points	≥ 6000	4000 – 5999	3000 – 3999	2000 – 2999	≤ 1999

Run For It

Dante has defeated the Queen of Mitis Forest and must now find his way out. The path is difficult, and he must watch his step if he intends to make it out of the forest alive.

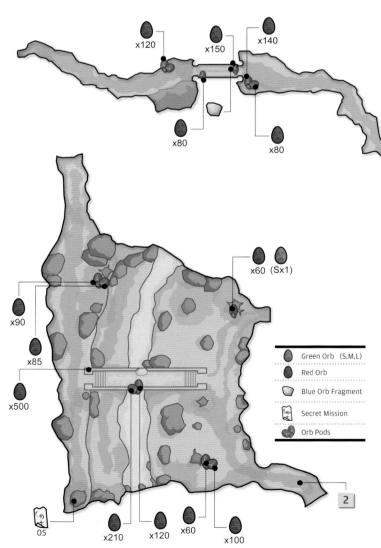

1 Ancient Training Ground

03_75   As you find your way up the path, a scene is triggered, introducing a new enemy, Fault. These demons will appear beneath you and drag you down to the Ruined Lowlands, a pit filled with demons that you must defeat in order to get out. Gilgamesh does a great job, taking Fault out with one hit.

If you're quick, you can kill a Fault!

Move forwards along the path and avoid the 3 Faults that appear. Go through the arched tunnel. When you reach the other side, a Red Seal will rise. You'll be confronted by 2 Scarecrows and 2 Chimera seeds, as well as 2 Faults. The Faults are stationary, so avoid their hiding places. Eliminate the Seeds and Scarecrows, and then continue up the path to the exit.

2 Lapis River

As you enter this area, a Red Seal will rise and you must get rid of 2 Mephistos and a Faust. You'll also have to contend with the Faults that appear. Take these demons out, and the Seal will fall. As before, Secret Mission 05: Sky Scraper is located in the south-west corner, but only Nero can complete this one, so ignore it. When you're ready, exit to the north-west.

Green Orb (S,M,L)
Red Orb
Blue Orb Fragment
Secret Mission
Orb Pods

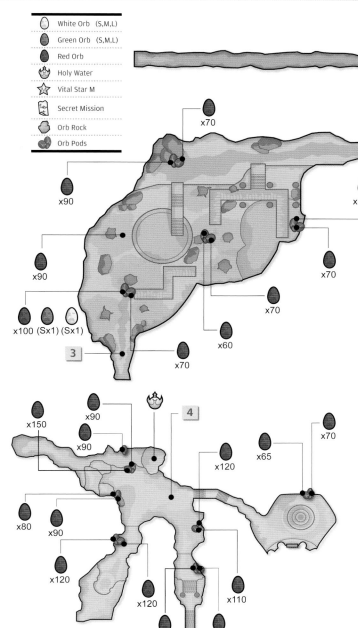

Legend:
- White Orb (S,M,L)
- Green Orb (S,M,L)
- Red Orb
- Holy Water
- Vital Star M
- Secret Mission
- Orb Rock
- Orb Pods

4 Windswept Valley

You're trapped behind yet another Red Seal in this area. Here, you must contend with 4 Chimera Scarecrows and 2 Chimera Assaults. Eliminate these monsters, and then proceed to the cliffs located in the north-west. Climb to the top using Air Hike or Kick Jump and then continue forwards to the exit.

5 Forest Entrance

03_76   In this area you'll find an Orb Stone and the entrance to Secret Mission 08: Royal Blocker, which only Dante can complete. There are plenty of Orb Pods to break as well but, other than that, this area is clear. When you're ready, go down the tunnel to the north-west and follow it to Foris Falls. Once there, Cross the bridge to the far side and a scene will be triggered, thus ending the Mission.

S Ranking Tips

❖ Devil Points Required: **42,500**

Minimum S Rank Requirements

Criteria	Rank	Value
Time	S	18:00 or less
Stylish Points	A	4403 or more
Orbs Found	S	75% to 94%
Bonus	-	No Item

With so few fights in this Mission, S Ranking Time and Orbs becomes quite important. In particular, pay attention to the opening area, Ancient Training Ground, as there are Orb Pods on the bridge above your path. You can get up there using a pedestal to the right of the small tunnel. The fights at Points 03 and 04 are the big ones in this Mission, so you need pull out all the stops to rack up the required Stylish Points.

There isn't a Boss at the end of this fight, so you'll need to get all your points from the enemies here. If you need more combat, allow a Fault to pull you down into the pit to face the enemies. If you do this, make sure you get the Orb Pods and Orb Drop that are down there. In this Mission, Sword Master is a great choice for your Style, especially using Dance Macabre on two or more enemies at once.

3 Ancient Plaza

When you enter this area, a Red Seal will rise and you must defeat 5 Assaults. There are also Faults in the area. The safest place to deal with the Assaults is in the small pit in the centre of the area. Jump in and immediately kill the Fault that appears. You'll now be free to deal with the Assaults without having to worry about a Fault appearing beneath you. When you've finished, exit to the north-east.

Destroy the Fault in this pit and you can fight the Assaults in peace.

Fortuna Castle

Mission Highlights

Item	Description
Battle Statue	Dante: SS Rank
Secret Mission 02*	Alley-Oop (page 235)
Secret Mission 03	Non-violent Resistance (page 236)
Secret Mission 09	Unbreakable (page 238)
Secret Mission 10*	Puppet Master (page 238)
New Weapon	Pandora
Boss Fight	Dagon

*Only Nero can complete this Secret Mission.

Ranking Objectives

Item	S	A	B	C	D
Time	≤ 28:00	28:01 – 31:00	31:01 – 35:00	35:01 – 45:00	≥ 45:01
Orbs (%)	≥ 95%	75% – 94%	60% – 74%	45% – 59%	≤ 44%
Stylish Points	≥ 11500	9500 – 11499	7500 – 9499	5000 – 7499	≤ 4999

A Chilling Encounter

Something has happened in the Castle to block Dante's path. In order to get out, he'll have to find the source of the problem and rectify it with Style.

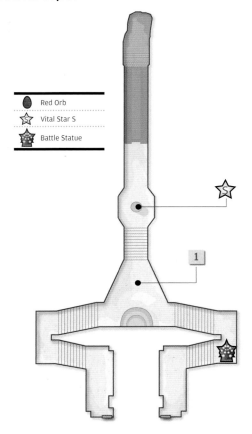

Red Orb
Vital Star S
Battle Statue

1 Foris Falls

Go up the stairs, where there are two paths. The door at the end of the right-hand path is blocked by a wall of ice. Head left instead and, mid-way up, you'll find a Battle Statue. This one requires an SS Rank for you to be able to destroy it. As soon as you've finished, continue up the stairs to the exit door.

2 Central Courtyard

Move down the walkway and a scene will be triggered, introducing a new enemy, Blitz. A Red Seal also rises. After you've seen off this demon, continue down the path to the exit.

When Blitz overcharges, he will try to grab you for the final explosion!

3 Grand Hall

03_77 When you enter the Grand Hall, a scene will be triggered, showing you that it's full of ice. You can't access the lower floor because of it, so head to the eastern side of the room. Just past the Emblem Switch is a door, which is your exit

To get the high Orb Drop on the column to the left of the Portrait of Sanctus, activate DT and use a triple jump to easily make it to the top.

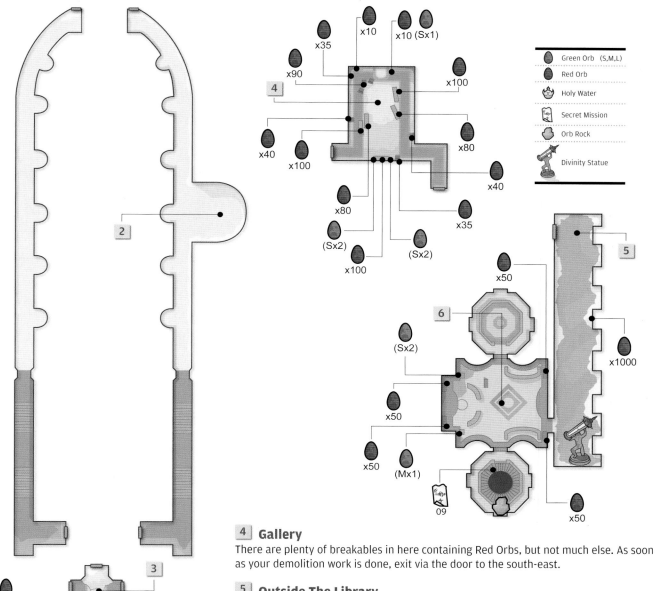

Green Orb (S,M,L)
Red Orb
Holy Water
Secret Mission
Orb Rock
Divinity Statue

04

4 Gallery
There are plenty of breakables in here containing Red Orbs, but not much else. As soon as your demolition work is done, exit via the door to the south-east.

5 Outside The Library
There's an Orb Drop on this small balcony. It's the same one that was here when Nero came through. You'll need Air Hike to reach it. After this, continue down to the Divinity Statue and the door.

6 Library
As you come in through the doorway, a Red Seal will rise and you'll come up against 1 Alto Angelo and 4 Bianco Angelos. Take these armoured beasts out, and the Red Seal will fall. You'll now notice a new room to the south that was not available to Nero. Enter, and you'll find an Orb Stone and a staircase leading down. At the bottom of the stairs is a door but, before you go through it, check to the left, where you'll find the marker for Secret Mission 09: Unbreakable. When you're done here, go through the door.

Turn away from the door to spy the marker for the Secret Mission.

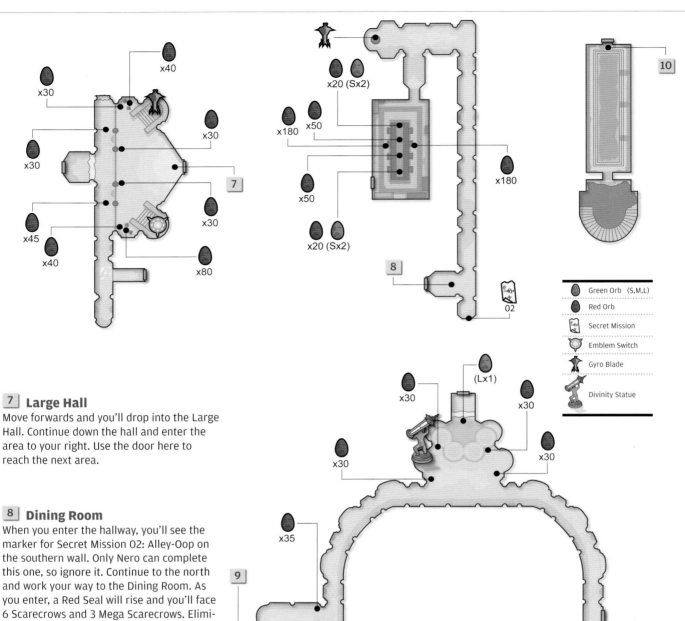

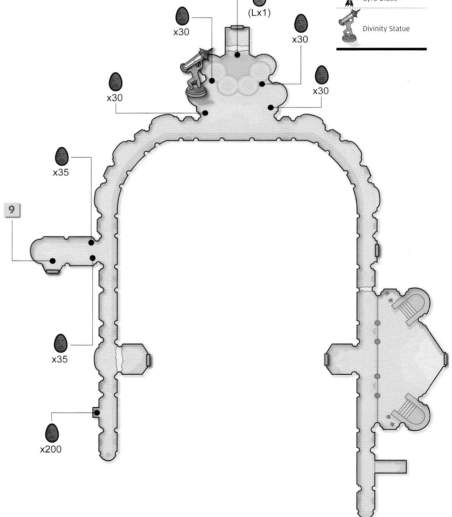

Green Orb (S,M,L)

Red Orb

Secret Mission

Emblem Switch

Gyro Blade

Divinity Statue

7 Large Hall

Move forwards and you'll drop into the Large Hall. Continue down the hall and enter the area to your right. Use the door here to reach the next area.

8 Dining Room

When you enter the hallway, you'll see the marker for Secret Mission 02: Alley-Oop on the southern wall. Only Nero can complete this one, so ignore it. Continue to the north and work your way to the Dining Room. As you enter, a Red Seal will rise and you'll face 6 Scarecrows and 3 Mega Scarecrows. Eliminate these demon puppets and then take the exit to the south-west.

9 Large Hall

There are breakables in this hallway, as well as two large Red Orbs hidden behind a breakable mirror at the southern end of the Hall. When you've finished, the exit is the door in the small alcove on the western wall, a short distance before the breakable mirror.

10 Torture Chamber

Here, a Red Seal will rise and you'll meet 5 Frosts. Destroy these icy beasts with your best moves to lower the Seal and then go south to the doorway. You'll find yourself in front of a large pit where the floor was destroyed by Nero. Walk forwards and fall to the area below.

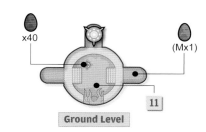

Ground Level

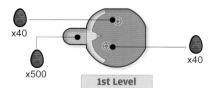

x40
x500

1st Level

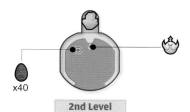

x40

2nd Level

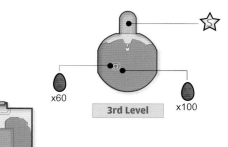

x60 x100

3rd Level

11 Spiral Well

On your way down to the bottom of this well, you'll pass several Jump Pads and large Red Orbs. When you reach the bottom, give yourself a few moments to use the Jump Pads to collect all the Orbs. From the 2nd Jump Pad, you can reach a ledge where a small alcove contains an Orb Drop. From the 3rd Jump Pad, you can reach a ledge that has an Orb Stone on it.

When you've finished collecting Orbs, drop back to the bottom of the well and activate the Emblem Switch, which you'll find in the small northern alcove. This activates a supercharged Jump Pad that will catapult you to the top, past the ledge you were originally on and on to the ledge above it. Once there, walk to the end of the catwalk to reach the exit door.

12 Master's Chamber

A Red Seal rises in this room, and you have 4 Scarecrows and a Blitz to deal with. The Blitz will appear after you've killed two of the Scarecrows. Behind the breakable mirror above the fireplace you'll find the marker for Secret Mission 10: Puppet Master. Only Nero can complete that particular Secret Mission, so ignore it. The exit is the door to the north.

13 Soldiers' Graveyard

03_79 Make your way down the stairs. Behind these is a small alcove, where you'll find the marker for Secret Mission 03: Non-violent Resistance. There are many breakables here as well. There are also two Orb Drops against the eastern wall. Finally, there is a large Red Orb on a spire projecting from the western wall. If you were unable to get the Gold Orb with Nero in Mission 05, it's available now. You'll need Trickster at Level 3 to get these hard-to-reach Orbs. There is a Divinity Statue here that you can use to refund enough Proud Souls to enable you to take Trickster to Level 3 for this task.

When you're ready, break the statue on the central column in the middle of this area. Stand on top of the column and face the spire directly across from you. Equip the Trickster Style. Now use Air Hike to double jump towards the spire and, at the apex of

Dante can reach the spire by using Sky Star with the Trickster Style.

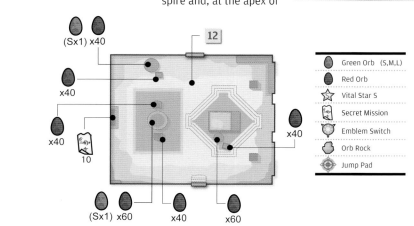

	Green Orb (S,M,L)
	Red Orb
	Vital Star S
	Secret Mission
	Emblem Switch
	Orb Rock
	Jump Pad

your jump, use Trickster's Sky Star to land on it. Face the Red Orb, double jump towards it, and then use Sky Star to dash over to the spire to get the Red Orb. If the Gold Orb is still here, use Air Hike and Sky Star to cross back to the middle spire, and then again, to reach the Gold Orb. When all this has been accomplished, exit this area via the door to the north-east.

Boss 11 Dagon

As with Bael in Mission 04, you must first deal with the Rusalkas. If a Rusalka grabs you, use Devil Trigger to break free. Once Dagon appears, attack him anywhere on his body, but his face is the real weak spot. You can climb on his back by moving

When Dagon is unconscious, use Gilgamesh's Real Impact for major damage!

to his side near his tail and then use Air Hike. Once on his back, use your most powerful melée attacks, before he throws you off. Rebellion's Round Trip is great for when he moves away from you. If Dagon ever freezes you, or grabs you in his mouth, you can immediately free yourself by activating Devil Trigger. When Dagon ices himself over, attack the Rusalkas and, from time to time, you'll get some Green Orbs.

Once the fight is over, you obtain a new gun, Pandora. You then find yourself on a ledge in a deep shaft. You'll remember this as the shaft in the Underground Laboratory in Nero's Mission. To end the Mission, step off the ledge and fall to the bottom.

S Ranking Tips

Devil Points Required: 70,000

Minimum S Rank Requirements

Criteria	Rank	Value
Time	S	28:00 or less
Stylish Points	B	8112 or more
Orbs Found	A	75% to 94%
Bonus	-	No Item

You'll want to S Rank your time, but there are several hard-to-reach Orbs that you'll want to forget about. This is a lengthy Mission, so there are plenty of enemies to battle with. When facing a Frost, make sure you destroy the healing ice it wraps itself in so that you can gain an instant Stylish Boost. If you kill Blitz before he can self-destruct, you get a huge boost in Style as well. When facing Dagon, using Rebellion's Round Trip is excellent for when he moves away. If you knock him unconscious, use Sword Master with Gilgamesh's Real Impact to inflict devastating damage and give yourself a huge boost in Style.

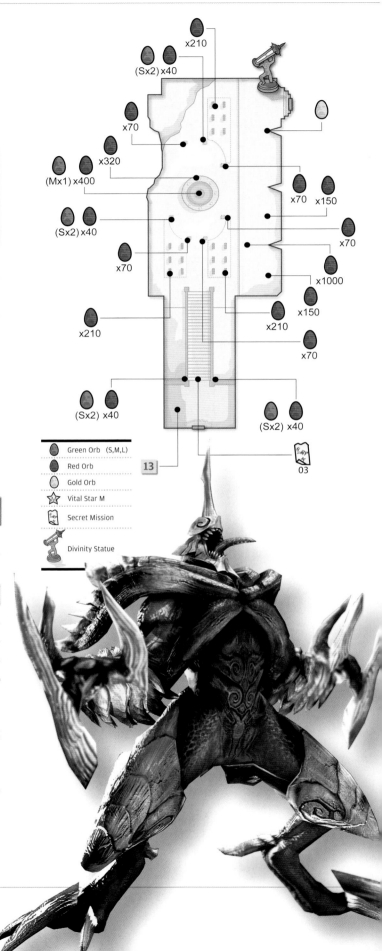

Green Orb (S,M,L)
Red Orb
Gold Orb
Vital Star M
Secret Mission
Divinity Statue

Mission 16

Inferno

Mission Highlights

Item	Description
Blue Orb Fragment	Quantity: 1
Battle Statue	Dante: S Rank
Secret Mission 04	Tracking Treasure Down (page 236)
New Weapon	Lucifer
Boss Fight	Berial

Ranking Objectives

Item	S	A	B	C	D
Time	≤ 25:00	25:01 – 28:00	28:01 – 33:00	33:01 – 40:00	≥ 40:01
Orbs (%)	≥ 95%	75% – 94%	60% – 74%	45% – 59%	≤ 44%
Stylish Points	≥ 10000	8000 – 9999	6500 – 7999	4500 – 6499	≤ 4499

Conqueror Of The Fire Hell

After the chilling events in the Castle, a little warmth would be appreciated. However, there is more than just a little heat waiting for Dante on the path ahead of him.

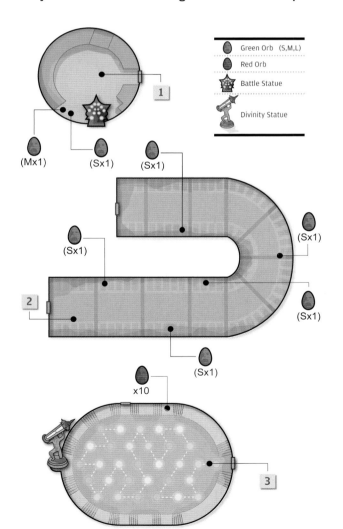

Green Orb (S,M,L)

Red Orb

Battle Statue

Divinity Statue

1 Underground Laboratory

You start this Mission in the midst of a poisonous gas that built up once the shaft sealed and the fan stopped turning. While you are in the gas, you will take constant damage from breathing it. This equates to 1 cell of your Health Meter every 12 seconds.

Even though poisonous gas fills the room, you have time to destroy the Battle Statue.

There are green orbs in this room as well as a Battle Statue. You'll need an S Rank to destroy this one and claim its Blue Orb Fragment. When you're done here, use the door found to the East to exit this room.

2 R&D Access

03_80 Move forward in this tunnel and a Red Seal will rise. You are faced with 3 Cutlass. Destroy them in a stylish manner. There are Green Orbs in the tunnel to replenish your Health, and each enemy you defeat also drops Green Orbs. You'll find the exit at the end of the tunnel.

3 Game Room

After a short scene, you find that the room is filled with Gladius. There are 12 in total, but you don't have to fight them. You can simply exit this room via the door to the North instead. When you are ready, take the door to the next area.

4 | Containment Room

As you enter this room, a Red Seal will rise and you face 12 Gladius and 2 Bianco Angelos. Use the shotgun to knock the Gladius to the ground where they are easier prey. Once you have killed all the demons, the Red Seal will fall. Jump up through the broken glass barrier, and use the door to the North.

5 | Foris Falls

You are now outside and away from the poisonous gas. You can breath easier for the time being. Once you climb the stairs to the upper level, you'll notice a broken railing. If you didn't get the Blue Orb Fragment that is here when Nero passed through, now is a good time to use Stinger with Dante to reach it. You can also use Pandora with Gunslinger to activate Argument and glide to the fragment. When you're ready, exit through the door.

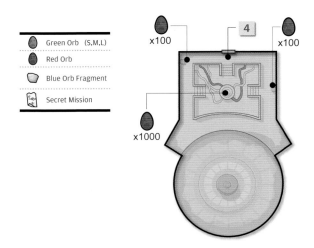

🟢	Green Orb (S,M,L)
🔴	Red Orb
⬜	Blue Orb Fragment
📄	Secret Mission

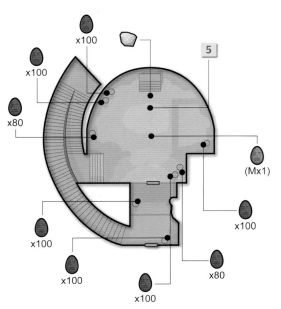

6 | Angel Creation

You are back in the poison gas, so be quick. As you enter the next room a Red Seal rises and you face 3 Bianco Angelos. Once you have done away with them, you'll find the marker for Secret Mission 04: Tracking Treasure Down. This is technically for Nero since the secret detecting Rusalka Corpse makes it easier. It is possible for Dante to complete this Mission, but it's best to save this one for Nero. Take the stairs in the Northwest to the upper area.

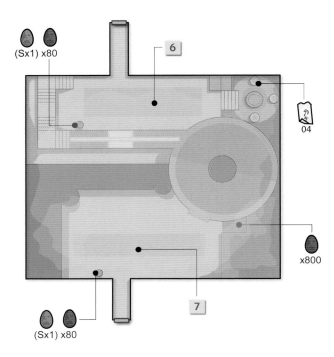

7 | Heavy Metal Assault

Move forward to the circular landing and walk past the break in the railing to the South to drop down to the lower area. Once there, a Red Seal will rise and you face 2 Alto Angelos and 3 Bianco Angelos. Dispatch these armoured monstrosities to lower the Seal, and then exit this area via the door you'll find to the South.

8 | Underground Laboratory

Here, you find that the poison gas has disappeared so you can finally breath a bit easier for the rest of this Mission. Walk into the shaft ahead and use the Jump Pads to reach the top. In this shaft you will discover ledges with breakable barrels on them. You can reach the ledges from the 2nd, 3rd, and 5th Jump Pads if you so choose. Once you reach the top, there is one more barrel to your right. Now head to the South to reach the exit.

9 | Grand Hall

Make your way up the stairs to the hall above. A short scene will inform you that the ice has been melted and you can leave the Castle. When you're ready, exit the hall by the Southern door.

To get the high Orb Drop on the column to the left of the Portrait of Sanctus, activate DT and use a triple jump to easily make it to the top.

04

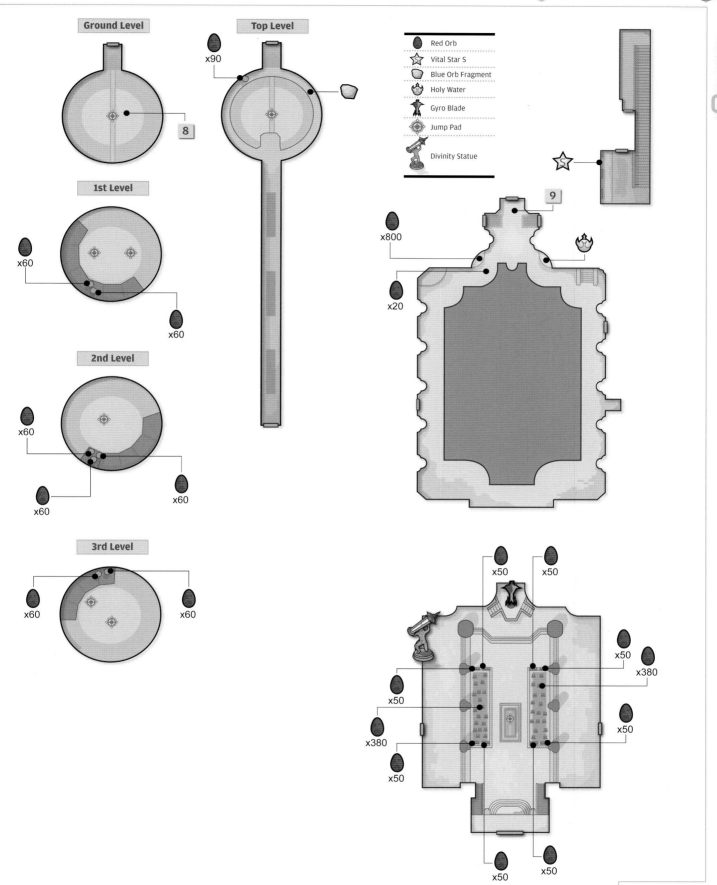

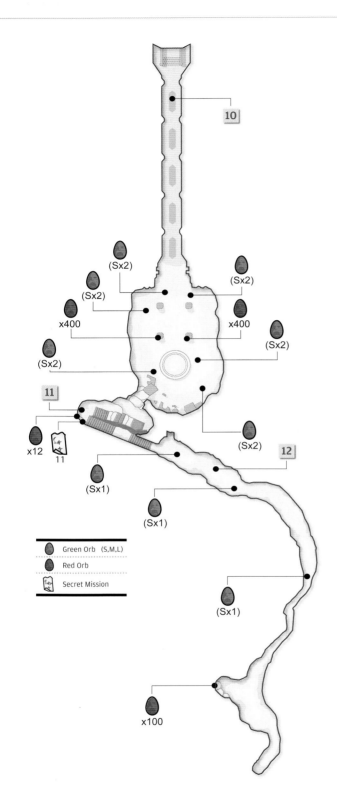

x400

x400

(Sx2)
(Sx2)
(Sx2)
(Sx2)
(Sx2)

10

11

11
x12

12

(Sx1)

(Sx1)

	Green Orb (S,M,L)
	Red Orb
	Secret Mission

(Sx2)

(Sx1)

x100

10 Fortuna Castle Gate

Once you make your way to the snow field, a scene will trigger that introduces a new enemy, Basilisk. These dog-like demons have a flaming head that they can launch at you. The head will quickly re-grow and they can repeat this attack. A Red Seal has risen making this a required fight. After you have destroyed these fiery beasts, there are two Orb Drops to be found on two of the taller columns here. Take the path in the south-west and go upwards.

11 Well Hidden Secret

Once you pass the long run of broken staircase, you'll come to a small landing with a large staircase to your left. This is the last staircase before reaching the top. On this small clearing, you'll notice small Red Orbs hovering against the back wall. These orbs lead to the marker for Secret Mission 11: Point of Impact which is located on a small hidden ledge above you.

Pandora's Argument makes it simple to reach this hidden Secret Mission.

The easiest way to reach this ledge is to stand at the top of the large staircase to your left. Equip the Gunslinger Style and Pandora. Now jump into the air and activate Argument. Once you have done so, glide over to the ledge. You'll have to fill the Disaster Gauge in order to do this. After you're done with the Secret Mission, make your way up the large staircase and enter the next area.

12 A Warm Welcome

Here you will be attacked by 3 Basilisk. Destroy these beasts and then continue onward to the left. After a bit of a trek you will finally reach the exit in the South.

13 Second Mining Area

03_81   Make your way to the large mining chamber and drop down to the bottom of the shaft. During the fall, you will pass a Jump Pad and you will find another one at the bottom. These weren't here when Nero came through, which is a clue that there is something secret here. The secret is a Blue Orb Fragment.

To reach the hidden fragment, face the first Jump Pad and use it to reach the 2nd one. Once you bounce from the 2nd pad, pull back on the Left Analog Stick and hold it back the entire time. Your goal is to land on a small ledge to the South. Once you are on this ledge, break the wooden barrier before you and then walk into the alcove to claim the fragment. Now, drop back down to the bottom.

Exit this chamber to the left and follow the tracks straight ahead to find an Orb Stone hidden behind a breakable wooden barrier. Next, follow the curve of the tracks to the south where you'll find a Divinity Statue and the exit.

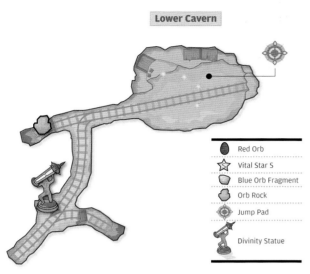

Lower Cavern

⬮	Red Orb
☆	Vital Star S
⬠	Blue Orb Fragment
⬡	Orb Rock
◈	Jump Pad
⚒	Divinity Statue

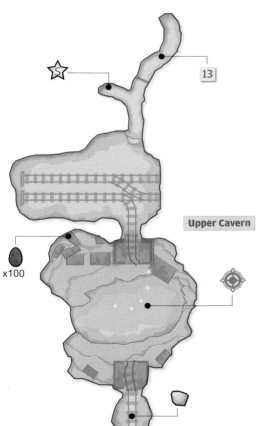

13

Upper Cavern

x100

Boss 12 **Berial**

A full strategy for getting through Berial can be found in the Opponents chapter. We will just offer you a few tips for this battle here.

When Berial's flames are out, attack him without mercy!

His head is his weak spot, so get close and jump up to attack it. Sword Master is a good Style for this fight. Gilgamesh does good damage and is a great weapon to use. When Berial is walking about the area, you have time to switch to Gunslinger and use Pandora's Revenge if you wish. When you do enough damage and extinguish his flames, he will be immobile for several seconds, so use this time to unleash a flurry of your most devastating moves.

Once the fight is over, a scene triggers and Dante gains a new melee weapon: Lucifer. After a brief Tutorial on your new weapon, go to the south to find the exit to end this Mission.

S Ranking Tips

Devil Points Required: **70,000**

Minimum S Rank Requirements

Criteria	Rank	Value
Time	S	25:00 or less
Stylish Points	A	8112 or more
Orbs Found	A	75% to 94%
Bonus	-	No Item

S Rank your time as usual but again, there are some hard to reach orbs that are better skipped. In particular the one on the high ledge to the left of Sanctus' portrait in the Grand Hall. You can get up there using Pandora. You'll have to fill the Disaster Gauge and equip the Gunslinger style. Then you need to use the Jump Pad in the centre of the room, and at the apex of your jump, activate Pandora's Argument and then glide over to the ledge and land on it. This is a lengthy procedure, so you're better off S Ranking Time and sacrificing those orbs. Just get the Stylish Points needed, and you'll S Rank the Mission.

Adagio For Strings

Mission Highlights

Item	Description
Blue Orb Fragment	Quantity: 1
Secret Mission 12	Steeplechase (page 239)
New Weapon	Yamato
New Style	Dark Slayer
Boss Fight	Angelo Agnus

Ranking Objectives

Item	S	A	B	C	D
Time	≤ 18:00	18:01 – 21:00	21:01 – 25:00	25:01 – 35:00	≥ 35:01
Orbs (%)	≥ 95%	75% – 94%	60% – 74%	45% – 59%	≤ 44%
Stylish Points	≥ 17000	13000 – 16999	9500 – 12999	6500 – 9499	≤ 6499

Regain Yamato

Yamato was taken from Nero by Sanctus and used by Agnus to open the Hell Gate. The sword once belonged to Dante's brother Vergil, and Dante means to get it back.

Green Orb	(S,M,L)
Red Orb	
Battle Statue	
Divinity Statue	

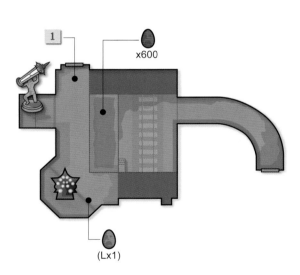

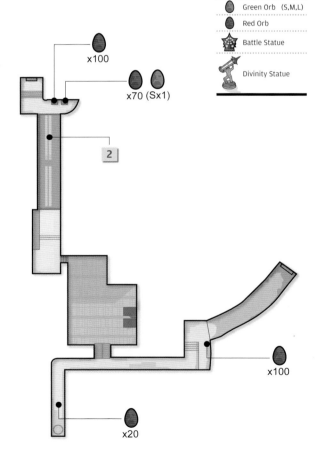

1 First Mining Area

There is a Divinity Statue in this room as well as a Blue Battle Statue for Nero. Drop to the lower level and claim the large Red Orbs in the water canal, then move down the eastern hallway to find the exit.

2 Port Caerula

Work your way across the drawbridge to the first dock. There, a Red Seal will rise and you face 7 Scarecrows, 2 Bianco Angelos, and 1 Alto Angelo. Dispatch this horde with demonic ferocity and the Seal will fall. Head up the ramp and you can find a large Red Orb to your right. Go left to enter the tunnel and find the door to the next area.

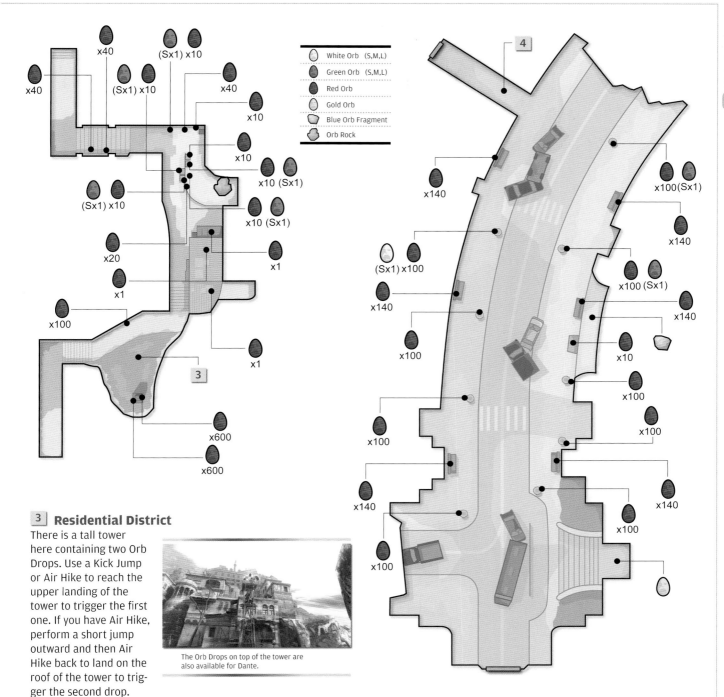

The Orb Drops on top of the tower are also available for Dante.

3 **Residential District**

There is a tall tower here containing two Orb Drops. Use a Kick Jump or Air Hike to reach the upper landing of the tower to trigger the first one. If you have Air Hike, perform a short jump outward and then Air Hike back to land on the roof of the tower to trigger the second drop.

Head to the north and go through the doorway. A Red Seal will rise and you are attacked by 2 Mephistos and 5 Assaults. Once you have done away with this pack of hellions, there is an Orb Stone you can destroy. The exit is up the stairs and to the north.

4 **Business District / Terrace**

03_82   Make your way to the street and head south. A Red Seal will rise locking you in combat with 12 Scarecrows, 2 Mega Scarecrows, and 3 Basilisks. Move about the street and destroy them all.

Once you've defeated that demonic army, you'll find a Blue Orb Fragment on the upper level of a building on the west side of the street. You'll need Air Hike and Trickster's Sky Star to reach it. Make your way to the "Restaurant-Cafe" where you'll see a Red Orb resting on the blue awning over the front door. Jump onto the awning. Equip Trickster style. Air Hike up so that your even with the upper balcony, then Sky Star over the railing. Claim the fragment and return to the street below. Make your way to the southern end of the street to exit this area.

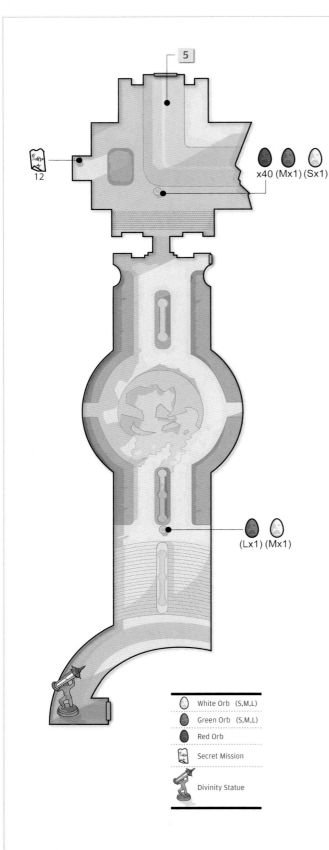

x40 (Mx1) (Sx1)

(Lx1) (Mx1)

	White Orb (S,M,L)
	Green Orb (S,M,L)
	Red Orb
	Secret Mission
	Divinity Statue

5 Opera House Plaza

On the Eastern side of this small area is an alcove with a trash bin. Break the bin to expose the marker for Secret Mission 12: Steeplechase. Next, go through the doorway to the south to reach the main Plaza. Here a Red Seal will rise and you must defeat 2 Mephistos, 2 Alto Angelos, and 1 Faust. After you have smoked them all, head south to find the door which leads to the next area.

Boss 13 **Angelo Agnus**

The full strategy for defeating this Boss is in the Opponents Chapter. Here are a few tips.

Gilgamesh is a great weapon for this fight as it does serious damage to Agnus rather quickly. You can destroy the enemies he summons

If Agnus grabs you to drain your health, activate Devil Trigger to break free.

to the fight for white orbs meaning Devil Trigger can be used freely during this fight. Sword Master is a great style to use. With Rebellion equipped, you can jump toward Agnus and attack him repeatedly while you are in the air. Once you've done enough damage to make Agnus dizzy, approach him quickly and unleash your most devastating attacks with Gilgamesh.

Agnus has two attacks that he uses to drain your health, so he can use it himself. When he attempts these, attack him quickly to interrupt them. If he does grab you with the weaker absorb attack, activate Devil Trigger to immediately break free. Once the fight is over, an elevator pad appears. Jump onto the pad to trigger a scene in which Dante gains Yamato and the mission ends.

S Ranking Tips

Devil Points Required: 100,000

Minimum S Rank Requirements

Criteria	Rank	Value
Time	S	18:00 or less
Stylish Points	B	11389 or more
Orbs Found	S	75% to 94%
Bonus	-	No Item

This Mission requires a lot of Stylish Points. While that number might appear high, there is a lot of combat in this Mission, so getting this many points or even more is not a problem. Sword Master with Rebellion and Gilgamesh are an excellent pairing to mow through the enemies and get the points you need. Use Real Impact with Gilgamesh when you can. It's particularly easy to use this manoeuvre on the Mega Scarecrows. When you face Agnus, he will often be motionless on the ground, and that is a great time to unleash Real Impact on him to inflict major damage and get Stylish Points.

Mission 18

The Destroyer

Mission Highlights

Item	Description
Boss Fight	The Savior

Ranking Objectives

Item	S	A	B	C	D
Time	≤ 10:00	10:01 – 12:00	12:01 – 14:30	14:31 – 17:00	≥ 17:01
Orbs (%)*	100%	100%	100%	100%	100%
Stylish Points	≥ 5000	4000 – 4999	3000 – 3999	2000 – 2999	≤ 1999

* There are no set orbs to be found in this mission. Automatic 100% given.

Confront The Savior

In this Mission, Dante faces The Savior in the skies above Fortuna City. The Savior means to destroy Dante at all costs, but Dante has other plans. The Hell Gate has been sealed, and Dante means to dispatch this demonic behemoth as well.

Boss 14 **The Savior – Part 1**

A full strategy for this fight is provided in the Opponents chapter. We will just outline the basics and give you a few tips here.

Suggested Preparation for Part 1

Item	Description	Status
Style	Trickster	Fully levelled
Melee Weapon	Gilgamesh	Kick 13 acquired
Gun	Shotgun	Standard
Ability	Air Hike	Standard

Start by concentrating on the Cores on his legs and back. Once the mission starts move forward to the first Jump Pad before you. On the next platform, go right to find another Jump Pad to use. When you land on the next platform, go right and look for the Red Jump Pad;

The Jump Pad on the right takes you to the Cores on the legs and back.

use it to reach the upper level. There, activate the Pulse Cannon to knock The Savior out and you will be placed on a different platform with two Jump Pads.

Take the pad on your right, and you find your first Core on the left leg. Destroy it, then go right to the next pad. Now you face the Core on the left wrist. Take it out, then use the pad to your right. Go right and down the stairs to the Core on The Savior's back and destroy it. Now walk towards the camera to find a Jump Pad on a fallen column. When you reach the next platform, there will be a Red Pad on your left and a Blue Pad on your right.

Take the Blue Pad to reach the next platform and the Core on his right leg. Destroy the Core, then backtrack to your left to the previous platform. At this point you are nearly out of time, but use the Red Pad to reach the upper area. There you will find the Cores on the right wrist and shoulder. Begin attacking the wrist Core until the Savior awakens, which causes you to fall to another platform.

The Blue Pad on your right takes you to the Core on his right leg.

The Laser Turret easily paralyses The Savior's arm.

Continue moving to your right using the Jump Pads that you come to. You will soon reach a platform with a Laser Turret. Activate it prior to his arm attack to paralyse that arm. Now, climb on the hand and run to the Cores and destroy them. Once you have destroyed the shoulder Core, target the forehead Core and begin firing. You can often damage or even destroy the forehead Core before you fall from his arm.

After the fall, you are on another platform. Again, move to your right continuously until you reach a Laser Turret. Time the activation of this Turret with the arm attack of the opposite arm you were just on. Once the arm is paralysed, climb on it and destroy the Cores. After you have destroyed the shoulder Core, attack the forehead Core to eliminate it too. Once all of these Cores have been dealt with, you begin the next phase of this fight.

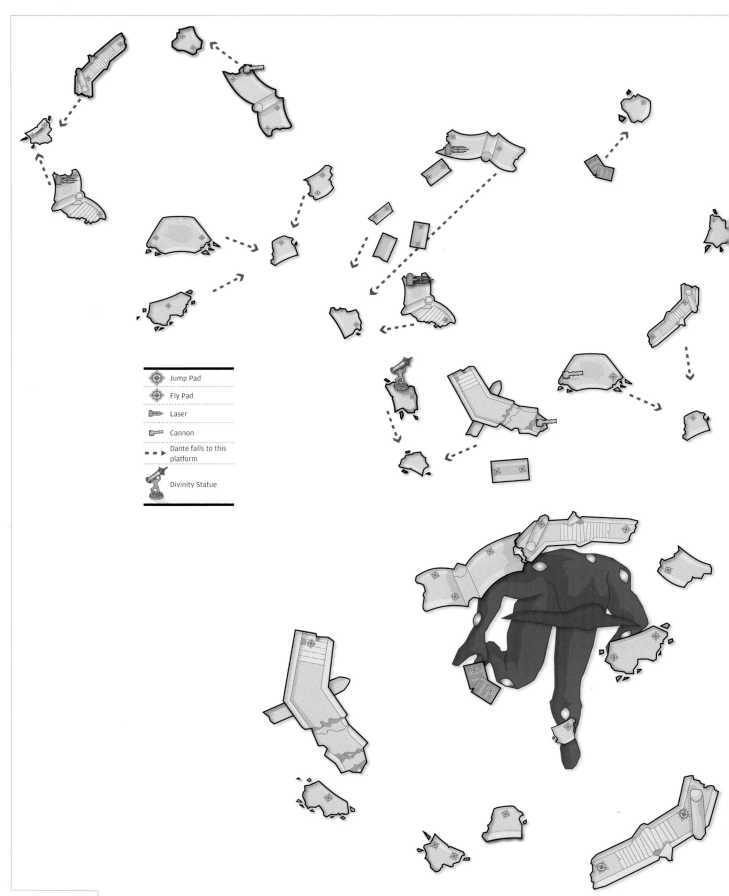

Jump Pad

Fly Pad

Laser

Cannon

Dante falls to this platform

Divinity Statue

Boss 14 **The Savior – Part 2**

The Savior immediately uses Final Flash, a powerful energy blast that you must avoid. As before, run to your right and use the

Suggested Preparation for Part 2

Item	Description	Status
Style	Trickster	Fully levelled
Melee Weapon	Gilgamesh	Kick 13 acquired
Gun	Pandora	Fully levelled
Ability	Air Hike	Standard

03_78   Jump Pads. Keep moving to your right until you reach a special central platform and trigger a scene. Do not stop moving until you trigger this scene! After the scene, the Savior's Health Bar is displayed. You can now attack him anywhere on

Pandora's Revenge does serious damage to the Savior!

his body to do damage, but the Core on his chest is especially weak. Once you deal enough damage, the Savior will fall unconscious. Pandora's Revenge is ideal for this task.

The Savior uses Final Flash again once his Health Meter is displayed, so move to your right and prepare to make your stand. You can attack the Savior from any platform in this area, but he will immediately destroy the smaller unstable ones, so pick your fighting ground carefully. Once you are ready, target The Savior

using Pandora's Revenge. Once the Savior begins attacking you, move to your right to the next platform and get ready with Pandora's Revenge.

Pro Tip!

The Savior doesn't always have to be directly in front you to be hit by Pandora's Revenge. You can often hit him while he is busy attacking the platform that you were on previously.

Once you have done enough damage to the Savior he will fall unconscious and you will drop to a platform with a Jump Pad directly in front of you. Use that pad to reach the Main Core. Equip Gilgamesh, activate Devil Trigger, and attack the Core furiously. You have 12 seconds to do as much damage as possible. When time is up, you will fall back to the regular platform route.

As before, move to your right and use Pandora's Revenge to damage the Savior when the opportunity arises. Once he is unconscious, attack the Main Core with all your might. Stick to this pattern for the duration of the fight, and the Savior will soon fall before you. Once he is defeated, a scene will trigger and the mission ends.

Gilgamesh's Real Impact is the attack of choice for damaging the Main Core!

S Ranking Tips

Devil Points Required: **38,000**

Minimum S Rank Requirements

Criteria	Rank	Value
Time	S	10:00 or less
Stylish Points	B	3778 or more
Orbs Found*	S	100%
Bonus	-	No Item

* No set orbs in this Mission. Automatic 100% given.

No Damage Option

Criteria	Rank	Value
Time	A	12:00 or less
Stylish Points	C	2723 or more
Orbs Found*	S	100%
Bonus	-	No Item
Bonus	-	No Damage

* No set orbs in this Mission. Automatic 100% given.

There are enemies to fight during the first part of this mission, and you can use them to boost your style. During the second part of the mission, it is only you and the Savior, so you'll need most of your Stylish Points to come early in the mission. With the excellent evasion techniques of Trickster, it is actually possible to get through this mission without taking damage and thus earning the No Damage bonus.

To do this, ignore all the enemies in the first part of the mission and concentrate only on the Cores. Once you get to the second part of the fight, remain very evasive and rely on Pandora's Revenge whenever it is safe. When you get to the Main Core, use Gilgamesh with Devil Trigger active to quickly take it out. Real Impact with Devil trigger does incredible damage to the Main Core as well as significantly boosts your Stylish Points.

The Successor

Mission Highlights

Item	Description
Boss Fight	Angelo Troops, Berial, Dagon, Echidna, Angelo Agnus

Ranking Objectives

Item	S	A	B	C	D
Time	≤ 30:00	30:01 - 34:00	34:01 - 40:00	40:01 - 50:00	≥ 50:01
Orbs (%)	≥ 95%	75% - 94%	60% - 74%	45% - 59%	≤ 44%
Stylish Points	≥ 12500	9500 - 12499	7000 - 9499	5000 - 6999	≤ 4999

❖ The Stairs Of Tribulation

Free from the bowels of the Savior, but still trapped inside, Nero must find a way to destroy his captor. Somewhere, further inside, Sanctus is hiding. With no other option before him, Nero moves deeper into the depths of his strange prison.

1 Roll The Dice

You start this mission in a small empty room. Go forward to the next area, and a scene will trigger. Once it is over, you are faced once again with the dice game. The rules are the same as in Mission 06 with only a few differences. This time, landing on a Blue space only triggers the Orb Rain, but not the Chests. The goal is the Purple space on the board, and you must reach it with an exact roll or via a Yellow space. The Yellow spaces will now warp you directly to the goal. Landing on a White space does nothing, and landing on a Red space will trigger an enemy fight, but not a laser trap.

Use High Roller to pick your number.

As before, you can select the number you want to roll by watching the top number displayed on the rotating die. The die goes through the same rotation sequences as before which is: 1, 4, 2, 6, 3, 5. To select your number, strike the die with High Roller. It's easiest to actually start the High Roller manoeuvre on the number prior to the desired number. For example, if you want to roll a 6, then start High Roller when you see the 2 appear. Using any other attack besides High Roller will result in a completely random roll of the die.

Reaching the Purple space will trigger a Boss fight. This mission is basically a Boss Rush where you must face 5 bosses in a row to complete the mission. When you are ready to begin, you need to roll a 4 from the starting location to reach the Purple space. The die must be activated before your first roll, so shoot it once to do so, then roll a 4 to reach the Boss space.

Boss 15 Angelo Troop

Deflecting the energy attacks of the Angelos results in their instant demise.

You face 4 Bianco Angelos and 1 Alto Angelo in this fight. Deal with these armoured monstrosities like you have always done. Buster is good to break the Biancos' shields and also for a powerful throw. You can use Snatch to get behind a Bianco where they are completely vulnerable to your attacks and Buster. If they use their energy attack, you can reflect the energy ball with Red Queen or a Level 1 charge shot to instantly destroy them all.

2 Turn Up The Heat

In this area you will find a Green Orb to the left of the building and a White Orb to the right. The Purple space is 6 moves away from the starting point. There is also a Yellow space 5 moves away. To proceed straight to the Boss, you need to roll either a 5 or a 6.

Boss 16 Berial

You faced Berial in Mission 02, so you know what to do. Use Snatch to stay in the air and close to his head. His head is weak to your attacks. Once you do enough damage to extinguish his flames, get close to his head and use Buster. Follow that with another Buster to his body on the ground. Keep the pressure on him, and he will fall to your might in no time.

Use Buster on his head once the flames have been extinguished.

3 Chill Out

There are Green Orbs to the right and left of the building. On the playing board, the Purple space is 7 moves away this time. However, there is a Yellow space only 4 moves away. If you need more Green Orbs, you can hit a Blue space to trigger the Orb Rain by rolling a 3 or 5. If you want to go straight to the Boss, then roll a 4 to land on Yellow and warp to the goal.

Boss 17 Dagon

You faced Bael in Mission 04 which is identical to this beast which Dante faced in Mission 15. The same techniques apply. Attack the tentacle wenches, the Rusalkas, to draw Dagon out in the open. If one of the she demons grabs you, use Devil Trigger to free yourself. If you knock a Rusalka unconscious, use Buster to pull Dagon out of the shadows immediately.

When he is unconscious, using Buster on his tongue leads to a devastating attack.

Move around Dagon and attack him furiously. If he catches you in his mouth, activate Devil Trigger to break free. If he goes unconscious, use Buster on his tongue to inflict major damage. When he ices himself over, attack the tentacle wenches to release orbs, occasionally you will get Green Orbs when you do this. You can also climb on his back and stand there to deliver multiple melee attacks before he shakes you off. Once he is down, the Warp Pad will appear to take you to the next board.

4 Snake In The Grass

There is a Green Orb to the left of the building and a White Orb to the right. The Purple space is 9 moves away on this broad, but there is a Yellow space which is only 4 moves away. If you're ready to go straight to the next Boss, then roll a 4 and you will be taken there immediately.

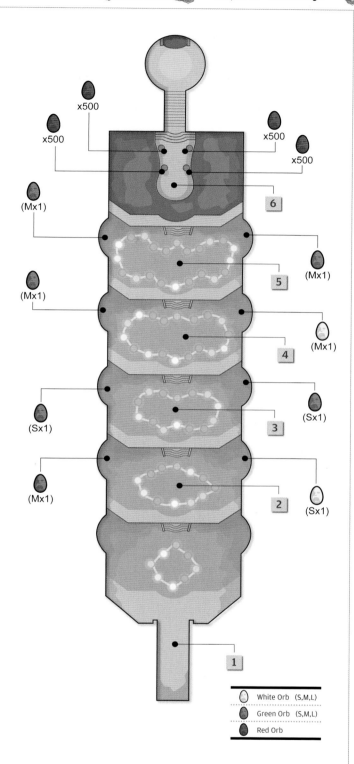

x500

x500

x500

x500

(Mx1)

6

(Mx1)

5

(Mx1)

(Mx1)

4

(Sx1)

3

(Sx1)

(Mx1)

2

(Sx1)

1

White Orb (S,M,L)
Green Orb (S,M,L)
Red Orb

Boss 18 **Echidna**

There are Orb Pods in this area that you'll need to break if you're shooting for 100% on orbs for your Mission Rank. As for Echidna, she's the same as she was in Mission 07. Use Snatch to get close to her female body when she is in Snake form and attack her. If you knock her female body unconscious, use Buster for a special attack and good damage.

A well-timed Charge Shot will stop her Dragon dive attack.

When she dives at you in Dragon form, either evade, use a Charge shot to her open mouth, or a well-timed High Roller to phase through the attack. When she is Enraged, you can use Buster to stop her dive attack as well. When she is in Birthing form, attack the Seed Tube with Buster. When she is grounded, avoid the tentacles and attack her body. Again, if she goes unconscious, use Buster. Keep the pressure on her, she will soon fall and the Warp Pad will appear.

5 | A Final Study

There are Green Orbs to the right and left of the building if you need them. The Boss space is now 11 moves away, but there are Yellow spaces 5 and 6 moves away. To get directly to the Boss on this board, roll a 5 or 6 and you are there.

Boss 19 **Angelo Agnus**

🖵 | 03_83   You fought him once before in Mission 09. This time he will summon Basilisks to the fight. As before, use Buster on the enemies he summons for a special attack against Agnus. When Agnus is dizzy, use Buster on him to initiate a damaging special attack. He uses two different health absorb attacks. Quickly attack him if he attempts these to stop them. If he grabs you with the weaker health absorb attack, activate Devil Trigger to break free. Evade as needed, and attack him viciously to bring him down.

When Agnus is dizzy, approach him quickly for a Buster attack.

6 | The Final Door

There are four small columns that you can break for Red orbs on the small platform on which you now stand. Ahead of you is the final door of this area and the exit. There is a weak barrier covering this door, so attack it with Red Queen to shatter it, then walk through the opening and you end this mission.

S Ranking Tips

◀◆▶ Devil Points Required: **90,000**

Minimum S Rank Requirements

Criteria	Rank	Value
Time	S	30:00 or less
Stylish Points	B	9001 or more
Orbs Found	S	75% to 94%
Bonus	-	No Item

There aren't many Orbs to be found in this mission, so make sure you don't miss the few that are here. Check the map to make sure you get them all. You've got 5 Boss Fights to overcome, but you've fought them all before. Use the same tactics you did in the previous mission, and you'll easily get the needed Stylish Points for S Ranking the mission.

La Vita Nuova

Mission Highlights

Item	Description
Boss Fight	Sanctus Diabolica & The False Savior

Ranking Objectives

Item	S	A	B	C	D
Time	≤ 3:15	3:16 - 5:00	5:01 - 8:30	8:01 - 13:00	≥ 13:01
Orbs (%)*	100%	100%	100%	100%	100%
Stylish Points	≥ 5500	4500 - 5499	4000 - 4499	3500 - 3999	≤ 3499

*There are no set orbs to be found in this mission. Automatic 100% given.

Destroy The Evil Sanctus

Sanctus, transformed by the power of the Savior, holds Kyrie's life in his hand. Nero promised Kyrie he would free her from this hellish prison, and that is a promise he means to keep!

Boss 20 Sanctus Diabolica

As in Mission 11, you must destroy the shield and his Halo before you can damage Sanctus. This time, however, he has the Sword of Sparda. He will often use the sword to block your attacks after you have broken his shield. When this happens, get close, use Buster to break his guard and then immediately attack him before he recovers. This will break his Halo. When his Health is full, you have 10 seconds to attack him before the Halo is restored. When his health is down to 50% or less, you will only have 5 seconds.

Buster can stop his Sparda Stinger in its tracks.

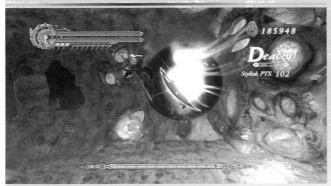
When he blocks with Sparda, you must use Buster to break his guard.

When his Halo is down, activate Devil Trigger and attack him quickly. Before his Halo is restored, make sure to use Buster for maximum damage. Keep up the cycle of breaking his shield, breaking his sword block, and breaking his Halo for the duration of the fight. When his health is low, he will begin to teleport to the ground after the shield is broken. Once on the ground, he will use Sparda to attack you. Once his health is very low, he will use Sparda Stinger which is a very devastating attack. You can evade these attacks or you can use Buster to deflect them. Deflecting them leads to a devastating counter-attack of your own. Activating Devil Trigger will augment these counter-attacks.

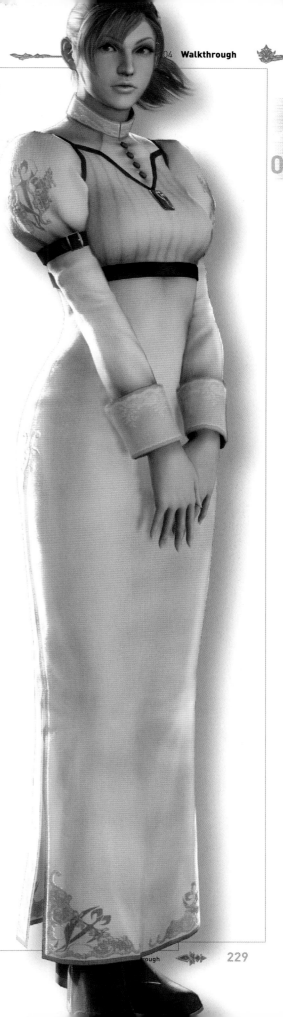

The False Savior

After you have defeated Sanctus a scene will trigger. Once this is over, you will face the False Savior. He only has two attacks both of which you must stop with Buster. He starts with a right hand punch. Time the punch as it comes down and use Buster to deflect it. He then follows with a left hand strike that you also need to deflect with proper timing. Once you have dealt with both of these, approach his head and use Buster once more to end this once and for all.

Ending The Game

Once the scenes have played out, the Credits will roll. You aren't done yet! You are presented you with a mini-game while the Staff Credits roll. You must protect Kyrie from the attacking Scarecrows. If she is hit once, you fail and the credits continue on by themselves. If you manage to stop all the enemies from attacking Kyrie, you will unlock a Bonus movie "Epilogue 02".

 03_84 Here's a tip, don't bother trying to kill the Scarecrows, just use Streak to push them all back and away from Kyrie. You only need to keep them at bay for 1 minute and 31 seconds. There is a small countdown timer at the top centre of the screen showing you how much time is remaining. Good luck!

Make it this far, and you're only 3 seconds away from success!

Congratulations, you have beaten Devil May Cry 4 and unlocked many things. For a full run down on all there is to see, do, and unlock in Devil May Cry 4, please refer to the Extras Chapter.

S Ranking Tips

◆ Devil Points Required: **33,000**

Minimum S Rank Requirements

Criteria	Rank	Value
Time	A	5:00 or less
Stylish Points	A	4500 or more
Orbs Found*	S	100%
Bonus	-	No Item

* No set orbs in this Mission. Automatic 100% given.

There is only Sanctus to get your Stylish Points from in this mission. The time limit is very tight for S Rank (3:15 or less), so shoot for A Rank and then boost your Stylish Points to compensate. There are no set orbs to find, so that is an automatic S Rank for orbs. Rely heavily on the special Buster attacks when Sanctus's shield and halo are down, and make sure to activate Devil Trigger before using Buster. When Sanctus begins using Sparda Stinger, time his incoming attack and use Buster to deflect it. This inflicts heavy damage and gives you a major boost in style.

Chapter 05

Extras

This is where you'll find the complete walkthrough for every Secret Mission and also for the Bloody Palace bonus game. You'll also learn about all the unlockables and some little secrets that Devil May Cry 4 contains. If you haven't beaten the game at least once, we advise you to avoid this chapter, as there are plenty of spoilers inside. When you're ready, dive in and find out all that there is to unlock and discover in this magnificent game.

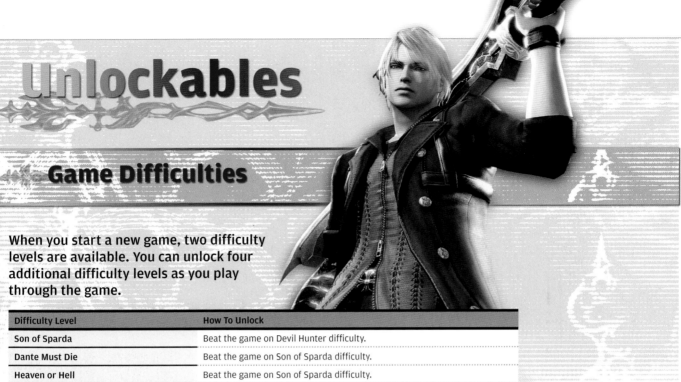

Unlockables

Game Difficulties

When you start a new game, two difficulty levels are available. You can unlock four additional difficulty levels as you play through the game.

Difficulty Level	How To Unlock
Son of Sparda	Beat the game on Devil Hunter difficulty.
Dante Must Die	Beat the game on Son of Sparda difficulty.
Heaven or Hell	Beat the game on Son of Sparda difficulty.
Hell and Hell	Beat the game on Dante Must Die difficulty.

In Son of Sparda mode, your attacks do 15% less damage (x0.85) and enemy attacks do 75% more damage (x1.75).

In Dante Must Die mode, your attacks do 30% less damage (x0.70) and enemy attacks do three times the normal amount of damage (x3.00).

Heaven or Hell mode is a special difficulty level. Although you get a ranking at the end of each Mission, the rankings are not displayed on the Total Ranking screen. However, these are remembered by the game and a "New Record" display will inform you if you do better the next time round.

In Heaven or Hell mode, all enemies die with one hit, whether from a sword strike or gunshot. But don't get too excited yet. Nero and Dante will also die in one hit. To make things a little more bearable, you're given three Gold Orbs to revive you

As shown on the screen, you have three Gold Orbs to make it past your enemies.

if you die. The Gold Orbs are displayed to the right of your Health Meter. One will be used automatically if you die. You can't use Gold Orbs from your Item list in this difficulty mode.

Once all three automatic Orbs have been used, it's time to "Abandon All Hope". At this point, you have the usual options of retrying the Mission or continuing the current one. As with standard gameplay, continue points are observed. For example, just before a Boss Fight, you'll cross a continue point. If you die during the Boss Fight, you can select continue to restart the Boss Fight from the beginning.

Hell and Hell is identical to Heaven or Hell mode, except that only Nero and Dante die in one hit. All enemies have normal health and, as in standard gameplay, must be killed. Enemy actions and the amount of damage they take are dictated by the Son of Sparda difficulty mode.

Story Theater

Epilogue 2 can be unlocked by protecting Kyrie.

The Story Theater is available from the start of a new game. Each time you view a new cut scene in the game, it's added to the Theater for immediate replay. However, Epilogue 2 is one special movie that can be unlocked, if you protect Kyrie while the ending Staff Credits are rolling after you've beaten the game. You must protect her for 1 min 31 secs. A small timer at the top centre of the screen shows the amount of time remaining.

> **Pro Tip!**
> Don't bother trying to kill all the Scarecrows as you protect Kyrie. Simply use Streak to keep them at bay for the entire time.

Gallery

The Gallery is unlocked when you beat the game once in either the Human or Devil Hunter difficulty. As you continue to beat the game in the other modes of difficulty, you will unlock new Gallery elements for viewing.

Gallery Element	Description	How To Unlock
History Of DMC	Slide show of the DMC series.	Beat Human or Devil Hunter difficulty.
Game Clear Bonus Art	6 high resolution CG pictures.	Beat each of the six difficulty levels.
Character Images	29 CG pictures.	Beat Human or Devil Hunter difficulty.
Publicity Artwork	12 CG pictures.	Beat Son of Sparda difficulty.

History of DMC

This slide show consists of pictures and text that explain the entire DMC series from DMC1 to DMC3.

Game Clear Bonus Art

Each difficulty level has a unique, high resolution CG picture associated with it. Beat each difficulty level to unlock all six Game Clear pictures.

Available Game Clear Artwork

Artwork	Description	How To Unlock
The Two Heroes	Dante and Nero sitting on a couch.	Beat Human difficulty.
The Cast	Composite picture showing Agnus, Gloria, Kyrie, Credo, Nero, Dante, Trish and Lady.	Beat Devil Hunter difficulty.
The Demons	Composite picture showing Chimera Seeds, Echidna, Berial, Bael and Dagon.	Beat Son of Sparda difficulty.
Demon Invasion	Composite picture showing Dante and Nero surrounded by all the enemies and Bosses in the game	Beat Dante Must Die difficulty.
The Ladies of Devil May Cry	Composite picture showing Lady, Kyrie, Gloria and Trish.	Beat Heaven or Hell difficulty.
Light From the Demon Blade	Picture showing Nero's DT demon holding Yamato. A reflection of Dante's DT form can be seen on the blade.	Beat Hell and Hell difficulty.

Each time you beat a difficulty level, a close-up of the corresponding picture will be displayed on-screen with a note of congratulation. After that, the full image is unlocked in the Gallery. In addition, once you've beaten the Son of Sparda difficulty mode, the Title

The Game Clear Artwork also treats you to a new Title Screen.

Screen image will begin using the Game Clear artwork as its background. The artwork rotates randomly.

Congratulation Messages

How To View	Message
Beat Human difficulty.	Prequel doesn't mean you can be a newbie.
Beat Devil Hunter difficulty.	Guess you aren't some casual gamer.
Beat Son of Sparda difficulty.	You know how to make me look good!
Beat Dante Must Die difficulty.	You've got some big demon balls!
Beat Heaven or Hell difficulty.	Man, you need to get out more.
Beat Hell and Hell difficulty.	Now that's what I call raising a lot of hell!

You get special Congratulations for clearing a difficulty level!

Character Images

This is a collection of 29 small images of various characters and Items in the game.

Publicity Artwork

This is a collection of 12 GC pictures that were used to promote the game.

Available Character Images

Image Number	Description
No. 01	Nero
No. 02	Nero in DT form (1)
No. 03	Nero in DT form (2)
No. 04	Red Queen
No. 05	Blue Rose
No. 06	Kyrie
No. 07	Credo
No. 08	Agnus
No. 09	Gloria
No. 10	Dante with Rebellion
No. 11	Dante with Gilgamesh
No. 12	Dante with Pandora
No. 13	Dante with Lucifer
No. 14	Dante in DT form (1)
No. 15	Dante in DT form (2)
No. 16	Rebellion
No. 17	Ebony & Ivory
No. 18	Coyote-A
No. 19	Gilgamesh
No. 20	Trish
No. 21	Lady
No. 22	The Scarecrows
No. 23	Bianco Angelo
No. 24	Frost
No. 25	Assault
No. 26	Blitz
No. 27	Mephisto
No. 28	Berial
No. 29	Echidna

Available Publicity Images

Artwork	Description
The Man With The Devil Bringer	Close up of Nero with Red Queen and Devil Bringer
Clash!	Nero and Dante fighting with Rebellion and Devil Bringer
Nero and Dante	Nero and Dante standing back to back before a Hell Gate
Red and Blue	Close-up shot of Nero and Dante
Dante and Nero	Nero and Dante facing each other
Three Guns	Nero and Dante fighting with guns
Nero Image 1	Hand drawn image of Nero and Devil Bringer
Nero Image 2	Hand drawn image of Nero with Red Queen
Devil Trigger Nero	Hand drawn image of Nero in DT form
Dante Image 1	Hand drawn image of Dante grabbing Rebellion (close-up)
Dante Image 2	Hand drawn image of Dante grabbing Rebellion
Dante Image 3	Hand drawn image of Dante grabbing Rebellion sitting down

Super Characters

When you've beaten the Dante Must Die difficulty level, you'll unlock the super versions of both Nero and Dante. These are identical to the normal character models, except that you're allowed unlimited use of Devil Trigger.

Using the super characters allows unlimited DT!

Secret Missions

There are 12 Secret Missions hidden throughout the game. Each one has a set task that you must accomplish in order to clear the Mission, where-upon you're rewarded with a Blue Orb Fragment. You can attempt a Secret Mission at any time once you've found it, but some of the Missions are more easily cleared later in the game when you have upgraded abilities or certain Key Items.

All Secret Missions are set to the Son of Sparda difficulty level, regardless of the difficulty level at which you attempt them. You can't attempt a Secret Mission in Heaven or Hell, or Hell and Hell, mode. Please refer to the walkthrough for the exact location of each Secret Mission marker.

Look for the markers that indicate that a Secret Mission is available.

Secret Mission 01

Title	**Annihilation**
Available	**Mission 02**
Objective	**Destroy all demons within the time limit!**

A mid-air Buster throw aimed at the enemies below is an advantageous move.

03_85   There are eight Scarecrows in total that you must destroy within the 60 sec time limit. The best method of attack is to get close to a pair of these beasts, and then use Snatch to pull others nearer to you. Once you've got them bunched together in groups of three or four, unleash heavy combos, but avoid attacks that repel the enemy.

There's some advantage to be gained by your jumping into the air and using Buster to throw the Scarecrow back down. This will damage all the enemies below in one go. After a throw, follow up with Split or Double Down to come crashing down on to the group of Scarecrows. We also recommend that you use Exceed in your attacks.

Secret Mission 02

Title	**Alley-Oop**
Available	**Mission 04**
Objective	**Successfully execute five mid-air Busters without touching the ground!**

Good timing and rhythm will allow you to achieve the coveted five mid-air Busters.

03_86   In this Secret Mission you must perform a Buster while airborne five times in a row, without touching the ground. If you do touch the ground, then your Buster count will be reset to 0. You have a total of eight Scarecrows to work with. Only four will be on-screen (max) at any one time. Unlike Secret Mission 1, you won't want the Scarecrows to bunch up when you perform Buster, since this will damage them and lower their HP. This means that you can't throw them quite as often. You can throw a Scarecrow with Buster three times before it dies.

The Air Hike ability makes this far easier to accomplish. Simply double jump in the centre of the area, and then perform a Snatch. As the Snatch is finishing, release your Lock-On (RB | R1) immediately and perform the Buster. To get all five in a row, you need to get into a smooth rhythm of Snatch, immediate Buster, back to Snatch, immediate Buster, etc. There should be hardly any pause after the Snatch. Enemy Step can help if you find yourself losing height. As soon as you perform a Snatch, use Enemy Step right away to gain height, and then perform another Snatch quickly, before the Enemy Step animation ends.

Secret Mission 03

Title	**Nonviolent Resistance**
Available	**Mission 05**
Objective	**Raise you stylish rankings without using attacks!**

Use Enemy Step to boost your Style.

Finish your Style Rank with a Hold and a Taunt!

03_87 This Mission requires you to raise your Stylish Rank to C without attacking the enemy. It seems impossible at first sight, but you can do it with evasions! The key is to use Tight Evades so that you evade an enemy attack within five frames or fewer before it strikes you. This will boost your rank. However, the presence of the Frost makes this quite difficult.

An easier solution is to wait until after Mission 08 before attempting this, when you have the Aegis Shield. If you use an enemy as a shield to block other enemy attacks, you get a Style boost. Even easier if you use Enemy Step! A successful outcome with Enemy Step will net you 150 Combat Points (CP). 500 points are needed to get past the E Rank (which is not displayed) and another 700 to get past the D Rank to reach C. The CP Timer for Enemy Step is 2.5 secs, which means you won't get CP for 2.5 secs after succeeding with Enemy Step, so there's nothing to be gained by performing it over and over again in a short time.

The key is to use Enemy Step, then run around the room to avoid damage. A hit taken will lose you two ranks in Style which, in this case, means you're reset to 0. Keep using Enemy Step until you reach the D Rank, then grab and Hold an enemy with Aegis Shield. If possible, position yourself in a corner, so you won't have to worry about attacks from behind. Once you are holding the enemy, perform a Taunt to boost your Style and then wait for the enemy attacks to come in and get blocked by Aegis Shield. Taunt has an CP Timer of 10 seconds, so you'll gain no advantage by performing successive Taunts, because they won't be counted for 10 seconds.

You also have the option of waiting until Dante is available and then attempting this Secret Mission using Royal Guard. When you Royal Block an attack, you get a Stylish boost, but it has to be a Royal Block, since that is the only block that nullifies all damage. Taking damage reduces your Style rank by two levels.

Secret Mission 04

Title	**Tracking Treasure Down**
Available	**Mission 06**
Objective	**Find all the hidden Orbs!**

The Orb Drops are scattered around, but they'll be triggered if you stand where one is hidden.

03_88 Although both Nero and Dante can complete this Secret Mission, it's easier to do it with Nero because of the Rusalka upgrade to his Devil Bringer arm, which glows when you're close to a secret. The task before you is to find 99 Red Orbs. The hidden Orbs are in Orb Drops scattered about the rooms. There are two types, small and large. A small drop is worth 30 and a large drop 60 Orbs.

There are eight possible locations, but only four are used during an attempt. These four are split into two small and two large drops. As you walk around the room, pay attention to Nero's arm. It will glow brighter as you get closer to a hidden drop. Please refer to the map for all eight possible locations.

Main Hall - Upper Floor

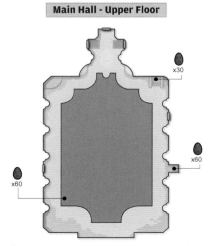

Main Hall - Lower floor

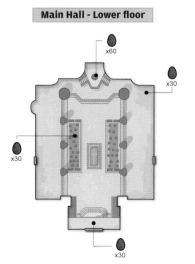

Main Hall - Basement

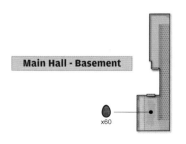

Secret Mission 05

Title	**Sky Scraper**
Available	**Mission 07**
Objective	**Reach the goal by rising to the top!**

Getting on the ledge provides the proper angle for you to use the Grim Grip for the last Jump Pad.

☐ 03_89   You have 60 seconds to use the Jump Pads and Grim Grips to reach the top of the shaft where the Blue Orb Fragment is waiting. There are five Jumps Pads to negotiate, and with Air Hike the task becomes much easier.

Use Jump Pad 1 on the ground to get started. When you reach the apex of your jump, immediately use Hellbound twice to enable you to cross the two Grim Grips and reach Jump Pad 2. At the apex of the launch from Jump Pad 2, use Hellbound on the two Grim Grips to reach Jump Pad 3.

When you reach the apex of the launch from the 3rd Jump Pad, you'll find a fence around Jump Pad 4. On your fist launch from Jump Pad 3, use Red Queen to strike the fence and make an opening. Fall back to Jump Pad 3. On the next launch, now that the fence is broken, you can easily make it to Jump Pad 4.

At the apex of the launch from Jump Pad 4 use Hellbound on the single Grim Grip. The goal here is to land on the ledge behind the Grip. Using Air Hike makes this a simple matter. After you've been pulled past the Grip, Air Hike over to the ledge. Once there, turn and face the Grim Grip again. Use Hellbound on the Grip so that you're pulled to the final Jump Pad. At the apex of the launch, push forwards on the Left Analog Stick to land on the upper ledge and claim the Blue Orb Fragment.

Secret Mission 06

Title	**Vermifuge**
Available	**Mission 10**
Objective	**Eliminate all the Chimera before the Scarecrow is taken over!**

Deposit the Scarecrow in the back near the Ruined Church and then take out the Chimera Seeds.

☐ 03_90   You're required to destroy all the Chimera Seeds before they take over the Scarecrow. Furthermore, you're not allowed to kill the Scarecrow. In a straight fight, this might prove daunting but, fortunately, there's a little trick you can use to make this one of the easiest Secret Missions of all.

As soon as you acquire the Aegis Shield from Mission 8 you will gain the Hold ability. Right at the start of this Secret Mission you should perform a hold on the Scarecrow. Once you've got him, run to the back of this area and up the stairs to the Ruined Church. Use double jumps to speed things up and avoid the Chimera Seeds. Having made it to the Ruined Church, drop the Scarecrow and then go back and kill the Chimera Seeds. The Seeds will not pass the top of the stairs, and the Scarecrow is very slow in coming back down. This technique gives you plenty of time to kill the Chimera Seeds at your leisure. To kill the Seeds in one hit, use Buster.

Secret Mission 07

Title	**Free Running**
Available	**Mission 12**
Objective	**Reach the goal without falling through the vanishing floor!**

Using Pandora's Argument, you can easily fly over to the Blue Orb Fragment!

☐ 03_91   This Secret Mission can prove quite difficult. The Mephistos are very aggressive and will often try to knock you off the platforms, thereby ending the Mission. Luckily, there is a special trick to this that makes them incredibly easy to deal with. Wait until you've got Pandora after Mission 15 and then replay Mission 12, while ensuring you upgrade Gunslinger style to Level 4 (max). This increases the length of the Disaster Gauge. If necessary, refund Orbs from previous purchases in order to max Gunslinger out.

Equip Pandora at the start of Mission 12, when you are confronted by the Scarecrows. Double jump into the air and use the Gatling gun (Jealousy) to shoot the Scarecrows while you're falling. Fire repeatedly in order to fill the Disaster Gauge. As soon as it's full, start Secret Mission 07, which is located just outside the first room of Mission 12.

Make sure you have Gunslinger style equipped, then double jump off the platform. At the apex of your jump, activate Argument (the flying missile machine). With a full Disaster Gauge, you have plenty of time to fly across the chasm below and reach the Blue Orb Fragment lying on the ledge in front of the exit door. As you do this, ignore the Mephistos, and don't fire any missiles, as this will deplete your Disaster Gauge.

Secret Mission 08

Title	**Royal Blocker**
Available	**Mission 14 (Dante only)**
Objective	**Successfully execute a Royal Block five times!**

Time it right and a Royal Block is yours.

03_92 Because this Mission needs the Royal Guard style, only Dante can accomplish it. The challenge requires that you perform a Royal Block five times in a row. A Royal Block is when you block an incoming attack within five frames of the impact, i.e. 0.08 seconds before the attack strikes you. When you've succeeded with this, you'll hear an explosive blocking sound and a bright red flash will encircle Dante. This sound is much louder and the flash much brighter than a regular Block, which is deployed outside the five-frame window of opportunity.

There are two Mephistos in this Mission's room. Start by killing one, so that you have just one to deal with as you attempt the Royal Blocks. The Mephisto has four attacks, two of which are easier to Royal Block than the others. Try your Royal Block on the Point attack and the Spin Slash, both of which it performs by staying close to you. If the Mephisto moves away, your best course of action is to move, evading the beast until it reverts to the Point or Spin Slash attack. If you're hit, or you regular Block the attack instead of using Royal Block, then your Royal Block count will be reset to 0 and you'll have to start all over again.

It helps if you hold the block button and wait for the attack to come. Just before the attack lands, release the button quickly and then press and hold it again. In this way, with good timing, you'll have no problem Royal Blocking the attack, and you'll find it easy to get into the rhythm of it.

Secret Mission 09

Title	**Unbreakable**
Available	**Mission 15**
Objective	**Eliminate all enemies without taking damage and without being captured by a Fault!**

Use Pandora's Argument for an easy win in this Secret Mission.

03_93 This Mission can be as difficult or as easy as you like! To make it super simple, switch to Gunslinger style with Pandora equipped as your gun. Then just double jump into the air and, at the apex of your jump, activate Argument and fire missiles until Argument is cancelled. Repeat this sequence - a double jump followed by Argument and missile firing - over and over again, until all the enemies are dead. A very straightforward way of claiming your Blue Orb Fragment.

Secret Mission 10

Title	**Puppet Master**
Available	**Mission 05**
Objective	**Manipulate the Gyro Blades and raze everything to the ground!**

Be quick and you can break all five statues.

03_94 Only Nero can complete this Mission, since it requires the use of the Gyro Blades. To meet this challenge, you have two minutes to break five enchanted statues. It's helpful to do a walkthrough of this Mission first so that you know where the statues are. There are two in the main hallway, one in the area with the Divinity Statue near the door, one in the area with the Emblem switch and one directly opposite that area, in the small alcove from where a door leads to the Grand Hall.

This is all pretty straightforward. Activate the Gyro Blade, and then strike it twice with Red Queen to power it up. Hit the blade with Buster to set it in motion. When you get near the statues that are off to the side and out of the main hallway, move the Gyro Blade using Buster on its own (don't power it up) in order to have better control. Single-strike power ups are also good for moving the blade in a short, controlled burst.

Secret Mission 11

Title	**Point of Impact**
Available	**Mission 16**
Objective	**Use Pandora to destroy distant objects!**

Good timing allows you to break both statues with time to spare.

 03_95 Only Dante can complete this Secret Mission. If you're having trouble reaching the ledge where the Mission's marker is located, simply activate Devil Trigger and use Dante's DT enhanced triple jump to make it to the ledge. As soon as the Mission starts, you have 30 seconds in which to use Pandora's Revenge (laser cannon) to destroy two statues. These are placed at opposite ends of the area, making it impossible to run to them, so only Pandora's long range Revenge can get the job done. It helps to have the ability Speed, so make sure you purchase it before trying this Secret Mission.

The hardest part of this Mission is aiming Pandora in the right way. You can't adjust the aim from left to right so, before you can activate Pandora, you have to be pointing directly at the statue. When the Mission starts, don't adjust the camera but instead run immediately to the North and down the long flight of stairs. Try to keep to the middle of the stairs when you go down and, as you descend, the camera will centre itself behind you automatically. If you manage to hold your position in the middle of the stairs while moving, the camera, hence your aim, will be in the right spot for Pandora. The moment you reach the bottom of the stairs, stop right away, press and hold RB | R1 and then activate Revenge. Do this correctly and the laser will destroy the statue, and you'll still have 15 seconds left.

Now run back to the South and into the small room. Again, don't adjust the camera as it will auto-adjust for you. Run all the way to the door of the room, stop dead, press and hold RB | R1, and then activate Revenge. When you do this the right way, you'll destroy the second statue with nearly 3 seconds to spare.

Secret Mission 12

Title	**Steeplechase**
Available	**Mission 17**
Objective	**Reach the goal without taking damage!**

Using Pandora's Argument allows you to glide over the lasers unscathed.

 03_96 This Mission can be difficult, unless you know a little secret. The easiest way to breeze through it is with Gunslinger at Level 4 plus Pandora. Make sure you fill the Disaster Gauge at the start of Mission 17, and then enter this Secret Mission. Dante can't use the Key of Cronus to slow time so, instead, double jump into the air and activate Pandora's Argument at the apex of your ascent. You will be off-screen, but you can still guide Dante over the top of the lasers! As you do this, you'll see the shadow of Pandora on the floor, so use that as your guide as you steer Dante to the far side of the room and claim the Blue Orb Fragment.

Bloody Palace

Bloody Palace is unlocked after you've beaten the Devil Hunter Difficulty mode. The palace consists of 101 rooms. The objective is to make it through each level, one after another, with no break or save. You're not allowed to use Items and, if you die, you must go back to the beginning and start again.

You'll face a host of enemies at each level and there is also a Boss Fight every 20 levels. You'll confront Berial at level 20, Bael at level 40, Echidna at level 60, Angelo Credo at level 80, Angle Agnus at level 100 and, finally, Dante at level 101. You can play as either Nero or Dante and, for both, super characters and Automatic modes are allowed.

Bloody Palace is set to the Son of Sparda difficulty up to Level 80. After Level 80, it switches to Dante Must Die mode, and the enemies can use DT. Furthermore, it's a timed event, in which you start with two minutes and then must earn more time as you play through. Each enemy you defeat has a set time value that it will add to you total, and each stage also has a Stage Clear Bonus that adds a fixed amount of time to your tally. Finally, a No Damage Bonus doubles the Stage Clear Bonus time.

Timer bonus per enemy type

Bloody Palace Timer bonus

Enemy Type	Time Bonus
Scarecrow (Leg)	5 seconds
Scarecrow (Arm)	5 seconds
Mega Scarecrow	15 seconds
Bianco Angelo	10 seconds
Alto Angelo	20 seconds
Mephisto	10 seconds
Faust	20 seconds
Frost	10 seconds
Assault	10 seconds
Blitz	30 seconds
Chimera Seed	2 seconds
Cutlass	15 seconds
Gladius	2 seconds
Basilisk	5 seconds

About stylish rank

The Stylish Rank acts as a multiplier for the timer bonus you gain for defeating the various enemy types.

Time Bonus Multiplier

Stylish Rank	Multiplier
E	x1.0
D	x1.1
C	x1.2
B	x1.3
A	x1.4
S	x1.5
SS	x1.75
SSS	x2.0

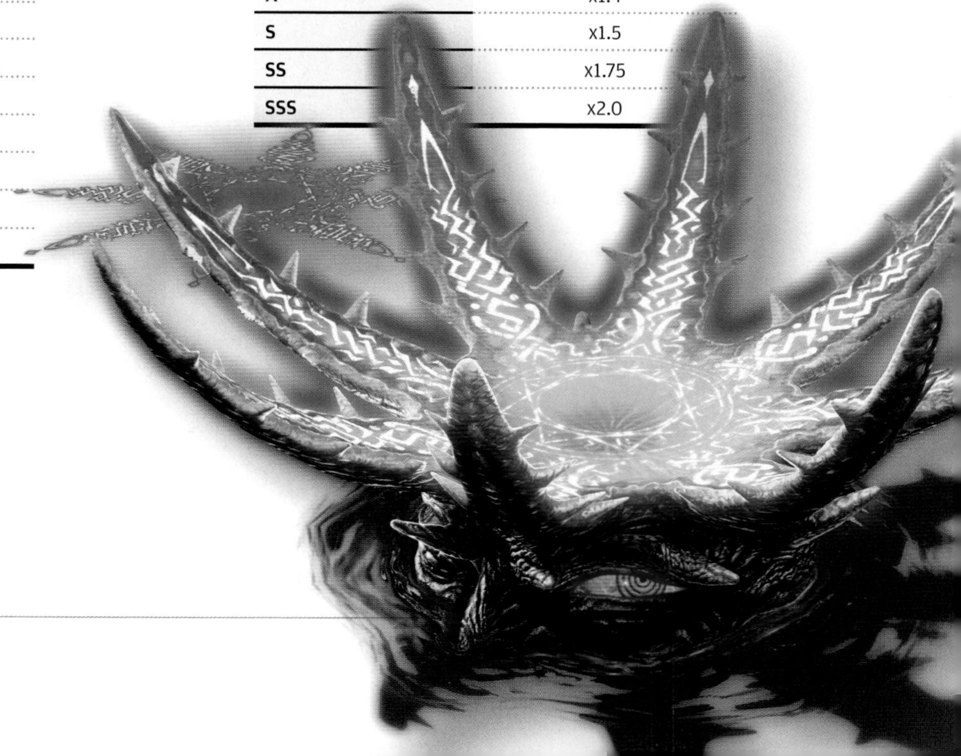

Stage specific time bonus

Upon successfully clearing a stage, you will also receive a time bonus, together with a helpful timer boost when entering a boss stage.

Normal Stage Time Bonus

Stage Number	Time Bonus
Stage 1 to 19	15 seconds
Stage 21 onwards	10 seconds

Boss Stage Time Bonus

Stage	Entering Bonus	Clear Bonus
20	30 seconds	120 seconds
40	30 seconds	120 seconds
60	30 seconds	120 seconds
80	30 seconds	120 seconds
100	30 seconds	120 seconds
101	60 seconds	300 seconds

Things to Remember

Nero's Exceed Gauge

It's worth getting into the habit of fully revving up the Red Queen as you finish each stage. When all enemies on a stage are defeated the timer will stop, allowing you to make your way in your own time to the warp plate at the centre of the arena. Use this brief respite to charge the Exceed Gauge fully in preparation for the next stage. This guide will always assume that you have a fully-charged Exceed Gauge at the start of each stage, so make sure you charge it routinely!

Dante's Disaster Gauge

Periodically, this guide will instruct you to charge the Disaster Gauge in order to unleash Pandora's Gunslinger attacks at a later stage, in order to save time and health. Use the Extreme Jealousy technique (see the Advanced Combat Techniques in the Combat Chapter for a full explanation) to hold a weak enemy up in the air, while firing continuously with PF262: Jealousy to charge the gauge quickly.

Charge Shot Combos

During this guide the use of a Charge Shot Combo will sometimes be suggested. This involves holding a Charge Shot throughout a combo and releasing it once it reaches level 2 or 3, usually as a powerful finisher to an aerial combo. For a more detailed example, see Advanced Combat Techniques in the Combat System Chapter.

Jump Cancelling

Jump Cancelling is the key to stringing together big combos to keep you airborne for long periods. It's also essential if you want to repeat a particularly powerful or useful attack quickly, as in the case of Extreme Jealousy. For full details on Jump Cancelling, see Advanced Combat Techniques in the Combat System.

Royal Strike

When facing a Blitz, you can use a special technique known as a Royal Strike to make light work of stripping the Blitz of its electric shield. To perform this manoeuvre, approach the Blitz while its electric shield is up. You need to have Royal Guard style and Gilgamesh equipped. Once you are close, press **Y** | △ to perform a strike. After pressing **Y** | △, press **B** | ◎ immediately to perform a Royal Block. You have to be quick and you must perform the Royal Block the instant the strike is in motion.

Use a Royal Strike to strip the Blitz of its electric shield.

If you perform this manoeuvre correctly, you'll strike the Blitz and trigger the electric shock. However, since you'll follow this immediately with a Royal Block, you'll also block the electrical tendril used to give you a shock. This will nullify all damage received while at the same time damaging the Blitz. This powerful technique can quickly strip a Blitz of its electric shield.

Bloody Palace Stage 1 - 20

Arena (external appearance)

Stage	Enemy set	Total No	Remarks
1	Scarecrow (Arm) x 3	3	Start - Easy beginning
2	Scarecrow (Leg) x 4	4	
3	Scarecrow (Arm) x 3, (Leg) x 3	6	
4	Frost x 2	2	
5	Bianco Angelo x 2	2	
6	Mephisto x 3	3	
7	Gladius x 6	6	Recover Devil Trigger here
8	Chimera Seed x 9	9	Recover health here
9	Chimera Seed x 9 Scarecrow (Arm) x 3	12	Recover health here
10	Scarecrow(Arm, Leg) x 12	12	Mid-Boss 1 - Scarecrow Festival
11	Assault x 2	2	
12	Mega Scarecrow x 2	2	
13	Bianco Angelo x 2 Assault x 2	4	
14	Faust x 1	1	
15	Bianco Angelo x 2 Alto Angelo x 1	3	
16	Scarecrow (Arm) x 3 (Leg) x 3 Mega Scarecrow x 1	7	
17	Alto Angelo x 2	2	
18	Blitz x 1	1	
19	Basilisk x 4	4	
Garden of god's punishment: Flame			
20	**Boss: Berial**	1	Boss battle 1 - Time addition before boss battle, health recovery after battle

Nero   Things start off nice and easily with a group of just three Scarecrows. A Red Queen Combo with Buster will finish each one effortlessly.

Dante   Whenever you are faced with an easy group of enemies, make absolutely sure that you use the opportunity to charge Dante's Disaster Gauge with Pandora. To protect yourself while charging the gauge, use Extreme Jealousy or repeated blasts from Revenge.

Nero   Deal with the group of four Scarecrows in the same manner as you did in Stage 1. It might be sensible to remain airborne, beyond their striking range, and kill a Scarecrow with an aerial combo and then immediately Snatch another one up.

Dante   Once again, use these weak enemies as a means of charging the Disaster Gauge. If you use the Extreme Jealousy technique against these enemies, you'll end the stage with a full Disaster Gauge. This will come in very useful later on!

Nero   Now that the number of enemies has increased, it's important to make sure you stay well out of range of their attacks. Use aerial combos against this group of Scarecrows, staying airborne while using Jump Cancelling as you attack and Snatching a new enemy up into the air each time you kill one.

Dante   Stay off the ground and outside the Scarecrow's attack range. Launch an attack on each one with an Aerial Rave, using Jump Cancelling to preserve height.

STAGE 4 — Frost x 2

Nero By ensuring that you rev up the Exceed Gauge fully when you end each stage, you can begin a new stage with a devastating attack. Run forwards immediately and grab the nearest Frost with Snatch. Perform an EX Level 3 Rising High Roller, once the Snatch has connected, and do as much damage as you can with an aerial combo. You can keep Frosts in the air with an aerial combo until they die; use Jump Cancelling to make sure you stay airborne. As soon as one Frost has been dealt with, repeat the process on the next.

Dante Switch over to Gilgamesh and jump up immediately at the nearest Frost. It's very likely that it'll attempt to shoot you down with an ice shot, so use Full House to dive straight in and nullify the attack. Upon landing, throw the first two strikes of Gilgamesh Combo A and tag on Kick 13. Repeat this sequence of dive-kick, combo and Kick 13 on each of the enemies to see them off quickly, while at the same time making sure they can't attack you.

STAGE 5 — Bianco Angelo x 2

Nero As soon as the stage begins, run forwards and get behind the Bianco Angelo on the right, and then deploy Red Queen Combo A Exceed strikes continuously. After eight strikes the enemy will be knocked down, so get back into range at once and finish the job with a few more strikes and an optional Buster. If you're really quick you'll take care of one Bianco Angelo before either of the enemies gets a chance to attack. As soon as you've taken care of one enemy, repeat the process on the other.

Dante Switch immediately over to Rebellion and Dark Slayer style and rush towards and behind the nearest Bianco Angelo. Attack the enemy with a repeated cycle of two Rebellion strikes into two Yamato strikes. This endless series of strikes will do a reasonable amount of damage and make it impossible for the enemy to counter-attack. When the first Bianco is out of the way, repeat the pattern on the second.

STAGE 6 — Mephisto x 3

Nero You can make very short work of these Mephistos with Charge Shot combos. Upon starting the stage, get a Charge Shot ready and Snatch repeatedly to remove your target's defensive veil. As soon as you've removed a Mephisto's veil, power in with a Charge Shot combo. Repeat the process for each of the three Mephistos.

Dante Switch to Swordmaster and equip Coyote-A and Gilgamesh. Dante can make very short work of these flying enemies; jump up into Enemy Step range of the nearest Mephisto and fire a rapid volley of Jump Cancelled shotgun blasts. After around three of these ultra-close range shots the enemy's defences will fail, so, the moment the creature falls to the ground perform Gilgamesh's Real Impact to kill it instantly. Repeat the process for each enemy, winning yourself a very rapid victory and an easy No Damage Clear bonus.

STAGE 7 — Gladius x 6

Nero Snatch and Buster are the order of the day here. As soon as the stage begins, Snatch a Gladius out of the air, press 🅱 | ◎ for Buster and then hold Lock-On to throw the Gladius at another. Repeat this process to see off the whole enemy group; ensure that your target is close when you throw a Gladius, so that you don't miss. Listen out for the small audio cue these enemies give before attacking, which will allow you to anticipate incoming danger and evade accordingly.

Dante Coyote-A shots are devastating against these enemies from any range! Blast them out of the air with shotgun blasts and then, using Gilgamesh Full House, quickly reach the spot where each Gladius falls. As you land, a couple of Gilgamesh melée strikes are all it takes to kill each enemy. An alternative method is to select Swordmaster and Lucifer, summon as many blades as possible, and then arrange them in the Climax formation. This will kill a Gladius instantly if it makes contact.

STAGE 8 — Chimera Seed x 9

Nero These creatures will not attack you right away, so use this time to quickly kill as many as you can with Buster. Jump into the air, Snatch an enemy and immediately destroy it using Buster. Remaining in the air will ensure that you're completely out of range of their attack.

Dante For a quick, easy and damage-free victory over these enemies, perform Over Drive repeatedly from a distance. If you start the repetition immediately, none of the Chimera Seeds will get a chance to attack.

STAGE 9 — Chimera Seed x 9, Scarecrow (Arm) x 3

Nero Go after the Scarecrows first, as the Chimeras will not attack you for a while after the stage has started and will only start looking for a Scarecrow to possess when they start moving. As the stage starts, run forwards immediately to meet the first Scarecrow and, to speed things up, kill it as soon as it appears with a Red Queen Combo flowing into an aerial combo. Quickly target and attack the next Scarecrow you see and despatch it in a similar fashion. By this time the last remaining Scarecrow will have been possessed by a Chimera, so use a Charge Shot to make the Scarecrow's vines stop whipping and move in for the kill. After you've taken care of the three Scarecrows, stay airborne and Snatch all the remaining Chimeras to Buster.

Dante Repeat the same pattern you used in the last stage. Keep well away from the enemy group, mow them down continuously with Drive and win an easy, No Damage Clear bonus.

STAGE 10 — Scarecrow (Arm) x 6 (Leg) x 6

Nero This is where Enemy Step comes in very handy. After opening the stage with a big attack, such as EX Level 3 Streak, jump up and remain in the air so that these enemies can't attack you. Use the way the gang bunches up to your advantage by jumping off the rabble with Enemy Step, while attacking using Jump Cancelled combos.

Dante Use this opportunity to acquire some major time bonuses! Switch immediately to Gunslinger. Equip Pandora and press **B** | **◎** to change into PF594 with Argument. As soon as you're ready, fire two missile volleys with **B** | **◎**. Next, switch to Swordmaster and fire off Drive and Over Drive, keeping your distance. When you've only a few enemies left, start charging the Disaster Gauge again, using the Extreme Jealousy technique.

STAGE 11 — Assault x 2

Nero Assaults are no problem when they haven't got a gang of their friends to back them up! As soon as the stage starts, run forwards and to the right. An Assault will materialize. As soon as you see the enemy, position Nero behind him and launch your own assault of Exceed Red Queen slashes. Keep striking the Assault until he keels over, then immediately Snatch and launch the enemy into an aerial combo to finish the job. Simply repeat the actions on the other Assault for a painless victory.

Dante This couldn't be easier. Switch over to Dark Slayer style and rush forwards to meet an Assault as it pops out of the ground. Commence your attack with a repeating cycle of two Rebellion slashes into two Yamato slashes. Although this cycle makes it impossible for the enemy to attack, it also doesn't succeed in knocking it away. The enemy is therefore forced to stand and take the hits until it dies! Having quickly seen off the first Assault, turn your attention now to the second one, using the same technique to dispatch it.

05

STAGE 12   Mega Scarecrow x 2

Nero The great thing about these enemies is that their slow speed prevents them regrouping after being blasted apart. In this situation, run forwards immediately and attack the Mega Scarecrow furthest away from you. Launch it into the air and perform an aerial combo, ending with Calibur. The Calibur strike will blast the enemy towards the outer edge of the arena, so you can punish it to death with any combos you like without risk of the other enemy sneaking up and attacking.

Dante With Swordmaster and Rebellion selected, rush forwards at once and use Stingers to blast the enemy directly in front of you to the edge of the arena. As soon as they're there, switch to Gilgamesh, performing Real Impact to kill them instantly. Repeat the process on the other Mega Scarecrow to obtain an effortless, No Damage bonus.

STAGE 13   Bianco Angelo x 2, Assault x 2

Nero Assaults and Bianco Angelos fight like cats and dogs. While they squabble among themselves, pick out an enemy that's out on its own and attack it from behind with Exceed Red Queen slashes. Repeat the process for each enemy. All enemies in this group are weak against attacks from behind.

Dante Assaults attack more frequently than Angelo troops, so target the Assaults first. Switch to Dark Slayer and, to quickly see off the Assaults, use the same attack from behind with two slashes of Rebellion into two strikes with Yamato. It's worth noting that Yamato sword strikes can't be deflected by enemy shields. This 'Rebellion strikes into Yamato strikes' sequence will make a mess of any shield-bearing enemy. Use the same technique of attacking from behind on the Angelos so as to quickly clear the stage.

STAGE 14   Faust x 1

Nero Charge Shot combos are very effective against this enemy type. As soon as the stage commences, begin by holding a Charge Shot and rip at the creature's cloak repeatedly with Snatch. You don't need to move Nero in order to avoid the Faust attacks, so you can use your left thumb to hit **B** | Ⓞ to Snatch, while you hold **X** | Ⓟ and **A** | Ⓧ to jump the Faust attacks with your right. When the cloak is removed, perform a combo, ending with a level 3 Charge Shot, and then the Faust will recover his defence. Simply repeat the cycle again to win the stage.

Dante Select Swordmaster and Gilgamesh. Rush instantly towards Faust, while holding a Charge Shot with your shotgun, then jump up and fire a series of blasts at close range to quickly remove its cloak. Five or six of these blasts are usually needed to breach the Faust's defences; as soon as its cloak has been removed, perform Gilgamesh Real Impact twice to despatch the enemy in short order.

STAGE 15   Bianco Angelo x 2, Alto Angelo x 1

Nero Immediately upon starting, hold **X** | Ⓟ to prepare a Charge Shot. Take evasive action and then wait for the Angelos to assume their formation for launching an Energy Ball attack. Make sure you have the middle Angelo of the formation in your sights, (press Ⓛ | L3 to change Lock-On target) and as soon as the Energy Ball is launched release **X** | Ⓟ to repel the attack and kill the trio instantly.

Dante You have a choice here; either wait for the Angelo troops to get in formation for the Energy Ball attack, and deflect it with a melée attack of your own, or select Dark Slayer and use the 'Rebellion into Yamato sword strike' sequence against each enemy in turn. Either method you choose will see off these enemies quickly.

STAGE 16 Scarecrow (Arm) x 3 (Leg) x 3, Mega Scarecrow x 1

Nero Run forwards immediately and target the Mega Scarecrow that appears in your path. Launch it into an aerial combo, and then blast the enemy to the outer edge of the arena with Calibur. Follow up with your most powerful attacks (in DT if you already have it) to finish the Mega Scarecrow off before his smaller friends arrive. As soon as you've taken care of the Mega Scarecrow, turn your attention to the smaller minions - stay in the air and attack with aerial combos, using Enemy Step to preserve height.

Dante Select Swordmaster, Pandora and Rebellion. Rush immediately towards the Mega Scarecrow that appears in the middle of the arena and blast it towards the far, outer edge, using Stingers. When you get to the edge, switch to Gilgamesh and perform Real Impact. After the move connects, you may need a further couple of melée strikes to see the enemy off. When the Mega Scarecrow is dead, use the remaining Scarecrows to charge your Disaster Gauge, using the Extreme Jealousy technique. There are enough enemies here to recharge the Disaster Gauge fully.

STAGE 17 Alto Angelo x 2

Nero Use your Devil Trigger here. Break down an Angelo's shield and deal massive damage with the DT Buster. Once you have broken one enemy's shield, continue pressing the attack by repeating the DT Buster until the enemy's dead. Using up your Devil Trigger to kill one of these guys is well worth the gauge cost.

Dante Switch over to Dark Slayer and use Yamato to shatter these enemies' shields quickly. You can actually use the 'Rebellion into Yamato' cycle covered previously to attack both enemies at once. When you break an enemy's shield, try using Swordmaster and Gilgamesh's Real Impact to finish the job quickly.

STAGE 18 Blitz x 1

Nero Upon starting this stage, Blitz will stand in the middle, inactive. Use this brief pause, before the action starts, to fire off as many level 1 Charge Shots as you possibly can. As soon as you fire one Charge Shot, begin charging the next in order to keep up a continuous firing rate. Blitz will start to zap around the arena in the form of lightning, appearing every so often to attempt a striking attack, so keep moving! As soon as he appears, make sure you evade and fire off a Charge Shot. When Blitz's lightning Armor is removed by the Charge Shots, activate Devil Trigger and use the Buster to throw him. If you catch him repeatedly with DT Buster while his Armor is down, you'll make short work of him.

Dante Switch to Swordmaster and Gilgamesh. Coyote-A or Pandora are effective in removing the Blitz's lightning Armor. Given the choice, it's probably better to use Coyote-A, as speed and mobility are important in this fight. When the Blitz loses its lightning shield, reach its position quickly using Full House, activate Devil Trigger and perform Real Impact repeatedly for as long as Blitz remains defenceless.

STAGE 19 Basilisk x 4

Nero Run forwards immediately and launch the first Basilisk you meet into an aerial combo. Instead of killing it in the air, deploy Buster so that you can use the Basilisk to launch a projectile attack at another. Repeat this process and you'll make light work of this stage.

Dante Switch quickly to Gunslinger and Pandora. Jump into the air immediately, as high as possible, switch into PF594: Argument and fire off a volley of missiles. Deactivate PF594 immediately after the attack to conserve the Disaster Gauge and mop up the remaining enemies using melée strikes.

STAGE 20 Boss: **Berial**

🖥 | 03_38
03_39

Please refer to the Opponents chapter for a full strategy for this Boss Fight.

05

Bloody Palace Stage 21 - 40

02:24:55

Arena (external appearance)

Stage	Enemy set	Total No	Remarks
21	Frost x 1, Mephisto x 2	3	
22	Frost x 2, Faust x 1	3	
23	Frost x 2, Assault x 3	5	
24	Assault x 3, Basilisk x 4	7	
25	Assault x 3, Blitz x 1	4	
26	Blitz x 1, Basilisk x 4	5	Recover health here
27	Frost x 2, Bianco Angelo x 2	4	
28	Assault x 2, Gladius x 8	10	Recover Devil Trigger here
29	Blitz x 1, Gladius x 6	7	Recover health and Devil Trigger here
30	Assault x 6, Frost x 4, Blitz x 1	11	Mid Boss - Assault-Type Festival
31	Mephisto x 3, Chimera Seed x 7	10	Recover health here
32	Faust x 1, Scarecrow x 3	4	
33	Mephisto x 2, Mega Scarecrow x 1	3	
34	Mephisto x 6	6	
35	Mephisto x 3, Frost x 1	4	
36	Faust x 1, Scarecrow (Leg) x 2	3	
37	Mephisto x 2, Assault x 3	5	
38	Mephisto x 2, Blitz x 1	3	
39	Faust x 1, Chimera Seed x 5	6	Recover health here
Garden of god's punishment: Snow			
40	**Boss: Bael**		Boss battle 2 - Time addition before boss battle, health recovery after battle

STAGE 21 Frost x 1, Mephisto x 2

Nero At the beginning of the stage, run forwards and attack the Frost first. The aim is to use a combo to blast the Frost as far away from the Mephisto pair as possible and as quickly as you can. It's important to remember that executing a launcher directly after a Snatch against a Frost will guarantee that the enemy is lifted off the ground. Take care of the Frost with aerial combos, and then use the same Snatch/Charge Shot set-up that was described for Stage 6 against the remaining Mephistos.

Dante Switch to Swordmaster, Coyote-A and Rebellion. Rush in quickly and attack the Frost with a rapid barrage of repeated Stingers until it dies. Now turn your attention to the Mephistos and switch to Gilgamesh. Use Enemy Step cancelled Coyote-A shots to remove their cloaks quickly and kill each one with a Gilgamesh Real Impact, once their true form is revealed.

STAGE 22 Frost x 2, Faust x 1

Nero Once again, take advantage of the slow-moving nature of the Faust to quickly attack the Frosts before the Faust has a chance to close in and attack. Use EX-Act and aerial combos as much as you can when attacking the Frosts in order to dispatch them quickly. When they're overcome, use Snatch to remove the Faust's cloak and attack its true form with a combo ending in a Charge Shot.

Dante Sticking with Swordmaster, Coyote-A and Gilgamesh, rush forwards immediately and perform a Gilgamesh Real Impact against the Frost on the right. As soon as the move connects and you land, finish the job with a Full House or two. Keep an eye on the Faust as you rush over to the second Frost; attack this enemy with the same sequence. If you're quick, you'll have time to unleash a Real Impact before the Frost can escape from its cocoon! When the Frosts are out of the way, remove the Faust's cloak with Jump Cancelled Coyote-A shots and repeat Gilgamesh Real Impact once its defences are breached.

STAGE 23　　Frost x 2, Assault x 3

Nero　Have a Charge Shot ready from the start. Shortly after the stage begins, an Assault will pop up out of the central warp plate. Snatch this enemy and use a Buster to throw it at the group to damage the other enemies. At this point use your Charge Shot to scatter the group, and then Streak towards the one that ends up the furthest away from the rest of the enemies. Keep holding Charge Shots while Streaking at the enemy until it dies. You can then just continue using Exceeded Streaks against the enemies, while using Charge Shots to add damage and prevent incoming attacks.

Dante　As none of these enemies give cues, allowing you to judge attacks accurately, simply power in with a barrage of Stingers until they're all dead. The first Assault will pop up out of the middle of the arena, so rush in and attack it from behind with Stingers. The same goes for the Frosts. If you keep the pressure up with Stingers, a Frost will not be able to attack you. Any Assaults that stray too close will also get caught by the Stinger barrage.

STAGE 24　　Assault x 3, Basilisk x 4

Nero　As you start this stage, Snatch the first Assault you see and kill it with an aerial combo. The Assaults and Basilisk enemies will fight amongst themselves, so use this opportunity to pick off the Assaults by Snatching them away from the group one at a time. When the Assaults are dead, stay in the air and kill the Basilisks with Snatch into Buster.

Dante　Switch to Swordmaster and Rebellion. As soon as the stage starts, perform Over Drive to take care of a Basilisk in the distance, at which point an Assault should rush towards you. Use a barrage of Stingers to quickly see it off. Attack each Assault with Stingers and the Basilisks with Aerial Rave. Keep moving and varying your attack patterns so that the Basilisks find it difficult to target you.

STAGE 25　　Assault x 3, Blitz x 1

Nero　The Blitz doesn't appear immediately, so use this time to kill a couple of Assaults, Snatch and launch each one into an aerial combo to see it off. Once the Blitz arrives it will attack anyone, so use this to your advantage by keeping the last remaining Assault alive - the Blitz will target the Assault instead of you.

Dante　The Assaults will pop out of the ground in a straight line in front of where you are, just begging for an Over Drive! Deploy this continuously for as long as possible before switching over to a rapid barrage of Stingers to rid yourself of the Assaults swiftly. When the Blitz appears, switch over to Coyote-A and Gilgamesh. Remove its shield with Coyote-A blasts before going in for the kill with as many Devil Trigger Real Impacts as you can.

STAGE 26　　Blitz x 1, Basilisk x 4

Nero　Target the Blitz right away and ignore the Basilisks completely. Keep firing Charge Shots at the Blitz. The Basilisks won't attack you at this point but will concentrate on the Blitz instead. Once the Blitz's defences are down, activate Devil Trigger and repeat Buster as many times as you can, firing Summoned Swords at the same time. Allow the Blitz to go berserk and attack the Basilisks, which makes your life easier as all you have to do is mop up the mess.

Dante　As soon as the stage begins, perform Over Drive. The Basilisks will launch fireballs at the Blitz as your Over Drive connects, which will weaken its shield significantly. When the Blitz starts moving, use Coyote-A shots to disable its shield. Activate Devil Trigger and deploy Gilgamesh Real Impact as many times as you can. When the Blitz goes crazy, either attempt to kill it with shots or evade until it self-destructs. Don't attempt to attack the Basilisks while the Blitz is in its crazed state, or you will be at risk of a very heavy attack.

05

STAGE 27 Frost x 2, Bianco Angelo x 2

Nero Take care of the Frosts first, each with Snatch into an aerial combo. Staying airborne is your best defence against most of the Bianco Angelo's attacks. As soon as the Frosts are dead, attack each Bianco from behind, using EX-Act slashes to dispatch them quickly.

Dante Unleash a constant and rapid barrage of Stingers against the Frosts. If you have time, you may want to connect a Real Impact when a Frost is knocked down. Keep up the barrage and the Frosts will be unable to attack you, while the Stinger's fast motion will stop the Biancos being able to

launch a sneak attack. When the Frosts are dead, switch to Dark Slayer and, as you attack from behind, use a continuous cycle of two Rebellion strikes into two Yamato strikes. This method makes it impossible for a Bianco to counter-attack or to escape the combo.

STAGE 28 Assault x 2, Gladius x 8

Nero Snatch and throw Gladius at other Gladius or Assaults. With skilful timing, and by using these living swords as weapons, you can clear this area quite easily.

Dante Ignore the Gladius and power into the Assaults with a rapid barrage of Stingers, listening out for the metallic ring the Gladius give when they're about to strike. Use this as your cue

to evade. Once the Assaults are dead, use Coyote-A to blast the Gladius out of the air and then use Stingers to chase and attack.

STAGE 29 Blitz x 1, Gladius x 6

Nero Although throwing Gladius at Blitz will weaken his lightning armour quickly, there are simply too many Gladius flying around at once to make targeting accurate. You are therefore advised to stay in the air to avoid Blitz's attacks. Throw the Gladius at each other, but aim to kill all but one. One Gladius kept alive will confuse Blitz's target-

ing. From this point, use Charge Shots to remove his armour and then, when his defences fail, go in for the kill using DT Buster repeatedly.

Dante Switch to Swordmaster, Coyote-A and Gilgamesh. Fire Coyote-A repeatedly to blast the Gladius out of the air and use Full House to reach the

location of each of them, so that you can kill them with melée strikes. Aim to kill all except one Gladius; the one that's left will confuse Blitz's targeting. Use Coyote-A to remove the Blitz's shield before striking at it repeatedly with Devil Trigger Gilgamesh Real Impact.

STAGE 30 Assault x 6, Frost x 4, Blitz x 1

Nero Starting with the Frosts, Snatch and Launch the first Frost so that it emerges into an aerial combo. Use Roulette Spin and Buster to throw the enemy at another Frost. Repeat this sequence in order to take care of the Frosts and when the Assaults come in, activate Devil Trigger and attack continually with DT Streak to prevent them launching a counter-attack. A useful tactic is to

bunch the enemies up along the edge of the arena and continue attacking them with Streak (using DT if you have it). Finally, when confronting the Blitz, weaken its shield with a Charge Shot Level 3, followed by some more Charge Shot Level 1s. Then go in for the kill with DT Buster, while firing Summoned Swords.

Dante Pressurise the Frosts constantly with a rapid barrage

of Stingers and, whenever you get the chance, launch Real Impact against any downed foe. Activate Devil Trigger against the Assaults and use DT Stingers the same way. Keep piling on the pressure so that they don't get a chance to attack you. When the Blitz appears, use Coyote-A to blast away its shield before going in for the kill with as many DT Real Impacts as you can muster.

STAGE 31 — Mephisto x 3, Chimera Seed x 7

Nero Pile into the Chimera Seeds immediately with an EX Level 3 Streak and then clear up the mess by jumping above the group and killing each Seed with Snatch to Buster. The Mephistos will show up shortly before you've killed all the Seeds. Be sure to kill all of the Chimera Seeds before you commence battle against the Mephistos. Snatch the cloak off and use a Charge Shot combo on each Mephisto to nullify the chances of being interrupted by one unannounced attack after another. The key is to watch all other Mephistos carefully as you Snatch at your target. Just jumping will suffice to avoid their attacks, so keep watching out carefully for their signals and audio cues, and you'll score a No Damage clear bonus.

Dante Switch straight into Swordmaster, Coyote-A and Rebellion. Perform Over Drive against the Chimera Seeds repeatedly, and from as far away as possible. Should any Seeds manage to advance towards you, just distance yourself from them again and let them have it with Over Drive. As soon as they're dead, use Enemy Step cancelled Coyote-A shots quickly to blast every Mephisto's cloak away. As soon as you've removed a cloak, switch to Gilgamesh and deliver a two Gilgamesh Combo A strikes, Kick 13 into a Full House combo to make a quick kill, at all times retaining your mobility.

STAGE 32 — Faust x 1, Scarecrow x 3

Nero The Faust's attacks are infrequent compared with those of the Scarecrows, so target these minnows first. When they are out of the way, deal quickly with the Faust using Snatch and Charge Shot combos. To speed things up here you may want to use Devil Trigger when attacking either enemy type. You can kill the Scarecrows or the Faust and still have half of your Devil Trigger gauge left.

Dante As soon as this stage begins, perform Over Drive repeatedly to see off the Scarecrows before they have a chance to do anything. When the Scarecrows are dead, use Enemy Step cancelled Coyote-A blasts to remove the Faust's cloak before going in for the kill with Devil Trigger Real Impact.

STAGE 33 — Mephisto x 2, Mega Scarecrow x 1

Nero Rush in and attack the Mega Scarecrow first. The slow-moving nature of the two Mephistos will ensure that they're unable to keep up with you if you blast the Mega Scarecrow round the edge of the arena. But if you want to speed things up against the remaining Mephistos, you can remove their cloaks instantly by activating Devil Trigger and firing a Maximum Bet.

Dante The Mega Scarecrow will not attack very often, so destroy the Mephistos first by removing their cloaks with Enemy Step cancelled Coyote-A blasts and then, once one of the creature's true from is revealed, with a Real Impact. When the Mephistos are dead, turn your attention to the Mega Scarecrow. Providing you keep up a barrage of strikes, it won't be able to attack you. Use this to your advantage and charge the Disaster Gauge as much as you can, using Extreme Jealousy, before ending the stage.

STAGE 34 — Mephisto x 6

Nero As these Mephistos bunch together in a group, you can use the secondary explosive effect of Charge Shot Level 3 to defrock a large number of them in one hit. Use a combination of Charge Shot Level 3 and Snatch to weaken their defences before powering in with a big EX-Act enhanced or Charge Shot combo.

Dante Target any Mephisto immediately and remove its cloak with Enemy Step cancelled Coyote-A shots. When one of them has been downed, deliver a 2 Gilgamesh Combo A strikes, Kick 13 into Full House combo to kill the creature, while maintaining the ability to evade out of the sequence should you see an attack coming. Repeat this sequence for all six Mephistos to clear the stage quickly.

STAGE 35 — Mephisto x 3, Frost x 1

Nero The Frost will stay cocooned and inactive in the middle of the arena for quite a while, so long as you make sure you don't venture too close. Use the time to take care of the Mephistos and break their defences with a combination of Charge Shot Level 3 and Snatch, before powering in with a big combo.

Dante Let the Mephistos come to you, but keep away from the Frost at this point. Once the Mephistos have made their way to your side of the arena, use Enemy Step cancelled Coyote-A shots at close range to destroy one of the creatures' defences, and then finish the job with Real Impact or a Kick 13 combo. As soon as

the Mephistos are out of commission, deploy a rapid barrage of Stingers to deal damage to the Frost, while at the same time stopping its attacks before they can get started.

STAGE 36 — Faust x 1, Scarecrow (Leg) x 2

Nero As you start this stage you'll see a Scarecrow appear on either side of you. Choose a side and then attack the Scarecrow in such a way that it is blasted across the arena. Use Streak repeatedly. Replicate the technique against the other Scarecrow. The aim is to stay on the move and keep away from

the Faust. When the second Scarecrow is no more, turn your attention to the Faust and strike hard at its true form after breaking its defence with Snatch and Charge Shots.

Dante Ignore the Scarecrows that appear beside you and rush forwards towards the middle of

the arena. As soon as the Faust appears, remove its cloak with Jump Cancelled Coyote-A shots and eliminate the creature instantly with Devil Trigger Real Impact. De-activate Devil Trigger and kill the Scarecrows with combo strikes. Charge your Disaster Gauge fully, using Extreme Jealousy if you need it.

STAGE 37 — Mephisto x 3, Assault x 3

Nero A good way of attacking the Assaults, while all the time staying on the move to avoid the Mephistos' attacks, is to use Streak continuously to blast them around the edge. Once you've taken care of the

Assaults, use Snatch or Charge Shots to remove the Mephistos' cloaks before powering in with a big combo on each of them.

Dante Switch to Gunslinger right away and perform PF666:

Omen, which kills the Assaults and leaves the Mephistos at death's door. Hurry over to the Mephistos and deliver a Gilgamesh Full House to each of them, wiping them out.

STAGE 38 — Mephisto x 2, Blitz x 1

Nero The Blitz's zapping around the arena will help weaken the Mephistos cloak armour. But before attempting to fight the Blitz, be sure to kill both Mephistos with a Snatch and Charge Shot routine. The worst thing that can happen is if a Mephisto knocks you out of your Devil Trigger Buster

against the Blitz, so make sure they're eliminated.

Dante Speed is very important here! Disable the cloak of a Mephisto quickly, using Enemy Step cancelled Coyote-A shots before killing the creature with a 2 strikes of Gilgamesh Combo A, Kick 13, and finally

a Full House. Aim to kill these creatures as quickly as possible because, when the Blitz appears on the scene, it will do its best to mess up anything you do. Having dispatched the Mephistos, concentrate on the Blitz. Remove its shielding with Coyote-A before striking at it with Devil Trigger Real Impact.

Nero   Make clearing the Chimera Seeds stage your top priority! When the stage starts, a pair of Chimera Seeds will appear right next to you. Use Buster to kill them instantly and then run to the other side of the arena to the other bunch of Seeds. The Faust will have appeared at this point, so quickly jump above the second group of Chimera Seeds and Snatch to Buster all of them. A final set of Chimera Seeds will now appear in a row in the middle of the arena. Use the EX Level 3 you've stored to plough through the group and finish them off quickly with Snatch to Buster cycles. Once the stage is cleared

of Seeds, focus on the Faust using Charge Shots and Snatch to weaken its armour before going in for the kill.

Dante   A pair of Chimera Seeds will appear in your location as soon as the stage begins. It's very important that you kill these as fast as possible with combo strikes. As soon as you kill the nearby Seeds, target the ones on the far side and use Over Drive to kill them. If you're fast enough you'll clear the stage of Seeds before the Faust arrives. When the Faust appears, use Coyote-A to remove its cloak, and then attack its true form with Devil Trigger Real Impact. With the Faust gone, all that remains is to use Over Drive from a long distance to kill the final set of Chimera Seeds and obtain a boost to your health.

STAGE 40   Boss: **Bael**

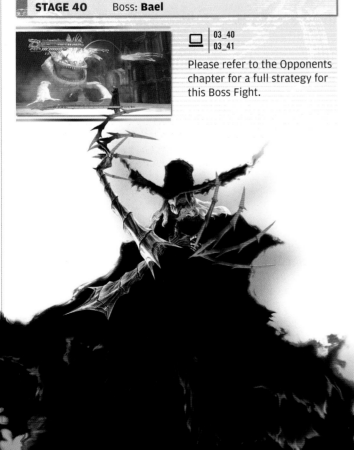

📺   03_40
    03_41

Please refer to the Opponents chapter for a full strategy for this Boss Fight.

Bloody Palace Stage 41 - 60

`02:24:55`

Arena (external appearance)

Stage	Enemy set	Total No	Remarks
41	Chimera Seed x 10	10	Recover health here
42	Chimera Seed x 4, Scarecrow(Leg) x 2, Chimera-Scarecrow(Arm) x 3	9	Recover health here
43	Chimera-Assault x 4	4	
44	Chimera Seed x 6, Gladius x 6	12	Recover health and Devil Trigger here
45	Chimera-Assault x 2, Blitz x 1	3	
46	Chimera Seed x 4, Basilisk x 2	6	Recover health here
47	Chimera Seed x 5, Bianco Angelo x 2, Alto Angelo x 1	8	Recover health here
48	Chimera Seed x 6, Scarecrow(Leg) x 1	7	Recover health here
49	Chimera-Assault x 3, Faust x 1	4	Recover health and Devil Trigger here
50	Chimera Seed x 15, Scarecrow(Arm, Leg) x 6, Assault x 6, Mid Boss - Parasite Festival	28	Recover health here
51	Scarecrow(Arm) x 6	6	Recover health here
52	Scarecrow(Leg) x 3, Gladius x 9	12	Recover Devil Trigger here
53	Mega Scarecrow x 3, Frost x 2	5	
54	Scarecrow(Arm, Leg) x 5, Alto Angelo x 1	6	
55	Mega Scarecrow x 1, Faust x 1	2	
56	Mega Scarecrow x 1, Alto Angelo x 2	3	
57	Scarecrow(Arm, Leg) x 4, Mephisto x 3	7	
58	Mega Scarecrow x 1, Basilisk x 5	6	
59	Chimera-Scarecrow(Arm) x 2, Mega Scarecrow x 1, Chimera Seed x 4	7	Recover health here
Garden of god's punishment: Dragon			
60	**Boss: Echidna**		Boss battle 3 - Time addition before boss battle, health recovery after battle

05

STAGE 41 — Chimera Seed x 10

Nero Jump up above the group of Chimera seeds immediately and, while remaining airborne and completely out of range of their attack, Snatch to Buster each one in turn. This technique will bring you swift

victory and an easy, No Damage bonus.

Dante As soon as the stage starts, execute Over Drive. Continue repeating this move until one or more of the Seeds start

advancing towards you. Attack with Stingers at close range before mopping up any remaining enemies with additional Over Drives.

STAGE 42 — Chimera Seed x 4, Scarecrow(Leg) x 2, Chimera-Scarecrow(Arm) x 3

Nero At first, ignore the three Chimera-Scarecrows. Jump up above the Chimera Seeds and Snatch to Buster each one, making instant kills. Next, target the Scarecrow (Leg)s and kill each one quickly with a decent combo. Finally,

move on to the Chimera-Scarecrow (Arm)s. Use a Charge Shot to stop the parasites' attack, and then kill each one with a combo.

Dante Once again, Over Drive is your best friend. Keep

your distance and launch Over Drive repeatedly at the group of enemies. If any Seed starts to advance to your position, kill it off quickly with a rapid barrage of Stingers.

STAGE 43 — Chimera-Assault x 4

Nero The absence of audio or visual cues makes these enemies extremely difficult to predict. Use Charge Shot Level 1 repeatedly to disable the parasites, before moving in for the kill with a ranged attack, such as EX Streak or Shuffle. If you find yourself surrounded, just move as far as possible out

of the way and resume fire with Charge Shots.

Dante As these enemies don't give you any sort of clue as to when they are going to attack, don't waste time trying out clever defensive tactics. Switch over to Pandora and Rebellion and disable the parasites with

a PF013: Epidemic shot (the explosive area damage will also hurt the parasites) before powering in with a rapid barrage of Stingers. If this enemy group becomes too hot to handle, activate Devil Trigger and perform DT Stingers instead.

STAGE 44 — Chimera Seed x 6, Gladius x 6

Nero Snatch and throw the nearest Gladius immediately to kill another. At this point, employ a sequence of Snatch to Buster to evade and to take care of any Gladius that stray too close. To deal with the Chimera Seeds without the risk of getting hurt, jump above them and,

while airborne, Snatch to Buster each one.

Dante Select Swordmaster, Coyote-A and Lucifer. As you start the stage, hold your position and summon a full set of Lucifer blades. Execute the Climax Command and allow the

Gladius to target your position before evading. The Climax formation will kill any Gladius that comes into contact with it. Continue this cycle of summoning blades and executing Climax to see off the enemy group safely.

STAGE 45 — Chimera-Assault x 2, Blitz x 1

Nero When fighting the Assaults, use Charge Shots to stop the parasites' attacks and power in with a ranged attack, such as EX Streak. The Blitz will appear as soon as you kill one of the Chimera-Assaults. Make sure both Assaults are dead before you start fighting the Blitz, since Chimera-Assaults have a nasty

and annoying habit of breaking your Buster combo against it.

Dante Switch to Pandora and Rebellion. Use Pandora's PF013: Epidemic shot to disable the parasite that's attached itself to an Assault before powering in with a barrage of Stingers. Repeat the cycle of PF013: Epi-

demic to Stinger barrage to see off both enemies quickly. Once the Blitz appears, switch over to Coyote-A and Gilgamesh, and remove the Blitz's lightning with Coyote-A blasts before going in for the kill with Devil Trigger Real Impact.

STAGE 46   Chimera Seed x 4, Basilisk x 2

Nero   Jump up immediately above the group of Chimera Seeds and Snatch to Buster each one to make instant kills. The Basilisks will try to get involved shortly after your attack run starts, so just add them to the mix. If you deploy Snatch to Buster repeatedly in mid-air you'll be victorious in no time and gain an easy No Damage bonus.

Dante   At the beginning of this stage the Chimera Seeds will be dormant. Use the opportunity to kill the Basilisks quickly with a solid ground to air combo on each of them. As soon as the Basilisks are out of the way, use Over Drive or a barrage of Stingers, depending on the distance, to rout the Chimera Seeds and gain a health boost.

STAGE 47   Chimera Seed x 5, Bianco Angelo x 2, Alto Angelo x 1

Nero   Go for the Chimera Seeds first. The Angelos need a few moments to set up their attacks, so use the time to kill the Chimera Seeds with Snatch to Buster. When they're dead, check whether the Angelo trio are about to execute their Energy Ball formation; if so, repel the Energy Ball with a Charge Shot, killing all three of them instantly. If the Angelos fail to assume their Energy Ball formation, don't waste time waiting for it. Use your Devil Trigger to kill the two Bianco Angelos, and then deactivate Devil Trigger. Finally, break the Alto Angelo's shield and kill it using Buster.

Dante   As you start this stage you'll have time to fire off two Over Drives to kill the Chimera Seeds in the distance. After the second Over Drive, evade the Angelos and ward off any remaining Chimera Seeds with Stingers. With the Seeds dead, either repel the Angelo Energy Ball attack, or keep up a combo cycle while attacking from behind with Dark Slayer, or you can knock them down and attack them with Real Impact.

STAGE 48   Chimera Seed x 6, Scarecrow (Leg) x 1

Nero   When this stage begins, activate Devil Trigger straight away and execute a Charged Maximum Bet. This projectile attack will mow down the line of Chimera Seeds, leaving you with just a small mess to clear up. Jump above the enemies that remain and slay them with Snatch to Buster.

Dante   As soon as you see the Chimera Seeds fall into position, deploy Over Drive repeatedly. Since the enemy group is ranged in a straight line, they won't stand an earthly against such an assault.

STAGE 49   Chimera-Assault x 3, Faust x 1

Nero   As Chimera-Assaults are nigh impossible to read when in a group like this, you're advised to take these guys out first with Charge Shots and ranged attacks. When the Assaults are dead, kill the Faust by using Snatch to remove its cloak and attack it with a big Charge Shot combo.

Dante   The Chimera Assaults will attack constantly and without supplying cues. Use Pandora to disable the parasite attacks and then power in with a barrage of Stingers against each of the Assaults. When the Assaults are out of the way, kill the Faust by disabling its cloak with Enemy Step cancelled Coyote-A blasts, followed, once its defences have been breached, by a Devil Trigger Real Impact.

STAGE 50 — Chimera Seed x 15, Scarecrow (Arm, Leg) x 6, Assault x 6

Nero Initially, stay up in the air as much as possible, using Snatch to Buster to take care of the Chimera Seeds and aerial combos to deal with the Scarecrows. When the Assaults make their presence felt, use a cycle of Charge Shots into DT Stinger in order to stop the parasite attack, while dealing damage to the whole group. If you maintain the sequence of Charge Shot, Streak and Snatch to Buster against any remaining Chimera Seeds, this enemy group will capitulate.

Dante Use Over Drive in the first instance to attack the enemies in the distance. Immediately thereafter, when the Assaults enter the scene, switch over to a rapid barrage of Stingers to see off each one quickly. The Chimeras will target the Assaults, so don't worry about them sneaking up on you. Once the Assaults are out of the way, continue attacking the remaining Chimera Seeds with Stingers. Some dormant Scarecrows may be left over. If so, use this opportunity to charge the Disaster Gauge with the Extreme Jealousy technique.

STAGE 51 — Scarecrow (Arm) x 6

Nero Simply move around the arena, activating and killing each Scarecrow in turn. Stay off the ground and perform aerial combos to win yourself a quick and easy No Damage clear bonus.

Dante Move around the arena, activating and killing each Scarecrow in turn, and charge the Disaster Gauge fully before you finish the stage.

STAGE 52 — Scarecrow (Leg) x 3, Gladius x 9

Nero None of the enemies here are particularly threatening, but be careful not to be swamped by them. As you begin the stage, grab the nearest Gladius and throw it at another. Repeat this move until you have cleared the arena of swords.

Stay airborne so that the Scarecrow can't attack you.

Dante Switch Immediately to Gunslinger and perform PF666: Omen to see off the group of Gladius. When the next two Gladius arrive, switch to Coyote-A to knock them out of the air. Kill the two remaining Gladius without delay, before using PF262: Jealousy shots against the remaining Scarecrows to eliminate them, boosting the Disaster Gauge at the same time with a small charge.

STAGE 53 — Mega Scarecrow x 3, Frost x 2

Nero Exploit the slow-moving nature of the Mega Scarecrows by separating them and attacking them individually. When two are dead, a pair of Frosts will appear. Activate Devil Trigger quickly, killing the last remaining Mega Scarecrow and one of the Frosts. Against the final Frost, use ground-based combos interrupted with Snatch to prevent it attacking you. You'll notice from this point onwards that Frosts can easily escape your aerial combos, so keep this Snatch cancel technique in mind!

Dante Switch to Swordmaster, Pandora and Rebellion. Use Stingers to blast a Mega Scarecrow to the outer edge of the arena. Launch it from here, use the Extreme Jealousy technique to charge 1/3 of the Disaster Gauge, and then kill it with a Gilgamesh Real Impact. Repeat the process for the other two Mega Scarecrows and when the Frosts appear attack with a barrage of Stingers. If they start getting rowdy, activate Devil Trigger and use DT Stinger instead.

Nero   Concentrate at first on taking care of the Scarecrows, as the Alto Angelo will target and attack them as well. As soon as the Scarecrows have been dispatched, defeat the Alto with attacks from behind and deploy Buster when it blocks. When its shield is shattered, use Buster quickly to eliminate it.

Dante   Go after the Alto Angelo first. The Scarecrows' attacks can be read, so keep an eye (and ear) open for any of their attacks from the rear while you launch an attack on the Alto with a barrage of Stingers. You can disable the Alto's shield with a frontal barrage of Stingers but, if you need to speed things

up, activate Devil Trigger, switch to Dark Slayer and use a sword slash cycle as you attack from behind. As soon as the Alto is dead, use the Scarecrows (with the Extreme Jealousy technique) to give the Disaster Gauge a full charge.

Nero   Keep your distance from the Mega Scarecrow lying on the ground at the far side of the arena. Stick to the outer edge and kill the Faust first. Use Snatch to remove the Faust's cloak and attack it with big Charge Shot combos. Two cycles of this sequence will see it off. Once the Faust is out of the way the Mega Scarecrow will wake

up. This creature is nothing but a huge punch-bag; just keep the combos coming so that it can't move.

Dante   Switch to Swordmaster, Coyote-A and Gilgamesh. The Mega Scarecrow's attacks are infrequent, so rush straight past it and disable the Faust's cloak using Enemy Step

cancelled Coyote-A blasts. As soon as the enemy has been downed, activate Devil Trigger and perform Real Impact to kill it. A salvo of strikes will prevent the Mega Scarecrow from attacking, so push it to the edge of the arena with Stingers and perform another Real Impact.

Nero   Run straight past the Mega Scarecrow and attack the Angelos first. Strike at them, forcing them to block and then use Buster to weaken and eventually break their shields. After shattering an Alto's shield, use Buster over and over again until it dies. Repeat the process on the other Alto, while activating Devil Trigger to speed things up.

With the Altos out of commission, you'll be free to kill the Mega Scarecrow. Aerial combos, frequent use of Roulette Spin, plus Busters, will wrap things up nicely.

Dante   As the Mega Scarecrow attacks infrequently you can allow the Altos to come to you. Activate Devil Trigger and

use DT Stingers against them, switching over to Real Impact should you get the chance. Once the Angelos are out of the way, power into the Mega Scarecrow with a constant barrage of strikes to prevent it attacking. Give the Disaster Gauge a full charge, if you haven't already done so, before setting about to kill the Mega Scarecrow,

Nero   As Mephisto attack cues can be easily read, target and attack the Scarecrows first. While you're attacking, listen out for the high-pitched whistle that signals an imminent Mephisto attack. When the Scarecrows are out of the way, turn your attention to the Mephistos. If they're bunched up together,

it might pay to use Charge Shot Level 3 - its secondary explosive blast is very effective at weakening their protective cloaks. A combination of Charge Shots and Snatch will break down their defences, enabling you to go in for the kill with a strong combo.

Dante   Switch to Gunslinger and Pandora. Wait until the Mephistos get close to your position and unleash PF666: Omen. This will kill all the Scarecrows, leaving the Mephistos for you to Stinger quickly to death.

05

STAGE 58 Mega Scarecrow x 1, Basilisk x 5

Nero Rush in right away. Jump above the group and deliver a cycle of Snatch to Buster. This sequence will knock down all the enemies in the area and seriously damage both the Basilisks and Mega Scarecrow, hitting them at the same time. If the Mega Scarecrow survives, deploy regular combo strikes

and aerial combos to kill it without risk to yourself.

Dante Use Aerial Raves against the Basilisks, ridding yourself swiftly of any that stray too close. At all other times, a barrage of Stinger round the outer edge of the arena can mow down a number of these enemies in one go, preventing their attacks. When the Basilisks are dead, use the Mega Scarecrow to charge your Disaster Gauge via the Extreme Jealousy technique.

STAGE 59 Chimera-Scarecrow (Arm) x 2, Mega Scarecrow x 1, Chimera Seed x 4

Nero Activate your Devil Trigger Immediately and fire Charged Maximum Bet repeatedly to decimate this group of enemies before they get a chance to get anywhere near your position. When your Devil Trigger has finished, run over to the far side of the arena, jump up above any remaining

Chimera Seeds and use Snatch to Buster on them to kill them instantly. Finally, see off the Mega Scarecrow. If you keep your attacks constant, it will be unable to counter-attack.

Dante Immediately upon starting this stage, select Gunslinger and Pandora and perform PF666: Omen to kill off the Chimera Seeds and possibly the Scarecrows too (depending on the Disaster Gauge value). Mop up any stragglers with Stingers before powering into the Mega Scarecrow.

STAGE 60 Boss: **Echidna**

03_42
03_43

Please refer to the Opponents chapter for a full strategy for this Boss Fight.

Bloody Palace Stage 61 - 80

Arena (external appearance)

Stage	Enemy set	Total No	Remarks
61	Bianco Angelo x 4	4	
62	Bianco Angelo x 3, Cutlass x 2	5	
63	Bianco Angelo x 2, Blitz x 1	3	
64	Bianco Angelo x 1, Gladius x 6	7	Recover Devil Trigger here
65	Alto Angelo x 1, Bianco Angelo x 7	8	
66	Alto Angelo x 1, Basilisk x 4	5	
67	Alto Angelo x 2, Blitz x 1	3	
68	Bianco Angelo x 2, Scarecrow(Arm) x 6	8	
69	Alto Angelo x 1, Frost x 2	3	
70	Alto Angelo x 2, Bianco Angelo x 10, Mid Boss - Angel Troop Festival	13	
71	Gladius x 16	16	Recover Devil Trigger here
72	Gladius x 10, Mega Scarecrow x 1	11	Recover Devil Trigger here
73	Gladius x 8, Frost x 1	9	Recover Devil Trigger here
74	Cutlass x 2, Basilisk x 4	6	
75	Cutlass x 3, Alto Angelo x 1	4	
76	Cutlass x 4, Gladius x 8	12	Recover Devil Trigger here
77	Basilisk x 10	10	
78	Basilisk x 4, Frost x 2	6	
79	Basilisk x 2, Cutlass x 2, Gladius x 4	8	
Garden of god's punishment: Armor			
80	**Boss: Angelo Credo**		Boss battle 4 - Time addition before boss battle, health recovery after battle

Nero   Strike constantly at the Biancos from behind with EX-Act enhanced Red Queen Combo strikes. Deploy Streak when you're surrounded and Buster whenever you have a clear chance to use it.

Dante   Select Dark Slayer and Rebellion. Enter the fray quickly and strike each Bianco from behind with the 2-strikes Rebellion into 2-strikes Yamato combo sequence. It will be unable to attack while you strike at it in this fashion. While this is happening, concentrate on watching the other enemies around you and, before continuing the sequence, jump as soon as you see any incoming attacks.

Nero   Focus on the Cutlass first of all. When a Cutlass jumps out of the ground to attack you, use Snatch immediately to pull it to the ground, where you can continue the assault with a Buster or combo. Repeat this process on the other Cutlass before activating Devil Trigger and attacking each Bianco from behind.

Dante   Select Dark Slayer. Attack and kill each Bianco by striking at it from behind with the 2-strikes Rebellion into 2-strikes Yamato sword combo sequence. As this is happening, you'll be open to attack from the Cutlass enemies so, while you strike at each Bianco, listen out for the whistling audio cue the Cutlass give before they attack. A double whistle warns you that an attack is imminent. After you've taken care of the Biancos, switch to Swordmaster, Coyote-A and Gilgamesh. Allow the Cutlass to circle round you while you hold a Charge Shot. If a Cutlass attempts a diving attack, jump backwards and fire a Coyote-A Charge Shot to knock it out of the air, at which point a Real Impact will kill the creature instantly.

Nero   Leave the Biancos alone and fire Charge Shots continuously at the Blitz. The Biancos will also lend a hand against this powerful enemy. Continue firing Charge Shots until its armour is removed. Activate Devil Trigger and continue the Assault with DT Buster, while tapping ✕ | ⓪ to fire Summoned Swords.

This method enables you to kill the Blitz before it goes berserk, leaving you to clean up the now weakened Biancos with combo strikes from behind.

Dante   Continuing with Dark Slayer, use the Rebellion to Yamato sword cycle to get rid of the Biancos as quickly as possible. Allowing them to live will put you at risk while you're trying to attack the Blitz. As soon as the Biancos are out of the way, attack the Blitz with Coyote-A shots to weaken its shield, and then deliver repeated Devil Trigger Real Impact.

Nero   Jump up straight away and begin the assault by executing Snatch into Buster on the nearest Gladius. Keep this cycle going until all the swords have died, leaving the lone Bianco for you to finish off with combo strikes.

Dante   Select Dark Slayer, Coyote-A and Gilgamesh. As soon as the stage starts, perform Slash Dimension C and use Full House to launch an assault on the Gladius on the ground, attacking as many as possible with Gilgamesh strikes. When you've taken care of the Gladius enemies, use the Rebellion to Yamato combo cycle to attack the Bianco Angelo from behind.

Nero   Take evasive action, while the Alto Angelo commands the Biancos to launch suicide strikes at you - just keep running, and avoid any direct combat. When all seven Biancos are dead, activate Devil Trigger to make quick work of the Alto Angelo.

Dante   The Alto Angelo will command each set of Bianco Angelos to launch suicide attacks on you. Take evasive action until there are no Biancos left, and then use strikes from behind to kill off the single Alto.

05

STAGE 66 — Alto Angelo x 1, Basilisk x 4

Nero Rush straight into the melée that's in full swing in the middle of the arena and jump up above the group. Snatch and Buster any Basilisk while in mid-air and the resulting throw attack will floor all enemies in the area; repeat this sequence, while staying airborne, to kill the Basilisks off quickly. When up against the Alto, force it to block by performing combo strikes and break its shield with Buster, whereupon you can repeat DT Buster until it dies.

Dante Select Swordmaster and Rebellion. As the stage begins, the Basilisks will target you immediately, so evade the barrage of fireballs as fast as you can and kill each Basilisk with an Aerial Rave combo. Remaining off the ground like this will keep you out of the way, safe from the Alto's attacks. When the Basilisks are dead, knock the Alto down and perform Real Impact to dispatch it quickly.

STAGE 67 — Alto Angelo x 2, Blitz x 1

Nero Fire Charge Shots continually at the Blitz to remove its armour and ignore the Altos when they arrive; concentrate solely on the Blitz and use DT Buster when its defence is down. Keep firing Summoned Swords while DT Buster is being executed and you'll kill the creature after three repetitions. When the Blitz is dead, see off the Altos by breaking their shields and performing Buster. Note that you can avoid any Alto Angelo attack simply by executing Shuffle. After an Alto has deflected one of your sword strikes, perform Shuffle immediately to snuff out any counter-attack.

Dante Select Swordmaster, Coyote-A and Gilgamesh. Weaken the Blitz's lightning armour with Coyote-A shots, and then perform 2 Devil Trigger Real Impacts when its defences are down. The pair of Alto Angelos will appear at this point. Concentrate on evading the now completely mad Blitz, while attacking with Coyote-A shots. When the Blitz is killed by your shots, or it self-destructs, switch over to Dark Slayer and strike at each of the Altos using the Rebellion into Yamato sword combo cycle.

STAGE 68 — Bianco Angelo x 2, Scarecrow (Arm) x 6

Nero The Scarecrows are slow moving, which makes it easy to keep an eye on them even while you're busy, so you can see off the Bianco Angelos first with EX-Act combo strikes from behind. Having got rid of them you can then take care of the Scarecrows, using aerial combos to keep out of range of their attacks.

Dante The Biancos are likely to dash towards you when this stage begins, so use the opportunity to mete out strikes from behind with the Rebellion to Yamato combo cycle while you're still some distance from the Scarecrows. When both Biancos are dead, use the Extreme Jealousy technique to charge up the Disaster Gauge.

STAGE 69 — Alto Angelo x 1, Frost x 2

Nero The Frosts will remain cocooned, so wait for the Alto to come to you. When it's in range, activate the Devil Trigger and use EX-Act enhance strikes and Buster to eliminate it quickly. As soon as the Frosts are awake, Snatch them and launch them as often as you can into aerial combos to stop them attacking.

Dante Switch to Dark Slayer and Rebellion. When the stage begins you'll see that the two Frosts are lying dormant in their ice cocoons. When the Alto dashes towards you, use the Rebellion to Yamato sword combo cycle to kill it quickly. Now, turn your attention to the Frosts. By constantly performing Stinger, you can attack them continuously while preventing their attacks on you. Use this approach on both enemies.

Nero   Attack the Bianco Angelos from behind with EX-Act enhanced strikes and kill them all off, at which point the Alto Angelo will appear. Wait for the Alto to issue the Energy Ball formation command and repel the projectile attack with a Charge Shot. Another set of Angelos will appear so, once again, wait for the Energy Ball formation and parry the attack, killing the group instantly.

Dante   Use Kick 13 to attack the Biancos from the rear. As soon as they've been knocked over, unleash a Real Impact, if you have time, or simply continue the assault with combo strikes into another Kick 13. After you've killed a couple of Bianco Angelos, an Alto will appear. Wait for the enemies to assume the Energy Ball formation and repel the attack. A final set of Angelos will now make

an appearance. Again, wait for the Energy Ball attack and repel the blast. This will destroy the whole group instantly.

Nero   At the start of this stage, activate Devil Trigger and use Snatch to Buster to throw the Gladius at each other. The Gladius replenish your Devil Trigger as you kill them, so aim to stay in Devil Trigger for the

whole stage to speed things up.

Dante   Select Swordmaster, Coyote-A and Lucifer. Summon a full set of blades immediately, using Pinup, and then arrange the blades in Climax formation.

Whenever a Gladius rushes in and connects with a blade it will be killed instantly, so you should repeat the sequence of summoning blades and setting them up around you with Climax to dispatch the enemy quickly.

Nero   Use Devil Trigger and Snatch to Buster cycles to throw the Gladius at each other. Once the Gladius are out of the way, rush in and destroy the Mega Scarecrow with combo strikes and aerial combos.

Dante   Use a combination of Lucifer Climax and Coyote-A shots to make short shrift of the Gladius. As soon as you've got rid of them, launch the Mega Scarecrow and charge the Dis-

aster Gauge using the Extreme Jealousy technique.

Nero   Snatch to Buster the Gladius until your Devil Trigger gauge is full and then attack the Frost. Snatch and launch the creature repeatedly to prevent it from attacking. Once it's dead, concentrate once more on throwing the Gladius at each other.

Dante   Switch to Gunslinger. Without further ado, perform PF666: Omen, using the Disaster Gauge charge from the previous stage. Pick off the remaining Gladius with Coyote-A blasts, while keeping your distance from the Frost. If the Frost

is still cocooned at this point, go on the attack using Real Impact. If it's already awake, use Stingers to blast it to the edge of the arena and, as soon as it's been floored, perform a Real Impact.

Nero   Rush forwards immediately past the Cutlass and towards the Basilisks in the

distance. Launch or Snatch to launch a Basilisk and perform a Roulette Spin, Snatch and finally a Buster. Repeat this sequence for all Basilisks, while listening out for the whistling audio cue the Cutlass give when they're about to strike. As soon as you hear a cue, perform a Side-Roll before using Snatch on another

target or chasing it with Streak. As soon as you're clear of the Basilisks, use Snatch to pull each Cutlass to the ground when it launches a diving attack. Kill it with an aerial combo into Buster. Activate Devil Trigger if you need it.

Dante   Switch to Swordmaster, Coyote-A and Gilgamesh. Use Kick 13 and Full House to attack the Basilisks. If any Cutlass attempts a diving attack, simply jump backwards and blast the creature out of the air with a Coyote-A shot. The moment it hits the deck, kill it instantly with Real Impact.

05

STAGE 75 — Cutlass x 3, Alto Angelo x 1

Nero   As soon as this stage commences, the three Cutlasses will attempt to attack from the ground beneath you, so jump away from this position and Snatch a Cutlass when it emerges. Kill the creature swiftly with an aerial combo and Buster before moving on to the Alto Angelo. Activate Devil Trigger and set up a Buster situation as soon as possible, either by knocking the Alto down or by breaking its shield. With the Alto gone, either use a Charge Shot to knock each Cutlass out of the ground or wait for one to emerge when on the attack, then catch it with Snatch. When you knock a Cutlass to the ground, use an aerial combo that includes Roulette Spin; the extra altitude will make it harder for the other Cutlass to reach you.

Dante   Rush towards the Alto Angelo and power in with a rapid barrage of Stingers, the aim being to force the Alto to the edge of the arena. Once in position, activate Devil Trigger and perform DT Stingers back and forth through the Alto. The Cutlass will try and attack you at this point, only to get caught up in your Stinger assault.

STAGE 76 — Cutlass x 4, Gladius x 8

Nero   Use a combination of Charge Shots and Snatch to Buster cycles to deal with the Gladius. Listen for the audio cues the Cutlass give and, whenever one jumps out to attack you, deploy either Buster or Snatch to Buster to destroy it. Charge Shot Level 3 is also very useful on this stage. If you shoot a Cutlass with a level 3, there's a strong possibility that the secondary explosion will eliminate the other Cutlass as well. Remember to give your Exceed Gauge a maximum charge fully before exiting the stage.

Dante   The key here is to attack the enemies through the defensive Climax formation. When the stage begins, summon the maximum number of blades with Lucifer and execute the Climax command. The aim is to make the enemies throw themselves into the Climax formation as they try to attack you. As soon as a Cutlass is caught by the formation, switch over to Gilgamesh to deliver a Kick 13 and then switch back to Lucifer to continue the sequence.

STAGE 77 — Basilisk x 10

Nero   As the stage begins you'll be surrounded by Basilisks. It's possible that they'll all attack you at the same time. If this happens, jump up and deliver an EX Level 3 Double-Down to scatter the group. Keep moving and use Streak frequently to mow down as many Basilisks as you can. After a successful Streak you'll be close enough to the enemy to enable you to Snatch and continue attacking with an aerial combo. Shuffle is very useful for evading incoming projectile attacks; watch out for the flash of light on a Basilisk's head before it fires and, with the help of Shuffle, simply sail through the attack.

Dante   Immediately after the start of this stage it's possible that the Basilisks will surround you and all attack at the same time. Jump up out of the ambush and power into the enemy group, using Stingers and DT Stingers as required. An alternative method is to activate Devil Trigger the moment the stage begins and perform Real Impact. With any luck, the move will connect as the Basilisks attack. Note: this is a high-risk strategy - and it's not 100% guaranteed!

STAGE 78 — Basilisk x 4, Frost x 2

Nero   Move into the middle of the arena and, when the Basilisks appear, repeat a Snatch to Buster cycle while remaining airborne, and damage all enemies in the immediate area. Activate your Devil Trigger against the Frosts and use a rapid barrage of DT Streaks to press home your attack while simultaneously preventing their counter-attacks.

Dante   Activate your Devil Trigger right away and perform DT Stingers against any enemy in the group. The aim is to bunch them up together, using Stingers, so that you can power into them around the outer edge of the arena. A sustained barrage of strikes will prevent the Frosts from attacking you. If you have time, use Real Impact against a downed Frost to kill it quickly.

Nero   Charge Shots work very well here! The Basilisks always stick close together, so prepare a Level 3 Charge Shot while Side-Rolling to avoid the strikes from the Cutlass. As soon as you have a Level 3 ready, fire it at one of the Basilisks. The secondary explosion will wipe out any other enemy in the vicinity (other Basilisks, most likely). Use Snatch and Buster whenever a Cutlass tries to get you with a diving attack. Alternatively, use Charge Shot Level 3 against the Cutlass to knock them out of the ground and

against the Basilisks to keep them at bay. Throw the final set of Gladius at each other to end this stage.

Dante   Attack the Basilisks first, as it's easier to read Cutlass attacks. Kill off each Basilisk with a Rebellion Combo into Aerial Rave. While attacking, keep an eye on the Cutlass and listen for their attack audio cues. As soon as you hear a cue, break off from the attack and evade before re-targeting your enemy. When you've taken care of the Basilisks, switch over to Lucifer. Summon a full set of blades and Climax to create a trap the Cutlass and Gladius will fall into whenever they attack. Each time a Cutlass is knocked out, use Gilgamesh Kick 13 or Real Impact to finish it off.

STAGE 80   Boss: **Angelo Credo**

🖥 03_44
03_45

Please refer to the Opponents chapter for a full strategy for this Boss Fight.

Bloody Palace Stage 81 - 100

Arena (external appearance)

Stage	Enemy set	Total No	Remarks
81	Scarecrow(Arm) x 3, Scarecrow(Leg) x 2, Mega Scarecrows 1	6	Enemies use Devil Trigger from this point onwards
82	Mephisto x 4, Faust x 1	5	
83	Frost x 4	4	
84	Chimera-Scarecrow(Arm) x 2, Chimera-Assault x 2, Chimera Seed x 12	16	Recover health here
85	Blitz x 2, Chimera Seed x 3	5	Recover health here
86	Bianco Angelo x 2, Alto Angelo x 1	3	
87	Gladius x 8, Basilisk x 4	12	Recover Devil Trigger here
88	Cutlass x 3, Bianco Angelo x 2	5	
89	Mega Scarecrows 3, Blitz x 1	4	
90	Scarecrow (Arm)(Leg)x 30, Mega Scarecrow x 3, Chimera Seed x 3, Mid Boss - Scarecrow Festival 2	37	Recover health here
91	Faust x 3	3	
92	Alto Angelo x 3, Bianco Angelo x 4	7	Recover Devil Trigger here
93	Assault x 7	7	
94	Chimera Seed x 6, Chimera-Scarecrow(Arm) x 3, Bianco Angelo x 2	11	Recover health here
95	Basilisk x 16, Chimera Seed x 4	20	Recover health here
96	Gladius x 8, Cutlass x 3, Bianco Angelo x 3	14	Recover Devil Trigger here
97	Mephisto x 6, Mega Scarecrow x 2	8	
98	Chimera-Scarecrow(Leg) x 2, Chimera-Assault x 2, Chimera Seed x 3	7	Recover health here
99	Alto Angelo x 2, Bianco Angelo x 44	46	
Garden of god's punishment: Insect			
100	**Boss: Angelo Agnus**		Boss battle 5 - Time addition before boss battle, health recovery after battle

STAGE 81 — Scarecrow (Arm) x 3,, Scarecrow (Leg) x 2, Mega Scarecrow x 1

Nero Things start off nice and simply here. Jump up over the group and kill the Scarecrows with aerial combos. Keep an eye on the Mega Scarecrow as you attack its lesser minions, in case it charges in with an attack. Air Hike to get away from it and then resume your attack on the Scarecrows. With the smaller enemies dead, move swiftly on to deal with the Mega Scarecrow, striking quickly to win an easy, No Damage clear bonus.

Dante Dash forwards immediately and blast the Mega Scarecrow to the edge of the arena. Once you've got it there, launch it into the air and charge the Disaster Gauge using Extreme Jealousy. Staying in the air like this will keep you safe from any attack. Your top priority here is to charge up the Disaster Gauge. As soon you have a full Disaster Gauge, finish off the remaining Scarecrows with aerial combos.

STAGE 82 — Mephisto x 4, Faust x 1

Nero Activate your Devil Trigger straight away and let fly with a Charged Maximum Bet. This projectile attack will de-cloak and immobilize any Mephisto in its path. Run towards the downed enemies and perform an EX Level 3 Streak. With luck you'll be able to kill two or three Mephistos instantly. Dispatch the remaining Mephistos using Snatch or Charge Shot to remove their cloak, and then power in with a powerful combo. The same technique applies to the Faust. Pay attention to its attack cues while you Snatch at its cloak and prepare a Charge Shot combo. Two cycles of this and it will die.

Dante Power straight in with Jump Cancelled Coyote-A blasts against any Mephisto. When the creature has been downed, use Gilgamesh for two strikes and continue with Kick 13 followed by a Full House to finish the job. Repeat the same sequence against all four Mephistos. When you move on to attack the Faust, use the shotgun to remove its cloak and then kill it with a Devil Trigger Real Impact.

STAGE 83 — Frost x 4

Nero The key to keeping these Frosts at bay is a combination of Charge Shot Level 3 and Snatch. Fire level 3 Charge Shots continuously. As soon as you shoot an enemy, chase it down using Streak and continue the Assault with EX-Act enhanced combo strikes, Snatch and then aerial combo. Frosts will find it easy to dodge Snatch from now on, so use Snatch only after you've downed a target with a Charge Shot Level 3. Keep up a constant string of Charge Shots, using Shuffle to avoid any projectile or pounce attacks.

Dante Select Swordmaster and Rebellion. Run with an Over Drive before powering into the nearest Frost with a rapid barrage of Stingers. Should the enemies try to surround you, activate Devil Trigger and use DT Stinger. A sustained, constant barrage of attacks will make it very difficult for the Frost to counter-attack, so keep piling on the pressure and victory will be yours in no time.

STAGE 84 — Chimera-Scarecrow (Arm) x 2, Chimera-Assault x 2, Chimera Seed x 12

Nero Mow down anything you possibly can straight away, using EX Level 3 Streak. Next, target the Chimera Seeds. Try and Snatch to Buster all of them before they enter Devil Trigger. As you Snatch up each one, remain airborne so as to avoid attacks (and if you can, try to start holding a level 3 Charge Shot here). Once you've taken care of the Chimera Seeds, use a combination of Charge Shot Level 3 and Shuffle to attack while simultaneously avoiding damage.

Dante Switch to Gunslinger and Pandora. With the full Disaster Gauge you've saved from Stage 81, unleash PF666: Omen. This will eliminate the Chimera Seeds, leaving you with a weakened set of Chimera Assaults and Scarecrows. The Chimera Assaults should be brought down to the ground near you. Kill them off quickly with Stingers before switching to ranged attacks like Over Drive and PF013: Epidemic for the remaining Scarecrows.

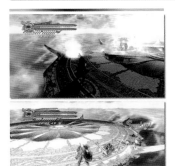

Nero   Charge a Charge Shot Level 3 immediately and let any Blitz have it. Keep track of the Blitz you attack by keeping your Lock-On activated. Deliver a couple more level 1 Charge Shots before moving in for the kill with 3 DT Busters and firing Summoned Swords. The Blitz will go berserk, so ignore it and let it self-destruct while you concentrate on firing a Charge Shot Level 3 and a couple more Level 1s at the other Blitz. Go in for the kill with DT Busters again. When this Blitz goes crazy, you can kill it off with

Charge Shots combined with Summoned Swords, leaving you safe to Snatch to Buster the set of Chimera Seeds and gain a health boost.

Dante   Switch to Swordmaster, Coyote-A and Gilgamesh. It's well-nigh impossible to accurately predict the movements of these enemies in order to evade. While Pandora will quickly weaken the Blitz's lightning armour, lack of mobility will get you into serious trouble. Your best bet is to jump constantly and rain down

shotgun blasts from above. As soon as a Blitz stands, continue to use Jump Cancelled shotgun blasts at close range. When you've removed a Blitz's shield, get in close using Gilgamesh Full House, then activate Devil Trigger and perform Real Impact as many times as possible. When a Blitz goes into berserk mode, stay high in the air and rain down shotgun blasts. As soon as the two Blitzes are eliminated, use a ranged attack such as Drive to destroy the Chimera Seeds and restore some health.

Nero   Start charging a Charge Shot immediately and take evasive action until the Angelos assume their Energy Ball formation. As soon as the Energy Ball is fired, release the Charge Shot to repel the attack and kill all three enemies instantly.

Dante   If this Angelo troop assumes its formation quickly for the Energy Ball attack, use the repel technique to see off all three enemies at once. Don't wait too long for this situation to arise. The tried and tested Dark Slayer style 2-strikes

Yamato into 2-strikes Rebellion combo cycle is also effective when attacking each Angelo from behind.

Nero   Initially, either stay in the air throwing the Gladius at each other, or power into the set of Basilisks with an EX Level 3 Streak. Snatch and combo any enemy knocked down by this attack. Ensure that you charge and release Charge Shot Level 3 continuously, while attacking both enemy types. The

secondary explosive effect will knock any Gladius out of the air instantly.

Dante   Switch to Swordmaster, Coyote-A and Rebellion. While maintaining forward momentum, which makes it difficult for the Gladius to target and attack you, unleash

a rapid barrage of Stingers to mow down the Basilisks. Having eliminated them, switch over to Lucifer, summon a full set of blades and execute the Climax command. If you keep repeating this sequence the Gladius will be killed the instant they try to attack you.

Nero   Target the Cutlass enemies first. Begin by holding a Charge Shot and, as soon as a Cutlass jumps out of the ground to attack, release the shot and rush over to where it has fallen. Hold your position for a moment and you'll notice that one Cutlass is about to attack directly beneath you. Deploy Shuffle to knock a second Cutlass out, leaving you free to deal with both of them with combo

strikes or aerial combos. Repeat this process for the third Cutlass and then use EX-Act enhanced strikes from behind to deal with the Angelos.

Dante   Select Dark Slayer and Gilgamesh. Dash forwards immediately and attack a Bianco with a 2-strikes Gilgamesh into 2-strikes Yamato combo cycle, quickly killing it before moving on to the other and repeating

the process. Switch to Swordmaster and Lucifer in order to deal with the Cutlass, summon as many blades as you can and perform the Climax command without further ado. When a Cutlass attempts to jump at you, the Climax formation will knock it out of the air, at which point you should move swiftly over to its position and kill it with a Kick 13 or Real Impact.

STAGE 89   Mega Scarecrow x 3, Blitz x 1

Nero   When you start this stage, wait for the Blitz to appear and then knock the three Mega Scarecrows down. Launch the nearest Mega Scarecrow with an EX Level 3 Rising High Roller and deliver as big an aerial combo as you can. Once it's downed, use Streaks to blast the enemy around the edge of the arena. As for the other two Mega Scarecrows, make repeated use of aerial combos, finished off with Buster, until they're dead. Remain airborne, as this will make it harder for

the Blitz to reach you with its attacks. When the Mega Scarecrows are dead, hold a Charge Shot Level 3 and fire it at the Blitz, and then start charging and releasing level 1 Charge Shots until its shield is broken. Now, activate Devil Trigger and attack with DT Buster, while firing Summoned Swords.

Dante   Speed and a perfectly executed Real Impact are both very important here. Select Swordmaster, Coyote-A and Gilgamesh. When the stage starts,

the Blitz will explode on to the scene, knocking all three Mega Scarecrows over. Move quickly over to the nearest one with Gilgamesh Full House before killing it with a couple of combo strikes into a Real Impact. Repeat this sequence on the other two Mega Scarecrows. Finally, turn your attention to the Blitz; remove its lightning shield with Coyote-A blasts and repeat Devil Trigger Real Impact when its defences have been breached.

STAGE 90   Scarecrow (Arm, Leg) x 30, Mega Scarecrow x 3, Chimera Seed x 3

Nero   As soon as you see the Mega Scarecrow, blast it to the edge of the arena with Streak before launching it into an aerial combo. Use Roulette Spin as much as you can to see it off quickly. Once you've destroyed the Mega Scarecrow, return to the group of normal Scarecrows and use constant Exceeded Streaks and Charge Shots until each one dies. A level 3 Charge Shot, together with its explosion, will kill a Scarecrow outright, unless it has used its DT. Repeating this sequence

- killing a Mega Scarecrow as soon as it appears and unleashing Exceeded Streaks against the crowd - will make a real mess of this group of enemies, especially if you use your DT. Finally, Snatch to Buster the three Chimera Seeds as they appear and win a health boost.

Dante   Things start off very quietly - just a pair of Scarecrows and a single Mega Scarecrow. Use the Mega Scarecrow to give the Disaster Gauge a full charge, using the

Extreme Jealousy technique. Things may seem slow, but will speed up when the stage gets busy. As soon as the gauge is fully charged, kill off these three enemies and, when the next set arrives, use Over Drive to attack continually from a distance. Keep this strategy going for as long as possible. The Scarecrows move slowly, so you'll be able to keep them at bay for quite a while. When things get too busy, select Gunslinger, jump up and then fire missile volleys with PF594: Argument.

STAGE 91   Faust x 3

Nero   Speed is of the essence here! Use Enemy Step cancelled Snatch quickly to remove the Faust's cloak and, as soon as it's been downed, activate Devil Trigger and perform Showdown, while firing Summoned Swords. Apply this sequence to all three Fausts to clear the stage quickly.

Dante   It's good to have a little breather at last. Select Swordmaster, Coyote-A and Gilgamesh. A single Faust will appear in the middle of the arena, so remove its cloak with a rapid, close-range volley of Enemy Step cancelled Coyote-A shots. As soon as its defences collapse, use a Gilgamesh Full House to

get in close and perform Real Impact; activate Devil Trigger before the first Real Impact strike and then de-activate once the move is finished in the interest of conserving DT. Simply repeat the process as each Faust appears and gain a swift victory and No Damage Clear bonus.

STAGE 92 Alto Angelo x 3, Bianco Angelo x 4

Nero Use Buster to attack and eventually break an Alto's shield. If you find yourself being ambushed, use Shuffle to evade while you attack. As soon as an Alto's shield is broken, kill it by activating Devil Trigger and repeating Buster, while firing Summoned Swords. Repeat this process, but allow one Alto to survive. When the group of Bianco Angelos arrives, the sole remaining Alto will command them to launch a suicide strike at you. When the Biancos carry out this command, resume your attack on the Alto.

Dante You regain your health at the end of this Mission, so go all out with Stingers and DT Stingers against the group of Alto Angelos, leaving one alive so that when the Biancos come in they will be ordered to mount a suicide strike (gain health here). Avoid the suicide strike and finish off the last Alto with another barrage of Stingers.

STAGE 93 Assault x 7

Nero It's very difficult to read Assaults and evade their attacks, so it's not worth bothering! Just power in constantly with Streaks and, if you find your strikes being repelled, switch over to Shuffle to continue the attack, evading as you go. As soon as your Devil Trigger gauge has received sufficient charge, activate and continue to press your attack with a continuous barrage of DT Streaks.

Dante As Assaults have no reliable cues for you to use for evasion, we advise you to just power in before they get a chance to mount an attack. Select Dark Slayer and Rebellion and, immediately, attack any nearby Assault with the 2-strikes Rebellion into 2-strikes Yamato combo chain. Keep this chain going, as any Assaults that stray too close will also be caught by it and be unable to attack. Activate Devil Trigger as soon as you can, while keeping the chain going and you'll make short work of this little army before they have a chance to attack or activate Devil Trigger.

STAGE 94 Chimera Seed x 6, Chimera-Scarecrow (Arm) x 3, Bianco Angelo x 2

Nero If you have any Devil Trigger left, activate and fire Maximum Bets at the first set of enemies to appear. Continue the stage, using Snatch to Buster to target and kill Chimera Seeds, while charging and releasing Charge Shots at the Chimera Scarecrows. Keep this cycle going until all the enemies are dead and the Biancos arrive. Use EX-Act enhanced strikes from behind to quickly see off the pair of Biancos.

Dante Select Swordmaster, Pandora and Rebellion for another nice and easy stage. Stand back and, the moment the first batch of enemies appears, use Over Drive to attack from a distance. A second set of enemies will appear on your left. Again, use Over Drive, switching over to Pandora should any of them try to advance. Keeping your distance, simply repeat this sequence to see off the whole set. Then, as soon as the Biancos appear, switch over to Dark Slayer and, while attacking from behind, use the Rebellion to Yamato combo cycle, while charging the Devil Trigger gauge, to dispatch them quickly.

STAGE 95 — Basilisk x 16, Chimera Seed x 4

Nero Activate Devil Trigger and repeat the DT Snatch to DT Buster sequence while remaining in mid-air above the Basilisks on the ground. This sequence will knock down any Basilisks in the vicinity. Repeat it for the second set of Basilisks and then use Snatch to Buster on the final group of Chimera Seeds, winning yourself a health boost.

Dante Switch to Swordmaster, Coyote-A and Rebellion. As soon as the stage begins, perform Over Drive and then activate Devil Trigger and let rip with a barrage of DT Stingers. There's a health recovery at the end of this stage, so don't worry about this approach; just keep up the barrage of Stingers until all the Basilisks are dead. When the set of Chimera Seeds appears, perform another Over Drive to catch them, plus some of the new group of Basilisks, in one fell swoop. Once again, go all out with Stingers until the second set of Basilisks capitulates, leaving you to perform one final Over Drive assault against another set of Chimera Seeds and claim your health restore.

STAGE 96 — Gladius x 8, Cutlass x 3, Bianco Angelo x 3

Nero See off the set of Gladius quickly by throwing them at each other with Buster, mixing some Charge Shots in to speed things up. As for the Cutlass, you can use Charge Shot Level 3 to blast them out of the ground or Snatch to pull them out of the air when they attack. Once you've downed them, use Streak to push the downed beast away from the other Cutlass, and then complete the job with an aerial combo finished with Buster.

Dante Switch to Swordmaster and Lucifer here. Summon blades and execute the Climax command within the Gladiuses' path. Flying into, or attacking, the position of this formation will kill the Gladius instantly. When they are out of commission, repeat the tactic against the Cutlass set. As soon as a Cutlass is blasted out of the air by Climax, switch over to Gilgamesh to deliver a Kick 13 combo, Real Impact or rapidly Stinger with Rebellion.

STAGE 97 — Mephisto x 6, Mega Scarecrow x 2

Nero Instead of using Snatch to disable the Mephistos' cloaks individually, use Charge Shot Level 3 to instantly remove the cloaks of multiple enemies in one go. As soon as the enemies are down, activate Devil Trigger and attack them using combo strikes and Buster. When combating the Mega Scarecrows, keep going with constant attack strings to charge the Devil Trigger and, at the same time, prevent them from counter-attacking. Aerial combos, using Roulette Spin, often prove useful as well.

Dante Speed is paramount here - select Swordmaster, Coyote-A and Gilgamesh. Run in quickly and remove a Mephisto's cloak using Jump Cancelled Coyote-A shots at close range. Attack the weakened form with a 2-strike Gilgamesh into Kick 13 finished with Full House. This combo sequence, when used instead of Real Impact, gives you more of a chance to evade if you need to abort the attack, and still does enough damage to kill each creature in a single cycle. As soon as the Mephistos have been killed off, use a knockdown attack followed by a Real Impact to see off the first Mega Scarecrow. Finally, use the second Mega Scarecrow as a means of charging the Disaster Gauge, using Extreme Jealousy if possible prior to killing it.

Nero   Deploy a sequence of Charge Shots and DT Streaks to disable the parasite attack, before chasing the enemy down with repeated strikes. After a successful Streak, make sure you launch a Charge Shot to disable the creature's parasite before unleashing another Streak. When confronting the final set of Chimera Seeds, simply jump above them and repeatedly Snatch to Buster to kill them and recover some health.

Dante   Select Swordmaster, Pandora and Rebellion. Once again, Over Drive is your best friend here, so open the stage with an Over Drive strike against the enemies that appear on the far side of the arena. Continue the stage, using Over Drive for long-distance attacks and switching to PF013: Epidemic shots if any enemy manages to advance. Finally, a set of 3 Chimera Seeds will appear, so just use Over Drive to kill them from a distance, enabling you to claim an easy health recovery.

Nero   Thankfully, this stage is surprisingly easy! You're faced with a set of three Alto Angelos, who will order each group of five Bianco Angelos that appears to launch suicide attacks. The five Biancos will charge at the edge of the arena and die, giving you time and health bonuses each time it happens. Keep running to evade this attack sequence until all the Biancos are dead and, finally, shatter the shields of the Altos and kill them with Buster attacks.

Dante   Allow the Altos to order the Biancos to launch suicide strikes. To all intents and purposes, this is a bonus stage for boosting your health and remaining time capacity for the boss fights ahead. When the Altos' supply of Bianco troops dries up, use any powerful method you like, such as knockdown to Real Impact, to see them off quickly.

03_46
03_47

Please refer to the Opponents chapter for a full strategy for this Boss Fight.

03_52
03_53

Please refer to the Opponents chapter for a full strategy for this Boss Fight.

Tidbits

Mission Names

The names of the Missions are borrowed from existing religious traditions as well as from the works of the Italian poet, Dante Alighieri, in particular Dante's Divine Comedy, written during the first part of the 13th century.

Mission 02 La Porte de L'Enfer

Literally translated as "The Gates of Hell", this is a sculpture created by the French artist Auguste Rodin. It depicts the opening section of Dante's Divine Comedy.

Mission 05 Trisagion

The Trisagion, literally translated as Thrice Holy, is a hymn of the Divine Liturgy in the Catholic faith. It is considered one of the oldest prayers in the Catholic religion.

Mission 11 The Ninth Circle

In Dante's Divine Comedy, this is the last and most wicked Circle of Hell, located at the centre of the Earth. Interestingly enough, Dante is guided through the Nine Circles of Hell by the Roman poet Virgil. If you've played DMC3, you'll recognize "Virgil" as the name of DMC's Dante's brother.

Mission 16 Inferno

The Inferno is the opening section of Dante Alighieri's Divine Comedy.

Mission 17 Adagio For Strings

Adagio for Strings is a piece of classical music composed for a string orchestra, written and arranged by American composer Samuel Barber in 1936. It is considered to be Barber's most popular work.

Mission 20 La Vita Nuova

La Vita Nuova, literally translated as New Life, is another book written by Dante Alighieri. This small work is a collection of love poems.

In-Game Tricks

Fill The Library Early

You'll find it easy to fill the Library entries for character actions at the Power Up menus. Simply refund all your Proud Souls, and then buy an ability. Refund the purchase immediately. The act of buying an ability, even if you refund it, enters that ability into the Library.

Nero's Combo B

If you perform Nero's Combo B to the final ground stab, there are three possible endings. In each, he will rest the sword on his shoulders and say one of the following: "Too easy", "Whoo", and "Hmph".

Maximum Red Orbs and Proud Souls

The maximum number of Red Orbs you can hold is 9,999,999. The maximum number of Proud Souls is 999,999.

Now that's a lot of Orbs!

Infinite Climbing

This is a neat, easy-to-use technique that will help you gain max height in your aerial combat manoeuvres. To apply it you need Enemy Step and Snatch with Nero. Double jump into the air, then perform a Snatch. As the Snatch finishes and the enemy is being drawn closer, hit the jump button immediately to perform Enemy Step. This will make you jump off the enemy and higher into the air. While this is happening, perform another Snatch right away, followed by another Enemy Step. If you do this over and over again, you can go on ascending until you hit the game's built-in ceiling.

Sequence Breaking

03_97 At the Start of Mission 5, you can backtrack to the Grand Hall and get on to the chandelier without the Wing Talisman, netting you a Vital Star (L) and a Holy Water. To accomplish this, you need Nero with Air Hike and Calibur.

Get on the first ledge...

...then jump to the ledge above it.

Double jump toward the chandelier...

...and a well timed Calibur will get you there.

Begin by standing under the archway near the Divinity Statue. Use a Kick Jump to reach the first ledge of the archway above you. Now, jump out and use an Air Hike back towards the archway to reach the second ledge above you. Once on the upper ledge, hold RB | R1 to stop yourself walking off the ledge. Turn the camera with the Right Analog Stick so that you're facing the Chandelier.

When you're ready, release RB | R1 and then double jump towards the Chandelier. At the apex of your double jump, fire Blue Rose two or three times to stay suspended in the air. As you fire Blue Rose, input the command for Calibur (RB | R1 + back to forward on the Left Stick + Y | △). If you do this correctly, you'll streak forwards and land on the chandelier. You can now claim the Vital Star and Holy Water. However, you can't trigger the breaking of the Chandelier, since you don't yet have the Wing Talisman.

Dante's Office

If you unlock the movie, Epilogue 02, by protecting Kyrie as the Staff Credits roll at the end of a game, you'll notice quite a few small treats. The movie takes place in Dante's Devil May Cry office. Fans of DMC3 will remember this room well. Mounted on the wall behind Dante are several Scarecrows, to the right and, to the left,

Dante's magazine is a monthly periodical.

The current month's edition has articles on Lady......

...and Ebony & Ivory.

The magazine is familiar with Devil May Cry 4!

the Sword of Sparda. While Dante is sitting at his desk, he's reading a magazine entitled Two Handgun: Monthly Magazine. On the left-hand page is a layout featuring Lady, with the title heading of Devil May Cry 4. On the right-hand page is an article about Ebony & Ivory. The movie finally ends with a classic Charlie's Angel pose. Smokin'!

Nero and Dante's Taunts

03_98
03_99

When you Taunt an enemy with Nero or Dante, they will perform a special action and often say something to tease the enemy. The Taunts change, depending on your Stylish Rank.

Nero's air guitar Taunt will play until interrupted.

Dante dares the enemy to engage in a "Showdown".

Nero's Taunts

Stylish Ranks E, D, or C
Nero Bows and says "Shall we dance?".
Nero makes a 'come here' gesture with his hand and says "Come on".
Nero puts his hand to his ear and says "What'd you say?"

Stylish Ranks B or A
Nero performs a quick martial arts hand gesture and says "Come on".
Nero pulls out Blue Rose, says "Bye-bye", spins the gun and puts it in the holster.
Nero sticks Red Queen in the ground and does an Exceed rev while saying "Starting to heat up".
Nero draws the thumb of his left hand across his throat and says either "What's up" or "Gone".

Stylish Ranks S, SS, or SSS
Nero says "Come on", and then performs an infinite loop of air guitar.
Nero waves his hands in the air while saying "Hey, hey, hey, come on babes".
Nero Claps his hands over his head and says "Ok, this may be fun".
Nero drops down on his right knee and slowly spreads his arms out before him.

Dante's Taunts

Stylish Ranks E, D, or C
Dante makes a 'come here' gesture with one hand and says "Come on".
Dante makes a 'come here' gesture with both hands and says "Come on".
Dante bends forward, claps his hands, and says "What's up?"

Stylish Ranks B or A
Dante stretches both arms out to his sides and says "What's up?"
Dante makes a fast 'come here' gesture with one hand and says "Come on".
Dante makes a fast 'come here' gesture with both hands and says "Come on".
Dante draws back, while making a 'come here' gesture with both hands, and says "All right baby".

Stylish Ranks S, SS, or SSS
Dante laughs, and then points at the enemy while laughing.
Dante rest his right arm on his right leg, does a 'come here' gesture with his left hand and says "Showdown".

Credits

©2008 Future Press Verlag und Marketing GmbH
All rights reserved, including the right of
reproduction in whole or in part in any form.

Future Press
Verlag und Marketing GmbH
Barmbeker Straße 5a
22303 Hamburg, Germany
www.future-press.com

Publisher	Frank Glaser
	Jörg Kraut
Authors	Chris Andrews
	Vincent Merken
	Saur Dash
	Wil Murray
Editoral Assistant	Bruce Byrne
Illustrator	Wil Murray
Assets localization	Hirofumi Yamada
Creative Director	Jörg Kraut
Layout	Martin Adler
	Sven Kanth
	Tobias Koch

English edition	ACE Localisation
French edition	Evocati
German edition	Studio Mühl
Spanish Edition	Vertigo Translations

©2008 Future Press Verlag und Marketing GmbH

ISBN 9783940643131

Unit price: £ 11.99 • EUR 16,99

Thanks to
Lisa Andrews, Carlos Astorqui, Michael Auer, Carol Aggett, Antoine
Bailly, Jane Best, Florence Bethuys, Alistair Bodin, David Bugden,
Jean Bury, Steve Cartwright, Paolo Celso, David Corless, Priscille
Demoly, Lucinda Digweed, Richard Deavall, Trevor Howell, Rishi
Kartaram, Lars Kuehme, Marjon Leenen, Geoffroy Marty, Katja Marx,
Dominic Matthews, Patrick Melchior, Stefano Perelli, Elisa Ramos,
Joanne Rayment, Géraldine Saint Louis, Agata Samojlowicz, Chikako
Sasaki, Boris Schneider-Johne, Emanuele Scichilone, Davide Solbiati,
Kai Stüwe, Leo Tan, Henriëtte van Herk, Matt Warley, Carrie Williams
and Michael Pattison.

Special thanks to
Taki Enomoto, Emi Nakai, the Capcom Licensing Team, Mr. Kobayashi
and his team for their untiring support!